'On page 374 of this plum pudding of a book, the author tells how he suddenly became convinced that no one would want to publish it. Only international celebrities were accepted as autobiographers...

Bunkum (as they say) and balderdash... All you need is a lively life, a satisfying style or both.

MacQuitty, for sure, has both. His style is clean, plain prose of the old school, enriched with anecdotes, wise comments and tongue-in-cheek asides... He is an Ulsterman, but early in life (he tells us) he went south to kiss the blarney stone.

As for his life, it is a kind to take even a blurb-writer's breath away. After a childhood of Proustian security and serenity, MacQuitty spent his twenties and thirties as a banker in India and the Far East. He then went home to Ireland to become a farmer, but was inveigled into the British film industry, where he produced such pictures as *Above Us the Waves*, about submarine warfare, and *A Night to Remember*, about the sinking of the *Titanic*. In the 1950s he ran Ulster Television, on less money per year than one hour of drama costs today. He also published fifteen bestselling books of photographs, and built up an archive of 250,000 negatives. Then there was Buddhism, friendship, sex, cars and sport - as well as a continuum of deeply felt and endlessly revitalising family life...

...The book lives... by its contents, and above all by its author's urbane delight in life.'

Kenneth MacLeish   *The Sunday Times*

Other Books by William MacQuitty

As author and photographer:

Abu Simbel (foreword by I.E.S. Edwards, 1965)
Buddha (foreword by the Dalai Lama, 1969)
Tutankhamun: The Last Journey (1972)
The World in Focus (foreword by Arthur C. Clarke, 1974)
Island of Isis (1976)
The Joy of Knowledge/Random House Encyclopedia (major contributor, 1977)
The Wisdom of the Ancient Egyptians (1978)
Ramesses the Great, Master of the World (1979)

As photographer:

Irish Gardens, with Edward Hyams (1967)
Great Botanical Gardens of the World, with Edward Hyams (1969)
Persia, the Immortal Kingdom with texts by Roman Girshman, Vladimir Minorsky and Ramesh Sanghvi (1971)
Princes of Jade, with Edmund Capon (1973)
Inside China, with Malcolm MacDonald (1980)
The Glory of India, with commentary by Chandra Kumar (foreword by John Masters, 1982)

A LIFE
TO REMEMBER

William MacQuitty

QUARTET BOOKS

For my ancestors,
who gave me life,
and for my wife, family and friends,
who made it a life to remember

First published by Quartet Books Limited in 1991
Paperback edition first published by Quartet Books Ltd in 1994
A Member of the Namara Group
27 Goodge Street, London W1P 1FD

All photographs relating to the author's films are reproduced courtesy of the
Rank Organization and London Independent Producers Limited

Photograph on pages two and three: The Amritsar staff of the Chartered Bank
of India, Australia and China on the departure of the manager John Reid for
home leave in 1927. Left to right, garlanded, Radha Kishen, bank *shroff*,
D.C. Scott, accountant, W. McCulloch, relieving manager, John Reid, John Tullie,
myself, George Tolmie and Tulsi Ram, cashier. Kartar Singh sits at the managers' feet.

British Library Cataloguing in Publication Data

MacQuitty, William
A Life To Remember
1. Northern Ireland. Social life, history
I. Title
941.6

ISBN 0-7043-0217-9

Designed by Namara
Typeset by MC Typeset Ltd, Gillingham, Kent
Printed and bound in Great Britain

Acknowledgements

To begin with, I would like to thank the Chartered Bank of India, Australia and China, today the Standard Chartered Bank, in whose foreign service, from 1924 to 1939, I enjoyed in the Orient, with all its delights and horrors, the world, the flesh and the devil. The foreign staff then numbered less than three hundred, and few of my generation survive, but they were, during their sometimes very brief lives, greatly respected by the exotic peoples they served. The Chartered Bank always allowed strongly individual talents to flourish, and the tradition is clearly alive and well, for it was with them that John Major, Britain's youngest prime minister this century, received his earliest business experience.

Next I would like to thank my old friend Arthur C. Clarke, not only for writing the foreword but also for dedicating his latest book, *The Ghost from the Grand Banks*, to me; and Jan Capp who so successfully produced my first book, *Abu Simbel*.

Finally I wish to thank Naim Attallah for believing in the book enough to want to publish it; Peter Ford, who has placed his editorial and authorial skills at the service of the drafting process and treated my story with great understanding; and the staff of Quartet Books for seeing the book through the press.

Contents

Part Three: Chairman of Talents

Foreword

Bill MacQuitty's autobiography is one that has shouted to be written, and now I can at least claim some credit for starting him on his literary career.

We met first in 1952, soon after I had gained some small notoriety through my fledgling science-fiction novels. Bill was then actively engaged in movie-making and was looking for ideas. Though nothing came of this, we found that we had many interests in common and thus began a friendship that has already lasted for half my lifetime.

One of those interests was underwater exploration, and when my partner, Mike Wilson, discovered a wreck off the south coast of Ceylon, bearing thousands of beautiful silver rupees minted by the Moghul Emperor Aurangzeb, Bill gladly agreed to accompany us on a return expedition in the spring of 1962.

Unfortunately, before we could set out in our cantankerous little diving boat, *Ran Muthu,* I tried to use my head as a wrecking ball on a low doorway. Bill had already left and was in Egypt when he received news that the expedition had to be delayed. He stayed on in Egypt and became fascinated by the attempts then being made to save the magnificent temples of Abu Simbel from the rising waters that would result from the completion of the Aswan High Dam. By an unprecedented feat of engineering, the temples were eventually raised above the new water level, but Bill had conceived a much less expensive and in some ways more spectacular solution.

He proposed leaving the temples where they were and building a small dam round them – not to keep water out, but to keep water in. The level would be the same on each side, so the dam could be a light – and cheap – 'membrane' structure only a foot thick. It would separate the muddy Nile from a trapped pool of constantly filtered, crystal-clear water; visitors could look at the temples from observation galleries at various depths and would see them as distinctly as if they were in open air. (The monuments would also have been considerably safer under water, beyond the reach of sandstorms and graffiti carvers.)

This experience led to his first book, *Abu Simbel*, written in 1965 – a large lavishly illustrated history of the temples and the various schemes to save them. Not many authors begin their career at the age of sixty, and I am proud of the fact that Bill should have inscribed my copy 'To Arthur who started it all'.

Subsequently he produced almost a book a year – often very massive books indeed on a remarkable variety of subjects and illustrated with his beautiful photographs. Undoubtedly his most successful was *Tutankhamun: The Last Journey*, which sold half a million copies. His haunting photograph of the funerary mask was seen all over the world, for it was used as the poster for the 1972 exhibition of the tomb's treasures.

His latest book before this one, *The Glory of India*, reveals the beauty of a country for which he has a deep affection. He must be one of the very few who can recall the India of Kipling; for six years he was a volunteer in the Punjab Light Horse, trying to keep the peace in Amritsar. (The local residents' terror of the amateur cavalry may be judged by the chant that sometimes followed them: 'One hand for the reins, one hand for the saddle – which hand for the sword, O Punjab Light Horse?')

When we were very small boys, both Bill and I experienced technological confrontations which, if they did not determine our destinies, foreshadowed them in an uncanny manner. In July 1919, I was two and a half years old when the quiet of my little West of England birthplace, Minehead, was shattered by the loudest noise any of its inhabitants have ever heard. An enormous, torpedo-shaped machine, many times larger than one of today's jumbo jets, came roaring up over the horizon and headed out to sea. This Close Encounter so terrified me (I am told that I fled screaming into the house) that I have no recollection of it, but it may well have helped to turn my interests towards the conquest of space. Exactly fifty years – to the very month – after I had seen the airship R34 begin the first transatlantic crossing, I was on the other side of that same ocean, watching Apollo 11 leave for the moon.

Bill's parallel experience took place in Belfast in May 1911 – two weeks after his sixth birthday, when his father took him to Harland & Wolff's shipyard to watch the launching of the largest ship in the world, the *Titanic*. In 1957 – the year the space age opened – Bill paid his tribute to the ship he saw as a boy, when he produced the classic movie, *A Night to Remember*. Based on Walter Lord's book, it must remain the definitive story of the greatest of marine tragedies; no future producer will have *Titanic* survivors as technical advisers. Now he has lived to see the rediscovery of the ship he painstakingly reconstructed and sank in the movie studios.

I have dedicated my latest book, *The Ghost from the Grand Banks*, which gives a further twist to the *Titanic* legend by telling the story of an attempt to salvage the ship far in the future – 'For my old friend Bill MacQuitty – who, as a boy, witnessed the launch of RMS *Titanic* and, forty-five years later, sank her for the second time'.

It makes me happy to know that, following my advice, he has at the age of eighty-five completed his autobiography, *A Life to Remember*. This remarkable book spans the lives of five British sovereigns, two devastating world wars and the end of the British Empire. It covers the period from the twenty-horse teams that hauled the *Titanic*'s huge anchors from the foundry to the shipyards to the 100-million-horsepower engines that put men into space.

Finally, it gives me added pleasure to close this foreword with a tribute to Bill's remarkable family. Without Betty – herself an author and a trained economist – he could not possibly have done so many things in so many countries. Betty is one of those competent, unflappable persons who can even pacify chronic worriers such as myself. I still remember her driving me through obscure by-ways of Middlesex, promising that she would get me to the Concorde on time. (She did.)

The three children have embarked on strikingly different careers. Jane is an author and the wine correspondent of the London *Times*. Miranda is a doctor of marine biology and the author of five books. Jonathan is president of GenPharm International, a genetic engineering company.

It's been far too long since I saw them all together.

Arthur C. Clarke
Colombo
15 May 1990

Part One

A Luxury Tramp

1

The Ant in Amber

On 15 May 1905, at 5 St John's Avenue, Belfast, I was born in a caul, thought to be a good omen and to give me protection from death by drowning. The sequence of 5s in the date and address, moreover, made 5 my lucky number. My first love was my West Highland terrier, called Jap after the Russo-Japanese War. On sunny days I would lie on my rug with Jap, rapturously content, or be carried by my mother round the little garden to see where a blackbird had nested. At night our rooms were lit by lamps, and turf fires lent a country fragrance which reminded my mother of her old home in County Longford, for she had been a country girl and remembered how, each winter, every child at her village school had to take a turf every day for the school fire. Gas, though recently piped into our home, was confined to the stairs, where it hissed from fishtail burners and cast flickering shadows. I found myself the centre of a loving scene, my night clothes airing in front of the fire as Mother bathed me and Father warmed my towel. Then I would be cuddled and carried upstairs to my cot in their bedroom, where I said my prayers: 'God bless Mummy and Daddy, and Uncle William, and Uncle Robert in London, and Aunt Hartie in Australia, and all my cousins and my dog Jap.'

The warmth and security of this sheltered life suddenly shattered one day when Jap was run over. Like all our deceased family pets, he was sent to the taxidermist. He returned in a life-like resting position and was placed on the wide sill of the landing window. Whenever I was carried past him on my way to bed, his eyes twinkled at me in the gaslight, and as soon as my mother was safely downstairs, I guiltily disobeyed her warning never to leave my cot and tiptoed down to the landing to cuddle my strangely unresponsive love.

Mother, steeped in Irish folklore, remained a little superstitious and told many fairy stories. My favourite bed-time story concerned a family of mice that lived in a hole at the base of an old oak tree. Every morning Mammy Mouse would see Daddy Douse off to work, then tidy the house and give Baby Bouse his breakfast. One day she had to go out and do some shopping, so she warned Baby Bouse on no account to leave the safety of the burrow since a big cat that wandered about outside would gobble him up if he did anything so foolish. But Baby Bouse eventually grew tired of waiting. First he poked out his nose, and then, seeing no one about, ventured out little by little. At this point the wily cat pounced and gobbled him up. It seems odd that such a terrifying story should have been my favourite, or that my mother should have told it in the first place. The names stuck, however. I was known as Bouse, Father as Douse and Mother as Mammy Mouse.

We were a musical family. Our small house contained a piano, an organ and a pianola. My uncle, William Baird MacQuitty, a physician who lived with us and after whom I was named, played them all with enthusiasm, flooding the house with classical music, light opera and haunting Irish airs. My father possessed a magnificent bass voice, and he had at one time considered becoming a professional singer, though his natural caution led him to content himself with singing in the choir and at Masonic concerts. He was a small man and his nickname at the Model School, which he left at fourteen to become a printer's devil, had been 'Midge'. In 1885 he was working at the case, sometimes setting type for thirty-seven continuous hours, and all for a penny an hour. By the age of twenty-one, he had been promoted to managing director of W. & G. Baird, proprietors of the *Belfast Telegraph*, the largest newspaper in Ireland.

I did not go to school while we were at No. 5 as I had bronchial troubles. Fat children were thriving children, and I was skinny. My mother taught me my three 'Rs' and did her best to fatten me, but to no avail, though I did consent to eat mashed potato and mincemeat. This I would mix like sand and cement and make into pyramids into which I sank burial shafts. One of my favourite books was about ancient Egypt, and Rosetta Avenue, called after the famous Egyptian stone, was not far from our house.

When I was five we moved to No. 12 University Square, mainly because Uncle William's practice had grown and he was in great demand. As an undergraduate, William had won over thirty prizes, scholarships and exhibitions, many with first-class honours. It was a record whose brilliance was never equalled at the Queen's University, Belfast, and the Royal University of Ireland. Alas, before the year was out, he was dead from a massive cerebral haemorrhage. My parents could no longer bear the new house, so we shortly moved to Bangor. It was thought that the sea air there would be good for my chest. I now suffered from asthma and was being terrorized by a recurring nightmare.

Lost in a strange mountainous country, I climb, hoping to see where I am from the summit. I scramble almost to the top when a boulder, loosened by my approach, starts to roll towards me. I throw myself out of its way, but it is deflected back towards me, and no matter how I twist and turn, it follows my every move. I race to the bottom, hoping to be safe when I start up the other side, but then I see with horror the earth splitting and a great chasm widening before me. It is too wide to jump, and as I stand transfixed, the boulder strikes me in the back and hurls me into the abyss. I fall faster and faster, terror springing from every pore. I know I will not hit the bottom, for there is no bottom, but I am unable to waken myself. Suddenly the spell breaks. I sit up in bed, trembling and sweating, my heart pounding.

No. 89 Princetown Road, Bangor, overlooked Belfast Lough, where great steamers, coasters and the *Bangor Boat* paddle steamer came and went. Beyond the lough lay the Irish Sea, and beyond that the oceans of the world. Daily I walked round the rocky coast, searching the pools at low tide. After storms, conger eels and streamers of seaweed attached to huge mussels would be washed ashore to join the smaller creatures, crabs, prawns, sea anemones and little fish of the pools. Each day brought new discoveries. I learned to swim and my asthma melted away in the excitement of battling with this new element. I became hungry and started to grow; and I went to a small local school.

The whole of Ulster was at this time in a state of excitement at the final stages of the building of the largest ship in the world, the *Titanic*. Whenever I went to Belfast with Father, he would point out the huge vessel towering above the stocks of Harland & Wolff's vast shipyard. It seemed impossible to me that such a mountain of iron and steel could ever be placed in the sea and actually float. One day I watched teams of draught horses straining to haul just one of the ship's propellers from the foundry. 'How can they get it into the sea,' I asked Father.

'They lay the keel on a slipway leading to the sea,' he explained, 'and the ship is built on the keel. When everything is ready for the launch, tons of tallow, soft soap and train oil are used to grease the slipway. Hydraulic rams push the ship ever so slowly, and she begins to slide, going faster and faster until she reaches the water. You'll see for yourself when we go to the launch.'

The day of the launch was 31 May 1911, two weeks after my sixth birthday. The sun shone from a cloudless sky as we made our way to the press stand, which stood directly in front of the ship's bow. We could see Lord Pirrie, the chairman of Harland & Wolff, with his guests in a smaller stand to our left, the group including Pierpont Morgan, the American millionaire owner of the White Star Line. As well as the British Red Ensign, the ship therefore also flew the American Stars and Stripes. Signal flags reading 'Good Luck' fluttered above the throng of workers and spectators.

At five minutes past noon, a red flag was hoisted to warn the fleet of boats in the River Lagan to stand clear. Another five minutes went by before a rocket was fired and workers began to hammer at the restraining chocks. At 12.14 the firing of a second rocket reduced the vast crowd to silence. Would this huge vessel ever really move? All at once the workers on board gave a cheer in which the crowds on shore joined. The slide had begun. Every ship in the lough sounded its siren, the noise drowning the roar of the piles of restraining anchors as they were dragged along the ground. Slowly gathering speed, the *Titanic* moved smoothly down the ways, and a minute later was plunging into the water and raising a huge wave. I felt a great lump in my throat and an enormous pride in being an Ulsterman.

At Princetown Road my room was next to a box-room that contained unwanted relics going back to the time of my father's father, who had been a wine merchant in Belfast. None of it was ever likely to be useful, but no one had the heart to throw it out. There were trunks, tin-lined wooden boxes, leather portmanteaux and carefully shaped hat-boxes. In these lay wedding dresses, christening robes and baby shoes labelled with names, weights and dates; old letters, scrapbooks, postcard albums, faded photographs and well-preserved daguerrotypes. Stacked against the wall were bedsteads, silent witnesses to the arrivals and departures of my ancestors.

As I slowly explored this treasure house, I came upon a battered deed box. The key was attached to a loop of string. With mounting excitement I turned the reluctant key and prised open the lid. Inside, on faded silk, lay a strange assortment of trophies from long-ago travels: small clay figures from India, a water carrier, a snake charmer, a small brass statue of Vishnu, a serene ivory carving of the Buddha, a blue faience figure of Osiris and a small box covered with red velvet. Within the velvet box lay a block of amber, and within the amber was a black ant. I took the block to the window and held it in a shaft of sunlight.

The ant had not moved for 50 million years, since being engulfed in resin oozing from a deodar pine in Kashmir. I turned the block and saw how fiercely the tiny creature had struggled to free itself from the treacherous golden trap. Two of its six legs lay beside the bulbous abdomen and the delicate antennae rising from the large head were twisted in a desperate fight for freedom. I felt a kinship with the ant. I, too, was trapped by all that my birth decreed. I wondered if I could ever escape.

In 1912 my brother James was born. There was a sense of excitement and anxiety in the house and I was sent out to play in the garden. I saw Dr Campbell come and wondered why. Later I was taken to meet my little brother. My mother was sitting up in bed, holding a very red wrinkled baby, its mouth and eyes screwed up tight. 'Well,' my parents said, 'so what do you think of your little brother? Isn't he lovely?'

'Where did he come from?' I asked dubiously.

My father said, 'The doctor brought him in his black bag.'

'Is he bringing any more?' I asked.

They laughed and replied, 'We don't think so.'

I had no notion where babies came from, and I think my parents were as surprised as I was, my mother being then forty-two.

Bangor, with its summer crowds, was a favourite pitch for evangelists, and the holiday-makers enjoyed listening to the hot-gospellers as they thundered on about God, sin, Satan and the damned roasting eternally. They were gifted orators who knew how to grip their audience. Sometimes they preached in the churches with which Bangor was richly endowed. One preacher always commenced his sermons by asking the ladies to cross their legs. As soon as the rustling had died down he would roar, 'Now the Gates of Hell are shut!' He was noted for the large collections he extracted from his congregations.

We attended the Old Abbey Church, where my father sometimes read the lessons. He took round the collection plate until they stopped him doing so, for he sang at the same time and his mighty bass drowned the choir. It also occurred to the church committee that it rather looked as if he were singing for money. He would intone all the ritual, except for the Creed, where he refused to recite 'the resurrection of the body', which his brother the late doctor had regarded as an impossibility. Finally he lost interest after presenting the church with a beautiful set of individual silver Communion cups in the cause of hygiene. The parson tried them out, but the congregation insisted on a return to the communal chalice. My father, who had a great fear of germs and imagined *spirochaete pallida* lying in wait for him on every lavatory seat or in any cracked cup, was so disgusted by this superstition that he never returned.

My parents, though heart-broken at the prospect, decided I must go to boarding school. The idea was that being on my own should build my confidence. Rockport, only three miles away, was run by Mr Bing, whose son, Geoffrey Bing, was later the legal adviser to the government of Ghana. Amid many tears my mother finally sewed name-tags on all my brave new clothes and we drove to Rockport, the event coinciding with my eighth birthday. 'Your son is lucky to arrive now. We are just having a cricket practice. He will enjoy that,' said Mr Bing confidently.

My father quickly slipped me a surprise present, a boy scout's knife, and my mother, a Box Brownie camera, before they hurried away to conceal their emotion. Under the watchful eye of Matron, I then unpacked my carefully listed clothes from the new cabin trunk and transferred them to my chest of drawers and wardrobe.

'Now change for cricket,' Matron commanded.

I said, 'I've never played cricket nor worn long trousers before. Please help me.'

Gradually she got me into the long white trousers, cricket shirt and blazer, and strange white boots. Practice was in progress, and at the end of an over the young English sportsmaster beckoned to me and asked, 'What is your name?'

'William,' I whispered.

'William what?' he raised his voice.

'William MacQuitty,' I said, trembling with embarrassment.

The boys crowded around, grinning hugely.

'Say sir!' he thundered.

'Sir William MacQuitty,' I stammered amid yells of laughter.

The master lost his temper, picked me up and flung me into a holly hedge beside the pitch before turning his back to continue with the game. I extracted myself from the hedge and walked away. There was a path that led straight through some firs. I stopped and cut the trunk of one with my new knife and watched the resin ooze. The path wound down to the sea and I took off my boots and socks and, with rolled-up trousers, walked along the edge. I was shaking all over, but gradually the cold sea restored a little composure. Eventually I walked back and examined the globule of resin. Filled with anger, I promised myself that this ant would never be caught.

After my stint at Rockport, I went at the age of nine to Campbell College on the outksirts of Belfast. It was an imposing red-brick building with a tower from which there flew a large Union Jack. The First World War had begun that summer. My heart sank as my parents left me at the massive front door, but the initial shock was lessened by my Rockport background. Although cricket was compulsory, I managed to persuade the authorities that I would be better employed as a botanist, supporting my case by finding a new variety of early purple orchid in the grounds.

S.A. Bennett, brother of the author Arnold, was our science master, and with his backing I was allowed to pursue my search for new material beyond the school limits. This good fortune came to a sudden end when two ladies reported me for polluting the local reservoir, where they had observed me swimming naked. The head, known as 'Tulip' Macfarlane from his habit of biting his lower lip, gave me six of the best. As I bent to touch my toes, my eyes swept past a copy of the famous picture of Captain Oates leaving Scott's tent to die in the blizzard. Other masters had more exotic punishments. The French master, 'Bubbles' Hughes, so called because he bubbled and sometimes frothed at the mouth in fury, required the offender to put on lady's high-heeled, lace-up boots and parade up and down his study.

Bullying was a fact of life. New boys were taken from their cubicles down to the baths at night, stripped and made to stand on a chair and sing before being thrown into icy water. I once awakened gasping for breath as a penfiller of ammonia was squirted up my nostril. Sneaking was unknown, the silence equalling that of the Mafia. Self-help was all one could expect. I joined boxing, sabre-fencing, judo and gymnastic classes.

The war had brought changes. School prizes were replaced by certificates, lard was substituted for butter, salt herrings for fresh meat and, curiously, rice for potatoes. Certain of the changes were welcome, such as the waiters being replaced by cheerful, giggly waitresses. Boys spent sleepless nights trying to arrange meetings. The school gave no education in sex, which remained like an underground stream that bubbled delightfully to the surface from time to time. In Stricklands Glen, near Bangor, we hid in vantage points among the bushes from where we could observe love-making couples, sometimes almost close enough to touch them. One boy had an obliging sister who, in a loft above their stable, would reveal her twelve-year-old treasure in the light of a hurricane lamp. Despite all the temptation, sex remained much of a mystery and few ever achieved the real thing.

Macfarlane's health had been failing for some time and, by the time I was in the sixth form, he had retired, to be replaced by Colonel Gibbon, an English master from Dulwich. 'Duffy', as he was known, was a short burly man who stood no nonsense and exuded enormous vitality and enthusiasm. 'Well, MacQuitty, what do you want to do with your life?' he asked.

'I want to go to India, sir.'

'Your father expects you to follow him into his business, or better still in the footsteps of your famous uncle in medicine.'

'I know, sir, I'm sorry, but I want to see the world.'

'He won't pay for that.'

'I know.'

'How do you like Campbell?' he asked briskly.

'I don't like it, sir.'

'What's the problem?'

'We work to a fixed schedule, questions and answers are always to the book, there's no time for inquiring about matters important to me. The masters try to mould me into a shape which is unnatural for me.'

Duffy remained silent as he gazed at me speculatively. I've made a pompous mess of this, I thought. Suddenly he spoke: 'We'll make you a luxury tramp.'

I stared in bewilderment.

'We'll make you a merchant banker. Meantime use the school as you will. Attend whatever classes you fancy. You needn't do prep unless you wish, but I'll expect an essay from you once a week on any subject you choose.

I stammered my thanks. I could not believe my good fortune. After ten minutes' conversation with a stranger, my world fell into place. It had the simplicity of a miracle.

In the summer of 1923, with unemployment at its peak, I applied to the Chartered Bank of India, Australia and China. They replied that I must first have experience in a home bank and pass the Institute of Bankers examination. Immediately I asked for a post in the Belfast Bank, who replied that they already had over a hundred applications for nine vacancies and the examination was in six weeks' time. With Duffy's support, I went to Renshaws, a crammer for banking subjects, and enrolled with the Metropolitan College, St Albans, who for £10 guaranteed to continue coaching me by post until I passed. Their method was simple. They reduced the contents of all past papers to one hundred key questions on each subject and supplied their students with the answers. I worked day and night and, to my great relief, got a place in the Belfast Bank. This success softened my father's disappointment and he asked me if there was anything I wished to do before starting work. I said I would like to see the battlefields in Belgium and France. To my delight he gave me twenty sovereigns and his blessing.

On 15 August I sailed to Zeebrugge, where I saw the famous block ships and Big Bertha, which could fire a shell sixty miles. At Thiepval the remains of the Ulster Defence Force lay in tidy rows around their memorial tower, a replica of Helen's Tower, built by Lord Dufferin to commemorate the death of his mother. I asked the caretaker where I might find the grave of a friend, Holt Hewett, and he led me to it down rows of identical tombstones. I took a photograph for Holt's family and thought of schoolmates, their memorial photographs round the Central Hall but their bodies now here, a part of a foreign soil.

I continued through Ypres, Moere, Dixmude and along the banks of the Yser, finally retracing my steps to Poelkapelle, a Paul Nash landscape of stunted, splintered trees in a welter of shell-holes and abandoned equipment. The area was still being cleared and was guarded by barbed wire. I climbed through a gap and picked my way cautiously across a battlefield unchanged since the fighting, except for a blanket of long grass. In a shell-hole a boot and un unmistakable shank showed in the green slime. Farther on a greatcoat, half-hidden by the returning grass, still covered its owner's remains. In the distance, a party of Chinese were putting remnants of the dead into rough coffins. Farther along still, soldiers were collecting and stacking shells. I kept carefully out of sight and managed to pick up a German and a British helmet, two shell cases, some buttons and a bayonet.

Since I still had a few sovereigns left, I decided to travel home fourth class via Paris. The station master at Arras liked the Irish and let me sleep in a first-class carriage, with instructions to change to a fourth-class compartment as soon as the train started. Through the rolling fields of Flanders, the wooden seat was a throne that carried me to the Gare du Nord, the station of my French lessons, where the atmosphere was electric. At Lunns, in the Place de l'Opera, I arranged my ticket home. It was nearly closing time and Paul Mason, a sympathetic clerk, offered to take me to a hotel he knew in the students' quarter, in rue Casimir Delavigné, near the Luxembourg Gardens. I showed Paul my trophies and gave him the British tin hat. We had dinner in St-Germain and talked of many things, including how I might contrive to lengthen my stay in Paris. 'A lot of my American clients want to see the naughty side of Paris,' said Paul, 'but

I can't take them myself because of my position, though if you were the guide you'd collect 10 per cent from Madame and we'd split it half and half.'

'What do I do?'

'I'll introduce you to the clients and give you an addressed envelope to show the taxi driver. When you arrive, pay his fare and give the letter to Madame. Afterwards she'll give you the 10 per cent commission.'

I said goodnight to Paul and retired to my small wedge-shaped room in the attic. In the morning, a pert little maid brought me hot water, coffee, milk, bread, butter and a small portion of jam. After breakfast I strolled through the Luxembourg Gardens and at four o'clock picked up two Americans from Dallas who introduced themselves as Steve and Russell. It was their first trip to Paris. 'We're sure glad to have you along,' they said. 'You'll stay with us? We don't know our way around, don't want to miss anything or get taken for a ride.'

'Of course,' I said, 'you've got nothing to worry about,' wondering how on earth I was going to cope.

At the 'house', La Piscine ('the Swimming Pool'), I paid the driver and pressed the bell of the imposing front door. A heavily built man opened up and looked us over carefully. 'I have a letter for Madame,' I said in my schoolboy French.

He took the letter and asked us to wait in a grandiose hall with a thick red carpet and heavy swags of purple velvet that draped alcoves in which white marble nymphs solicited us with welcoming postures. In a few moments Madame appeared and led us into an even more ornate room, where we sat on heavily upholstered chairs. 'You will take champagne, of course?' she offered in French.

'*Mais oui*,' I replied, explaining this exchange to my Americans, who promptly responded, 'We ain't come here to drink.'

'It's customary,' I explained.

Fortunately four girls then arrived, bearing champagne and glasses. Their short dresses displayed their charms to fine advantage. Steve said, 'I want the blonde.'

'Boy, I go for the red-head with the big tits,' said Russell.

'Your friends are too hasty,' remarked Madame. 'First they must see La Piscine, for which we are justly famous.'

I explained to the boys that this was the most erotic spectacle in Paris, if not in the world, and we followed Madame upstairs, Steve and Russell meanwhile holding on to their girls. The lights were subdued in the large room she led us into, and in the centre was what appeared to be a swimming pool. As we peered over the surrounding parapet, we saw a placid sheet of water. We gazed down. The sole of a dainty foot appeared, followed by its fellow. It was as though we were lying at the bottom of a pool, looking up at a girl walking on the surface. More nude young ladies appeared in this upside-down fashion, which enabled them to display themselves from an unusual angle. 'Form the Crown of Queen Victoria,' commanded Madame.

The girls sat in a circle, facing inwards and extending their arms towards the centre. The sight of so many soft round bottoms with their centre-pieces flattened against the glass was, as Steve said, 'Awesome.' The boys watched spellbound as Madame order more and more exotic entertainment. At length, when she deemed the moment ripe, she made her financial arrangements. 'I think I can safely leave you now,' I said to my clients, who were too overcome to reply.

I nudged Russell, but he waved me away. Madame beckoned me discreetly and I followed her into her office, where she counted out thirty francs with precision. 'I have much enjoyed meeting *M'seur*, and I hope we may do more business.'

I thanked her and asked, 'How on earth does the Piscine work?'

'It is a simple system of mirrors which displays what is happening in the adjoining room. *Voila!*' she laughed. 'The gentlemen are so impressed.'

Paul and I divided the spoils later. 'How do you know we've got 10 per cent?' I asked.

'It's probably less,' said Paul, 'but it's a good start.'

Gradually I worked my way round a number of 'houses'. The House of All Nations, said to have been patronized by the late King Edward VII, claimed to supply girls from every nation. At Aux Fauns, the cheapest, the girls made sibilant noises to attract attention, but it was a free-for-all, the rule being that they could not proposition a client verbally. At 32 rue Blondell, the girls moved among the tables where the customers were enjoying a drink. Madame sat at a desk to the side, and drink and girl were paid for at the same time. Some of the more active girls earned extra money by picking coins off the edge of a table with their labia and, with a little more effort, cigarettes. Some wore nothing, others a sash or a small paper flag stuck on a navel or nipple. It all seemed very relaxed.

The Baby Show was another popular establishment. None of the girls were young, but they all dressed with ribbons and bows like little girls, and pouted and pretended. There was one most attractive girl, Susanne, and I asked her why she worked when she could obviously have married. 'I like making love and I get well paid for it. One day I will have my own hat shop. I want to run my own affairs, to be independent.'

'But,' I said, 'surely you'd be better off with the security of a husband, home and children.'

'My married friends are not so happy. They have to work very hard with the house, meals and children, and their husbands are unfaithful.'

'But they're doing good work, bringing up the children.'

'We do good work here. We listen to all the worries of our clients, we are better than priests at confessionals. Many men are ugly or misshapen and can find no one to make love to, but for us their money is the same, and so we give them contentment.'

I thought at once of Toulouse-Lautrec with his disabilities, finding solace in such company.

Alas, my time ran out. The Belfast Bank was calling me. While I was inside my father's office in Royal Avenue, telling him how much I had enjoyed my visit to the battlefields, an angry mob appeared outside in the street. 'Quick,' he said, and we dashed into the passage.

A moment later a shower of huge nuts and bolts, known locally as 'Harland & Wolff confetti', came through the plate-glass windows. We took refuge in the office of my father's cousin, Sir Robert Baird, which lay deeper inside the building. The commotion was nothing unusual, and while we waited for things to simmer down, Sir Robert, a jovial man who enjoyed a joke as much as my father, told us how he had once been the guest of honour at a printers' convention in Bulawayo, and made a speech lauding the town to the skies but at the end forgot what its name was. 'What do they call this God-forsaken hole?' he asked his neighbour. 'They were very good about it,' he said, 'and presented me with this.'

He reached inside a cupboard and produced an elegant grey topi. 'Might be useful to you in India, though why you won't work here, I can't imagine. We're all getting on, we need new blood. What's the matter with him, James?'

'He's like you, Robert, a bit wild and wants to see the world.'

'Enjoy it while you're young, my boy. That's what I did.'

Police and 'B' Specials had meanwhile opened fire and cleared the street. People emerged from doorways and went about their affairs, dodging behind horse-drawn drays and tramcars to avoid stray shots. On the whole, no one seemed greatly concerned about the 'Troubles'. They had become a way of life and might eventually fizzle out, it was thought, when the rapidly growing Catholic community outnumbered the smaller Protestant families.

When at last I stood before the Belfast Bank's heavy front door, it reminded me all too forcibly of those of my schools. Inside I was ushered into the presence of a ponderous man who obviously intended having his power and presence recognized. 'You are new here, MacQuitty, and you will find that we have certain regulations that you will have to strictly obey. You will find them on the notice board. Make sure that you see it every day as there will be changes and additions from time to time. For the moment, you will work with Mr Kerr. One of the staff will show you where he is.'

As I made my thanks, I wondered how such a mandarin could split infinitives. What luck, I thought. Harry Kerr, who had joined the bank about a year before, was a good friend of mine with whom I had boated on the lough and played rugby for Bangor. He welcomed me to his little room above the front porch, where he operated an addressograph machine. Here we stamped out names and addresses on metal cards which printed them on dividends, envelopes and so forth. Later we graduated to handling cash, counting heaps of silver coins into £5 paper bags, using five fingers for shillings and florins and four fingers for half-crowns.

After six months of this, and a lot of night work, I passed my Institute of Bankers Exam and reapplied to the Chartered, who told me to report for duty in London on 14 May 1924, the day before my birthday. The Belfast Bank were displeased at my short stay. The mandarin manager asked me whether I intended to grow a pigtail and what was wrong with Belfast? I tried hard to explain, but left him unconvinced. Harry was also eager to try for another job, and my father gave him the place he had reserved for me with the *Belfast Telegraph*.

Meanwhile my uncle Robert MacQuitty was alerted to find me safe digs in wicked London. He recommended the Toc H hostel, 23 Queen's Gate Gardens, South Kensington, where each member paid rent according to his ability. Mine worked out at £1 15s. (£1.75) a week.

I shared an attic with a postman and an out-of-work welder. An ex-naval chef cooked breakfasts and left hot suppers for us in a huge old-fashioned oven. Our job-master, Eric Challens, assigned us philanthropic duties as part of the deal.

The Chartered Bank's headquarters lay beyond the Bank of England at 38 Bishopsgate. After a brief interview with the chief accountant, Shem Jones, a pleasant Welshman, I reported to Miss Yirrel who had charge of current-account pass books. She was a tiny but strict lady to whom fell the task of breaking in new recruits. The work was undemanding: nine to five with an hour off for lunch, for which we received a 2s. (10p) luncheon voucher. The thrifty Scots, who formed the bulk of the foreign staff, sold their vouchers and brought sandwiches.

By the end of my first week I was beginning to relax. Life seemed much easier than in Belfast. At the hostel Eric Challens asked me what sort of job I would like. 'There's prison visiting, hospital help, caring for the elderly and various social services, including boys' clubs.'

'What do the boys' clubs do?'

'Chiefly boxing.'

'I'd like that,' I said.

'It can be a bit rough. The Venture was a corner pub, but two old ladies bought the licence and turned it into a boys' club, which upset the locals. The last fellow we sent down got beaten up.'

'I'll have a go,' I said.

'Here's the key,' said Eric. 'I thought Ireland would choose that. Best of luck.'

The Venture Boys' Club was on a corner of Portobello Road in a solid ornate building whose doors and windows were boarded up. The inside was dark. I groped for a switch and a naked bulb lit up, revealing chairs, a table, the remains of a boxing ring and sets of shabby gloves in a cupboard. A few boys came in. 'Who are you?' I asked.

'We're club members,' they chorused.

More arrived, and soon there were a couple of dozen ranging from teenagers to young men in their early twenties. We looked at each other in silence. 'Any of you box?' I asked.

They shuffled about and finally nudged one of their numbers forward. He was a stocky chap, about ten stone and five foot six. 'Like to have a round?' I suggested.

He did not reply, but took off his coat. I did the same, hanging mine on a rickety chair. I took off my shirt, and he did likewise, though reluctantly, his vest being full of holes. We put on the battered gloves, touched them and started to box. I weighed about eleven stone four and was just under six feet with a long reach, but within a few moments my confidence was shattered. Micky South, for that was his name, was a south paw and quick as an eel. His right foot, never still, took him in and out of range while his right fist jabbed away in a tornado of lightning strikes, some followed up by his sharp elbow. I was completely outclassed. My nose streamed blood. There were no rounds and the ring closed in as more and more members arrived. I fought as hard as I could, but saw no way of ending my humiliation until suddenly the members melted away including, to my great relief, Micky South. 'What's going on here?' asked a bulky policeman. 'You all right?' he inquired, looking at me closely in the dim light.

'Yes, sergeant. We were just sparring.'

'I'd get off home if I were you,' he said, staring at my blood-stained vest.

'Thank you, sergeant, I'll do that.'

When he left, I turned to get my clothes. They were gone. I was stunned. It was two long walks and a tube journey to get from Notting Hill to Gloucester Road. My money had been in my coat pocket and I was covered with blood. I went to the door. 'You chaps frightened of the police?' I shouted and went back inside.

In a few moments they were all there, and more besides, until the room was full. As they looked at me I felt like a creature from another world. Pulling myself together I said, 'The club will open three nights a week, Mondays, Wednesdays and Fridays. The sub will be tuppence a night and you pay as you come in.'

They looked at me, still in silence. I wiped my bleeding nose on the back of my hand.

'Someone has moved my clothes. Please put them back before you go. See you on Monday. Good night, good night, Micky.'

There was a scattering of 'good nights' and I was alone. Scarcely daring to look, I turned to find my clothes where I had left them. None of my money was missing.

It was bank policy to move potential foreign staff through as many departments as possible before sending them East. Having passed the Yirrel test, I was assigned to cancel currency notes issued by the bank in Shanghai. The tattered notes had a strange, appalling odour which conjured up visions of opium dens and brothels on the dimly lit waterfront of the Whangpoo river. There were many blanks in the great registers. I imagined notes hidden by seductive ladies against the day when their charms failed, or quantities of money being burnt at some mandarin's funeral for wealth in the hereafter. Next I was sent to the mail room where I worked with 'Piggle' Ogilvie, a short, tough Channel Islander who held no less than thirty-six hockey caps for England. Letters bearing colourful stamps arrived from every corner of the globe. The work came in batches, and during waits Piggle and I would play chess on a set concealed in a drawer between us.

The boys' club meanwhile flourished. The old ladies came and supplied new sets of gloves, new furnishings and boxing shorts, and singlets and shoes for the team that represented the club at matches. On Saturdays a lawyer friend gave free advice on problems, and on Thursdays we had a dance. A friend from the bank played the piano – another gift from the ladies – and members arrived wearing collars and ties and bringing their girls. Everything had to be correct, and as Master of Ceremonies I was expected to dance with every girl, which I thoroughly enjoyed. The members were lively, outgoing cockneys, full of high spirits liable to take fire if jealousy roused their fighting instincts. Fortunately the pianist was a good psychologist who would swing into a Paul Jones or other diversion before a situation became serious.

My chess contests with Piggle were cut short by the General Strike of 1926. We joined the volunteers. Piggle went on the tubes and I was sworn into the City of London Police, given a striped arm band, a whistle with a pea in it, a smart peaked cap and a short truncheon. This was worn suspended on its leather thong from the left brace button down the left trouser leg. It made standing uncomfortable and sitting impossible. I was given simple instructions, one of these being that if I hit someone over the head I should say to the magistrate, 'I aimed a blow at his shoulder, Your Worship, but he moved his head in the way.'

Thus armed and briefed, I was sent to direct traffic at the junction of Bishopsgate and Wormwood Street. First I watched the policeman I was to relieve. It seemed simple enough: so much traffic through Bishopsgate and then a shorter period for Wormwood Street. He surrendered his place to me with a broad grin. 'Mind you don't get run over,' he said.

'Not likely,' I grinned back.

I was surprised at the drivers' instant responses to my signals. Like the policeman in the Irish song of 'The Mountains of Mourne', 'I stopped the whole street with one wave of my hand'. It was good fun and within an hour I was an old hand, signalling with assurance. The traffic swept by in endless streams, abruptly stopping every time I raised my arm. At one of these moments a young man in a red Salmson sports car, a pretty blonde at his side, made a dash to get through. I maintained the dignity of the law. A screech of brakes and the bumper hit my left knee while the front tyre trapped my foot. I collapsed backwards, giving my leg what French ski instructors call a *torsion brutale*. By the time I was able to walk again, the General Strike was over.

Several members of Toc H had motor-bikes and I bought a 500-cc side-valve Norton with a fixed belt drive to the rear wheel for £11. You had to run with it to start the engine, and, as soon as you were travelling fast enough, drop the exhaust valve-lifter to restore the compression. If you wanted to carry a passenger, they had to jump on, too. I soon changed it for a special racing bike with a 350-cc Blackburn OHV engine with an alloy piston mounted in a special frame with lubrication to the primary and secondary driving chains. The bike came cheap as the owner had killed himself racing it at Brooklands. It had no name, so I christened it 'New Dawn'. My first use of my new and more docile machine was to visit my cousins Emily, Norah and Kathleen, the daughters of my Uncle Robert, who lived in Putney with their parents. Kathleen was a professor at the Royal College of Music, a brilliant pianist and the youngest professor they ever had. She gave recitals at the Wigmore Hall. She was also fond of horses and we often went riding on Sundays. She said she was sure there would be lots of opportunities to ride when I went East and I had better learn now.

On Saturdays the bank closed at one o'clock, and on summer Saturday afternoons I often rode my motor-bike down to the coast, grounds sheets and blankets tightly rolled and strapped to the tank, and David Lloyd, a bank friend, on the back. We bought broken biscuits and corned beef for 1s. 6d. (7½p), and after turning east along the shore to Saltdean, found shelter in the barn of a friendly farmer. Emerging from our overalls like butterflies from chrysali, we then drove back to Brighton, resplendent in blazers, Oxford bags and scarves knotted at the throat. The promenade was a great hunting ground, the boys apparently the hunters yet the girls controlling the game. The glance, the walk, the interest, the excitement were set against the blue sky and wide beach with cosy groynes and, eventually, nightfall to hide us in a gentle embrace. Our brief encounters seldom led to second meetings, but one day at a stop in Piccadilly I found myself being hailed. 'Hi!' Babs shouted.

She was an American student, very attractive, with straight blonde hair cut in a pageboy fringe, candid blue eyes and a small nubile figure. 'Get on,' I said. 'Where would you like to go?'

'Let's go to the country and fight for my honour,' she yelled in my ear.

I set off westward. Passing through Chiswick, my new 'fine-proof' aluminium silencer dropped off. I rushed back to retrieve it, but before I could reach it a bus ran over it, shattering it like glass. The bike thundered down the street, every head turning at the appalling racket. 'What shall we do?' I asked Babs.

'Go on,' she screamed above the din. 'My honour's worth more than your fishtail.'

Ten miles out we came to a sign: ALL THE STRAWBERRIES YOU CAN EAT FOR SIXPENCE. We walked through the scented fruit, picking as we went, until we reached the top of the field where a ditch hidden in long grass marked the boundary. I spread my coat for her to sit on while I foraged for the best strawberries. When I returned she was gone. I walked along the ditch, and suddenly there she was, stark naked, sunbathing in a little hollow. I sat beside her, unable to take my eyes off the fair hair between her thighs. 'I've got the straw-berries,' I wavered.

'You've got something I like better,' she grinned.

This first encounter with sex equality brought a surge of happiness at not being saddled with the sense of guilt so dear to Ireland. Time and place were always right for Babs. We made love in parks, cinemas, in doorways sheltering from the rain and on top of an open-top bus driving past Marble Arch. Our light-hearted affair came to an end when she returned to New York. Three months later I received a summons to appear at Chiswick Magistrates Court. The buff envelope and court document gave me a shock. Full of anxiety, I went to court, and learned to my great relief that it was the incident of the silencer, which I had by now forgotten. The magistrate asked if I wished to say anything to the charge of riding a motor-cycle without a proper silencer. 'I was taking my girlfriend for a long-promised ride,' I explained, 'and didn't want to let her down when the bus smashed my fine-proof silencer.'

The magistrate looked at me a little enviously, I thought, as he said, 'Young man, we must pay for our pleasures. The fine will be £2.'

A week later Shem Jones, the chief accountant, sent for me. My appointment to Amritsar had come through. I was given an appoint-ment with the bank's outfitters. 'You are travelling on the *Kaiser-i-Hind*,' they said. 'You will require one cabin trunk' – my old school one would do – 'one large tin-lined wooden chest and two suitcases. Besides ordinary clothes, you will require evening dress, a dozen stiff dress shirts, two dozen collars ditto, a dozen white shirts, mosquito boots and two tropical suits. The Indian tailor will copy as many more as your may require very cheaply. You will purchase your solar topi at Simon Artz in Port Said. We will do the packing and your luggage must be labelled, CABIN WANTED ON VOYAGE or HOLD NOT WANTED ON VOYAGE.' They were expert and thorough. I arranged for 'New Dawn' to be freighted on the same ship. I was given five days to make my farewells in Belfast. These were less trying than I had expected. Father was pleased that I was paddling my own canoe and earning £465 a year. Mother used her love and skill to hide her anxiety and sadness at a five-year separation. 'Be careful of snakes and bad friends,' she advised. 'Get plenty of nourishing food and wear warm dry clothes.'

I said goodbye to Harry Kerr, to Kathleen Bell, the girl next door, my first romance, to Paddy, the dog that had succeeded Jap, and to my brother James, now fourteen, who would have to look after my parents. Five years seemed an impossible period for any of us to comprehend.

2

Passage to Amritsar

As a bank official, expected to travel everywhere first class, I felt a distinct flush of superiority as I took a comfortable seat on the train at Victoria Station, at the start of my long journey to Amritsar. I was soon put in my place by discovering that the two other young men in the compartment would be travelling very much farther, one to Singapore, the other to Shanghai. At Marseilles, when we found that the ship would not sail till morning, my companions suggested an evening ashore. We stowed our luggage in our respective cabins and set off for the Old Port, where I was introduced to Bassio's, the renowned fish restaurant. Our next stop was a *cinéma cochon* in a large *maison de plaisir*.

The film was old and much splicing had made it shorter than the sound track, which was on a record. Passionate love noises accompanied the preliminary love meals while the final entrance of the outraged husband was augmented by ecstatic groans and cries. The lights went up and Madame appeared with girls and champagne. We drank under her professional eye, but desire was punctuated by hilarity. Madame had more to offer. She ushered us into a room with a large mirror. Cautioning silence, she switched off the light. We gazed into the silent darkness and suddenly a light went on in an adjoining room. We were witnessing the famous 'see-through' mirror.

A portly man entered with a voluptuous lady, who skilfully divested herself and her client of their clothes. Positioning him so as to give us all a good view, she proceeded to demonstrate the arts of love for which France has a well-earned international reputation. After the climax, the man rose, approached the mirror and appeared to look me straight in the eye. He flexed his arm muscles and gave an appreciative nod of masculine satisfaction.

Next morning I stayed on deck to watch our departure. Tugs took up the tow ropes and, with shattering blasts of her siren, the *Kaiser-i-Hind* gradually edged out of harbour. Soon the tow ropes were dropped and the engines picked up their monotonous throb. Marseilles fell astern and we steamed past the Isle of Dogs. Cassis followed, and there was a brief glimpse of Nice. After that we were out of sight of land and on course for Malta, where we were due to coal. On the advice of my companions, my deckchair, bought from a Moroccan vendor for 8*s.* (40p), had been placed on the starboard side where, sheltered from the wind by a funnel, I would get any sunshine going as well as additional warmth from the boilers, not to mention, it transpired, showers of smuts whenever the wind backed. Deckchairs became pieces of territory that were guarded with animal ferocity.

I walked round the deck to the bows. As I looked down, I forgot about the vast bulk of the ship behind me and felt like a seagull swooping over the waves. After a while I strolled to the stern. Twin screws thrust torrents of white water through the sea with an exhilarating power. 'I say, haven't we met before?'

By my side stood the same portly gentleman I had seen eyeball to eyeball in the see-through mirror of last night's escapade. 'No,' I replied, wondering, horrified, whether the mirror could possibly have worked both ways, 'I don't think so.'

'I know we've met somewhere. I never forget a face.

'Care for a drink?' I asked, hoping to evade the subject.

In the bar I learnt that he taught in a mission school in northern Siam. It must be an exciting country to be in, I said, but he replied that it was terribly boring, and very lonely. 'But aren't the Siamese girls delicious?' I asked.

'Oh, one must be so careful. Everyone knows what's going on. Absolutely no secrecy.'

'What of the ladies of the night?'

'Very tempting. "Golden flowers", they're called, but Europeans who succumb end up with VD, and a black dose into the bargain, except for one chap who always wore two condoms and kept his trousers on.'

'So how do you pass the time?' I asked.

'I love music,' he said and then, looking at me intently, he added,

'By God, that's where I saw you! At the Wigmore Hall. You were talking to Kathleen MacQuitty after her piano recital when I came up to congratulate her.'

'Kathleen's my cousin,' I said with relief.

'I'm so glad to have met you. She's my favourite pianist. Same again, steward.'

The P & O had the contract for carrying the mail. It made them feel superior to other Eastern lines and gave them an excuse to lord it over their passengers. Bells and loudspeakers herded us through the ship's routines. Evening dress with starched shirts and collars was *de rigeur* for dinner, irrespective of the temperature. The spotless decks and brass fittings were continually cleaned by dedicated Lascar seamen. Goanese stewards patrolled the decks to offer cups of *bouillon*.

After Malta, our next stop was Port Said, where East meets West at the entrance to the Suez Canal. I found it was possible to leave the ship here and rejoin it once it was through the canal and this allowed time to visit the pyramids. I decided I would abandon Simon Artz, where I was to buy my topi, since I already had Sir Robert's, and skip the performance of the famous, fortunate fornicating donkey in preference for the last surviving Wonder of the World. The Port Said to Cairo line passed through Ismailia on the northern shore of Lake Timsah, the 'Crocodile Lake', which was the centre of operations during the construction of the canal and where the austerely furnished house occupied by Ferdinand de Lesseps still stood. From Ismailia, the track ran beside the ancient canal that linked the Nile with the Red Sea in the days of the Pharaohs. Soon the train was passing mile after mile of date palms and orange and lemon groves, and I began to feel a rapture akin to my intimations in early childhood. The dates, clusters of golden fruit that hung gracefully beneath the dark green umbrellas of curving palm fronds, were far removed from the dark-brown squashed slabs one bought in the Belfast shops.

Cairo was bigger than I expected, and the station seethed with people carrying bundles of every colour and shape. Policemen with long canes yelled and smote to maintain order. Heavily veiled ladies clutched their children and belongings. As I struggled through the turmoil, I wondered if I had not been over-optimistic. Holding my bag tightly and keeping a wary eye on a tall white-robed Arab who seemed to be following me, I made for the exit. As soon as I stopped he introduced himself.

'My name, effendi, is Ahmed. I am a qualified dragoman, and if you require any service I will be glad to arrange it for you.'

I explained my wish to see the pyramids and rejoin my ship after it had passed through the canal, and he hailed a battered open motor-car and bade me sit beside him in the back. 'I will explain all as we go along.'

Our road led through busy streets crammed with carts pulled by people, donkeys, shamefully thin ponies and gaunt camels. Occasionally a dignified old man would come into view, sitting far back on his donkey. Gradually the turmoil of the streets receded, and then we drove through more open suburbs until these gave way to green fields intersected by water channels. Ahmed pointed to where, rising above the palms, the tip of the Great Pyramid appeared. Even at two miles' distance, it looked astonishingly large. Within minutes the green fields ended and the yellow-brown sands of the desert took over. The driver accelerated for the last hundred yards and we drew to a halt in a flurry of dust near the Sphinx. Ahmed swiftly dispersed a rush of donkey boys, camel men, vendors and guides and led me to the entrance of the Great Pyramid, helping me up the steep blocks. He introduced me to his friend Abdul, one of the guardians, and we stooped double to scramble down and then up through a low narrow passage that brought us into the majestic Grand Gallery. Beyond lay the burial chamber of black granite with a huge granite sarcophagus in which the mummy of Cheops had been laid in 2690 BC. I rested by the empty sarcophagus, the darkness broken by candlelight, in the heart of the largest man-made building in the world, built by the Pharoah so that his embalmed body might be secure until the resurrection. Without doubt the trappings of Christianity – incense, libations of holy water, altars, tonsured priests with vestments – were first woven in Ancient Egypt. In spite of all precautions, the mummy of Cheops was stolen and never recovered. The costly amulets and sacred jewellery, the gold and precious inscriptions that were to protect the Pharaoh on his long journey through the Underworld, did nothing more than make it attractive to thieves. I sat a long time in the darkness.

'We must go now,' said Ahmed, 'or effendi may miss his ship. But before we leave I will sing you the song that the blind harpist sang at the feasts of the Ancient Egyptians and which was found on the wall of a tomb in Luxor where it was written four thousand years ago.

> 'Spend a happy day and weary not thereof.
> Lo, none may take his goods with him,
> And none that have gone may come again'

Ahmed's strange Eygptian voice gave the song an awe-inspiring antiquity.

At the entrance the sun was blinding. I tipped the guardian who accepted with his right hand while his left continued to move his amber prayer beads one at a time. Observing my interest, he offered them to me to examine. I looked through them carefully, wondering if I should find another ant. There was still time for a long cool drink of fresh orange juice and a walk across to the Sphinx, known in Arabic as *Abu Hol*, 'Father of Terror', before Ahmed steered me safely into Cairo and through the endless bustle on to the train for Suez. I thanked him and tipped him handsomely. He invoked Allah to be with me on my way through life. The journey to Port Suez turned out to be surprisingly easy. I was waiting for the ship as she completed her passage through the seventy-nine miles of canal.

On Christmas Eve, as we sailed into the Red Sea, the air was scorching, and even though wind-scoops were fitted to the open portholes, the hot following wind made them useless. Christmas Day was celebrated with the same ritual as if we had been in a snow-bound Britain. Father Christmas came aboard, complete with sleigh drawn by wooden reindeers and a huge sack of presents for the delighted children. I felt sorry for him as he sweltered in his thick red robe and bushy white beard. That night we wore fancy dress to a traditional Christmas dinner, followed by a masked ball.

Early in the morning, festivities over, I walked to the stern and watched the twin torrents of foaming water, radiant now with phosphorescence as they lit up the depths in ever-changing patterns. I wondered how my family were spending their Christmas and to what extent they were with me, I with them. I thought of the amber beads running through the left hand of the guardian of the Great Pyramid and the Muslim belief that all is preordained by Allah. I could not credit it. Surely man had free will. A brain interpreted my five senses, a mind, a self, was programmed from the very beginnings of my line of life. There was the heart, the still small voice and the everlasting soul promoted by religions. Which was the real me? A slap on the back jerked me from my reverie. 'Not thinking of going overboard, I hope.'

It was the fourth officer, with whom I had become friendly. 'Not likely,' I said, 'but what would you do if I was?'

'Oh,' he replied, 'I always ask them to wait a few minutes until I get below!'

Next morning the sea was like glass and the bow waves spread in a vast 'V' as far as the eye could reach. From time to time we passed a dow filled with pilgrims bound for Mecca. As they waved to us, we waved back from our exalted position. The seamen rigged up a canvas pool and filled it with the clear water of the Red Sea. In spite of warnings from the 'Old Hands', I swam and sunbathed, enjoying such a novel winter experience. On the whole, passengers did not emerge until late afternoon because of their concern about sunstroke, and I wondered why the sun should suddenly become so lethal. Topis were worn and stewards served iced lime juice and ice cream. In the Mediterranean, a slow twilight had softened our journey into night, but now a huge fiery sun, magnified by the desert's dusty air, sank quickly in a blaze of glory that ended in the amethyst after-glow I had seen but disbelieved in garish postcards in Port Said.

At Aden we coaled, and the next day entered the Indian Ocean, where I saw my first whales. A school of six swam abreast of us, blowing columns of vapour into the air. Flying fish and dolphins took advantage of our bow waves to leap high out of the water and seemingly enjoyed the company of the big ship. That night I saw the Southern Cross: four bright stars in the shape of a cross on its side, just above the horizon.

The next day, one day out from Bombay, I made a point of rereading the Bank Agreement:

> On the occasion of your departure for the East, I beg to express the Directors' expectation that you will acquit yourself to their satisfaction in the discharge of the duties that will devolve upon you now or hereafter, and that by a steady regard for the interests of the Bank you will merit the Court's favourable notice.
>
> As soon as you arrive in Amritsar you will place yourself under the direction of Mr John Reid, the Bank's Agent there, who will be duly apprised of the terms of your Agreement.
>
> You are of course aware that it is the rule of the Bank that Officers of the Foreign Staff are not permitted to marry while holding the position of Sub-Accountant, and in acknowledging this letter you must signify your agreement to strictly observe this rule and also state that you are free from debt.
>
> Signed, Secretary

The bit about marrying did not bother me any more than the split infinitive. My mother had often told my brother and myself the story of some forgotten Irish sage who said, 'A good woman is like an eel in a sack of serpents. If you succeed in pulling it out without getting stung, what have you got? A wet fish.' It took some fifteen years to become an accountant.

There was a farewell party on the last night, and afterwards I took my final stroll to the stern. As I gazed at the boiling wake I suddenly realized that a couple of deckchairs were churning about in the glowing water. I thought for a moment that someone might have gone overboard, but more and more chairs followed and bobbed and drifted in our wake. I ran forward to see what was happening. A group of tipsy young men were venting their wrath at the disciplinarianism of the P & O Line and slinging over the side any loose objects they could lay hands on. The crew saved the ship's piano in the nick of time, and the culprits vanished, knowing it was too late for any retributive action. I was granted a last glimpse of my red deckchair as it floated astern – my involuntary offering to the Indian Ocean.

Putting on my sun helmet that auspicious New Year's Eve, and feeling like a freak in my new tropical suit, I went on deck. The ship towered above the Indians who thronged the port of Bombay's Ballard Pier. Beyond the crowd stood the Gateway to India like a large edition of Marble Arch. It's going to be worse than Cairo, I thought. I could do with an Ahmed. After much heaving and yelling, a gangway was pushed on board and, to my relief, a familiar face appeared near the front of the boarders. Sandy Young and I had been great friends in London until he was posted a few months ahead of me. 'Welcome to India,' he said in his broad Scots accent.

We went to breakfast, where he told me that one of the bank's clerks would see my baggage safely through customs and book it on the Punjab Mail to Amritsar. Meanwhile, tonight, we would see in the New Year together. I was booked into the Taj Mahal Hotel, and thither we drove in a horse-drawn Victoria. The hotel had a magnificent staircase that filled the centre of the building. My room, the largest bedroom I had ever seen, overlooked the sea. The staff, resplendent in uniforms and imposing turbans, were like something from the *Arabian Nights*. After the turmoil of the streets, it seemed unbelievably tranquil.

Sandy's guided tour took in the bank next. Here I was introduced to the Burra Sahib, the 'Big Master', then to the rest of the foreign staff in order of rank. The high ceilings were equipped with three-bladed fans that revolved at various speeds between slow, which barely disturbed the air, and fast, when papers had to be anchored down. I wondered whether the speed of a fan had anything to do with the temperament of the sahib beneath it. The Indian staff sat on stools at the counters, dressed in white, with long shirts hanging outside their trousers. The sahibs sat at polished desks, their *chaprassi*, or office servant, standing in readiness before them with pen, blotter, matches, a glass of water or whatever the master might need. A stream of clerks came and went, placing the folders, documents and, from time to time, telegrams on the already crowded desks. The cashiers squatted behind protective grills, ringing silver rupees on the marble floor to check for counterfeit coins. Outside the counters, the customers kept up an incessant chatter that made me wonder at anyone being able to work in such bedlam. As the Europeans pressed me for news from home, I did my best to respond while trying to hide my disastrous Bulawayo topi. The scene filled me with mounting apprehension. This type of banking was more than I had bargained for.

The Bombay Club had the grandeur of the Taj, but the immaculate stewards, in similarly splendid turbans and wide cummerbunds, moved more briskly. They whisked trays of drinks among the tables with alacrity and assurance. Round followed round, but I noticed that no payment was offered, no chits signed. The bar boy, the *kitmagar*, Sandy explained, wrote every order down in his book and presented accounts once a month. A suspicious member had kept his own tally for months, but could never fault the barman. Like many systems in India, it seemed impossible but it worked well.

Sandy had arranged to pick me up at the Taj to take me to the New Year's Eve dinner at Greens Hotel. I filled in the time till then by setting off to view the Towers of Silence. The drive took me through a shanty town where a mix of palm fronds, matting, flattened kerosene tins and broken planks were stitched together to form crude shelters. Despite the stench, squalor and open drains, people and children seemed remarkably cheerful. Before long we were in the better surroundings of brick houses, many with shops on the ground floor. Soon the road began to climb Malabar Hill and the driver pointed out the famous towers where a row of vultures sat along the parapets. Even as we watched, a funeral party approached, and the corpse, wrapped in a white sheet, was taken on a stretcher through the doorway. There was mounting excitement among the birds, and some minutes later they disappeared from the parapet to descend on to the exposed body. The mourners, when they came out, seemed perfectly composed. I asked my driver how long would it take the birds to conclude their gruesome meal. 'In one half-hour all gone, sahib. Sometimes longer if there are more dead peoples. Sometimes bits drop on road when too much.'

When he picked me up at the Taj, Sandy first made sure that I was suitably attired. I had put on my wool evening dress with starched shirt and collar. It passed muster. 'You're going to be hot in it, mind, but it'll be fine for Amritsar. They have fires there in winter.'

For the New Year's ball the ladies were dressed in glittering gowns, the men in full regimentals or tails. There was jollification, but I still found it daunting, sensing an aura of social distinction of a well-defined pecking order. Did I imagine it, I asked Sandy. 'Not a bit of it. You're witnessing the British caste system as laid down by the Heaven Born, the Indian civil servant. The Order of Preference is all in the *Blue Book* – status and salaries clearly set out and heaven help the hostess who gets her seating arrangements in the wrong order.'

At midnight streamers and balloons filled the air, the chimes rang out and everyone embraced and wished their neighbours a Happy New Year. The dancing continued until, in the small hours, we joined hands for 'Auld Lang Syne', a lump in every throat.

On the way back to our hotel, our Victoria drove through the city. On Bombay's pavements sleeping forms lay wrapped like corpses in the sheets that were their only privacy or protection from mosquitoes. Brahmini cows and bulls, like animals from a Christmas manger, reclined in graceful attitudes across the roads or munched garbage in the gutters. The open drains gave off their stench as the filth of the city waited for the coming of the untouchables to load up the ordure carts. Lastly our vehicle ambled through the Red Light quarter, known as 'the Rag', where ladies of the night waited for custom behind barred windows. In the soft light of oil lamps, they looked mysterious and alluring, the bars heightening the appeal. Some of them beckoned with a hand dropping from the wrist, the opposite of the European gesture of solicitation. 'We'll not stop,' said Sandy. 'They're poxed to the eyes.'

We reached the magnificent security of the Taj. 'See you for lunch,' said Sandy, 'and then I'll put you on the Punjab Mail. It leaves at 3.30.'

Up in my room I opened the window and looked out on the moonlit waters that linked Bombay with Bangor Bay. My five-year separation had hardly begun. It was the first day of 1927. Until I had completed a year, a month, a week and a day, I was fated to remain a griffin, a gauche newcomer.

At Bombay station, hoardes of passengers carried bundles, tin trunks, baskets, sacks and rolls of bedding tied with ropes and straps. The quotation 'Take up thy bed and walk' kept returning insistently into my head. My bed was waiting for me in a first-class compartment, at the door of which a Chartered Bank clerk stood patiently waiting to hand over my tickets and luggage receipts. Standing beside the clerk was a tall, gaunt man with a black beard and a neatly wound turban. He wore a white shirt over baggy white trousers. 'This,' said Sandy, 'is your bearer, who will see to your needs and look after your luggage. He is a Pathan.'

I looked at the man closely. He had fine eyes and returned my gaze with dignity. 'What is your name?' I asked.

'Allah Dad Khan, hazur,' he replied in a deep voice.

'What does "hazur" mean?' I asked.

' "The Presence",' said Sandy. 'Equivalent to "sir".'

We walked to the front of the train and admired the powerful engine whose great coupled driving wheels engaged the broad track. Everything was larger than at home. The first-class compartments spanned the width of the train. There were no corridors, for security reasons, and the massive doors locked on the inside, as did the windows. These, in addition to plain glass, had dark glass, gauze and wooden shutters. There was also a self-contained toilet compartment. This miniature fortress contained four berths, two up and two down.

'How long's the journey?' I asked Sandy.

'Thirty-six hours to Amritsar. John Tullie will meet you and take you to the bank bungalow. It's pretty primitive. Just right for the Irish!' Sandy chuckled.

We walked back through the jostling crowd. Water carriers called out, *'Hindi pani'* or *'Mussulman pani.'* Other vendors sold betel, hot tea, sweetmeats and food. Although the train was crowded, more and more people struggled to get aboard. The police ineffectually tried to restore order. At last a whistle blew and I waved Sandy goodbye.

Allah Dad had placed my bedroll on the lower berth, the upper berth being folded back against the side. On the opposite birth sat a colonel whose batman was arranging his kit. Allah Dad and the colonel's batman left at the first stop to sit in a third-class compartment. I had already taken a liking to Allah Dad, but felt embarrassed that an older man should be so obviously set on pleasing me. We were steaming through open country, the slums and turmoil of Bombay behind us. My companion had opened a book without speaking or even looking in my direction. Deciding to learn a little more about my employer, I opened my briefcase and began to read from a history of the Chartered Bank:

The Bank of India, Australia and China was founded by James Wilson, the third son of a family of fifteen who was born in 1805. On the 29th of September 1853, after many objections from the East India Company, the Bank received its Royal Charter. Since then generations of young Scotsmen, Englishmen, Welshmen and Irishmen forsook their homelands to join the Chartered Bank's Foreign Service. Their numbers have never been large, at no time as many as three hundred all told: but these men have encountered during their careers in the East, wars and revolutions, terrorists and assassins, plagues and famines, cholera, dysentery and malaria.

'Going far?' the voice of the colonel cut in.

As he put down the book he had been reading, I saw its title, *The Maltese Cat*, one of my favourite Kipling stories. I explained my position, delighted to have someone to talk to.

'How long do you do?' he asked,

'Five years.'

He took out a curved Peterson pipe, made in Dublin and similar to the one my father smoked. He filled it slowly, a mild interest lighting his cool grey eyes as he regarded me. 'You'll be joining the AFI.'

'What's that?'

'Auxiliary Force India. Your outfit's the Punjab Light Horse. The Adjutant's a decent chap. Captain Freer Smith. Lahore's their HQ. About twenty-five miles from Amritsar.'

'Do I have to join?' I asked, having been the only boy at Campbell who never volunteered for the Officer Training Corps.

'No,' said the colonel, puffing on his pipe, 'but every fit man does. We've only 60,000 British troops in India to 370 million Indians, and if there's any trouble, like a mutiny, we'll need all the help we can get. It's worth a go. You get a Waler and an allowance, and there are only a few drills a month.'

'A Waler?'

'Short for New South Wales, where we used to get the horses for the Indian Cavalry. They came in whaling ships – another reason for the name.'

Over dinner, the colonel offered his philosophy of India: 'The country has many good things and the Indians have unyielding loyalty to their friends and, considering we are foreign rulers, they accept us with grace and good manners. Treat them well and they'll do the same by you.'

At the junction for Bophal, the colonel left the train. Allah Dad came in, unrolled my bed and laid out my toothbrush, soap, face cloth and towel. When I had washed I sat on the bed and was just in time to stop him as he suddenly knelt at my feet and started to undo my shoelaces. 'Please don't bother, Allah Dad. I will do them myself when I turn in.'

'Hazur, it is customary, but as hazur pleases.'

He sounded hurt, and I realized that I must tread cautiously with this man and my new country. To my astonishment, Allah Dad returned to my carriage at each stop to see if there was anything I needed. In the morning he woke me with *chota hazri*, or 'little breakfast', on a small tray containing a teapot, a cup and saucer, a small jug of buffalo milk and a slice of toast thinly spread with butter from the same source. Both buffalo products were slightly rancid but not unpleasant. After I had washed, shaved and dressed, I went to the dining car for the main breakfast, and it was only when I was returning that a terrible thought struck me. Tomorrow I would be placed in charge of one, perhaps several departments, and I had never learnt my sixteen-times table. There were sixteen annas to the rupee, but the significance had never dawned on me. Bank ledgers run to 60 lines with a carry forward of several hundred digits, so how many times did 16 go into 479? One ignorant sub-accountant was well on course for making himself a laughing stock. To the rhythm of the wheels, I recited the new table. That night I went over it again and again till sleep overcame me.

It was dark on the second morning when Allah Dad woke me with *chota hazri*. We were two hours out of Amritsar. I dressed hurriedly and was still going over my table as the train slowed. Dawn broke as it stopped. The platform was thronged with the usual vendors, whom Allah Dad thrust out of the way as he lifted my baggage on to the platform. As he did so, a small reception committee advanced: two amiable Scots, John Tullie and George Tolmie, and Tara Chand, the chief clerk, who placed a garland of scented jasmine blossom round my neck in welcome. In a moment we were in a waiting tonga, and I looked anxiously around for my luggage. 'Not to worry,' said John Tullie. 'Tara Chand will see to it.'

The driver whipped the skinny horse through the already crowded streets at a spanking pace. 'That's the office,' they told me as we rattled past a dusty nondescript building, guarded by a red-turbanned watchman who leant on a long metal-shod pole.

Then we were in the bazaar, and I glimpsed coppersmiths' shops piled high with shining bowls, trays and pots. There were sweetmeats in pyramids and spices in mounds of colour; leather-workers with harness, shoes and sandals; fruit stalls with piles of oranges, bananas, raisins, dates; and over all an unforgettable pall of flies and a mingling of smells. We clattered out of the bazaar through the Hall Gate, one of thirteen that pierced the city wall, and up a slight rise over the railway bridge. The railway line divided the city from the civil lines and the road led to cantonments. About a mile farther on, we turned aside on to an earth road that wandered through fruit groves. Mango trees gave shade and here and there, red against the green, glowed stretches of roses, the raw material for attar, the essence of roses for which Amritsar is famous. Suddenly the tonga swung into a neatly kept drive flanked by rows of large chrysanthemums in earthenware pots, and pulled up with a jerk under the porch of the chummery, a dun-coloured bungalow with wide verandas. White-clad servants salaamed a welcome.

My room, just to the left of the porch, was about twenty feet square, with a high ceiling. Its two windows had gauze screens, and there was a big stone fireplace. A dressing table, chair and net-canopied bed completed the furnishing. There were three other doors, one of which led to a veranda where a cane long-chair with folding leg-rests awaited the sahib's weary moments. Another led to my bathroom, a concrete box with a three-foot zinc tub in the centre, a tall Shanghai jar and dipper in one corner and, in the other, a commode with a deep white enamelled pot, the assemblage constituting a 'thunder box'. A drainage channel in the floor led to a hole in the outside wall, and a small outside door gave the *mater*, the untouchable dirty-job man, access to collect the thunder-box receptacle to be emptied into a tank at the rear, then cleaned and returned to its original position. The contents of the tank were collected from time to time by the municipal night-soil department.

As I took in the scene, the little door opened and the *bheesti*, or water carrier, entered, carrying a four-gallon kerosin tin of steaming water, which he emptied into the tub. Salaaming deeply, he withdrew backwards, and Allah Dad came to help me off with my shoes, a gesture I allowed in deference to custom. Cold water was ladled from the Shanghai jar into the scalding water, and after testing it I lowered myself gingerly into the tub. Feet and bottom I managed to submerge, and with the dipper gave the rest a soaking. Standing up, I soaped all over and washed down with the dipper, a small brass bucket with a brass handle fixed on the inside. Seeing that I was finished, Allah Dad came in with a towel and was about to dry me when, custom or no custom, I took over.

The central dining room had a higher ceiling than the surrounding bedrooms. Around the ceiling, windows were let into the walls to catch whatever breeze was available in the hot weather, though now they were closed for winter. Over breakfast, I met the other chums of the chummery. Besides the two Scots, the solid, dependable, quiet John Tullie and the pawkier George Tolmie, there was a tall, dark Franco-Italian, Enrico de Andria of the Oriental Carpet Company, and John Hannay, box-wallah. Hannay, short, fortyish and energetic, was only with us temporarily while his own bungalow was being repaired. His bearer placed a plate of porridge in front of him with what looked like some hesitancy. '*Lao jao*,' he said – 'Take away. *Burra peg, lao*.'

A large whisky arrived with a jug of water. After two more generous measures, Hannay was ready for his day's work in the cotton goods section of the bazaar.

After breakfast I took a stroll round the compound. There was about an acre of ground surrounded by an open-work brick wall. Against this peaches, almonds and oranges grew in profusion. In front of the bungalow stood two magnificent mango trees. Round at the back, in the servants' quarters, some twenty-four servants with families and possibly dependent relatives lived cheek by jowl. There was stabling for six horses, each animal with its own *syce*, or groom. The caste system, for all its faults, created jobs, since the man who provided grass for the horse was not allowed to groom or saddle it.

As I breathed in the scents of the garden quietly, a flight of parakeets swept past me at eye level, red beaks contrasting vividly with bright-green plumage. Again and again they swooped and chattered across my path. I stood motionless, the thought clear in my mind: whatever happens, I shall never regret having come to this rewarding country.

3

The Griffin and the Sadhu

John Reid, the burra sahib, was a large, forthright, Aberdonian bachelor with penetrating blue eyes and a big nose. 'Welcome to Amritsar,' he said as he shook me warmly by the hand.

He had a questioning, humorous personality, and I took to him instantly. He was eager to hear the latest gossip from Head Office in London, and as we talked I noticed that a long black hair had come to rest on his nose. Instincively I leant across his desk. 'Excuse me, sir,' I said, 'but there's a hair on your nose.'

At the same moment as I seized the hair I realized to my consternation that it was growing. Instinct prompted me again. I plucked it out by the root. We stared at one another. 'I've always wanted to do that,' said John Reid, and laughed.

I joined in, though my heart was pounding. I could not believe what I had done within five minutes of meeting my new boss in his own office.

My desk in the banking hall was already piled high with ledgers. As John Tullie gave me my two keys, he explained that the larger one was for the main safe and I must keep it attached to my person at all times, even in the bath. The smaller one was for my desk drawer, which he duly opened. Inside lay a Colt .45 revolver. 'Is that thing loaded?' I asked,

'Of course,' said John.

The previous relief had apparently pulled to see, and a bullet, flattened on the marble floor, narrowly missed Tulsi Ram, the chief cashier. Behind my desk stood a rack of nine shotguns loaded with buck-shot and fitted with long bayonets. The guns were to be released to the bank guard in the event of an emergency. How would I know it was an emergency, I asked. No worry: I'd hear it coming a long way off. The doors would be locked and help summoned. After that we fought to the last man.

Tulsi Ram was a very fat man in a white dhoti that he wore wound round the body like a sarong, though with the back brought up between the legs and anchored in the waistband. A small pill-box cap sat on his head at a jaunty angle. 'Much welcoming sir dats,' said Tulsi, a huge smile filling his round face, when John Tullie introduced me.

Tulsi ended all his sentences with 'dats', short for 'that is'.

My next introduction was to D.C. Scott, the accountant, a short fat balding man who had the unenviable task of allocating the bank work between himself and three sub-accountants. Like John Reid, he was a bachelor and had a bungalow to himself. He gave me my list of jobs. By the time I returned to my desk, the pile of ledgers had grown even higher.

My *chaprassi* was Ram Nath, who spoke excellent English. He was a Brahmin, one of the Twice-Born, Highest of the High; a smooth, short, well-filled-out man who had, down the middle of his forehead, a smear of red enclosed between two smears of white – the emblem of Siva, the Preserver and Destroyer. I was to discover that he was a happy, secure and contented person. If sent on an urgent errand, however, he had a tendency to return very late, saying that even as he was hurrying through the bazaar, eager to complete his mission to my entire satisfaction, the shadow of a donkey fell upon his shadow, this defilement then making it imperative that he visit the temple for purification. In support of his account, a small amount of ash would be seen to have joined the sign of Siva on his forehead. Eventually I suggested that, whenever he went through the bazaar, he walked on the shady side of the street where no shadow might fall on his and where it would also be cooler. 'My sahib is greatly gifted with much wisdom,' he beamed with genuine delight. 'I will certainly take his advice in future.'

Now Ram Nath placed a huge ledger in front of me, before summoning the relative clerk, a young Sikh with bright intelligent eyes. 'Welcome to my country, sahib,' said the clerk, whose name was Kartar Singh, and who seemed a little surprised when I shook hands with him.

Kartar Singh's job was to call out the vouchers and cheques as I duly ticked them off in the ledgers. I then had to check the additions. My worst fears were soon confirmed. The casts came to large totals and it took me all my time to work the annas into rupees. From time to time errors crept into the books, as the clerks phrased it. It sounded rather as if cockroaches somehow managed to crawl inside when no one was looking. To admit a mistake involved a deeply hurtful loss of face. I soon found myself cultivating the sympathetic approach that, in this matter, we fought shoulder to shoulder to defeat a cunning enemy.

The bank remained relatively quiet until the doors opened and the customers entered amid a babel of chatter. George bellowed for silence: '*Chiprao!*' For a brief spell silence reigned, until the quiet murmur gradually increased and the whole pattern was repeated; and so it went on until lunchtime. The three of us then went upstairs to our small dining room, to have lunch brought in by bearers. Reid and Scot were driven home to their bungalows. Our rather thin onion soup, known as 'dishcloth and onion', was followed by salt buffalow hump with boiled potatoes and ladies' fingers. The last course was cheesy toast. After we had eaten, George and John disposed themselves on long-chairs with their legs up to take a siesta, while I ventured up on to the the flat roof, so gaining my first sight of the famous Golden Temple of the Sikhs, set in its 'Pool of Tranquillity' among the clustering streets and houses. Beyond the city walls I saw the flat countryside and the great shade trees marking the Grand Trunk Road. Kipling's country, I thought. The cool air carried a medley of smells and scents: spices, smoke from cooking fires, roasting meat, sewers, jasmin and orange blossom, all blended continually. Reluctantly I returned to the drab interior of the banking hall.

At three o'clock the doors were closed, and at five our tonga returned us to the chummery. On John's advice I took the Colt .45 back to get some practice, since I had never before fired anything more potent than a Diana air gun. After tea, John took me outside the compound where a thick plank was positioned against a bank of earth. I stood ten feet back, aimed at a paper target and pulled the trigger. The weapon's terrific kick nearly jerked it out of my hand and the bullet struck the top of the plank. 'Don't pull the trigger, squeeze it gently,' advised John, 'and aim below the bull's-eye. Hold it in both hands, if you like. It must remain steady.'

I tried again, and this time hit the target. After twenty minutes I had the feel of the weapon and was able to increase the distance. The snub-nosed bullet carried sufficient weight and velocity to knock an advancing attacker flat on his back. The lead, spreading on impact, could create a terrible exit wound. I wondered if I would ever have to use the revolver and what chance one would stand against an enraged Indian mob. Surely it could only make matters worse. 'You've a natural eye, Bill,' said John, who was, it so happened, corporal in charge of the Amritsar Detachment of the Punjab Light Horse. 'You'll make a great addition to the PLH.'

In vain I pointed out my peaceful nature and reluctance to become a warrior. It was a matter of security for the women and children, to escort them into the old fort. Apart from anything else, the chummery lay well away from any security zone and was therefore vulnerable to attack. Tika Ram, our Gurkha *chokidar*, or night-watchman, was old and could not be expected to do more than keep watch. Whatever my feelings, I realized that again I was faced by custom, and having slept on it I agreed.

On my third day, the burra sahib's *chaprassi* salaamed before me and said the burra sahib would like to see me. As I walked through the clutter of tables laden with ledgers and documents, I wondered if the summons could have anything to do with our first meeting and the alarming incident of the hair. John Reid looked up as I entered and waved me to a chair. 'You'll have received your duties from Scott. I'd like you to run through them.'

I listed them rapidly: 'Cash, current accounts, telegrams, main safe, godowns.'

'Good,' said John in broad Aberdonian. 'I want you to learn Urdu. It's most important that we know what our customers are talking about. Even more important that they know that we know. Once you've passed your exam, you'll receive an extra seventy rupees a month. We've a very good language teacher, Muni Lal. I'll arrange for him to be at your bungalow so you can have an hour with him each morning before you start the telegrams. It's in the first hour of the day that your brain's clearer, your memory sharper. You'll pick it up in no time,' he smiled.

'Thank you, sir,' I said.

I had thought my work load heavy enough already, but it was usual for a newcomer to be given the lion's share and the least attractive jobs. The telegrams themselves were delivered to the bungalow after office hours, and the decoded telegrams had to be on the Burra Sahib's desk to await his arrival next morning. These documents could, for the telegram sub, be the cause of many a weary hour late into the night or even through the pale dawn. The code books for decoding were kept in a black dispatch box, and the telegrams arrived as meaningless jumbles of letters or figures. One digit could indicate a document running to several pages, and there was a mountain of work as the various amounts, periods and dates were slotted into correct positions. A final check figure proved the correctness of the document, but this would sometimes be misread by the telegraph office and fresh advices then had to be cabled for in the middle of the night.

The Amritsar Club was a low single-storeyed white building set amid attractive gardens. Its thick walls were designed to keep out the summer heat and its arched pillars supported a veranda. The interior was dimly lit by small windows, and at night by modest supplies of electricity backed by hurricane lamps. There was a lounge, a small conservatory, changing rooms and, most importantly, the men-only bar. A sprinkling of cane chairs and tables made up the furniture, which could be moved outside in hot weather. The servants were amazingly attentive, and able to anticipate the needs of members to an astonishing degree. They were also incredibly loyal, despite low wages and a certain amount of abuse that they suffered from some members.

Any would-be member was required to be white and preferably in an acceptable occupation. Passing on both counts, I increased the male membership to twenty against seven wives and two elderly sisters. Like all clubs in India, the Amritsar Club formed the hub of the expatriate community. Here the ladies would discuss the problems of their lives, the inefficiencies of their servants, the dreadful dangers of dirt and disease and the even greater dangers of the thousands of alluring Indian girls whose lissome figures were concealed by the folds of extremely attractive saris, some of these made of material so fine that more was revealed than concealed. The famous *Kama Sutra*, first published in Amritsar, suggested an infinite variety of couplings concerned with pleasure indefinitely extended, and it was common knowledge that the only hair on the girls' nubile bodies grew on their heads. Hence the absolute need for the colour bar. The main consideration was to make the club a safe British haven in a vast and hazardous ocean.

In Amritsar, drinking began at sundown, unlike Bombay and the south, where drinks accompanied tiffin. Members were known to delay their drink until the precise moment. The basic measure was the *chota peg*, twenty to the bottle, a *burra peg* being double this and a *pau peg* half. Pegs were drunk in long glasses with ice and soda, the soda for some mysterious reason being considered pure, though made in the bazaar. With drinking under way, everyone stood his round, which accounted for a great deal of liquor. Whisked by John into the bar, I found myself welcomed as new blood, plied with drinks and questioned about home. The nostalgia for home was something that I found constantly strange in this marvellous country so full of exciting possibilities.

I paid for my round as soon as I could and tried to drop out in the one that followed, so provoking a wave of protest. It was part of the game to hold one's drink. The secret, John told me, was to hold your head very steady, and never let it droop or you'd drown in it. My most ambitious tipple in London had been a half of bitter. As I continued to refuse, they finally and incredulously asked, 'Why aren't you drinking?'

'I'm not thirsty,' I replied.

The remark followed me around and for ages I was described as the chap who didn't drink because he wasn't thirsty!

My *munshi* who was going to teach me Urdu, Muni Lal, rode into our compound on a bicycle, protecting himself from the early sun with a large black umbrella. From one of the handlebars hung a purple cloth filled with books. Muni Lal was a round-faced comfortable man of about forty, dressed in a loose white dhoti and an equally loose white turban. He wore black shoes, and black socks held up by violet suspenders. Allah Dad brought out two chairs and a table. Muni Lal placed the purple bundle on the table, opened it up and arranged the books carefully. 'Sir, which book would you like as your reader?'

'If it's convenient,' I replied, 'I would very much like *The Rubáiyát of Omar Khayyám.*'

'He is one of my favourite poets,' said Muni Lal approvingly, 'but you are the first of my gentlemen to ask for it.'

'He's a great favourite of mine, too,' I said.

'Some of his verses I find most difficult, and I am hopeful you may reveal their meaning to me.'

'Which one?' I asked.

Muni Lal beamed, obviously delighted. 'I will recite the most difficult,' he offered.

> 'Oh, Thou, who didst with Pitfall and with Gin
> Beset the Road I was to wander in,
>   Thou will not with Predestination round
> Enmesh me and impute my Fall to Sin.'

As his rather high-pitched voice came to the end, he looked at me. 'You are an Irishman, sir, and this is the translation by your famous countryman, Edward FitzGerald, 1809 born, 1883 died. We will read the original text, which has over four hundred quatrains. Jolly good stuff, much pleasure for me.'

Muni Lal was a Brahmin and religion a popular subject with him. It turned out that something was puzzling him greatly. 'In Amritsar,' he said, 'we use a lot of kerosene oil, which comes in a large tin. Our god Shiva, leaping through the flames in his eternal dance, is impressed on the metal of the tin and makes a fine picture to honour the Hindus and help sales for the British kerosene company. Yet when the Amritsar match factory introduced their new brand of matches and decided to honour the Christian religion by calling it "The Light of the World", there was so much trouble with the missionaries that the idea was abandoned.'

I could only comment on Christianity's bewildering variety of edicts and protest that I was much more interested in learning about his own philosophy.

'It is very complicated, but also very simple,' offered Muni Lal. 'I will first give you the simple case. Hindus believe that the world and everything in it is, when divided into its smallest particle, the same thing, which we call *Prana*, the 'Breath of God'. It seems that now your scientists are discovering this also. During our lives we build up *Karma*, a collection of our good and bad deeds. After we die we come back to this world to atone for our bad deeds or benefit from our good deeds. Eventually we hope to reach a state of *Nirvana*, when return to this earth is no longer necessary. As our sacred book, the *Upanishads*, says, "The Self is all knowing, all understanding, and to it belongs all glory." It is the pure consciousness, dwelling in the heart of all, the divine citadel of Brahma. There is no space it does not fill. We have great problems in discovering this truth because our senses sandwich us between time and space, which in reality do not exist.

Our smiles met as he repacked the books. 'I bring the four hundred quatrains tomorrow, sir,' my *munshi* called as he rode away between the long rows of chrysanthemums.

Our small community continued to produce its surprises. Although its life was based on life in England, that life was at least twenty years behind the times. The Europeans went in great fear of not doing the right thing, especially in their social rounds. One of my first tasks as a newcomer was to have personal visiting cards printed in the bazaar. These I then had to deliver myself to each married household. There was a box at the entrance of every house to receive these cards, and you had to be properly dressed while doing it; and to leave one card for the husband and one for the wife; and, if there were any daughters, one for each of them too. Only after this was achieved could you be invited to the household concerned, and you had to accomplish the manoeuvre without being observed. If any of the family happened to be in view, you sneaked away and came back when the coast was clear.

Our lives in Amritsar were socially and literally in the hands of Freddy Puckle, the District Commissioner, who was responsible for the security of the most seditious area in India. He had a large number of administrative functions, and to assist him in these were a number of magistrates and, below them, the *tahsildars*, who were primarily though not entirely revenue officers. It was remarkable how the hierarchical system spread so easily across the country and was so acceptable to the Indians, who could thus take their complaints step by step to the highest authority, for the District Commissioner was the King and Emperor's representative and was, with his wife, at the top of the social tree.

Freddy and Violet Puckle filled their position with charm and common sense. Having successfully dropped my cards, I was invited to dinner and found myself in a bungalow that was old and strong like the club, but furnished with a taste that showed a strong feminine influence. The ladies wore long dresses and jewels, the men starched shirts and black ties, and the servants seemed to derive a special dignity of their own to match the company. I found myself thinking of the Indian Mutiny, of the Jallianwalla Bagh and the continuing violence of the Freedom Fighters, and trying to visualize the scene should a mob suddenly storm this elegant bastion of the Raj. After dinner, the ladies withdrew, port, brandy and Madeira were passed, cigars lit and stories told. As a mere griffin, I kept very quiet, but felt curious about copies of *The Times* that were carefully laid out on a side-table. In the end I asked my host about them.

'They come out in batches from England every week,' the District Commissioner explained, 'and arrive with me a month old, but I always read them in the correct order, starting with Monday. No matter how eager I am to find out what has happened, I wait until Tuesday before opening the next paper.'

It seemed the most striking example of the yearning for the Old Country I had yet encountered.

The married ladies of the station in general found time on their hands, and found also, having thrown a *cordon sanitaire* around their brown sisters, that they themselves came in for the attentions of any sex-starved bachelors. Our lives were like those of goldfish in a bowl, and the faithful admirer could only, like a troubadour of old, sigh hopelessly for a love that might never be requited. Pursuing the ladies was known rather contemptuously as 'poodle faking' by the heartier sporting elements. It was not, in any case, an activity for which my bank duties left me any time. I did, on the other hand, have a sense of an empty space, an absence of affection, in my crowded life. One morning Enrico asked, 'Would you like a pup?' and produced a half-starved, sickly looking bull terrier bitch. 'It's no good to me. If you don't want it, I'll have it put down.'

The pup was only six weeks old and obviously taken from its mother far too soon. 'I'll keep it,' I said.

The vet advised that her only chance was to be fed with raw meat, minced very finely. This I did, and 'Lugs' – that being the name her sadly drooping ears suggested – throve on the diet. Allah Dad accepted the newcomer with good grace. I had the feeling that if I brought home a tame cobra, he would accept it just as readily. 'Allah Dad,' I asked, 'is not the dog an unclean animal to Muslims?'

'Yes, hazur, but it is hazur's bitch, and the *mali*, the gardener, will do the work for me.'

Lugs became a great companion and followed me on my morning rides. When she tired, I picked her up and she rode in front of me. She never gained her full weight, but was very frisky and probably more agile than her parents. A short while later I was given a West Highland terrier, Macwhusky, who brought back vivid memories of Jap. Macwhusky was very dignified and would challenge any pi-dog in the neighbourhood, whereas Lugs would simply lie down and roll over the moment danger threatened.

So far as our defence was concerned, we already had quite an armoury of rifles and shotguns in the chummery. I had put the Colt .45 in a drawer of my dressing table. In another drawer I placed fifty rounds of ammunition that John had provided. Nevertheless, if the servants did decide to turn disloyal, they could easily shoot the lot of us, or more simply poison us. Strangely enough, it was a thought that never worried me in the slightest. I felt far more concern over the wretched main-safe key, the chain of which I would loop through the handle of my zinc tub when I had a bath.

The greatest hazard I encountered in the bath in fact came about when, as I lay in the zinc tub, feet on the floor and torso flat on the bottom, soaping myself as best I could, Allah Dad came through the outer door bearing a bundle of cushions. As he passed the tub, a sleepy snake slithered from between the cushions and fell into the water. I froze. It was a three-foot Russell viper, whose tail sought purchase between my legs and whose small venomous head landed flat on my chest. The snake and I stared into each other's eyes. If only

I can remain absolutely still, I thought, it mightn't strike. Unlike the cobra, which only strikes in a predictable arc and hence is popular with snake charmers, a Russell viper is capable of striking in any direction to over half the length of its body.

A long minute went by before the viper, its forked tongue flickering, wove its way past my neck, its body slithering across my soapy chest. It slowed as it touched the floor, leaving a foot of tail resting on my shoulder. If I were our *mali*, I thought, I would now seize the tail and crack the viper like a whip. Slowly the tail slipped over the edge and the viper headed across the floor towards the outlet hole. 'Allah Dad,' I screamed, 'there's a snake in here.'

Allah Dad rushed in just in time to see the last of the viper vanish through the drain hole. We ran outside, but it never reappeared. It had probably turned aside into the cavity wall or some other refuge. 'What shall we do?' I asked Allah Dad. 'There may be more snakes under the bungalow.'

'We must call the *zamph*-wallah,' said Allah Dad decisively.

In due course the snake man came. He was a thin, wrinkled old fellow who proclaimed at once in a high-pitched voice that snakes abounded under our house. 'Watch, sahib,' he said. 'The snakes will come out presently.'

He sat on a sack and began to play shrill notes on his gourd pipe. I waited patiently. There was an air of suspense, but nothing happened, and after ten minutes I went inside. Twenty minutes later, Allah Dad called me and I watched from the veranda. The piping had grown louder and the snake-wallah held a forked stick and a cloth in his right hand. A cobra emerged slowly from one of the ventilator shafts. As I made a mental note that we must get new grills on all of them, the snake man, without ever ceasing his playing, pinned the cobra to the ground. In a trice he dropped his pipe and taunted the snake with the cloth, which it bit savagely. Quickly he seized it behind the head, picked it up and adroitly dropped it into the open sack, which he closed with a running cord. Motioning us to remain silent, he picked up his pipe and resumed the music. Within a few minutes a second cobra, the mate of the first, was slowly moving out through the broken ventilator to be caught by the same method.

'Are you not frightened of being bitten?' I asked.

'No, sahib, me bitten many times. My father also *zamph*-wallah. He bitten many time, but not hurting too much. Always make snake bite cloth first. After we take out teeth, no more poison, but good dancing cobra. When dancing finished, have mongoose fight. When snake too old, have special mongoose fight to death. Sahib like to see?'

'No, thank you very much. Are you not a Hindu? Do you not

worship the snake goddess?'

'Of course, sahib, and my snake goddess give me power over snakes, and thus I live.'

The first lethal shot I fired killed a kite hawk, known as a 'shite' hawk – a large bird that had become adept at grabbing a free dinner. It was in the habit of swooping on our meals as they were carried from the cook-house to the table across the rear compound. One day I sat in wait with the Colt, for if the hawk had seen me holding a shotgun, it would have stayed away. As he hovered about twelve feet above me, I fired and, to the great delight of the staff, brought him down stone dead. We collected our armaments and posed for a memorial photograph.

By this stage my colonel's prediction had come to pass. Trooper W.B. MacQuitty, Corps No. 781, had been duly enrolled in the Punjab Light Horse, as enrolment certificate No. 54, dated 15.1.27, confirmed. I had also been initiated into cavalry drill by Farrier Sergeant-Major Savin, or 'Spavin' as we called him in private. I acquired a rather tubby horse called Soupy, short for Soup Plates, whose name referred to the size of his feet. The uniform tunic had shoulder chains to prevent one's arm being cut off in battle. Helmet, boots, puttees, sabre, short Lee Enfield .303 rifle and bandolier completed the ensemble. The rifle was carried in a rifle bucket on the right of the saddle, and the sabre in a scabard on the left. Thus accoutred I attended drills, parades and firing practices on the range. Our strength was nine troopers, of whom I was the youngest and the least experienced. Our two weary Lewis guns seldom managed more than five rounds without jamming.

Six weeks after my enrolment, the Amritsar Detachment was ordered to report in full strength to Lahore, there to join in a ceremonial parade at which Lord Birdwood, Commander-in-Chief, Northern Command, would take the salute. It was alarming news. I was able to ride Soupy and had succeeded a number of times, while on the move, in drawing and returning the sabre to its swinging scabard. But to do this on a strange horse in Lahore before a vast concourse of the élite of the land sounded like another kettle of fish altogether. 'Don't worry,' said John. 'Spavin will fix you up with a quiet mount and we'll practice the drill till it's coming out of your ears.'

The great day arrived. With uniforms carefully pressed, boots, buttons and shoulder chains polished by our admiring bearers until they glittered splendidly in the sunshine, we arrived in Lahore. There

Savin met us and escorted us to the cavalry lines, where our mounts were lined up neatly. I inquired anxiously which was mine. 'Yours is Caesar, the quietest horse in the regiment,' said Savin. 'What's more, he knows the drill. All you have to do is sit tight, and Tullie and Tolmie'll be on either side of you in the rear file. And do try to get your bloody sabre back in the scabard without killing the animal.'

Caesar was a big handsome grey. He reminded me of Harkaway, an eighteen-hand black I had ridden in Putney – the horse used in a film about Dick Turpin's ride to York. Caesar answered instantly to the slightest touch of heel or rein, and had a beautiful walk and a soft trot. I began to feel a good deal calmer. As my father always said, none of his worst disasters had ever happened.

The parade was to be held on the race course, about a mile away. At last we formed up and moved out to take up our position with the other troops already gathered. The saluting base was stationed in front of the grandstand, on which hundreds of Europeans were gathered in all their finery, the grandstand itself flanked by a vast concourse of Indians. It was strange, amid all the calls for freedom from British rule, to find a display of British power so popular. Even our bearers seemed impressed, but it crossed my mind that we were all sitting ducks for a pot shot.

The column must have been nearly a mile long. It was interspersed with several bands, including Pathan pipers, and suddenly the bands struck up and we moved off at a slow walk, a splendid spectacle. The order came to draw sabres. We drew as one man. The long-drawn-out order, 'T-rrrot,' followed, and the column bounced into the uncomfortable ceremonial trot that was to carry us past the saluting post. To my delight, Ceasar anticipated all commands and needed no encouragement – unlike George's horse, which was frisky and difficult to control, or John's, which was equally restive. Fat chance of them helping me, I thought, as I moved firmly along, curb and snaffle held gently in the left hand and sabre proudly upright in the right.

The resplendent figure of Lord Birdwood in plumes was by now in view on the saluting base and the martial music increased in volume. An air of triumph surged through the column: the climax to days of preparation. It seemed to move through Caesar, too. I could feel the gathering excitement in his loins. He's really enjoying the show, I chuckled, and began to feel a firm affection for this splendid animal. All at once he slowed, slightly backing from our position. I urged him forward to no avail. John and George were powerless to help. Caesar switched his trot to a slow canter, passed them and drew steadily ahead. With sabre awry, I used both hands to try to restrain him. Despite my frantic efforts, he continued to canter until he had drawn level with our adjutant, at which point he promptly resumed his trot, step by step alongside the adjutant's horse.

We approached the dais, and the adjutant, with a magnificent flourish, gave the command, 'Present sabres.' In this I had no difficulty emulating my superior officer, who meanwhile totally ignored my presence; at which point I even wildly considered galloping off into oblivion, except that Caesar, locked into step, was not to be moved. At long last the parade ended. Thankfully I returned the sabre to its scabbard with professional precision and awaited my ignominious dismissal from the PLH. The adjutant was abrupt but fair. 'They should have known better than to give you my horse,' he said grimly. 'It won't happen again.'

The regular British Army in India was seldom seen, but lived a secluded life of its own. The atmosphere in the cantonments was circumscribed. The lay-out of the bungalows and barracks, the straight paths lined with whitewashed stones, did nothing to enhance the bleak surroundings. British other ranks (BORs) – NCOs and men – were drilled and paraded until it seemed they were mentally standing at attention. There was a parade for everything: church, doctor, rations, meals. The outside world was out of bounds. Not for them the joys of Amritsar city. Regiments came and went without leaving a trace. They moved in their own pool, which consisted of camp followers, the dedicated Indians who brought them morning tea, shaved them, fed them, looked after their innumerable pets – the dogs, monkeys and other animals that were a comfort to exiles longing for home; who laundered their uniforms and shone their buttons until the British Army in India was, if not the smartest in the world, without doubt the cleanest. The most renowned of the camp followers was the *bheesti*, the regimental water-carrier, made famous by Kipling in 'Gunga Din'. The least were the ladies who supplied relief in the bushes or the bull-ring. This under-exposure to the country gave the British soldier an almost god-like authority as far as the Indians were concerned, but in the eyes of the white civil population he was a common type, as socially unacceptable as the Indians or Eurasians.

My main contact with the army came at the rare intervals when the stocks of PLH ammunition needed to be checked. These were held in the Gobind Garh Fort, half a mile west of the Lahori Gate, built during 1805–9 by Ranjit Singh, who also built the massive wall round Amritsar. Solid and atmospheric with history, the fort still offered sanctuary. On my first visit, a section of artillery and a platoon of British infantry were in occupation, and the officer in charge handed me an acknowledgement form to sign. When I said I would like to check the boxes before doing so, he led me with poor grace to the magazine where the ammunition was stored. 'Sign here,' he said, proffering his clip-board a second time.

'I'd like to have the boxes opened first,' I said, feeling slightly nettled by his obvious distaste at dealing with someone he saw as an amateur.

'None of your chaps have ever asked for this before,' he huffed, as if I was doubting his honesty.

'You're always on the move,' I said. 'How do you know what mightn't have happened last year?'

He looked thoughtful. It seemed likely that he had taken over without checking the ammunition himself. He called the guard and the boxes were opened. Two were filled with brick. I did not report the matter, but new boxes were transferred.

Shortly after this I was invited to dine in the mess. If civilian dinner parties were ritualized by protocol, the army equivalent was even stricter. No matter how entertaining or intelligent a young officer might be, all conversation waited on the commanding officer and descended in order of rank. I found myself tense with the fear of letting the PLH down as I entered the mess and shook hands with the CO. My goodness, I suddenly wondered, should I have saluted?

'Glad you came,' said the CO. 'Your chaps have to see the women and children into the fort if there's trouble. Good thing too. We wouldn't know where to find 'em.'

'Thank you, sir, I hope it won't come to that,' I said in a rather squeaky voice, but began to feel a little easier, having survived the first hurdle. We drank sherry. Everyone else was in full regimentals, but since I did not have any, I wore my dinner jacket. When the mess sergeant announced that dinner was served, we moved in order of rank to sit at a long table that carried a phalanx of regimental silver gleaming in the candlelight. When the meal was over, the mess sergeant placed decanters of port, Madeira and Marsala before the CO, and these were circulated. No one lit up until the CO had started his cigar, and the conversation thereafter consisted of sport, which regiment had won what, what had happened to whom, news from home. Mention of women was barred, as, I fancied, were religion and politics. I kept quiet. There was no way the general opinion could be challenged in this setting. It would have been considered bad manners. I felt sorry for them, caught, as they were, in a web of custom, but the social mechanics of it worked. Their unquestioning belief in the regiment made them courageous in catastrophe and invincible in conflict. I went home greatly impressed by their régime, their obvious closed ranks and unquestioned self-sufficiency. Their aloofness towards the rest of the world made them all the more impressive when they did appear, marching behind their regimental bands and bringing order into the frenzied turmoil of our narrow streets.

Business at the bank was expanding and the allocation of work fell more heavily on me, the junior sub-accountant, who, since he was considered to be in better physical condition than the older hands, received little sympathy. Sometimes I despaired of getting through the endless tasks and spent anxious hours desperately trying to catch up.

With life beginning to put so much pressure on me, I thought it might be useful to consider yoga and asked Muni Lal how I might find a guru to teach me. 'This is not a matter for study,' said my *munshi*. 'It is a matter of knowing, like falling in love!'

'But,' I said, 'I know nothing of yoga. There must be someone who can help.'

'If you are really serious, sahib, many people will help you.'

'But how do I find them?'

'You will not find them. They will find you,' Muni Lal replied with effortless authority.

'But how will they know what I need and where I am?' I continued, more perplexed than ever.

'Sahib, to these people you are like a palm tree in the desert. As you advance upon the Way, and I know from our many talks that you have the seeds of this in your being, you emit vibrations, and even as a stone cast in still waters emits ripples, these emanations make it apparent that you are ready and they will come.'

'But when will they come, and how will I know them?'

'They will come when you are ready and you will know them as a child knows its father,' stated Muni Lal with final conviction.

Two months after this conversation, Allah Dad told me, rather distantly, that a *sadhu*, or holy man, and his *chela*, or attendant, were in the garden. They were seated in the shade of the mango tree. The *chela*, who sat on the *sadhu*'s left, looked about fifteen, while the *sadhu* seemed in his early forties. Both sat in the lotus position, backs straight, legs folded. The *sadhu*'s long black hair flowed over his shoulders. His mouth and face were gentle; his eyes, large and brilliant, were focused on mine. I seated myself opposite. Both remained silent, the boy looking down, immobile. I had by this time read several books on yoga and practised some hatha yoga exercises, which I had found practical and rewarding. Now I found myself thinking suddenly of the rapture I had experienced in earliest childhood. Could the seeds of this encounter have been planted in those far-off days?

Although the silence continued, I sensed that some communication was taking place with which it was impossible for me to interfere. I felt almost like a willing patient being examined by a first-class physician. There was an elation and a lightness, as if some load was being lifted. The garden scents seemed stronger, the colours more vibrant, the passage of time unmarked. Finally I surfaced. 'Thank you for coming,' I said. 'Can you help me to understand yoga?'

Another long silence, the *sadhu* replied, to my astonishment, in a soft Irish accent, 'Sahib, you were going to ask me why we have come. Our meeting was conceived before your birth. You have already travelled some distance along the Way, as your attitudes towards life and death reveal. The Way lies in you, exists only in you, as you and all life and matter exist only in the Supreme Creator of the Universe. It is useless to discuss the Unknowable.'

Silence overtook us again, but his eyes never left mine. At length I heard myself repeating my thanks to him for coming and asking how he had learnt to speak such fluent English with an Irish accent. For the first time I fancied I saw the trace of a smile. 'I was an orphan,' he said, 'and brought up in a convent run by an Irish Order until I became a follower of the Way.'

'What about Christianity?' I asked.

'All religions have certain similar aims, like the spokes of a wheel that link to the hub from different points, but their teaching demands faith and beliefs, so in spite of their common aim, they remain divided, each claiming to know the Unknowable and failing to see the clear bright light of Reality that has been in the Universe since the beginning, the laws of Nature which are the same for us all.'

'Can books help?' I asked.

'Yoga comes from within, like a rosebud expanding into a rose. The knowledge you need is already there. You must allow it to grow. It will grow at the speed at which you are able to receive it, and books may help to fertilize the soil. Your senses will help, but you must ride them like horses. They are not you. The Way lies deep in your own self. To it be true. There is no other existence.'

Silence fell again. I felt that I was being carried along in an invisible flood towards a limitless sea. 'Wake up, hazur, wake up.'

Allah Dad was holding my shoulder. I looked around. The garden was empty. 'When did the holy men leave?' I asked.

'I did not see them go, hazur.' His voice indicated disapproval. 'Hazur's bath is waiting.'

4

Hot Weather

The sparkling freshness of the lovely spring mornings began to fade.
By the end of April the fans slowly revolved at the office and the
sahibs' boiled and filtered drinking water was brought in empty
whisky bottles to be chilled in a zinc-lined box under a slab of ice,
protected from over-rapid melt by a wrapping of hessian. The hessian
and corks had an unforgettable musty smell from long service. I
suspected that once the thirsty sahibs had emptied the bottles, the
obliging *chaprassies* simply refilled them from the bank tap. Water was
ever a risk. Fractured sewers and mains seeped insidiously beneath
the scorched and cracking earth.

By May the heat had grown to be alarming. Metal exposed to the
sun could not be touched. Shade temperatures reached 120°F and
once our veranda thermometer showed 110°F at midnight. *Kus-kus*,
absorbent grass mats, were hung over doors and windows and
continually soaked by the sweating *bheesti*. I perspired in thin pyjamas
under the stifling mosquito net on my damp mattress. One night I
woke suddenly with a violent call of nature. I rushed to the thunder
box and let fly a fluid blast of diarrhoea flecked with blood. I had
dysentery.

The chummery swore by Dr J. Collis Browne's Chlorodyne, which
contained ether and opium. Ten drops in water offered great relief
even if it had little effect on the bugs. I reached a stage where I
needed to rush off every half-hour, expecting to pass an elephant but

emitting only a noisy blast with a sprinkling of blood. Gradually the disturbing symptoms subsided, to be replaced by an acute sinus infection that wracked my head and eyes with excruciating pain. For this I received nose drops and a warning from my doctor never to introduce a dirty finger into a clean nostril. The sinusitis ended abruptly with an internal explosion that voided thick brown evil-smelling clots down my nostrils.

I felt that a further blow was imminent. Sure enough, it came a week later: conjunctivitis of both eyes. Each morning the lids were sealed and crusted. The whites of my eyes were bright red when I managed to get them open. The doctor prescribed bathing them in silver nitrate, and eventually the infection responded. By now I had a healthy respect for elementary hygiene and understood why Hindus and Muslims were forever washing themselves and their cooking utensils.

Shortly after this, my doctor invited me to a round of golf. The Amritsar golf course boasted no grass. The hard-baked earth, with hummocks and mounds, provided a variety of hazards, and from time to time contact with a rock would send a ball savagely back at the golfer. Half-way round the course stood an old cistern, its water covered with a thick green scum. Here the doctor doffed his topi, swirled the green out of the way, dipped and drank deeply. I watched in dismay. 'The trouble with Europeans,' he said, 'is that they live sterile lives. The only way to overcome the bugs of India is to acquire a gradual immunity. A little dirt a day keeps the doctor away.'

I decided to replace my heavy bed and mattress with a charpoy, a frame of wood and string resting on four legs. A thin grass mat and a pillow completed my new bed. The charpoy was set in the middle of the lawn, its four feet in four bowls of water to prevent creepy crawlies from climbing into bed with me. Instead of pyjamas I wore a loin cloth. The chummery thought my ailment had affected my reason. 'We're in the middle of the worst civil unrest for years and you choose to sleep unprotected in the middle of the lawn where anyone could shoot you just with a shotgun from the road,' they chorused.

'I'd rather be cool,' I replied.

As I crawled under the mosquito net, I carefully placed my Colt .45 and a five-cell electric torch under the grass pillow before adjusting my loin cloth and lying on the grass mat. It was undoubtedly much cooler.

Our bungalow was surrounded by orchards and the nights were rich with changing fragrances: jasmine, orange, lemon. Night sounds also came to me in the scented air: the faint call of peafowl, the rising crescendo of the brain-fever bird, the dry rustle of the cicadas. Above the natural sounds came the calls of the watchmen, telling each other all was well. Tika Ram, our watchman, was a Gurkha veteran, retired from the British Army, who wore his kukri with confidence. During the First World War, he had decapitated eleven Germans on nocturnal visits to enemy lines, unfailingly returning with gruesome proof of his success.

Since snakes lurked in various places, I was always careful to search the ground before getting out of bed. Scorpions and hornets were also numerous and, unlike snakes, were unafraid of people. I learnt to keep my mosquito boots in bed with me after being stung by a huge hornet that had sought a resting place in one. It stung me under the big-toe nail and the pain was beyond belief. Allah Dad came to the rescue and massaged the toe with kerosene oil, which was his general cure-all.

Despite illnesses, the unrelenting heat and civil commotion, the five of us turned up for work day after day in various stages of distress. Throughout this trying period, John Reid proved to be a tower of strength. He was a heavy smoker who shook powerful cocktails and gave enjoyable parties. He took little exercise himself, as he suffered from chronic asthma and bronchitis, yet he arranged sporting events, including a walking race round our five-mile Circular Road for which he presented silver cups. We used to ride together, and in this more relaxed atmosphere I once asked him if he had ever thought of seeking a guru. 'I've thought about it,' he said, 'and I've read a great deal of Indian literature, including the *Bhagavagita* and the *Upanishads*. But what would the neighbours say if they learnt that the burra sahib of the Chartered Bank was standing on his head and contemplating his navel?'

'Let them say what they say. You're a Scot. I believe I could find a guru. He could come before the neighbours wake up.'

'Fix it,' said John.

The next time I saw Muni Lal, I said, 'I want a guru simply for hatha yoga, one who can cure my burra sahib of his chest complaints.'

'Is not a problem,' beamed Muni Lal. 'I have very chap. Of course, he is holy man, but he is also a doctor of medicines. He is Dr Ram Chandra. Of course, he is a little expensive, but he will certainly cure your sahib.'

I explained the need for secrecy, which was instantly appreciated. On the day appointed I rode to John's bungalow on my New Dawn motor-cycle. We waited together in the big lounge for the arrival of Dr Ram Chandra. No one appeared. John sent for his bearer. 'Has anyone arrived?'

'No one coming in, sahib, only old man in garden.'

'Tell him to come in here.'

'Not wanting to come in, sahib.' The bearer looked sheepish.

'Why not?'

'He says house unclean.'

We went out to the garden.

Ram Chandra, about fifty, thin and wiry with strong features and perceptive eyes, said, 'You sent for me, but I cannot enter your house nor can I treat you if you continue to drink and smoke. We can work on your veranda if you wish.'

John was a man of quick decisions. 'Agreed,' he said.

We sat on the veranda and talked. Yes, it was possible to restore the body; it was the servant of the mind. The air we breathed was the source of all life. We must learn to breathe properly, to relax and do exercises which would encourage these things.

We began the next morning. The side veranda was private and ideal. At one end was a large mirror, and in this we were instructed to study the positions. They would only look and feel right if correctly performed. With wonderful self-control, John gave up smoking and drinking. Ram Chandra, pleased with our progress, suggested that this could be improved if we exercised naked or with with a *rumali*, the Indian equivalent of a jock-strap. We settled for nudity and chuckled at the thought of the shock on our customers' faces could they only have seen the burra sahib and his chota sahib standing stark naked on their heads before the day's banking.

At the end of six months, John's asthma and bronchitis had departed, and so had our secret. Our most valued clients insisted on coming to see the ashram. John's fame spread and the bank flourished. Head Office was at first perplexed, but since the earnings grew steadily, the Chartered obviously had something their competitors lacked. Towards the end of his time in India, John would, every now and then, lie on a bed of nails with a plank across his chest and invite favoured clients to walk over it.

The blistering furnace heat pursued the sweltering population with increasing fury. At nearly the end of June, high winds rose and swept dust from the baking earth into swirling clouds. In vain were doors and windows tightly closed. The red torrent poured through tiny cracks and entered every nook and cranny of the darkened interior. Nothing was safe. Every drawer and cupboard was breached. My clothes, papers and precious belongings were coated in a fine film that seemed impossible to remove. The sun was hidden, and after the fierce wind had subsided, the dust hung on in the still air indefinitely.

'Nothing to be done till the rains come, and hopefully they'll be here soon,' said John.

We were by now all covered with prickly heat, the bright red spots of overworked sweat glands worn out with the desperate task of keeping body temperature normal. Heat stroke was not uncommon, even among Indians. The body temperature could rise rapidly and death follow unless the victim was plunged into cold water. Once, after a game of polo in Lahore, I undressed and was about to get into a warm bath when suddenly my skin went dry and I felt very hot and faint. I had a thermometer and took my temperature. It was over 104°. Unbelievingly, I shook it down and tried again. This time it was even higher. Fortunately there was a great Shanghai jar of chilled water with a brass dipper in the room, and I sluiced vigorously until my temperature miraculously dropped to normal.

The dust notwithstanding, I continued to prefer my charpoy in the garden, often soaking myself so as to cool off by evaporation. Another pest was the sandflies, tiny creatures small enough to get through the net and capable of producing an unpleasant fever. Sometimes I wondered how I managed to sleep at all, but in fact I slept quite well, and was more than surprised one night to wake up with a start at the sound of distant thunder. Huge cumulus clouds piled high in the sky were vividly lit with fork and sheet lightning. There was a patter of warm raindrops. Within minutes it had burst into a roar. Everyone was awake. The chummery left their beds and danced around in the deluge, which grew steadily colder. The dust vanished, the prickly heat retreated, the parched land rejoiced.

As temperatures dropped, the humidity increased. It became, in a way, even more trying. Circles of damp surrounded the iced *chota pegs*, writing paper stuck to the wrist and ink spread itself on damp paper. Bullfrogs calling unceasingly for mates added their chorus to my nightly orchestra. Sometimes a croak would be cut off in mid-note as a stealthy snake engulfed the serenader. Mosquitoes bred in any standing water. A broken bowl, an old tin, an undrained puddle swarmed with their emergent larvae. The water table was only a few feet below the surface, and soon the low areas became pools. We sprayed and drained and anointed ourselves with repellents, the most successful being a combination of kerosene oil and soft green soap. Still the mosquitoes, with their high-pitched whine, attacked us with the persistence of starving tigers. We tried to protect ourselves, but some always broke through our defences and were soon bloated with our blood; which made them easy targets for a quick smack that left a crimson splash on the wall. The memsahibs wisely stayed in the hills.

The rains affected social behaviour. Open shirts, shorts and sandals replaced starched white drill, collars and ties, though long trousers and mosquito boots were essential after sunset. With the cats away, some of the mice began to play. Everything in India flows towards sex. The land is drenched with it, the highly spiced foods designed, indeed, to fuel the flames. The carvings in temples revealed ancient wisdom in the endless erotic couplings of gods and goddesses who intertwined in a thousand voluptuous movements.

The other side to the almost irresistible temptation was, of course, VD, which was widespread. Pox doctors and quacks abounded, and curative pills and potions adorned every pharmacy, as did sheaths in a variety of colours, including black. Blue ointment and blue soap were sworn by, but alcohol, the great relaxer and courage inspirer, could overturn the most careful preparations and make a visit to the doctor for post-coital disinfection necessary – which, alas, was not always successful. Our own good doctor recommended abstinence. If that proved impossible, he counselled wearing a sheath, starting with a full bladder and, when finished, voiding the bladder and washing thoroughly with soap and water.

Amritsar was the final destination of the great caravans that journeyed down the Old Silk Road of Marco Polo. Kipling caught the atmosphere in his 'Ballad of the King's Jest' (1892):

> When the Spring-time flushes the desert grass,
> Our Kalifas wind through the Khyber Pass.
> Lean are the camels but heavy the frails,
> Light are the purses but heavy the bales,
> As the snow-bound trade of the north comes down
> To the market square of Peshawar town.

By the time the *kalifas* reached Amritsar, bales and frails were a lot lighter but purses a lot heavier, and the lusty camel drivers, having led their beasts through the lonely wastes, were ready for comfort. The ladies of Amritsar opened wide their doors to welcome them. Shades of Paris, I thought, as late one evening we visited the street of brothels.

The houses looked like their neighbours – wooden fronts, small verandas – but had a red-light aura of excitement. Courtesans have influenced history, and every city has its head lady. The most influential in Amritsar was a petite Muslim beauty whose features were like those of the Mumtaz Mahal that I saw in a miniature painting in Lahore Museum. I took an instant liking to her effortless air of authority and her obvious pride in her position. I spoke to her of the great houses of Paris, and she asked endless questions, which I answered to her great delight. Then I inquired why the ladies of India only wore hair on their heads. 'Just as our men are circumcized, it is in the interests of cleanliness,' she said.

'It must be painful,' I said.

'Ah, you want to know our secret?' she smiled. 'It is nothing more than a ball of sticky toffee which rolls the hair away. There are some old women who specialize in this service. They are very skilful, it is nothing.'

I turned the conversation to politics. 'What is going to happen to the British here?'

'You have been liked in the past, and even today the majority want you to stay. You have dealt more fairly with India than my Moghul ancestors, but Gandhi has stirred up the youth of the country and they see rich spoils for themselves. It will be a violent minority who make the country ungovernable. You are so few and so correct. My ancestors would have slaughtered any opposition, but you have the justice of the Raj to uphold. India is totally corrupt. We understand this. You cannot change us. So you will go, and when you go there will be much killing and settling of old scores and even more blood-letting between the Muslims and Hindus.

'Is there danger in Amritsar now?'

'Yes, but you will be safe.'

'Why?' I asked.

'Because you are an Irishman and have found freedom from the British.'

'But how will they know I am Irish? How do you know?'

'Foreigners have no secrets in India. You taught us the "game" and now we play it better than you.'

I held her hand as I said goodbye. She looked at me with her large dark eyes as if weighing me up. 'Come and see me whenever you wish. We are friends by the Grace of God. My name is Mala.'

'Friends by the Grace of God,' I repeated.

Life had begun to settle into the routine of a morning ride, office work, tennis at the club, followed by shower, change and a game of bridge, then home to dinner and bed. My mother had learned bridge from my father, and they both played a good hand and often held little bridge parties at home; sometimes they had played with me. I was grateful to them for having taught me, but I was also a little alarmed to find myself slipping so easily into the social round, especially when I was asked to be the club secretary and found my excuses overriden. I was still a griffin and expected to toe the line.

One of my duties was to arrange the club's future activities with the staff. I discussed these with the head boy at some length one evening, and after he left, Mrs Mullen, the wife of the manager of the Amritsar Distillery, who had been in India some thirty years, asked me what he'd been talking about. 'You mean you couldn't follow?' I said.

'Oh, no,' she replied. 'I expect my servants to speak English. I wouldn't dream of speaking to them in their own language.'

'But what do you do when you go out?'

'I never go out by myself, and my husband or *syce* deals with the matter.'

Mrs Mullen was by no means alone in this. It was one of the reasons why it was so difficult for servants who had known and respected a bachelor sahib to accept an English-speaking mistress who did not understand them and was filled with the advice and prejudices of the other ladies of the station. The old and trusted bearer frequently had to make his sad farewells.

Another of my duties was to supply the club wives with peafowl for their Christmas dinners. This I was happy to do, and it helped to mitigate their disapproval of my interest in the natives and their affairs. John Reid had been approached on several occasions with requests that MacQuitty be sent home before some dreadful scandal erupted. His invariable reply was that I was a first-rate worker and what I did in my spare time was my own affair. Since he was their banker, this usually ended the matter, especially after it became known that he had a guru himself.

Kartar Singh, my clerk, came from a farming family and knew the country. One Sunday morning we set off on the New Dawn, carrying a .22 Remington and a twelve-bore BSA shotgun with a variety of cartridges, including buckshot. There was always a chance of a black buck, and the farmers were glad to get rid of them as they ate the crops. We drove some twenty miles into flat country, mostly travelling along the hard *mutti* (impacted earth) roads of the canal network until branching off down a likely path. About a mile beyond a village, the narrow tracks petered out. We left the machine in the shade of a tree and walked across a stretch of ploughed land, criss-crossed with irrigation ditches and featuring here and there great stands of sugar cane. Buck were around in plenty, but they kept steadily out of range. Although we saw peafowl scuttling through crops of corn, it was impossible to get close to them, and perhaps this was just as well since by some they are considered sacred because they kill snakes, which curiously enough are also sacred. 'Do not worry,' said Kartar Singh. 'It's not good shooting them here. We might get into trouble. We'll get some after dark when they roost in the trees along the canal bank.'

Our bag was only four woodpigeons after a long day with a break for lunch with the friendly headman – curry, chapatti and tea. I had begun to retrace my steps to where we had left the bike when, peering round a stand of sugar cane, I saw a buck quietly grazing. Hastily changing my No. 5s for buckshot and scarcely daring to breathe, I waited while the buck grazed closer. When it was less than fifty feet away, I fired. The buck fell and then rose, and I gave it the second barrel. It went down again, scrambled up and started away, only to fall again. I tore after it and, in spite of its anguished pleading eyes, cut its throat. Kartar Singh, hearing the shots, came running, followed by two children in floods of tears. They were the headman's son and daughter. The buck I had killed was their pet doe.

We had tea with the headman, who accepted my abject apologies. 'It is a small matter, sahib. There are plenty more.'

I gave the children five silver rupees. Their tears dried and we were warmly invited to return soon.

We drove homeward, the doe resting on the tank, its legs tied behind my back. As darkness fell, we stopped on the canal bank and Kartar Singh, taking the Remington, vanished among the trees. There was a shot, followed by a dull thud, and another, followed by a wild flapping and squawking as half a dozen peafowl took to the air. Kartar Singh returned with two heavy birds. 'It's quite easy. You can get as many as you like. No problems at Christmas,' he said, slinging the birds over his shoulder.

When we got home, I skinned the doe, scraped the skin and dressed it with alum. I never shot another buck, nor for that matter any other four-footed animal, except to put it out of its pain. My blood lust had been obliterated by the look in the doe's eyes. Snipe, teal, widgeon, peafowl, partridge, pheasant and quail I remained quite happy to slay, perhaps because they lacked expression. I made sure that the buck's death was not wasted. We ate the venison and I had the skin made into a cushion, which I still have to remind me of my decision.

Not long after this, I was summoned in my capacity as a member of the Punjab Light Horse to dispatch two horses that had broken their legs at the Great Amritsar Horse Fair, made famous by Kipling in *Kim*. The horses lay amid the confusion of the fair. One, besides breaking a foreleg, had spiked its eye on a tent peg. The owners and helpers were holding down the struggling horses, but the ever-present mob of spectators made my approach difficult. I had been through the drill with Savin. The bullet needed to be aimed so it passed through the brain and down the spinal canal, thus destroying all nervous function and movement. An imaginary cross was drawn between the left eye and the right ear and vice versa. At this point the mouth of the gun was placed, and fired when the line-up with the neck was in the correct position. I was fortunate that in both cases a single shot sufficed. This act did not tally with the Buddhist respect for life, nor indeed with that of the Hindu, whose sick or useless animals were driven out and left to die in desert places.

Cold or hot weather, my typical day began with Allah Dad's '*Chay budgy gia, hazur*' – 'Six o'clock gone' – in his deep voice. He repeated the phrase till I was awake, but if this failed nudged me gently on the shin. Then he carried in a little table on which he put my cup of tea before lifting the mosquito net and looping it over its frame. Tea drunk, I pulled on my mosquito boots and went for my sluice from the Shanghai jar. Dried, I pulled on a cotton shirt and jodphurs. Soupy, carefully groomed, saddled and bridled, waited patiently in the drive. The *syce* stood to attention as I mounted. Lugs and MacWhusky were already romping around the garden and being scolded by the *mali* for knocking over his flowerpots. I walked Soupy slowly out of the compound and turned right down a road that led through groves of large loose-skinned oranges something like oversize tangerines. They were full of pips and rather watery, but easy to skin and eat as Soupy picked his way, avoiding the scampering dogs. The orchards ended in shade trees, and beyond them stretched open country.

The villagers got to know me and would often stop me to have a chat, and sometimes to ask my opinion in a dispute. If I suggested they see a magistrate, they would reply, 'You decide between us, sahib. My friend is a Muslim and I am a Hindu, and, you see, the magistrate will be for one or the other. Therefore we will abide by your decision.'

Whether my simple suggestions were ever followed I never knew, but since I always rode out in the same direction and never carried arms, I would have made an easy target for their wrath. The disputes were usually about water rights, money, ownership of land, animals or women. The courts were slow, and professional witnesses could be hired. Indeed, they sat on benches under the shade trees by the courts offering their services. Case files would remain at the bottom of the pile unless an offering was made to speed the progress. The wealthier Indians were extremely litiginous and lawyers and barristers had a good life. Democratic justice, so successful in Britain, was unsuited to a corrupt society where witnesses were concerned only with giving evidence that would benefit themselves, their families and friends.

Another custom was *dastur*. This meant that in every transaction, however small, some little perk was reserved for the vendor. Since it was the custom, no one paid it any attention until it over-stepped reason. Then the cook, or whoever had been challenged, would say there was some mistake and come back with altered figures. The bank did allow us to accept fruit or garlands, but only on special occasions, such as Christmas or festivals. Occasionally we would find money or a bottle of whisky concealed at the bottom of the basket, but such favours we always gracefully returned.

Once I was approached by a customer who asked me if I would use my influence to obtain finance for a friend who stood to make a lot of money. It became obvious that this was not in the interests of the bank, but he offered me a large sum for my services. Naturally I refused. 'Is it not enough, sahib?' he asked.

'No, not nearly enough.

He doubled his offer. I shook my head. 'How much, then, do you want?' he asked.

I told him. 'But that is a hundred times more than I hope to make myself,' he said in astonishment.

'Ah, yes,' I replied, 'but you will understand that I should have to resign from the bank and refund them for any loss they might sustain. I would also have to provide myself with sufficient income to make my retirement possible.'

He grinned with relief. 'Sahib, it is said of your country that it is full of saints and scholars. I hope we may be friends.'

'By all means.'

The story seemed to have got around the bazaar. It was, at all events, the last time I was offered a bribe.

The earth was moving steadily towards the winter solstice. The thick-walled bungalows slowly surrendered their heat and I exchanged the cold charpoy on the lawn for a bed on the veranda. This allowed me the benefit of fresh air and the sounds and scents I had grown to like. On particularly cold nights, I wore a balaclava helmet and covered the blankets with a padded quilt. The days were bright and sunny, the skies blue and clear. It was an incredible change from the horrors of summer.

The *mali* filled the garden with flowers: rows of potted chrysanthemums and zinnias, and beds of sweetpeas, canna lilies, nasturtiums and roses. For some reason the only flowers we did not seem to be able to grow were carnations. The hard-worked *bheesti* carried endless supplies of water from the well in his goatskin bag.

It was the dinner-party season. Each household carefully chose compatible guests for enjoyable evenings. Unfortunately our small community did not make for variety or exceptional conversation, though the people who ran the country – police, doctors, teachers, judges, magistrates – all had wondrous experiences to relate, even if these were not always suitable for the ears of the ladies. It was not, in any case, done to 'talk shop'. Dress was inevitably evening.

Hospitality followed a disciplined ritual. Guests, invited at eight for 8.30, were welcomed with short drinks and small eats. At 8.30 the *khitmagar*, or butler, would announce, 'Dinner is served.' Place cards, carefully laid out in the precise order of the *Blue Book*, nestled among elaborate flower arrangements beautifully prepared by the *mali*. Bearers stood behind each chair, ready to move it into position as the guest sat down. The servants were genuinely fond of parties and gave their best to make each a success.

At the announcement of dinner, the head of the chummery would escort the leading lady into the dining room, placing her on his right. Sherry was served with the soup, white wine with the fish, red with the meat, a sauterne with the sweet, followed by finger bowls of warm water on which floated a scented flower. Finally, fruit and nuts were placed on the table. After the desert, the ladies retired to the drawing room for coffee and liqueurs. The men relaxed with cigars and circulated decanters of port, Madeira and Marsala. It was customary to tell slightly *risqué*, often dull stories, but it was important to appear attentive whenever a senior held forth. After thirty minutes or so, on an almost imperceptible signal from the chief guest, the host would suggest we join the ladies. Conversation in the presence of the ladies was formal and continued until the head lady announced she must leave for home. Everyone remained seated until she rose, and then respectfully followed her out, making their appreciative adieus.

As a bit of one-upmanship, I had ordered a large porcelain jar of Chinese ginger from Moti Lal, our local grocer. It came supplied with an elegant fork for spearing the strangely shaped ginger, and the half-gallon jar, tall and magnificent, became a feature of our dinner parties. To one of these we invited the District Commissioner, Freddy Puckle, and his wife Violet. All went smoothly. The conversation flowed around such harmless topics as local sports and memories of home. Eventually the jar of ginger was brought in and placed before the first lady. Violet plunged the fork into its now depleted depths and landed a morsel on her plate. Glancing down I saw to my horror that the curiously shaped ginger was not ginger at all but a dead lizard, either a casualty from China or more likely one of our own. Allah Dad, standing behind my chair, took in the scene and in a twinkling, before anyone had time to realize, leant over as if to brush up some crumbs and swept the plate with its gruesome victim on to the concrete floor. All was set to rights, Violet plunged again, and to my relief came up with a piece of ginger which she pronounced most delicious.

At one stage the mystery of the gradual reduction of the contents of our sherry decanter began to exercise us. Apart from dinner parties, we never drank sherry, yet the level went steadily down. Late one evening, when there was only a quarter left, we decided to add a small contribution of our natural fluid to top it up. Imagine our delight as the sherry continued to go down until at last the decanter was empty. Then I sent for the *khitmagar*. 'Khitmagar, who has been drinking our sherry?'

'Every night, sahib, cook is putting a little in master's soup.'

The big annual event in Amritsar was the New Year's Eve Ball. Members, including out-station visitors, arrived at 10.30 to find the club transformed with coloured lights, strings of paper decorations, a four-piece band from Lahore, bright fires, champagne and a *kala jugga*. The *kala jugga*, literally 'dark place', was a standard provision for all dances. Here amorous and would-be amorous couples could flirt between numbers. Here, too, bereft men sought their missing partners for the next dance. As club secretary, it was part of my duties to dance with the senior ladies and keep the social machinery in top gear. This I attempted to do, fortifying myself with occasional visits to the male-only bar. Towards the end of the evening, the band played the 'Blue Danube', and I found myself in the arms of a voluptuous lady from a lonely up-country estate. She was wearing a white gown, trimmed with gold and glittering with sequins. I rather fancied myself in an old-fashioned waltz, and we whirled around the room in fine style. The music when it stopped had brought us close to the entrance to the *kala jugga*. She guided me into its darkest recess. 'Strauss is so wonderfully romantic,' she whispered as we sank down on a deep couch. 'What a wonderful evening.'

She turned towards me, her splendid bosom pinning me in my corner, a hand sliding behind my head. Suddenly I felt an overpowering desire to sneeze and choked it back. We continued in our soft embrace while I wondered how soon I could decently free myself. She was slightly tipsy, and I began to wonder how her hard-drinking, jealous husband would react if he found me in his darling's arms. Gradually I had a terrible sense that all was not well. Something warm and wet was trickling down my face. My God, I thought, she's started to cry. The flow continued. What on earth had happened? She must have noticed it too. 'I think perhaps we should go back,' she whispered.

Thankfully I rose, drying my face with my handkerchief. As we moved into the light, the cause of the mysterious flow was only too apparent. I had suffered a nose-bleed. Her spotless gown was streaked with blood, my shirt equally crimson. The implication was there for all to see. We stumbled back into the *kala jugga*. 'What shall I do?' she sobbed.

'Go to the ladies' room,' I hissed. 'Tell the *ayah* you have had a nose-bleed and ask her to send for your husband to take you home.'

'But you?' she gasped.

'I'll slip into the changing room. My bearer has clean shirts.'

And so it happened, and by a miracle no one was any the wiser. But there was a sequel, two months later. About every ten days I had another nose-bleed, often very heavy, and the doctor advised me to consult Surgeon Sohan Singh, pupil of the famous Jullunder Smith, one of the first surgeons to remove cataracts. He was renowned for smoking a Burmese cheroot while operating.

Sohan Singh was a dignified Sikh in his fifties with a fine grey beard. He examined me carefully and said, 'You have a projecting broken bone in the back of your nose and it is pressing on an artery. The bone should be removed. If you like, I will do this tomorrow morning. I shall be operating and can see you at ten o'clock.'

I accepted his offer, but on the way home reflected on the dangers of such an operation, with infection rife and all manner of foreign bacteria lurking in an Indian hospital. The following morning, having arranged my temporary absence with the bank, I set out fearfully. The Amritsar General Hospital was a red-brick building, a product of the Raj. Its large compound, filled with charpoys, was where the cataract patients were cared for by their families. January and February were the cataract season, when the air was cool and free from dust and people came from all over the Punjab to be operated on by Sohan Singh.

The surgeon was in the lecture theatre, addressing his students, who sat in mounting tiers around him. He explained the operation he was about to perform on me, and they listened with rapt attention. It came as a surprise to me to be on show, but I appreciated their interest and was happy to be making my small contribution to science. Sohan Singh motioned me to a stool in front of him, adjusted his head mirror and light and peered up my nostril. Micky South would have had a good laugh at this, I thought.

'This is an unusual injury,' said Sohan Singh. 'How did you come to damage your nose?'

I explained that I thought I had done it boxing.

'Ah,' he said, 'you Irishmen, always fighting.'

'Oh, no,' I said. 'I was just teaching boxing at a boys' club in London.'

'How can a teacher get hurt? You must have liked boxing.' His eyes twinkled. 'This is a very short operation. You will feel nothing, not like in your boxing fights,' he smiled. 'Hypodermic syringe, please.'

His assistant handed him the syringe, which I noticed had an exceptionally long needle. 'You will feel nothing but a little prick,' he said.

The little prick was followed by two more, and while we waited for the anaesthetic to take effect, he went over the ground again and showed the students the long shears he would use to remove the offending bone. The theatre was packed, the students remarkably silent and attentive. Good chaps, I thought. Another assistant appeared with a tray of additional instruments and a kidney dish that he held at the ready for the flow of blood. Sohan Singh inserted the shears. I felt them grip the bone. 'Keep quite still,' said Sohan Singh.

There was a horrible crunch, a blinding pain, and tears streamed down my face. Terrified to move, I remained frozen. 'Can you feel something?' asked Sohan Singh.

'Yes,' I said.

Sohan Singh took the syringe and squirted a couple of drops on to his tongue. 'This is water some wicked student has substituted. Bring me a fresh bottle of cocaine.'

I was reinjected; the pain subsided. Said Sohan Singh, 'You may stay in the hospital and go home later, but come and see me in one week's time. I am cross with my students. I will deal with them when you are gone.'

My nose healed quickly and Sohan Singh was pleased. I said I would very much like to watch him operate. 'You can do better than that,' he suggested. 'You can help with an amputation. We are short of a man in the theatre.'

I followed him apprehensively into the changing room and put on an operating gown and mask. I comforted myself with the thought that it was probably something small. After all, he was an eye specialist. The theatre was a lofty room with tall windows. The patient, a small thin man, already lay on the operating table. On his right leg at the knee was a dreadful growth the size of a football. 'It is a severe sarcoma,' said Sohan Singh. 'The leg will be amputated from the hip, thus avoiding dividing the femur.'

He introduced me to the young Indian house surgeon, who was very deferential and told the patient I was the doctor sahib from

Ireland. The poor patient clutched my hand, greatly comforted, and continued to hold it tightly as the cotton mask was placed over his mouth and nose and the anaesthetist dripped ether on to it from a cloth-wrapped bottle. After a brief struggle, the patient lost consciousness and the surgeon asked me to take charge of the leg. As I manipulated it in accordance with his instructions, he deftly cut along a blue pencilled line, exposing the femoral artery, which he ligatured in two places before dividing the great vessel. The blood remaining in the leg was massaged back into the patient and the leg began to cool. While the operation proceeded, an orderly walked round the theatre with a fly swatter, killing flies on the walls, on the patient, or wherever they alighted. At last the leg came free. The weight was more than I bargained for and I almost dropped it. The orderly stopped swatting and fetched a deep bucket, into which I lowered the emaciated limb with its dreadful burden. 'Please take his hand again,' said the surgeon. 'It will comfort him when he comes round.'

I took the patient's hand and, as he came to, I said, 'It is all over and you'll soon be well again,' though I thought his chances slim.

One is accustomed to seeing pieces of animals hung up in butchers' shops, but the closeness to live action, the participation, the weight of the leg and the fact that, for good or ill, it would never be part of the man again, was a reality that brought home the value of life. I was still in a state of shock when Sohan Singh escorted me into his eye operation theatre.

This theatre was larger and held three operating tables. The patient's eye was anaesthetized with drops of cocaine before Sohan Singh made a neat semi-circular incision round the top of the iris and, with gentle pressure, forced the opaque lens out of its socket. The operation lasted a bare two minutes, and then a large pad of cotton wool was placed over the eye and bandaged into place while the surgeon moved to the second table and a new patient replaced the first. His assembly-line approach managed to deal with the tremendous work load of the vital two months most successfully. After a week, the bandage would be removed and the patient would be able to count the number of fingers the doctor held up to his previously useless eye. There must, of course, have been failures, but the crowds of people who came bore witness to the success rate. I thought that part of the cure lay with the support given by the patients' families, who nursed, fed and comforted. The little family groups cooked and chatted round their anxious member as they awaited the great day

Shortly after this experience, Allah Dad said that a man was waiting to see me. I went out, and there, standing in the drive and supported by a couple of rough crutches, was my amputee patient. He had brought me some mangoes and thanked me, with tears running down his cheeks, for doing the operation. He was a poor farmworker, his life consisting of a hopeless struggle to pay off debts incurred for his family and from which he would never escape. But at least he had escaped from his terrible leg, and his tears gave way to broad smiles as I talked to him. He looked much better and, despite his protests, I gave him money to help him on his way. I explained to Allah Dad that all I had done was hold the leg, but he commented, 'Many people are hoping that hazur will continue to visit hospital.'

5

Kim

Winter and the brief spring passed all too quickly. My second hot weather smote with relentless force. This time it was even worse, but knowing what to expect I managed to get a week's leave. Eric Gordon, a piece-goods wallah recently arrived in Amritsar, took some leave at the same time. He was an excellent companion: slim, dark-haired, intelligent, cheerful and, like me, from a family with a medical background. His father, a Manchester doctor, had wanted him to go into medicine and join the practice, but Eric opted to see the world. His father's parting gift was an old Morris Cowley coupé with rumble seat, highly suitable for a Manchester doctor though rather a curiosity in the Punjab. Very much wanting to try it out, we decided to drive to the native state of Chamba, a hundred miles east of Amritsar in the great sweep of the Himalayas which stretches from Samarkand to Bhutan. Chamba was governed by a maharajah in autonomous splendour, and the district was said to abound in game, especially cheetah and snow leopards, both of which species enjoyed the maharajah's protection.

Suitcases in the rumble seat, bedrolls strapped to the wings and a well-filled ice box on the running board, we set out. The Morris Cowley was cramped. Even with its windows wide open it soon became terribly hot. A couple of hours' driving brought us to the foothills, where the road narrowed and began to wind between stony outcrops. Stunted trees clung to the cliffs above the river gorges, and the hills were scarred with deep channels from millennia of snow melts. We came to the steep climb to the hill station of Dalhousie, named after the Governor-General of India whose policy was to recognize the independence of the native states, and here spent the night. The scent of pines and wood smoke, the fresh cool air and the comfortable hotel seemed reassuringly alpine.

Greatly refreshed next morning by an English breakfast – porridge, kippers, bacon and eggs, toast and marmalade, tea – we set out to trek to Chamba with four local carriers. We found ourselves following behind them through what is possibly the most beautiful forest in the world. The trail was easy, the air exhilarating, and we made good progress. Eleven miles from Dalhousie we came to a *marg*, a green open sward with a lake in the middle, set amid majestic dark-green cedar forests. We stopped for lunch beside the lake, which was remarkable for a floating island said to change position daily. The story intrigued me. I decided to stay for a while after lunch to see if I could spot any sign of movement. I handed Eric my shotgun, and he went ahead with the carriers, leaving me to catch up later. The sun was pleasantly warm. Light shimmered on the lake. The island remained motionless. When I awoke, the sun was lower in the sky. I looked at my watch: three o' clock. I had slept two hours.

Hastily I set off along a path through woods full of wild flowers. Here and there were little clearings and an occasional wooden shack could be glimpsed between the trees. I pressed ahead, hoping the party was waiting for me, but the light was fading and I wondered how long it would take to reach Chamba. When I heard the unmistakable low snarl of a cheetah I began to wish I had kept the shotgun, notwithstanding the extra weight. I hurried on and the snarling stalked behind me. Half-running, I arrived at a fork in the trail and searched in vain for an indication of which path to take for Chamba. Perhaps both went there. I choose the left fork.

Another mile of half-running, half-walking, and I was benighted. To judge by the orchestrated snarls, the cheetah had now been joined by several companions. Thoroughly frightened, I thought of climbing a tree, but imagined that cheetah might well be better climbers than I was. By this time I seemed to have lost the trail, but then I saw, to my great relief, a faint light about a hundred yards ahead. I stumbled towards it and eventually made out a small shack with a partly open door, through which a fire in a stone hearth was visible. In Urdu I called: 'Is anyone there?'

An old woman emerged from a side-room and stared. 'Could I stay the night?' I asked her.

She was small and bent, but moved easily, and when I asked again, she turned and went back into the room. Since there was a charpoy near the fire, I sat on it, assuming her husband was in the room and she was consulting him on this unexpected visitor. I stretched out and fell asleep, and woke at dawn, feeling very cold. The fire was dead. I called out my thanks to the old woman, who remained firmly behind her door, left five rupees on the stone hearth and retraced my steps until I had once again picked up the trail. Fortunately I soon came across some men gathering wood and found I was only two miles short of my destination.

In the final approach to Chamba, I crossed the Ravi River by a ramshackle bridge and climbed to the small plateau on which the town stands, beautifully situated amid snow-capped peaks. Eric was there to meet me, greatly relieved to see me at last. 'Thank goodness you made it,' he said. 'We're invited to dine with HH this evening, and to play bridge afterwards.'

The rest-house overlooked the river, which tumbled in a series of cascades over boulders on its way to Lahore and the distant Indian Ocean. A level maidan stretched in front of the maharajah's palace, and here two prisoners slowly drew a heavy roller across the cricket pitch. They said they were quite happy to be out of gaol. When I asked why they didn't run away, they showed me the heavy chains that encircled their waists and linked to their ankle irons. 'You could get your friends to file them off,' I suggested.

'No, sahib,' they replied. 'Everyone knows us. Anyone who tried to free us would be punished.'

There were no guards, and the prisoners had wound thick bandages around their ankles to prevent chafing.

In the evening we presented ourselves at the palace, to be welcomed by the vizier and his officials, all clearly delighted that there were guests for dinner. The maharajah, HH Raja Ram Singh, was a short, stout man of thirty-eight with a whimsical sense of humour and a tendency, Eric had already been informed by the British Adviser, Colonel Coldstream, to pursue the local ladies. After a dinner rounded off with a large helping of halva covered in gold leaf, we retired to the card room, where the card table, placed centrally, was laid out with two new packs of cards bearing the royal coat of arms and four leather-bound bridge scoring blocks with a similar design. It emerged that Eric and I were expected to match our play against HH and the vizier. HH promptly won the cut, the vizier dealt, the courtiers crowded around. They chattered among themselves and were generous in revealing our hands to our opponents. But this was all to the good, since Eric had also been warned by Colonel Coldstream that HH could not abide to lose. Our one concern was therefore to make his optimistic bids come true. We reached a stage in the game when HH's opening bid was six no trumps. 'Very bold play, Your Highness,' chorused the admiring courtiers.

It took some skilful discarding, but we managed to lose every trick. HH was beside himself with joy.

Chamba has a wealth of old temples, and its glorious situation makes it a happy abode of the gods. Eric, a great nature lover, would take himself off on long country walks while I roamed the narrow streets, relaxed by an unhurried way of life that made a welcome contrast with seething Amritsar. The great trees around the town, the sparkling river, the silence of the surrounding mountains made our world of frantic finance seem as remote as a bad dream. Why not stay, adopt the contemplative life, take things easily, go for thought instead of action? I stood on a high bank above the river, turning these notions over in my mind, when I had a sense of being observed, though I had noticed no one else in that part of the valley. I turned to see two figures seated in the shade of a pine. As I drew closer, I recognized the *sadhu* and his *chela*. The *chela* looked modestly down as before. The *sadhu* gazed at me with his sharp eyes. 'You have been a long time coming,' he said.

'It's only by chance I am here,' I replied.

'There is no such thing as chance. You came here, as you will return to Amritsar, but you will not be the same person. You are travelling the path.'

'What path?'

'The path to self-knowledge. The path that reveals the unreality of the material world and leads to freedom of the mind.'

'What should I do now?'

'Relax, be receptive. That is all.'

'When will I see you next?'

He never replied. I met his glance for a long time until he looked down and I felt it was time for me to go.

Three days later we left Chamba at daybreak. On the way back to Dalhousie, our carriers were curious to see where, according to my account of getting lost, I had spent the night. There was no hut that they knew of, and no one lived close to the trail. With some difficulty I retraced my steps, but eventually came to a point I identified as the place where I rejoined the trail. 'The little house is over there, about two hundred yards back from the path,' I said.

We picked a way through the bushes. 'Here's the place,' I said. 'I'm sure of it.'

'There's no house,' said Eric.

We pushed through the undergrowth, and all at once Eric called out, 'Here's your money.'

On a blackened stone lay my five rupees.

Ah, yes, there had once been a house here, the carriers said, but it burnt down many years before. An old woman and her bedridden husband perished in the flames.

Some people have explanations for such happenings. I have none. All the way back to Dalhousie I was filled with an extraordinary feeling of being part of the giant pattern of nature, at one with the towering mountains and their eternal snows, with the great deodar pines and the grassy meadows, the flowers and the birds, the animals and the people. I was a small cell in the body of creation. All I needed to do was relax and be receptive.

A week after returning from Chamba I went down with a high fever. In spite of sweating profusely under a pile of blankets, I continued to shiver with cold. 'You have malaria,' said a charming young locum, at that point in charge of the practice.

He prescribed quinine to kill the parasite and phenacetin to reduce the fever. The thought crossed my mind of the ancient Romans going to the marshes to catch malaria to cure themselves of syphilis, the *spirochaete palida* not being able to survive high temperatures. By the end of a week I was no better. Blood samples showed I had the malignant variety, while my temperature had risen to 105°. I could read from the anxious faces around me that this was not good news. Allah Dad slept within earshot, and every time I stirred was at my side in a moment. The young doctor called in each day. 'I am giving you the maximum daily dose allowed by the British Pharmacopia – thirty grains of quinine bi-hydro-chloride,' he said. 'But it's very disappointing. You're not responding, not responding at all,' he added with a sigh. 'If you were fit to travel, I'd recommend you to go to a hill station.'

I could see that he thought little of my chances and a European death always caused much concern. I was still quite strong mentally. 'You are quite right,' I said. 'I will go to the hills. Allah Dad is capable of getting me there.'

The doctor, relieved, shook hands warmly and warned me to continue with the medicines.

'Allah Dad,' I announced. 'We leave for the hills.'

'Well spoken, hazur.' His face lit up.

John Reid also agreed. 'Murree is easy to reach. Take the night train to Rawalpindi, then a car up to Murree. They make the best beer in India and the Cecil's a fine hotel. Wish I could come too.'

I began to feel better. I tried to stand, but collapsed like a sawdust puppet. Allah Dad half-carried me to a chair. In the mirror I saw the face of a stranger, gaunt and haggard with ten days' growth of black beard. I had lost two stone.

There were vague impressions of a tonga ride, wrapped in my old school tartan rug; of a bottle of Black Label Johnnie Walker that Allah Dad thoughtfully took along; of a tumbler full of whisky before settling for the night in my bedroll in a railway carriage. Then nothing until we pulled into Rawalpindi.

Sitting on the station platform, I watched a huge red sun rise over the plain and felt for the first time that I had a chance of beating these malicious invaders. An ancient open Buick took us up the winding road to Murree, 7,000 feet above the heat-hazed plane. As we travelled alongside a steep gorge, a sudden impulse seized me. I gathered up all my medicines and, to Allah Dad's alarm, threw them over the edge. If Mother Nature wanted me, I resolved, she could have me.

The Cecil had no vacant rooms, but they found me a little bungalow perched above a cliff. I lay on a long-chair on the small veranda and for the first time felt hungry. Allah Dad brought me my topi. 'A present for *you*,' I said. 'I'll never wear it again. Fetch me some porridge and cream.'

Over the next few days, as I soaked up the warm sunshine in the bracing pine-scented air, I contemplated my enemy. The doctors lacked weapons. The malignant malarial parasite multiplied at enormous speed, producing in a few days half a million of its kind within each cubic centimetre of blood. It killed by destroying the red blood cells. There were 370 million Indians who must have been infected time after time. Why weren't they all dead? Obviously because they'd become resistant. Therefore why shouldn't I do likewise? If I was to work in India for five years, I'd need to take my health in hand. I thought about the gurus. We lived in our minds, so how many kinds of 'me' inhabited my mind? The conscious, the sub-conscious, the instincts, the gut feeling, the feeling in the bones, the heart. Which was the real me, and since I was a part of nature created by the God of all things, was I more important in the scheme than the malarial parasite or its unwitting servant, the anopheles mosquito, without whose cooperation it couldn't exist?

I continued to lie in the sun and added Guinness to my diet. On the fourth day I was still weak and partially deaf from the quinine, but I felt better in myself and hoped the invaders were on the retreat. The following day Allah Dad brought me a telegram. It read: 'Tolmie transferred to Peshawar please report for duty tomorrow, Scott.'

What a nerve, I thought. A dying man summarily recalled by a lazy accountant. Then I thought further, here's a chance to prove your new attitude. What have you to fear? 'Allah Dad,' I said. 'We return tomorrow morning. Order the car and pack.'

'But hazur is not well. Should stay till better.'

'Allah Dad, *I* am all right. It is my body that is a little weak and that will soon recover.'

Allah Dad went off reluctantly to make arrangements.

The drive down was uneventful. I enjoyed the sunshine and felt no need for a topi. In the train I experienced a strange flow of power, weak but under control. Back at the office I was still too feeble to move about. I sat and signed everything set before me. Kartar Singh and the clerks were a great support. It was Scott I felt sorry for. He was a bureaucrat, a man with small vision, a cog in an old-fashioned piece of clockwork, an example of the law that allows an employee to reach to one level above the job he is capable of handling. Unable to rise higher, they then arrange their petty kingdoms to the best of their capacity.

The IMS doctor came to visit me. 'My locum didn't expect you back,' he said, 'but here you are.' He regarded me thoughtfully. 'I think you will enjoy India.'

I agreed wholeheartedly. Moti Lal, my grocer, chemist and supplier of everything in the Hall Bazaar, gave me a tonic and a bottle of black Italian pills called Essanophle, which he said would be excellent for the present stage. I continued to recover, but it took six months before my body was back to its normal self.

'We're a man short for a party in Lahore. How about coming along?' asked John Tullie one morning.

'I'd love to,' I said, for the puzzle of where he took off to at weekends had long intrigued me.

'You won't need your bearer. We'll stay at Faletti's Hotel,' he said. 'Come on your motor-bike and I'll take your clothes. It's all very informal.'

Lahore lay twenty-five miles west of Amritsar on one of the most beautiful stretches of the Grand Trunk Road, originally laid out in the sixteenth century and later remetalled by the British to form a magnificent 1,500-mile highway linking Calcutta with the Khyber Pass. The armies of the Raj had marched along it to relieve Lucknow, Cawnpore and Delhi. Kipling celebrated it in *Kim*, as did the great Irish poet Thomas Moore in *Lalla Rookh*. I felt I was joining good company as I sped along the central strip, passing sweating bullocks and buffaloes as they strained to draw heavy loads along the earth tracks edging the tarmac. Large shisham trees lined the road at close intervals, sometimes joining overhead and providing shade for travellers. It stimulated the adrenalin to open the throttle and let the bike have its head, but I needed to remain alert. Indian drivers had no concept of a hazard. They were given to dozing on top of huge loads of straw and letting the bullocks or buffalo choose their own way, often to wander on to the tarmac. Overcrowded buses, their passengers clinging precariously to the roofs, swayed and rocked, hooting maniacally at any placid animals which crossed their path. The drivers regularly swerved on to the earth tracks to pass, leaving in their wakes billows of dust to blind anyone travelling in their wakes.

Bicycles were ridden by all manner of people. Bundles dangled from handlebars, umbrellas were held aloft against the sun, the bikes wobbled from side to side. Tongas and closed carriages kept up a brisk pace under the over-used whips of their drivers, and foot porters bore heavy burdens on heads or backs. Surveying the scene with indifference, camels stalked disdainfully by on the final stages of their long journey from beyond the Khyber. Here was real Kim's country, I thought. The road ran straight until a bend took it over a canal that today marks the frontier between India and Pakistan. After that it continued in a straight line until it passed the red sandstone walls of Shalimar Gardens and entered Lahore.

Faletti's Hotel stood on the Upper Mall, close to the museum in front of which 'Zam-Zammah', Kim's gun, mounts guard. John was there ahead of me and the hotel bearer had laid out my clothes. My room was high and airy. It had an electric fan, and the blessing of running water meant it had its own bath and WC. It came as a shock to find all this civilization so close to Amritsar, but Lahore, after all, was the cultural capital of the Punjab. It housed the Governor, the High Court, Lahore Cathedral, the King Edward Memorial Hospital, the Punjab Club, the Masonic Lodge and the offices of the *Civil Military Gazette* where Rudyard Kipling formerly worked as assistant editor. His poem 'If', in a plain black frame, had hung on the nursery wall of my Belfast childhood and his books had been one of my delights. Now I was present where he had been, seeing what he had seen. But at this point John arrived to interrupt my thoughts. There was time for a *chota peg* in the bar before setting off for our party.

With John on the pillion, I drove down a well-kept road flanked by bungalows enclosed behind high hedges. There was never a sign or smell of an open drain. 'Turn in here,' instructed John.

I swung in at an open gate and stopped the bike in front of a red-brick house. A compound, shaded by luxurious trees and with a well-watered lawn, had succeeded in remaining green despite the heat. A long table, already thronged with guests, occupied the far end of the garden. 'They're in fancy dress!' I exclaimed in concern.

'Tie a handkerchief round your head and go as an accident,' John suggested. Fortunately I had a large handkerchief with me, and quickly tied it on while John gathered up a guard's cap that was lying on the veranda table and put it on at a jaunty angle. We went forward and in an instant were swept into a circle of golden boys and girls, animated, vivacious, eager to ply us with hospitality. Conversation rippled round the table, and the Welsh-sounding lilt of the Eurasians, said to derive from the Welsh missionaries who taught English in the early days, mixed distinctively among the scattering of European guests.

Eurasians were roughly as numerous as the British in India, and until the opening of the Suez Canal, which enabled white wives to make their way out to India in great numbers, they and the Indians suffered no colour bar. Alas, the subsequent invasion of relatively unsophisticated memsahibs, fearful of competition, soon put a stop to this friendly state of affairs. The exciting results of matches between British and Indians were unjustly relegated to a caste unacceptable to either race. Deprived of their rightful place in a so-called democratic society, they strove to establish themselves in the British way of life. They ran the railways, entered the police force, the post and telegraphs, the public works departments. They formed their own clubs, one of which, the ubiquitous Burt Institute Railway Club, was highly popular with the sahibs, especially once their wives were safely packed off to the hill stations.

The daughters of Eurasian families worked, like their brothers, in responsible positions in hospitals, schools, hotels and other essential services. They were noted for their femininity and prettiness. The actress Merle Oberon, later Lady Korda, who once worked on the Calcutta telephone exchange, epitomized the startling beauty of many young Eurasian women. Their slightly idiosyncratic construction of sentences and use of words added to their charm in the same way as English spoken by French girls becomes an attractive asset.

Our conversation blossomed, though I seemed to detect beneath the flow of friendliness a note of deference to the 'men from home'. Opposite me was seated a slim fair girl of my own age, dressed in a gym tunic as a schoolgirl and carrying a satchel. Her companion was an elderly army captain of stern, possessive mien. My eyes kept coming back to her, and from time to time her grey eyes caught mine and I was aware of a quiver of a smile hovering about her lips. After dinner there were games, and I found myself paired with her for hide-and-seek. She spoke perfect English, and as we hid in the shrubbery, waiting to be found, I said I'd very much like to see her again but supposed her husband would object. 'Oh, he'll object all right, but he's not my husband. Anyway, he goes back to his regiment on the Frontier next week.'

The news set my pulse racing. Some chemistry was at work. It seemed simple enough, but I felt a sudden tightening in the gut, a deep response. It was an emotion I had never experienced before in relation to a woman. When I told her about the New Dawn, she said she had never been on a motor-bike. 'Would you like a ride?' I asked. 'Could I see you home?'

'Why not?' she smiled.

'What about the army?' I asked.

'That has nothing to do with you. I belong to myself.'

When the time came to go, she perched side-saddle on the pillion. 'You'd be safer astride with a foot on each footrest,' I said.

She swung her right leg round in an agile arc and rewarded me with a glimpse of fair pubic hair. 'You'll need to guide me,' I said.

We moved out of the drive and accelerated through the almost deserted streets, bathed by then in the light of a full moon. Skirting the old city, we crossed the Ravi River, broad and slow-moving, a great silver gleam. On the far side of the bridge we turned down an earth road and arrived at a massive gate where an old man stepped out from the shadows. 'You live here?' I asked.

'No, this is Shahdara, the tomb of Jahangir. It's my favourite place. Leave your bike with the watchman. It will be quite safe. No one comes here at night. They say it's haunted.'

Through a small doorway we entered a large garden filled with the odour of jasmine and other scents I could not place. In the centre stood the magnificent tomb of the emperor, a vast square of marble and coloured stone, tall minarets at each of its four corners. An ornamental pool reflected the dream-like quality of the building. Around the outer wall were open rooms, a caravanserai where visitors had rested once upon a time.

She took my hand and led me up a marble staircase to the flat roof. 'It may well be haunted,' she said. 'If dogs are brought up here they become terrified, jump over the parapet and are dashed to pieces on the ground.'

We climbed a minaret and looked down on the Ravi and all the city. We were alone in paradise. I said, 'I don't even know you name.'

'Everyone calls me Kim, "Little friend of all the world". I don't know yours either.'

'Bill,' I told her.

We went down again and entered the tomb chamber. Here absolute silence reigned, but I felt comfortable and thought that Jahangir might perhaps be pleased with company after 360 years in his lonely cenotaph. We sat on the inlaid marble plinth surrounding the sarcophagus and leant against the ninety-nine names of God inscribed along its sides. After a while Kim said, 'I'm going to take a nap. I often sleep here. It's cool and I like the smells.'

Stretching herself out, she used her satchel as a pillow and immediately fell asleep. I looked at her and thought about the extraordinary events of the evening until suddenly I too felt tired, slid down beside her and closed my eyes.

'Time to go.' Kim was shaking my arm.

Dawn was breaking as we hurried back through the garden. I tipped the watchman, and Kim remounted the pillion, swinging her satchel. 'What have you got in there?' I asked, wondering why I hadn't done so sooner.

'Kipling's *Jungle Book*.'

'Can I see you again next week?'

'Perhaps,' said Kim thoughtfully, 'but I'm not sure it's a good idea – not for either of us.'

'Where can we meet?' I implored.

There was a silence. I felt as if my fate was being arranged in some far-distant place. 'Be at Kim's Gun at sunset next Saturday,' she said in a low voice, 'but don't wait if I'm not there, for in that case I shan't be seeing you again.'

As we reached her home, a cold chill ran up my spine. The captain was waiting by the gate. 'Don't speak to him,' Kim commanded.

She dismounted and walked past the captain and into the house, but he came towards me. 'You are public school, are you not?' he queried in a crisp military tone of voice.

I nodded.

'You might behave like a gentleman.'

Was he going to hit me, I wondered, but as he came closer I saw he had been crying. After a long silence he turned away and stood leaning on the gate.

'You're a dark horse,' said John Tullie over a very late breakfast, 'snatching the Belle of Lahore from under the captain's nose. I wonder he didn't shoot you.'

'Why is she called the Belle of Lahore?' I asked.

'Oh, she's enormous fun. She works for the dental clinic, so meets everyone, but she's very much her own girl. How did you get off with her?'

'She'd never been on a motor-bike and I offered her a ride home.'

'Well, you certainly took your time. I got tired of waiting.'

'She showed me some of the sights.

'Lucky chap,' said John.

The week passed slowly before I once again found myself travelling the Grand Trunk Road. After changing at Faletti's and adjusting the straps to hold my folded tartan rug on the pillion, I set off for Kim's Gun. Dusk was falling as I arrived. Of Kim there was never a sign. She's not coming, I thought, and I don't blame her, for what can I, a mere chota sahib with nothing but a motor-bike, offer such a popular girl? Yet I felt a great ache, a great loss. Despite her instructions that I shouldn't wait, I decided I'd give it half an hour. Then I felt a slight hand on my shoulder and turned. Kim was wearing a slim striped dress and looked so cool and sophisticated that I felt humble and unworthy. 'I wondered if you'd come,' I said.

'I wondered too,' she replied. 'Anyway, here I am.'

She sat on the pillion and directed me to a small restaurant whose owner was Italian. It was his first restaurant and he was eager to please. He made French mustard for our steaks and produced a cassata for desert. I ordered a bottle of Beaune. Kim ate with a good appetite, and after Amritsar I found the food delicious. I felt tense, but over coffee began to relax and to answer her questions. Later I asked her about her own life. It was a hungry exchange. Her parents lived in Bangalore. She had married at seventeen, had had a baby daughter, had divorced her husband. She was country-born and bred, had never been out of India, spoke several Indian dialects fluently and knew the country intimately. No wonder she was called Kim. When I asked her what she wanted out of life, she said, 'I don't know, but I must belong to myself, to mine own self. People I meet want me to play their game. I feel like the old lama searching for his river in *Kim*. I suppose it's a search for something which has meaning for me. It could be all wrong for someone else.'

'I feel the same,' I said. 'Like a diamond with many facets which people want to grind down to a flat surface to mirror their own ideas.'

'You're pretty conceited too. Diamond indeed!'

'I should have said a very rough diamond, only then it wouldn't have had any facets.'

Kim guided me back to where she lived. We drove down a quiet street with an L-bend and came to where a watchman with a stout stick stood guard. There was a steep staircase on the side of the highest building, and up this we went, turning in at a door on the top floor. Inside was a small apartment: kitchen, bathroom, living room and bedroom. 'It's very small,' said Kim, 'but it's all I need. I use the bedroom only in winter. Now I sleep on my roof.'

She led the way up the outside stairs to a flat roof on which was a large bed, a table and a couple of cane chairs. There was no mosquito net. 'I thought you lived in the house where I left you last week,' I said.

'That was a friend's. This is mine. I couldn't afford a bungalow.'

'What about a mosquito net?' I asked.

'We don't have many mosquitoes in the city, and if I hear one I put my head under the sheet.'

Wasn't she frightened, I asked, that anyone could come up the outside stairs and get on to the roof in the night? She agreed that they could, if they got past the *chokidar*, but added that her only visitor was a lonely old colonel. 'He tries to take me for a ride in his staff car,' she said. 'I meet everyone at the clinic, and since they're generally nervous, I try to cheer them up, and then they ask me out. Some even want to marry me,' she grinned.

'What about tomorrow,' I asked. 'Are you free?'

'Would you like me to be?'

'Oh, very much.'

'We could have a picnic.'

'What time shall I call for you?' I asked.

'It's late. Why don't you sleep here?'

To my surprise I heard myself saying I had no pyjamas.

'I never wear any,' said Kim. 'In fact, in the hot weather I never wear pants. It's hot enough as it is.'

'Are you sure it's all right my staying,' I stammered.

'It's cool here and it's a big bed. You'll be quite safe. I'm turning in.'

With a graceful movement she slipped between the sheets, leaving her dress on the chair and her head half-covered. I sat for a while, wondering what to do next, finally also slipping quietly between the sheets. Overhead the stars shone brightly, and faint sounds came from the sleeping city. I fell asleep quickly, as if it was the most natural thing in the world. Suddenly I was wide awake. There were footsteps on the stairs. I nudged Kim, who wakened slowly. 'Only the colonel,' she said. 'Lie still, say nothing.'

She slid down by my legs. In the moonlight an erect military figure emerged from the stairs and came towards the bed. The colonel sat down on the chair. 'My dear,' he said, 'I couldn't sleep and wondered if you would humour an old man and come for a drive.'

I lay still as a mouse. The colonel must have felt that something was amiss. He produced a torch and shone it in my face. After a brief silence he muttered, 'Mistake, mistake,' and went slowly back down the stairs.

Kim surfaced. 'Poor old chap, he'll worry like anything but I'll tell him I let someone have the flat while I was away.'

In a few moments she was asleep again. I looked up at the friendly moon, thought how it would soon be over Bangor and wondered what my parents would make of my present situation. Then, with a feeling of happiness and enormous freedom, I fell asleep too.

The muezzin calling the faithful to prayer from the mosque of Wazir Khan awakened me. I was alone. Round the roof ran a parapet that enhanced the seclusion of the high building. I looked over the edge to see other roof-top sleepers emerging from their shroud-like covers. Kipling's 'City of Dreadful Night' was facing a new day. It did not look too dreadful to me. I slipped on my trousers and went down. Kim was just emerging from the shower. 'Help yourself,' she said.

By the time I finished showering she was carrying a breakfast tray up to the roof. Coffee, toast, butter, marmalade and fruit lay on the table. 'It looks marvellous,' I said, 'almost better than the view.'

'I was lucky to get this flat,' she said. 'It's a new block beside the Old City, but private. I don't think the neighbours realize I overlook them. They can't see me, at any rate. If you still feel like a picnic, we'll shop in the Anarkali Bazaar after breakfast.'

We entered the bazaar by the Lahori Gate. Overflowing stalls lined the narrow streets on either side. It was similar to Amritsar, even down to having thirteen gates and a Golden Temple, but shopping was a new experience for me. In Amritsar the task was left to the cook, who would have been deeply offended had I attempted to deprive him of this most important office.

The Anarkali Bazaar was more ornate than that of Amritsar. The houses were higher and adorned with fretted woodwork and elegant balconies with shuttered windows. Beggars sat at their appointed sites, the blind, the diseased, the crippled and, in one case, a small fat man in a little low-wheeled cart. I looked more closely as he held up his brass begging bowl. His arms and legs had been broken and the bones reset at right angles. His bright eyes looked at me through a tangled mat of black hair. 'What on earth happened to him?' I asked Kim.

'Ram Dass was made a professional beggar when a child. His parents were too poor to take care of him, so he joined what is regarded here as an honourable profession. It is a terrible price, but he has a place above the others. He earns his own living. People talk to him. He is a part of the community.'

She dropped a coin in the brass bowl and received a warm smile in return. A young boy in a loin-cloth, who pulled the cart with a rope, smiled as well as he trundled his charge away.

1905. Mother, Father, Nurse and me with Jap, my West Highland terrier

1911. Myself aged six

1911. RMS *Titanic* before her launch on 31 May

1957. Laurence Beesley, a *Titanic* survivor, talks of his experience

Edith Russell, a *Titanic* survivor and frequent visitor during the filming, had a sharp eye for detail and became a close friend of our family

1957. Director Roy Baker discusses a scene in the boiler-room with Geoffrey Unsworth, director of photography, and Bob Asher, first assistant director (*background*)

Fourth officer of the Titanic, Joseph Boxhall, and Commander Grattidge, captain of the *Queen Mary* and *Queen Elizabeth*, my advisers on *A Night to Remember*, discuss a point whilst Kenneth More and I listen

3 July 1958 – the première at the
Odeon Theatre, Leicester Square

14 April 1984. Edwina MacKenzie,
a ninety-eight-year-old survivor,
cuts the cake at the *Titanic*
anniversary ceremony held on
board the *Queen Mary*,
now permanently berthed in
Los Angeles

1927. Tika Ram, my Gurkha *chokidar* (watchman), who slew eleven Germans with his kukri in World War I

Amritsar 1927. Allah Dad, my friend and bearer, with his son

1929. Freedom fighters picket the bank in the Hall Bazaar, Amritsar

8 June 1928. Bob Leete landed a Gypsy Moth in Karachi to win the *Daily Mail* £1000 prize for the first light-aircraft flight to India. This led to the founding of the Lahore Flying Club where I obtained my pilot's 'A' licence

1927 The Amritsar detachment of the Punjab Light Horse on parade; Farrier Sergeant Major Savin *(extreme right)* and Trooper MacQuitty *(extreme left)*

Budh Gaya, the sacred site of the Buddha's enlightenment

Ravena, the ten-headed demon king of Ceylon, is burnt at the festival of Dussera. He stole Sita, the beautiful wife of Rama, who subsequently killed him with the help of the monkey-god Hanuman

Lugs, my bull terrier bitch
with the Grand Prix
Salmson and me in front of
the chummery, Amritsar

Kim in Gulmarg, Kashmir

I followed Kim as she wove her way among handcarts – some of them loaded with tubs of offal – donkeys carrying ancient men, porters burdened with produce and an occasional camel unperturbed by the market frenzy. Several stall-holders called out to her and she exchanged banter. For a moment it put me in mind of Portobello Road. At length she stopped at a fruit stall piled high with pyramids of beautifully arranged pomegranates, oranges, loquats, lemons, bananas. Quickly she made a selection. Bargaining was swift, and we moved on to the baker for fresh chapattis, then to the cooked meats for koftas, spiced meat balls, and kebabs of lamb on wooden skewers between onion and peppers, broiled over charcoal embers fanned into heat with an elegantly woven palm frond. The sweet-meat stall was heaped with pyramids of white milk-cakes, made from milk simmered until it became a thick dough and then scented with rose water; with halvas of irresistible fragrance; with rossi gullas, gulab jamins and jelabies saturated with syrup. Finally, at the spirit store, we bought bottles of Murree beer, brewed by the Dyer family, whose general made such fateful history at Amritsar during the rebellion of 1919. Wherever the British Army went, it concerned itself with supplies of good water and good beer. 'How do we keep the beer cold?' I asked.

'I have a waterproof bag and put the ice and bottles in that with the glasses wrapped in a cloth.'

Eventually we slung the bottle bag round my neck, wedged the basket between us and set out for Shalimar Gardens, which I had passed the previous day, and left the bike with a guard at the main gate. Inside the massive sandstone walls, fountains played down the centre of a long narrow stretch of water leading to a white marble pavilion. The blue sky was reflected in the water and on either side stretched vast green lawns scattered with ancient trees. Beyond the pavilion the water flowed down a carved marble sluice into a large square tank divided in two by white marble walks leading to a central platform surrounded by two hundred fountains. At each corner stood small identical white marble pavilions. Beyond, a similar arrangement stretched to the furthermost wall. The contrast with the hot and dusty bedlam outside was breathtaking. 'I'd never have imagined that those old walls concealed anything like this,' I said.

'It ought to be good,' said Kim. 'It was designed by Shah Jahan, who built the Taj Mahal. He laid out the gardens in 1637 and some of the trees are very old. My favourite is a buttress tree on the far lawn. It's a lonely old tree, but it has the advantage that people can be seen approaching, and since Indians are quite shy, it's quieter.'

I spread my old tartan rug, that had kept me warm in Campbell College, between two high flanks of the tree and opened the picnic.

'The emperor would be glad to join us,' I suggested.

'Don't be too sure,' said Kim. 'Muslims hadn't much time for women. Muslim women are not supposed to have souls, so they don't get to heaven, which on the other hand is filled with houris – delightful nymphs – as well as wine and tobacco. But it's a very powerful religion. I hope you never see a Muslim-Hindu riot.'

'Which faith has your approval?' I queried.

'Oh, mine's simple. I don't believe God exists as a separate sort of person. I believe God is existence. Everything is God, including my brain and conscience, which tell me to love everyone. He's an inside not an outside God. Manufactured religions are too political.'

I spoke of talks with my *munshi* and the Hindu philosophy which also saw God in everything, and how I had been fascinated by the Secret Doctrines of Madame Blavatsky and felt drawn towards the Buddhist philosophy.

'I've news for you,' said Kim. 'Annie Besant has just celebrated Madame Blavatsky's golden jubilee by launching a new messiah, Krishnamurti, in Madras. Annie's quite a girl. Although she's British, she started the Home Rule Movement and was elected first president of the National Congress.'

'So she's the cause of all our trouble.'

'Well, a bit. All these do-gooders end up in politics.'

As we sat on, the fountains flashing in the sunlight and doves cooing from the walls, I wondered how we had got into a philosophical discussion. What was life about anyway? I repeated my thought aloud. 'It's about living,' said Kim, 'and it's time we got moving.'

'When may I see you again?' I asked.

'Perhaps in October. The clinic moves to Kashmir for the summer, and I go with them.' My heart sank at the unexpected news and my face must have shown my dismay. 'Don't worry. Hundreds of girls stay in Lahore, and there are big dances at the Burt every Saturday.'

We drove back in silence. I gave her the basket and the bag with the empty beer bottles. She stood silent and then bent forward swiftly to kiss me on the lips. 'Goodbye,' she said. 'When I know where I'm staying I may write.'

I drove away before she could notice my tears. This is absurd, I thought. A divorced woman with a child. What would my Calvinistic ancestors have thought, let alone my father and mother, who had counterpointed the warmth of my upbringing with the idea of the finger of scorn that was pointed at all transgressors? Why was I so upset? It was as if a door to a golden world had opened an instant, then swung to and shut me out.

6

Wings and a Trance

Back at Amritsar, Allah Dad and the dogs greeted me with affection. My bath was ready. After a *chota peg* I began to decode the cables. They brought startling tidings. Tullie was to proceed on a long-awaited furlough and be replaced by Mr W. Hendrie from Singapore. Mr J. Darnley was to be added to the Amritsar staff from London to fill the gap left by Tolmie when he was transferred to Peshawar. Suddenly I was to be the longest serving sub-accountant in Amritsar. When Enrico came in, I told him the news. 'I'm off too,' he said. 'Like to buy my car?'

A practical chap, Enrico. 'Of course I would,' I said, 'but can I afford it?'

He saw I couldn't resist and eventually, with the sale of the New Dawn, I became the proud owner of a Salmson identical to the one that had run me down during the General Strike.

'You'll have to take over the Punjab Light Horse,' said John Tullie. 'I cleared it with the CO some time ago. It's no good protesting. No one else will do it and I've got to get away.'

Farewell parties proliferated, with a great deal of drink and sentiment, but I found myself awaiting the arrival of my new mess-mates with some apprehension. *Ek dum*, 'in a breath', my companions were to change. People came and went quickly in India, many to the tiny British cemeteries where leaning tombstones bore witness to their failure to make old bones.

The new car was meanwhile great fun and a feather in Allah Dad's cap, his sahib having thereby risen into the car owners' league. Kartar Singh liked to sit beside me. We could talk more easily than on the bike, though I could see that he regretted the passing of the New Dawn and the chance it offered of roaring along tiny paths in the countryside. One day, as we drove on an 'air-eating trip' – the Indian expression for taking the air – he told me he was soon to be married. 'But you're younger than I am,' I said. 'What do you want to get married for?'

'A family arrangement. I know the bride and I'll be happy with her.'

My goodness, I thought, all my friends are leaving me. Something of my feelings must have shown, for Kartar Singh added quickly, 'I shall be the same with you, sahib. It will make no difference. Will you come to my wedding?'

'Of course,' I said, 'but I know nothing about your ceremonies, or your religion for that matter.'

'That's easy. I'll take you to the Golden Temple whenever you wish.'

The Golden Temple was only five minutes from the bank, and, as we walked along the crowded street, Kartar Singh told me how the Sikh religion was started by a Hindu guru called Nanak, who didn't like the multiple Hindu deities. 'He believed in one God, like the Muslims, and sought union with him through love and devotion. Subsequent gurus compiled a book of all their writings called the *Granth*. The tenth and last guru, Gobind Singh, created the Khalsa, a pure militant brotherhood marked by the five Ks: *kes*, long hair; *kangha*, a comb; *kara*, an iron bracelet; *kacha*, short pants; *kirpan*, a dagger. The surname Singh means Lion. We're renowned as warriors,' he said with a chuckle.

'What about priests?' I asked.

'We have no priests. Anyone can take the service. At my wedding my bride and I will walk round the *Granth* four times. Like your Bible, it is the centre of our religion.'

After informing the guard that we had no tobacco or alcohol in our possession, we took off our shoes and passed through the Gate of Prayer. The Golden Temple stands in a large tank from which Amritsar takes its name, Amrita Saras, the 'Pool of Tranquillity', whose waters are bounded by a wide pavement of white marble and shaded cloisters from which a marble walkway leads across to the temple. The temple itself is quite small, its lower part of delicately carved white marble. The upper part, including the four minars and central dome, is of gilded copper inlaid with flowers and designs. The effect was dazzling, the brilliant white contrasting with the glittering gold against a vivid blue sky and every detail reflected in the tank. I stood a long time, fascinated by the vividly changing patterns in the water. Finally we crossed the walkway and entered the temple.

Upstairs was a richly embellished shrine where an elderly Sikh, reading from the *Granth*, paid us no heed as we walked slowly round, admiring the delicate carving on the walls and panels. But ever and again we were drawn back to the great open book resting on its silk cushion. It must have measured more than four feet across. The atmosphere had none of the erotic mysticism of the Hindu temples nor, it occurred to me, the musty, faded aura of the cathedrals of the West. There was a sparkling cleanliness, simple and refreshing. As we left we were offered halva. 'It is a kind of blessing,' said Kartar Singh.

Bill Hendrie turned out to be a slender, gentlemanly Scot with a dry sense of humour and a sensitive disposition. He lacked Tullie's robust attitude to life, but I took to him quickly. He was engaged to be married, lived quietly, and became popular with the golfing community; and as a good horseman he was swiftly welcomed into the PLH. Since he had a concern about his health and diet, cook tried to get food that he liked, but his lunch was often only an apple and a glass of milk.

Joe Darnley, straight from the London office, was short, sturdy and shy. He wore glasses, was a good pianist, cultured and rather solitary. I took over Tolmie's desk and Darnley took mine. He shared with Hendrie a faddiness about food and dosed himself with tonics, including a thick dark mixture of malt and cod-liver oil. His room was at the rear of the bungalow, and early one morning he came to me, worried by something he had witnessed. 'A scruffy old man brought a cow,' he said, 'and milked it under my window into a dirty old kerosene oil tin. I thought I should let you know that your bearer was watching and did nothing.'

'Oh, that's all right, the old man's our milkman and Allah Dad keeps an eye on him to see he doesn't water the milk. The tin's quite clean. We use them for everything.'

'Don't we get milk from the dairy?'

'What dairy? We could use tinned milk, but the chaps don't like it, or buffalo milk, though we do use buffalo butter.'

'I don't like that either,' said Joe. 'Couldn't we at least have brown bread? It's very unhealthy to eat nothing but white bread.'

'I'll ask cook,' I said.

'The *khansama* produced brown bread the very next day. It looked good but had a slightly curious flavour. 'That's the wholemeal,' said Joe with satisfaction, 'all the goodness of the bran and wheat germ. You don't know what you've been missing.'

We enjoyed the brown bread and brown toast for more than a couple of months until, one day, Joe noticed a yellow lump in the middle of a slice. 'What's that?' he asked.

'I've no notion,' I said. 'I'll ask Allah Dad.'

'Hazur, only Allah and baker know what is in the bread,' was Allah Dad's comment.

We decided to call on the baker.

Makhan Singh received us cordially. His hair and beard were tied up in a green cloth as he kneaded a mass of yellowish dough in a wooden trough. 'We've come to see how you make your brown bread,' I said.

'Sahib, I am just now making.'

'But this is white bread, Makhan Singh.'

'Making everything good,' said Makhan Singh as he reached for a bottle on a small shelf above his head. Skilfully he withdrew the cork with his teeth and carefully poured a little of the tar-like substance it contained on to the dough. A moment's vigorous mixing and there was our brown bread. 'What's in the bottle?' I asked.

'Brun dye from Germany, much expensive,' beamed Makhan Singh.

Overhead hung several thick ropes that puzzled me until I looked closer and found they were long clusters of living flies surrounding coarse string. 'What do these cords do?' I asked.

'Sahib,' said Makhan Singh, looking at me incredulously, 'they for keeping flies out of bread.'

I looked more closely at the busy swarms. 'What do you put on the cords?' I asked, with a horrid feeling that I knew already.

'Dung,' said Makhan Singh.

Cow urine and dung: the heavenly panacea for all the ills of India.

No word from Kim. I tried to console myself by plunging ever more deeply into the life going on around me. The bank's flat roof gave me a grandstand view of the city. In the bazaar merchants and traders from all over Asia mingled with the 160,000 citizens: Afghans, Kashmiris, Nepalese, Baluchis, Bokariots, Tibetans, Persians, Turkomans, Yarkandis, all in their picturesque national costumes, stalking through the throng with poise and dignity. The older men were particularly careful about their appearance, hair and beards carefully dressed to set off their stern features.

Down in the side-streets and alleyways I spotted more intimate scenes. Here, for instance, a dentist plied his trade. His instruments, contained in the wooden box on which he sat, included a pair of large forceps; a hand-drill turned by pushing a ring up and down the shank, and several bits; a small hammer and wooden pegs for knocking out teeth that defied the forceps; a couple of files; a cloth on which to bite; and opium to rub on a gum to deaden pain. As I watched, a patient squatted in front of him, and after some bargaining clenched his teeth on the folded cloth. The dentist took his hand-drill, adjusted a small bit and, to my astonishment, commenced drilling a hole in the middle of the man's upper front tooth. He then repeated the operation on its fellow. Next he produced a small tin from which the patient choose two gold rivets that were duly hammered home. When I took the chance to ask the dentist why this was done, he said, 'it is to beautify the teeth, sahib, and to show he speaks the truth. I can also do silver.'

Following on my excursion with Kim to the Anarkali Bazaar, I began to explore our own. 'Where does the meat come from?' I asked, looking at the abundance and variety of joints hanging in the meat market and covered with their quota of flies.

'Just at the back, sahib,'

At the rear I found the slaughterhouse. As in the days of ancient Egypt, the animal had its feet tied with a slip-knot so that, when the rope was pulled, it brought the four feet together and the beast fell helpless to the ground. The butcher then cut its throat, skinned and quartered it and removed the edible offal, watched all the time with apparent composure by other sacred cows awaiting their turn. So much for sacred cows. Little wonder Hindus and Muslims came to blows.

Their differences continued in death. Muslims were buried, but Hindus, except for young children, were cremated. The practice of cremation went flatly against all economic sense. Some millions of tons of wood were used annually to cremate bodies that could have added to the fertility of the soil, and since no firewood was left for cooking, this had to be done with cow dung; and that should have gone back to the soil.

One day, as I walked towards the ghat, a funeral procession passed me. At the front four men carried a bier on which lay the body of a child wrapped in red cloth and bound with cord. At the entrance of the ghat, the group divided, the men going with the body while the women remained a little way off. The women's voices rose and fell in a gentle tide of sympathy for the bereaved mother. Inside the ghat, funeral pyres burned, and I could see the outlines of bodies through the hot flames. Here and there heaps of grey ash marked the sites of the previous day's pyres. In one corner, more wood was being stacked round a shrouded figure. Watching the scene stood a *sadhu*, a lean man with matted hair and a long beard. Round his neck hung a string of sacred beads, and his penetrating look of understanding and silent presence contrasted strangely with the wailing of the mourners.

The bearers carried the bier through this fearsome scene to a well on the far side of the ghat, away from the fire, and placed it on the ground. The father spoke to an attendant. Arrangements were made in low voices. The attendant left the group and returned with mattock and spade. Working slowly, he cut through the hard, dry ground until a grave less than a yard deep was dug. Gauging the size of the body with his eye, he shaved down the ends of the opening with the narrow spade, scooping up the fallen earth with the mattock. At last it was ready.

The bier was carried to the open grave and the father unwrapped the cloth, revealing the pretty face of a little girl who looked as if she slept except that the eyes were open. Helped by his relatives, he gently lowered the child to the bottom of the shallow grave. The attendant bent down and removed some earth with his hands to make more room for her feet. The father knelt and, reaching under his daughter's blouse, broke a white band of cloth which was next to her skin. He looked at her intensely but without tears for a long moment, then quickly crumbled the warm earth over her face and body till all was hidden.

In their colourful assertion of life, the Indian festivals gave us holidays from banking and were conveniently spaced at two-monthly intervals. Holi, a saturnalia at the vernal equinox, was celebrated by squirting or throwing red water over everyone. It was great fun, especially for the young, and Europeans invariably got splashed if they ventured on to the streets. 'What does it mean?' I asked Kartar Singh, who looked a bit sheepish.

'It represents the flow from the womb of nature,' he explained.

'And what about the Dussera festival, the one with the giant figures?'

'It celebrates the victory of Rama over Ravana, the wicked king of Ceylon who stole Rama's beautiful wife Sita. The king was in the shape of a *dussera*, a ten-headed demon, when Rama, with the help of the monkey god Hanuman, killed him. So each year Ravana with his ten heads is burnt.'

The huge forty-foot effigies of Ravana were constructed of wicker, stuffed with straw and beautifully clothed in glittering garments. The fingers were made of fire-crackers and fireworks filled the body. The figures' ten heads were built in a pyramid of six, three, and one on the top. At night, when ignited, they spouted fire intermingled with bright flashes, loud detonations and clouds of smoke, to the delight of the cheering good-natured crowds. It seemed astonishing that people so poor would spend so much time, money and difficult work in creating these giants, only to burn them.

'What about Diwali?' I asked Kartar Singh.

'Diwali is the festival of light in honour of Lakshmi, goddess of prosperity, very important for the bank,' he grinned. 'It's held on the new moon of Kartik. All the houses are outlined with little clay lamps. Lamps are also launched in tiny wooden boats into lakes and rivers. The longer they stay alight, the better will be the fortunes of their owners.'

'And the Sikhs?'

'They don't believe any such nonsense. We believe in loyalty, justice, truth, honesty, impartiality and gratitude. We do not believe in caste, sacred rivers, hypocrisy, nor do we drink wine or smoke. If we carry out all these things properly, I think we are the best people in the world. Like Muslims, we serve one God.'

'And the Muslim festivals?' I asked.

'The big ones are Mohurram and Bakar Id, but they're not jolly like Hindu festivals. The first is mourning for Husain and Hasan, murdered grandsons of Muhammad, and the second is the sacrifice of a pet animal in memory of Abraham's sacrifice of Isaac, who in the Koran version is Ishmael, the son of Hagar. Since neither of them were sacrificed, I don't know why they do it.'

'When do these happen?'

'Always a different date, because of their lunar calendar of 354 days, which makes each New Year's Day always eleven days earlier than the previous one. It's rather confusing, but you won't miss them. They make much noise – a great *tamasha*.'

As it happened, I was invited to celebrate Bakar Id by Muslim friends. The family gathered in their small courtyard where a wretched snow-white kid was trying to hide behind a tree. It had been a family pet for three months, and the children were thoroughly upset. I asked why they didn't buy an animal from the bazaar. 'It has to be a pet and live with us, otherwise it would not qualify for a sacrifice,' explained the father.

A basin of water was brought by his wife and placed on the ground. 'It is for the kid to drink. We cannot take its life until it has drunk.'

The kid remained firmly behind the tree. Finally an uncle caught it and carried it to the basin, holding its head above the water. It refused to drink, so he pushed its head under. The eldest son, a thin boy of fifteen, then appeared with a large kitchen knife while the uncle held the kid down and offered its throat to the knife. The boy stood silent. It was his honour, but I could see he had no heart for the deed. After encouragement from his mother and exhortations from his father, he made a light stroke across the kid's throat, producing a trickle of blood and frantic struggles from the animal. His father, upset by such a loss of face, strode over and held the kid while the uncle severed the neck to the backbone. In a few moments, all was over. The carcass would be skinned and cut up, some pieces kept and the remainder given to the poor.

The whole business left me with an acute sense of horror. The sufferings of the wretched animal, prolonged by its amateur butchers, the destruction of the trust and genuine affection between the family and the animal, seemed to have made a mockery of good faith. The ghastly ritual seemed totally unjustified. Rich people sacrificed large animals, and those with no yard kept the animal in the house and sacrificed it in their bathrooms. I spoke of my qualms to one of our clients, a wealthy carpet merchant, Nur Khan.

'Ah,' he said, 'Mr MacQuitty, you seem to forget that your Christian religion is founded on the crucifixion of Christ. The Roman Catholics eat His body and drink His blood at the Eucharest. Protestants do the same at Holy Communion. It is not His message of love that is the foundation of your Church, it is your salvation through his sacrifice. Your religious orders all wear the cross of the crucifixion. In the Spanish Inquisition, hundreds of thousands were burnt alive to save their immortal souls. Our customs are hallowed by long tradition. The Jews have the same ritual. But at least we both stop short of human sacrifice.'

As I sat at my desk, thinking over Nur Khan's words, my *chaprassi* brought me a blue envelope postmarked 'Gulmarg'. My heart gave a sudden leap. I laid the letter on one side and went on with my work until I had an opportunity to slip up to the roof. Then I sat down on the parapet and opened the letter. The blue paper it was written on matched the envelope. Kim wrote of Gulmarg, the beauty of the place, her work and the type of people she was meeting. It was a friendly and objective message and ended simply 'Kim'. I read and reread it and finally put it in my pocket and went back down to work with a lightened step.

The hot weather was again exhausting. Whenever a local holiday gave us a long weekend, Eric and I would head in the car to our nearest hill station, Mussourie. The road there ended at the foot of a bridlepath to the town. Here we hired ponies and their *syces*, and when we came to steep ascents, the *syces* would hang on to their ponies' tails to encourage them from behind. As we rode up, we would watch the stocky hill porters heaving impossible loads up steep short-cuts. They used headbands and short forked sticks to steady themselves. By placing the stick beneath a load, they could snatch a rest from time to time. They tackled anything: great sacks of grain, cabin trunks, sideboards. One even had on his back an upright piano supported by another porter pushing from behind. At the top, they would unstrap their burdens and lie flat on the ground while their fellows walked up and down the backs of their legs to loosen the muscles.

Visitors who did not ride were taken up in dandies, open litters carried by four dandy-wallahs, or doolies, closed litters. At the top, heavy rickshaws with folding leather hoods provided quick and comfortable transport, drawn along by two barefoot coolies and pushed by two more. When the sahibs were in a hurry, the rickshaw coolies raced one another. No matter how wet or cold the night, they were always there, waiting to take revellers home. Princes and important people had their own elegant rickshaws with splendidly uniformed attendants who, for all their finery, still ran barefoot.

As at Chamba, the most enjoyable feature of the hills was the cool sparkling air. On our morning walks 7,000 feet above the valley, we gained heavenly views of the Dun and, beyond, the Siwalik Hills rising from the great plain. When the monsoon was breaking, the sun shone through the downpour drenching the plain. 'Eric,' I said, 'rain is falling on a divided, dissatisfied people concerned with nationality, politics and religion, and here is a magnificent example of the equality with which nature treats mankind.'

'What about your malaria, in that case?' asked Eric. 'Nature doesn't give a cuss for us. We got here by our own contriving.'

On one occasion we managed to reach Simla, the most glamorous of all the hill stations, the summer headquarters of the Viceroy ever since Lord and Lady Dufferin, whose estate I used to visit in Ireland, first went there in 1888. At the end of March, the Viceroy, the Supreme Legislature and government departments would pack up and leave Delhi for Simla with their mountains of files, so beloved of the Indian bureaucrats, who, I came to be convinced, believed that writing down any intention automatically achieved it. It said much for the local administration that the country apparently got on just as well when the government was away from Delhi as when it was present.

Simla frothed with fun at the headquarters of the famous Black Hearts Club and the Gaiety Theatre. There were dances galore and parties at Viceregal Lodge. It was full evening dress every night, the only anxiety that of being left out. The fact that it worked was amazing: that 370 million could be governed in such a way. The 'Heaven Born' seemed cut off from the reality of the Indian life around them, as was emphasized by the Simon Commission, which consisted of eight British Members of Parliament, none of whom had any connections with India, 'so that their decisions would be impartial'. The commission was sent under the chairmanship of Sir John Simon to adjudicate on India's fitness for independence, but Great Britain's exclusion of Indians from the commission was regarded in India as sheer social arrogance. The commission was therefore boycotted from the start. The usual welcome arches put up in every Indian village came to bear the words 'GO BACK SIMON'.

We stayed at the Charleville Hotel, where by tradition a bell was rung at 4 a.m. to enable naughty couples to regain their own beds. On our last morning I left Eric, who decided to laze, and climbed Jakko Hill to see the view of the snow-capped Himalayas from its summit. On my way down, I rested on a fallen deodar. Something made me turn. A few yards to my right were two seated figures, their backs towards me. They seemed familiar. I stood up and walked in front of them. They were indeed my *sadhu* and his *chela*. I spoke to the *sadhu*, but there was no reply. He sat in the lotus seat, his eyes open. Again I spoke. Again there was no response. At this point the *chela* spoke for the first time since I had met them, saying in Urdu, 'He is not here, sahib, he cannot answer.'

I looked closely. There was no movement, no breath. I touched his brow. It was cold as ice. 'How long has he been like this?' I asked.

'Since sunrise.'

'What is he doing?'

'He seeks knowledge.'

'What knowledge?'

'I do not know.'

'Shall we meet again?'

'I do not know.'

I gave the *chela* five rupees. 'Please offer your *sadhu* my respects and wish him well.'

I walked slowly back to the hotel, wondering how it was that I kept running into this curious pair in this huge country. 'Do you think they're following me about?' I asked Eric.

'Not on your life. If they were after your money, they'd be much more direct. Take your Amritsar guru, Dr Chandra – he never makes any bones about it. Those chaps are in rags. They like the cold, they're looking for something. They don't work, they live in their minds, they get well thought of and plenty of offerings. Better life than a lot of us. Who knows? Maybe they're right. It's all relative.'

The Amritsar summer dragged on. Our weekly PLH parades were enlivened with slow chukkas of polo and paper chases. A final innovation was my idea of firing revolver blanks to burst balloons tied to the jumps in the manage, a mud-walled enclosure on the maidan where the horses were schooled. I had by now acquired a second horse, Ginger, a lively chestnut mare, good for polo but highly strung. On my first jump she broke her martingale, threw her head back just as I fired and caught the blank wad behind her ears; then fell stunned on the far side of the jump, to the delighted cheers of the Indians who always crowded round the manage to see what the 'Punjab Lat Hass' was up to. Even elderly plump Hindu gentlemen taking their pet quail for a morning walk joined in the merriment at my downfall.

The rains had filled every depression with water, enabling mosquitoes and frogs to swell the nightly chorus and render sleep more difficult. One night a coppersmith bird, no bigger than an English robin, was putting out an endless series of *tonks* very like the noise made by striking a copper bowl with a wooden mallet. First puffing itself up to twice its normal size, it then let out all the air in a sudden rush to create this devastating sound. Not to be outdone, a brain-fever bird joined in with its even more irritating song, starting low on the scale and gradually ascending until its voice finally broke on an absurdly high top note. For a space there was a blessed silence before the whole performance started again from the beginning. Meanwhile, in the distance, *chokidars* called to one another that all was well.

Lying awake, I began to reflect again on my foolhardiness in making myself so vulnerable, not only to natural hazards but to the fury of the terrorist groups: a sleeping figure within twenty yards of a public road and only an ancient Gurkha for protection. Admittedly the Gurkhas were the finest soldiers in India, perhaps the world. Strange that they should follow Buddhism, a philosophy of peace. But was all well? Where was Choki? He should have passed on patrol before now. I slipped on my canvas mosquito boots, took my flashlight and loaded Colt from under the grass pillow, lifted the mosquito net and shone the torch on the grass to check that no reptiles were lurking.

Choki was behind the bungalow, bent over a kerosene tin heated by a small fire. He looked up as I appeared. 'What are you doing, Tika Ram?'

He gave an endearing grin. 'Making rum, sahib.'

How was it done, I asked.

'First, put *kutcha* sugar in water, cook, leave for some days till bubbles stop. Light fire again, but not too much, no boil. Put three sticks inside for little *bowli* glass to sit and on top big *chatti* of cold water.'

He lifted the large basin to show me. The finger bowl inside it, safely above the fermented liquor, was half full of alcohol that had condensed on the cold base of the big *chatti* and dripped down. The distilling system was certainly ingenious. If the forces of the law became interested, they would find nothing but utensils in normal everyday use. 'Do you drink it all yourself?' I asked.

'No, sahib. Some to wife and some to sell. Wife still works hard for *derzi* [tailor] with Singer.'

At about this time my life was suddenly brightened by an invitation to join the Lahore Flying Club as a founder member, the club having been inspired by Bob Leete's historic flight when he won the *Daily Mail* £1,000 prize for piloting the first light aircraft to fly from London to India. He had made landfall at Karachi on 8 January 1928, arriving in his de Havilland 60 Moth with its Cirrus Mark 2 engine. Because I could only get to Lahore at weekends when everyone else wanted to fly, my instruction never lasted longer than fifteen minutes. I had only completed six hours when, after making a couple of good landings, Bob Leete said, 'Try one on your own.'

I had expected a good deal more time on dual control before being trusted solo with the club's aircraft, and since Bob received a fee of 150 rupees for everyone who got their 'A Licence', I wondered for a terrible moment whether he was short of cash. Then it occurred to me that he might presume I had put in more flying time than I had, since he had seen me around for four months. As I wondered what to do, Bob stepped down from the plane and wandered off to the hanger. I was too ashamed to get out and follow, especially with all the Sunday members watching. With a tight band of fear around my stomach, I opened the throttle and taxied slowly to the take-off point.

The Gypsy Moth layout was simple: a spring-loaded air-speed indicator on the port wing-strut, a central joystick, rudder bar, spring-loaded tail trimming wheel, rev counter, petrol gauge, speaking tube, headphones and throttle, all controls duplicated in the front cockpit. The engine had four in-line upside-down cylinders. A fourteen-gallon gavity-flow fuel tank was in the top wing, rubber shock absorbers were on the landing wheels, and there was a tail skid. I lined up for take-off, conscious of all eyes watching even as I had watched others go solo for the first time. As I gave full throttle and lifted the tail, I missed the well-known figure in the front cockpit with his capable hands and feet on the controls and his reassuring voice over the headphones. Freed from his extra weight, the Moth leapt off the ground, and before I could adjust to the new sensation, I was half-way round the airfield on my first solo approach.

'Go round as many times as you like before landing,' had been Bob's final instruction, but my strongest instinct was to touch down promptly so as not to prolong the anxiety. I throttled back and put the nose into the normal glide position. The lightened plane seemed to float indefinitely, but slowly the ground came nearer until I was able to distinguish blades of grass – the sign it was time to ease the stick back. To my horror, the nose immediately lifted. Quickly I pushed the stick forward. The plane hit the ground with a thump, bounced back into the air, and finally came to a halt after a series of giant hops.

Bob came running out. Maybe he'd taken a look at my log book, I thought. 'Terrible landing. Very sorry,' I said.

'Any landing where the pilot can get out of the plane is a good landing.'

'I've only done six hours, you know.'

'I realize that,' said Bob. 'I go on performance. Judge Gordon Walker has logged forty hours, and although he's extremely careful, I won't let him go solo till I'm satisfied he can do it. You'll get your "A Cert" after another six hours.'

Six hours and ten minutes of flying time later, I completed my tests and received my 'Fédération Aéronautique Internationale, British Empire, Aviator's Certificate', signed by the chairman and secretary of the Royal Aero Club, and henceforth, to my great delight, would be able to carry passengers. This will be a big surprise for Kim, I thought. She'll be my first passenger if I have anything to do with it.

Tension, always close to the surface in Amritsar, rose with the arrest of three young Sikhs who had thrown bombs in the Delhi Assembly. The bombs had not exploded, but the trio were regarded as national heroes and a *hartal*, or general strike, was proclaimed. The police were out in full strength, the units of the Auxiliary Force India were ordered on standby and regular troops took over key positions. Orders came that I was to take the Amritsar Detachment through the city. It went against the grain. Up to that point our policy had been to maintain a low profile.

The following morning I placed myself at the head of my small troop. We were fully accoutred with sabres and carbines – shoulder chains burnished, helmets cleaned, uniforms neatly pressed, bandoliers polished, harness shining, bits sparkling. As we jangled through the Hall Gate to the bazaar, I wondered what on earth I should do if an upheaval started. What chance would we stand in a narrow crowded street where anyone could strike at us and disappear? Sabre drill was simple enough, but always performed at a gallop. Here, at close quarters, we would need to slash, but slashing had never been a part of the drill. I wondered why it had never occurred to me to ask about it.

John Lobb's police were everywhere, carrying their stout *lathis*, heavy staves shod with brass to make a simple but powerful extension of the London bobby's truncheon. Cracked down on bare feet or occasionally swung at an arm or shoulder, they were effective in crowd control. As we trotted through the Hall Bazaar, we were treated with cheering, jeering and a chant that went:

> *Ek hat men jean,*
> *Ek hat men ras.*
> *Kan hat men tulwar?*
> Panjab Lat Hass!

> (One hand on the saddle,
> One hand on the reigns.
> Which hand holds the sword?
> Oh, Punjab Light Hass!)

Not that we were dreaded or especially unpopular. When all was said and done, we were well known to the business community, but as we passed along the narrow street I could not avoid thinking of General Dyer and Captain Briggs, only ten years or so before, taking that same route and leading fifty Indian troops against a mob of 20,000, the police force demoralized and the civil administration in paralysis. What nerve and cold courage it must have taken to penetrate so deeply into lawless territory where killing, looting and arson reigned freely. As for ourselves, having made a circuit of the town hall, we retraced our route and emerged unscathed through the Hall Gate to a sympathetic reception from our servants.

It was a great relief that the operation to show the flag went off so smoothly, and I wondered again at the way in which such an apparently peaceable people could all at once become so wildly ferocious at certain points in their history. Again it occurred to me what an extraordinary achievement it was that a handful of British managed to hold such a vast politically and religiously divided country in relative tranquillity. I hoped our Amritsar Detachment had made its small contribution.

Not long after the *hartal*, news came that Gandhi was to pass through Amritsar on his way to Lahore. I mentioned to Kartar Singh that I should very much like to see this important person. Gandhi was clearly the key figure in Indian politics. His voice swayed millions. He popped up in unexpected confrontations with the Raj and was constantly being put in gaol for his pains. A week later, as we were checking the ledgers, Kartar Singh remarked, 'Gandhi will be passing through at four o'clock.'

We slipped away to the crowded station where the stationmaster escorted us to a good position. After a long wait, a train appeared in the distance. 'This is the one,' said the stationmaster.

We moved closer to the edge of the platform. The train slowed and we found ourselves carried along by the crowd, which had already spotted the Mahatma's carriage. With Kartar Singh's help, I pushed through the throng, and there was Gandhi, sitting cross-legged, wrapped in a shawl and eating what looked like a lettuce leaf. With his big ears he had me thinking of a leprechaun seated on a magic mushroom and from time to time eating a piece of it. He was unimpressed, I thought, by his chanting admirers, who hailed him as Mahatma, 'the Great Lord'. His policy of *satyagraha*, soul force and civil disobedience, had, as he said, been 'a Himalayan miscalculation' that led to murder and riots by people who disregarded his appeals for non-violence and continued a reign of terror. Addressing his listeners now, he exhorted them to refrain from violence, and was still calling for *ahimsa*, the way of non-violence, when the whistle blew as if to underline his final word and the train pulled out of the station to cries of, 'Long live Gandhi, long live the Mahatma, death to the British!'

'So what do you think of him?' asked Kartar Singh.

'I like him,' I said. 'He's a rebel, and so am I in a small way.'

'You may be right,' said Kartar Singh, 'but there will be mass killings if the British leave.'

'Don't you want the British to go?'

'No. India is a corrupt country, and the corruption remains unchecked until it reaches the most junior British civil servant, and there it stops. We walk in freedom because of the British. If they go, justice will go, and with it will go what you call playing the game. No one will be safe.'

'We're not safe now,' I said. 'What about Saunders, the young police officer recently shot in cold blood when he was walking to his house in Lahore? The murderer who shot him was not in any danger.'

'Yes, but you played the game, you celebrated his death by a memorial football match in Lahore.'

'And,' I said, 'we all had to have anti-tetanus injections. Nevertheless I like the man Gandhi. I like him for wearing his loin-cloth when he mixes with the mighty, for spinning cotton and trying to get the people to return to a simple life, and especially for his support of the outcasts.'

'But he is your greatest enemy.'

'I don't think so. Sooner or later we must leave India, as we've promised, but Gandhi will give us an excuse for going sooner, before we get caught up in the appalling difficulties that will come with freedom. Already Abdul Ghaffar Khan has raised an army in the north. How can Muslims and Hindus select a joint leader? He has to be either Hindu or Muslim, and neither side will wear it unless it's their own man.'

'And what of the Sikhs?' asked Kartar Singh. 'We will want our own leader too.'

I also asked Allah Dad what he made of Gandhi. 'Hazur, he is a Hindu first. He is looking for himself, for his next life. He has not got ordinary love for other people.'

'But he is always fasting and helping the untouchables.'

'Hazur, he has only changed the name. They are now "Children of God", but to Hindus they are still outcasts.'

'He lives in poverty,' I offered.

'Hazur, it is a poverty we would all like to share. His every wish is granted, he has an army of attendants. He loves himself.'

'How will it end?'

'He will spill blood, much blood.'

John Reid and I continued our daily yoga exercises. John had become something of an adept and Dr Ram Chandra was pleased with his progress. He was able to swallow several yards of white bandage and then withdraw it, thus cleansing his stomach. He could also pass a finer bandage up his nose and out of his mouth or down the other nostril, drawing it backwards and forwards. I thought this unlikely to make any difference to his health, but he maintained that part of his improved condition could be attributed to these cleanings. I knew that experts could submerge themselves and draw in and expel water through the anus, but I stuck to breathing, posture and exercises, generally endeavouring to relax and stretch every part of my body as far as it would comfortably go.

John had made the second of two trips to Amarnath, the sacred cave in the Himalayas where venerable yogis, some believed to be more than a century old, lived in the solitude of the vast mountains. He had come across three adepts living in extreme austerity. 'What do they do?' I asked.

'They say they act as transmitters, sending good thoughts to mankind. One whom I touched was in a frozen trance. The others, though almost naked, were warm. They claim to be able to generate heat by circulating energy in a figure-of-eight pattern through their bodies. They certainly had need of warmth. Their cave was a lofty cleft in the side of the mountain and gave little shelter at 15,000 feet.'

'They had no fires?' I asked.

'Yes, a small fire, just two logs set end to end with a glow where they met. Beside this was a brass *lota* used for melting snow for drinking-water. There did not seem to be any food. They have some weeks to wait before the thousands of pilgrims arrive, and snow still lay outside the cave.'

'What do you suppose they were really up to? Making a living out of the faithful?' I asked.

'I think exactly what they say. After all, where do our thoughts come from? Suddenly you get a new idea, something you've never thought about before. Where does it come from? Then occasionally you are aware of liking a person before you've even spoken to them, perhaps through some body-language beyond speech, or perhaps through some sense of smell so faint you're unaware of it.'

I had to tell John that I didn't like the implications of telepathetic perceptions or occult mysteries. It seemed to me that there were enough wonders in the ordinary business of living, and that trances, levitations and so on didn't seem to make the world a better place to live in. We had many such conversations that arrived at no conclusion, for what can one know of the unknowable? But we were both in better health and stronger for our practice of yoga.

Ram Chandra suggested that the time had come for us to try complete meditation, which had the objective of isolating mind from body – not in a state of trance but in a withdrawal from the world. To achieve this we sat cross-legged on the ground in the lotus position (though I found that any comfortable position served equally well), fixed our attention on the least stimulating idea or object one could imagine, and continued to hold the mind relentlessly on its target until it drifted into an area of oblivion. The exercise did seem to induce tranquillity. The idea of oblivion already held an appeal for me. If there was life after death, it would, in my view, have to be pretty good to better oblivion. The Buddhist prayer, '*Om mani padme hum,*' literally, 'The jewel in the lotus,' represented the idea of a drop of water on a lotus flower falling into the lake and losing itself in its original source: the eternal recycling of nature.

One day, as I rose from my session of meditation feeling light and refreshed, I glanced in a mirror on the veranda wall. It reflected the veranda but not me. John had already gone into the house. I shut my eyes tight and backed down into the cane chair again. Once I had been able to stop trembling and been able to reassure myself by feeling each of my limbs in turn, I shakily stood and, keeping my eyes resolutely away from the mirror, got in the Salmson and drove home. The experience left me badly frightened and I spoke about it to Dr Ram Chandra. 'You should not have attempted this,' he said. 'It is very dangerous. Some force for evil might have entered your body.'

'But,' I said, 'surely this is exactly what you've been teaching us to achieve. How can it be dangerous?'

'It's like driving your car. You must be in control, otherwise it runs away and kills you. You have to learn to drive.'

'How could any such force enter my body?'

'Thoughts are always entering your body, as do more material things. The child never loses its parents. Even after their deaths, they are still part of the child. The dead lover remains not only in the mind but also in the body. You talk of feeling things in your bones, in your heart, in your liver. This is quite correct. These things acquire space in your body. When they are good they are comforting. The dead continue their lives through the living. But when they are bad they can torture and destroy. Your Bible has accounts of Christ driving out devils. There are many mad people in the world. Even in your country they are described as being possessed.'

'What am I to do now?' I asked.

'You must advance slowly. You have done well. Apply what you have learnt to your way of life, and when the time comes for another step, a guide will be there to help you.'

'How shall I recognize the guide?' I asked.

'You will know him. My work with you and John Reid is coming to an end. You have nothing to fear, you will not be separated again. Life has much in store for you. Follow the way and go in peace. As the Buddha says, "Be a lamp unto yourself." '

'How can I know that this thing will not happen again?'

'Because no matter how far you travel, I shall be close to you.'

'At school I once learnt a poem by Emerson. It was about Brahma.'

'What does he say?' My guru was looking serious.

> 'They reckon ill who leave me out;
> When me they fly, I am the wings;
> I am the doubter and the doubt,
> And I the hymn the Brahman sings.'

'He is very wise, your poet,' said Ram Chandra.

7

The Luck of the Irish

The Grand Prix Salmson, a hopeless car for India really, was nevertheless Allah Dad's great pride. It had its place on the shady side of the bungalow, where he would polish the bright red torpedo body and metal fittings till they shone like new. One one occasion, as we drove to the bazaar, he jumped out before I could stop him and walloped an unfortunate cart pusher, who, startled by the roaring monster, had spilt a load of oranges across the road. For better or worse, Allah Dad's sahib could do no wrong. The situation was not of my choosing. Milton's 'He that is low need fear no fall' was more to my liking.

Meanwhile Kim had returned from Kashmir. I resumed my pilgrimage along the Grand Trunk Road, being due at Zam-Zammah at dusk. The Salmson was fast, and would be comfortable for Kim, I reflected. It had a fixed drive without a differential gear, so the rear wheels turned together and there was no loss of power through wheel-spin, which made for dramatic cornering. It had no doors and only a tiny wind shield. There was a bulb horn on the running-board on the driver's side, and a starting handle permanently in position. Then, as I drove, suddenly it occurred to me that my blessed anonymity was at an end. There was no other car in the district like the Salmson. Wherever I left it, the world and his wife would know that there was MacQuitty. I already had a reputation for being a loner:

Down to Gehenna or up to the Throne,
He travels fastest who travels alone.

The sun was still up when I drove down the Mall, which meant I had time to book our old table at the Italian restaurant before doubling back to Kim's Gun. Soon it was dark. As I bent down to switch on the side-lights, a familiar voice asked, 'What on earth have you got here?'

Kim was wearing a white linen dress with a belt, and she looked as cool and capable as ever.

'My car. I swapped it for the bike.'

'It's fun,' said Kim, hopping in, 'but what an awful colour.'

Although she had been away half a year, we seemed to take up exactly where we left off. Over dinner I told her about my trips to Simla and Mussourie.

'Oh,' she said, 'Kashmir's much better. It's a real country, set in a vast valley, with high meadows and tumbling streams full of snow trout. European flowers and fruit flourish, and by the Dal Lake are gardens more beautiful than Shahdra and Shalimar.'

'It's a pity there's nothing nearer,' I said.

'Oh, but there is. You're just beside the Kangra Valley. It's not high country, but it's lovely, and there are rest-houses and *dak* bungalows where you can stay. Have you tried a *dak* bungalow? They're one of the best things the British did. Staging posts for the mail – *dak*. Simple square rooms with a charpoy, table and chairs, and a small bathroom, but all in good positions. Like the missions, the government picked the best sites.'

We talked and lingered over coffee before driving back to her flat. As I parked the glaring red torpedo of the Salmson outside I was aware that it stood out like a beacon. I helped Kim to alight and stood silently, but as she started up the stairs, she asked over her shoulder, 'Did you remember your pyjamas?'

'What about the car?' I asked. 'Isn't it a bit obvious?'

'You are a funny thing. What does that matter?'

'People might gossip.'

'What if they do? I am my own person. Let them gossip.'

An extraordinary sense of freedom swept over me. Later, as we looked up at the star-filled sky, she said, 'I have been away so long I'd almost forgotten your smell.'

'Do I smell so bad!'

'Of course not, but we all have smells – very faint, because we've almost lost the use of our noses.'

'So the reason I'm attracted – terribly attracted – to you is because of your smell?'

'I think so, but fate has a lot to do with it too. That's why I didn't want to meet you again. As I said at the time, it may not be good for us, but now it's fate, I'm afraid, so there's not much I can do about it.'

'I'm grateful to fate, if that's what it was, for bringing us together. It's made me very happy.'

'I hope you're right,' said Kim. 'Anyway, I'm going to sleep,' and she promptly did.

In the morning, as we sat having breakfast, I asked casually, 'Would you like to fly over Lahore this afternoon?'

She looked at me in astonishment, and that afternoon, when I took Kim out to the plane at the club, she did not want to climb in at first. 'Is it safe?' she asked. 'It feels very flimsy,' poking a finger through the fabric.

Fortunately we were too far away from the clubhouse for anyone to see the incident, and anyway we were always patching the old skin. I strapped her into the front cockpit, adjusted her helmet and head-phones and took off. It was a gusty day, with bumps here and there, and in the middle of one particularly severe drop she slipped down in her seat so that her feet became wedged against the rudder bar; and since the rudder bars were connected, I could no longer move mine. And since her headphones had pulled out of the connecting tube, she couldn't hear my screams to her to get back up in her seat. My hands shook and my stomach froze as we headed over Lahore, across the Ravi River and above Jehangir's tomb.

Desperately I fought to gain height as Lahore slipped away behind us and, directly ahead, the Himalayas rose in all their majesty, the Moth's ceiling being, as I kept reminding myself, less than 9,000 feet. Eventually we reached 5,000 feet, and I set the tail trimmer, unstrapped my harness and lent over the cowling, hoping to grab Kim's helmet. Suddenly she sat up. Her panic had evaporated and she was looking about herself with interest, pointing out the Hima-layas with delight. Praying she would stay put, I headed for home, and still shaking, managed a perfect three-point landing and got out. But Kim refused to budge. 'Take me up again,' she demanded.

'You promise to sit up?'

'Yes. I was only frightened at first.'

Going up again would be good for me too, I thought, and this time I headed towards Amritsar where there was plenty of flat space for emergency landings. Kim chatted away on the headphones as if she had been flying all her life. Over dinner that evening I confessed she had been my first passenger. 'No wonder I was scared,' she said. 'I never will be again.'

Our annual AFI field day consisted of contests between the different detachments: shooting, tent pegging and a two-furlong race. Some of us stayed in camp, and Eric and I were quartered in a bell tent. We had to feed, groom and harness our horses, attend all parades and receive praise or blame for our efforts. As I had entered for the scurry, I had sent Soupy off two days early to be walked by his *syce* along the canal road to Lahore. He arrived in fine form, and I was delighted when I was drawn for the fifth race and given a cloth bearing the numeral '5' to be tied on my chest. It augured well, my lucky number coming up twice. I backed myself heavily both ways.

Soupy and I made a good start and led the field for the first furlong, but after that his bolt was shot. Horse after horse galloped past us, but my lucky number survived and we came in fifth. The following day included the shoot, and at midday beer was served to the troops. I was by now a full corporal and fancied that a third stripe could be within my reach. When I noticed that my adjutant and the colonel, sitting with their ladies in the shade of a banyan tree, had not been served, I hastily grabbed a tray and four mugs of beer and prayed I would get there first. As I came up to their table I transferred the tray to my left hand and swept off my helmet with a graceful d'Artagnan gesture to honour the officers' ladies in their long feminine dresses. Too late I realized my gaff. The ladies smiled; my adjutant coloured; the colonel looked pleased, as if scoring a point. 'Thank you, corporal,' said the adjutant, and added after an ominous pause, 'Next time remember your salute.'

I never did get my third stripe.

But there was a far sadder end to the field day. When I returned to Amritsar, the *syce* greeted me, weeping and shaking with terror. As instructed he had started to walk poor Soupy home slowly along the canal road, but at nightfall had been frightened by evil spirits and galloped to the nearest rest-house, where the unfortunate animal collapsed and died.

'Soupy was an elderly horse,' I said, trying to comfort the man, 'and he had a very happy life.'

He threw himself at my feet, sobbing as if his heart would break.

'Allah Dad,' I commanded, 'take the *syce* to his family and tell them he is forgiven.'

Next morning I received a sequence of three telegrams from the Public Works Department:

SIR YOUR HORSE IS LYING DOWN HERE IN SICK CONDITION. PLEASE SEND ASSISTANCE.

SIR YOUR HORSE IS EXPIRING HELP URGENTLY REQUESTED.

SIR YOUR HORSE HAS EXPIRED PLEASE HAVE BODY TAKEN AWAY.

Additional parades were making it impossible for me to see Kim, but she promised to come down to Amritsar instead and show me the Kangra Valley. The Saturday she was due to arrive by train, I reached the station in good time and, as I waited, asked the stationmaster about the 1919 troubles. 'We had terrible time, sahib,' he said, 'mob destroying government property. Killing hundreds of Indians, including stationmaster and employees, smashing telegraph office and ticket office before help coming. Also killing Europeans, setting fire to many, many buildings and looting shops. Army saving situation.'

'You think the army acted rightly?'

'What else to do? Gandhi always talking peace, but only trouble coming. We have work to do and families, we keep trains and telegraphs running. These are wild peoples. They would not be seen when the Moghuls ruled. They fight British because British are full of fair play and listen to everybody.'

When the Lahore train came in, Kim stepped down with a small suitcase that I took from her and stowed in the tightly packed tail space behind the seats. We left Amritsar immediately and travelled east along the Dharmsala road, which was a smaller version of the Grand Trunk Road. Already the frenetic pace of Amritsar was left behind, and soon the road narrowed and began to wind between low hills. The River Beas tumbled past on a wide stony course, and after a few miles it was running faster, with small cliffs on either side and large boulders scattered in its bed. Slowly we climbed to a thousand feet and, rounding a corner, gained a view of the snow-capped Himalayas.

The road wound beautifully through the hills. It had white stone markers, low parapets on corners or beside steep drops, and was well designed. Certainly whatever criticisms the Indians levelled at the British, these did not include roads, railways or canals. Eventually we reached Kotla with its rest-house on high ground commanding a splendid view across the River Beas. Our room was simple and had a pleasant veranda with long-chairs. We moved in our things before walking to the end of the garden to watch the sun vanish behind the hills, draining the colour from the scene as it sank. Later it suffused the sky with a red glow that gradually died away. The night was cool and windless, the only sound the flowing water. The *kansama* brought out a table and chairs and asked what we would like for dinner. 'What have you got?' I asked.

'Mulligatawny soup, roast chicken, potatoes and brinjal, custel brun.'

'Very good,' said Kim. 'Have you soda pani?'

'Just bring, memsahib.'

We drank our whiskies with great contentment, and after dinner sat and watched the stars grow brighter and a new moon slowly rise. It was extraordinary that such an atmosphere of utter contrast could lie so close to the teeming cities of Lahore and Amritsar. It was hard to believe that out there were striving nations, battling armies, competing religions and the endless confusions of political convictions. 'It's so peaceful here, they seem to be so isolated. How do they manage it?' I asked Kim.

'Like Swiss mountain villages, they are self-contained. Here even more so. There are sugar-cane and tea plantations not far away.'

'Is this what Gandhi wants?'

'Yes, but his spinning and weaving of local cotton cloth was also an anti-British cotton-piece goods campaign, and his Gandhi home-spun cap became a far from peaceful emblem.'

'Yet you're a fatalist, so wasn't all this bound to happen!'

'I'm in good company. The Christian God's omnipotent, ruling all the affairs of men, and in Islam fate is the inexorable power known as Kismet that transcends all the physical laws of the universe. That's why Muslims accept wealth or poverty with indifference.'

'I simply don't accept that I'm not "the master of my fate, the captain of my soul". I can't prove it, but I don't see what the point of living would be if it were all prearranged. It would be so dull for God, rather like the Lord's Prayer must be getting. All that "Lead us not into temptation". Why would He? And "Give us this day our daily bread". Why shouldn't we earn it?'

'I think you're a conceited small boy. You should listen to your Omar Khayyám. He was the greatest fatalist of them all.

'Oh come with old Khayyám, and leave the Wise
To talk: one thing is certain, that life flies;
    One thing is certain, and the Rest is Lies;
The Flower that once has blown for ever dies.'

In the morning we walked along the hill road towards Kangra and saw logs being dragged by oxen up a steep bank from the river to be loaded on to ox-carts and taken to the local wood store. There we watched seasoned wood being cut into planks by two men, one holding a double handle on the lower end of a long saw, the other standing on a framework above him and pulling it up, most of the cutting being achieved on the down stroke. At midday we found a pool with a flat boulder and decided to swim in the afternoon, then to climb a narrow path leading up to a small temple that overlooked the River Beas. I had taken the lead when all at once I was confronted by a cobra slithering down towards me. The snake and I both stopped in our tracks. The cobra raised its head and, with a sharp hiss, expanded its hood. My legs felt very exposed since I was wearing *chaplis* – open Indian sandals – and a pair of shorts. As I was carrying a stick, I felt I could have slain it. 'Don't touch it,' said Kim. 'Keep still and wait.'

I made no move. The cobra gradually lowered its head and, with a swift movement, continued its way downhill. 'Snakes never touch you unless they're frightened or you hurt one,' concluded Kim.

I told her about the Russell viper in my bath.

'You were jolly lucky. It must have been drowsy.'

The temple had a bronze tiger in the forecourt and, round the back, an empty inner shrine. There was a powerful presence in the air. I wondered if fate was feeling thwarted.

Three days after returning from Kotla, I was stopped on my morning ride by two young Sikhs. The dogs sniffed at their shoes suspiciously. 'Sahib,' said the taller of the two, 'may we ask question?'

'Yes,' I answered, accustomed by now to being stopped and asked questions.

'Sahib,' the man continued, 'this is private matter. If you do not wish to answer, we will finish.'

I observed them more closely. They were in their mid-twenties, intense, strained, but resolute. Freedom Fighters, I thought. I nodded.

'You Irishman. Irish have won freedom from England. What for us to do to win freedom for India?'

'You know that I am in charge of the Punjab Light Horse.'

'Yes, sahib, but you also banker and your job is taking memsahibs and children into fort, not fighting us.'

'Do not kill anyone,' I said. 'It is not necessary. There are very few English left in India and they will leave you as they left us. Then, like us, you may find that the change is not necessarily for the better.'

'Better for us, sahib.'

'If you kill, not so,' I said. 'The Brtitish are stern fighters. If you kill one, many more will come. But they are also a proud people, and if the majority of Indians wish them to leave, they will not stay.'

'We have no choice, sahib, we must sacrifice ourselves in the cause of freedom.'

'But Gandhi, your great leader, is continually ordering you to use peaceful disobedience, but no bloodshed. You are violating everything for which he stands.'

'He won us nothing. He is put in prison. Many of us are gaoled. We must fight.'

'There are 370 million people in India and only 60,000 British troops. If your people wanted the British to go, they could not stay. You are speaking for a tiny minority. What do you think will happen to the Sikhs when the British leave? The Hindus and Muslims vastly outnumber you.'

'It will be time to think of that when the English have been driven out. That is first step.'

'You asked me a question and I give you the same answer as your leader. Do not kill. You are great sportsmen. You understand fair play. Play fair with your people and ours.'

They remained silent as I rode away.

The bank godowns were being picketed. Members of the National Front lay in the road, and the bullock-carts, with their loads of Manchester cotton-piece goods, could not move out. Police were called, but as soon as they dragged one lot of prone figures away, others took their place. Outside the bank, a large crowd gathered, shouting 'Inqulab Zindabad!' – 'Long live the revolution!' Customers anxious to get their money out in case the bank stopped payment pushed against the closed doors. As soon as we opened for business, they rushed to the counter, clamouring for their savings. Tulsi Ram heaved his vast bulk over to my desk and said, 'Sahib, many peoples want to take money and we have only five lacs in safe dats.'

'Who has the greatest claim?' I asked.

'Fazal Ali wants 25,000 rupees from current account and three lacs from deposit dats.'

'Send him to me and tell the rest that all will be paid.'

I could hear Tulsi Ram's mighty voice booming across the banking hall that all would be paid before adding some remarks of his own which provoked a laugh from his now quieter customers. Bidding Fazal Ali sit, I asked what I could do for him.

'Sahib I have a large deal which I must complete today and so I need to withdraw my money.'

'But your three lacs on deposit are not due for two months.'

'Other times, sahib, you have let me withdraw money without interest. Is this different?'

'No, Mr Ali, you may draw all your money now, but on one condition.'

'What condition, sahib?' he asked nervously.

'That any money you withdraw today may not be redeposited today.'

Fazal Ali agreed immediately, with evident relief though somewhat shamefacedly.

The cash counters in India being on the floor, Fazal Ali pushed himself through the throng and sat opposite Tulsi Ram, cross-legged behind his grill and well briefed on what to do in the event of a run on the bank. I took the chance to get in touch with the Government Bank of India and our neighbouring banks for funds, but they were all in the same boat. Rumour of a British collapse had led to a general withdrawal.

Tulsi began to pay Fazal Ali, handing over the first lac in 100-rupee notes; ten neat wads with a hundred notes in each. With trembling fingers Fazal Ali began to count, but in his excitement failed to reach a tally. The crowd became impatient, but Tulsi reassured them and the sight of so much money had a soothing effect. The next wad was passed across. 'But these are only 10-rupee notes,' objected Fazal. 'I require larger notes.'

'Very sorry, but larger notes must be kept for other customers as well as you.'

Amid a murmur of approval, the counting continued, and soon Fazal Ali was surrounded by little stacks of notes. Two of his clerks joined him and protected the mounting piles with encircling arms and legs. Finally Tulsi opened the 1,000-rupee bags of silver and began to ring each rupee on the marble floor before passing it over. 'I cannot accept silver,' protested Fazal Ali.

'Everybody will accept silver,' said Tulsi, surrounded by nodding heads.

The ringing of the silver had a calming effect, but the process was interrupted by the arrival of Fazal Ali's chief clerk with news of looting in the bazaar. The din outside the bank confirmed his story. The bank guard had already taken up positions at the door, bayonets fixed and guns loaded with buckshot, five heavy lead balls to a cartridge. By now Fazal had stopped counting and was leading his heavily laden clerks to the door. A quick look outside at the frenzied mob in the Hall Bazaar decided him to hurry back. 'Mr Tulsi Ram,' he said, 'I have changed my mind. I will not take the money today. There are too many people about. I will come for it later in the week.'

Tulsi Ram, his face wreathed in smiles, brought me the news. Our contigency scheme had worked. I said, 'Please tell Fazal Ali that, in accordance with our agreement, we cannot take back the money today, but that he may stay until the bank closes, and provided that he places it on deposit for two months, it will be accepted.'

Fazal Ali sat near the guards, complaining bitterly that the bank would not accept his money. The crowd drifted away. The run was over.

It was always a relief after these fraught incidents to climb into the Gypsy Moth and soar into the blue sky. All man's inhumanity to man was left on the ground as I swooped and spun in the blue firmament. Back at the club, our good Judge Gordon Walker, an elder brother of the Labour MP, Patrick Gordon Walker, was taking his first solo at last. His circuit was perfect, his approach meticulous. Not for him, I thought enviously, the problem of the lighter plane. Then, just as he was about to touch down in the most perfect landing we had ever seen, he decided to go round again. 'That's what you should have done,' said Bob Leete.

Another perfect circuit with a superb approach, but no landing. 'He's a perfectionist,' said Bob.

Forty minutes later, the good judge was still making perfect approaches. The light was fading, fire engine and ambulance were standing by. The judge, after all, was an important member of the Raj establishment. Bob stood out in the field to wave him down, but still the judge kept going. At last, as it was nearing sunset, he made a perfect landing and expressed surprise at our concern.

The club had prospered. Two more Moths had been bought, but since we needed to increase our income it was decided to offer 5-rupee joy-rides. The scheme was most successful in Lahore, and it was decided to take the circus to other cities, Amritsar being the first. Air navigation in India is easy. The pilot simply follows the railway lines. At Amritsar we installed ourselves on the polo ground, where I found I was more in demand than Bob, for my customers knew that I had to be in the bank on Monday. We kept making a circuit of the Golden Temple and more and more people queued as they heard glowing accounts from elated passengers who had made a safe return.

Late in the afternoon, Tulsi Ram, until that point watching rather nervously, decided to venture a trip. 'Get in,' I said, and buckled the straps round his great girth. 'Are you comfortable?' I asked as we rumbled off.

'Very comfortable dats, much enjoying,' came his voice over the headphones.

I gave the engine full throttle, lifted the tail and we bumped across the field. Some yards past the point of no return, I realized I had underestimated Tulsi's weight, the wheels were still holding firmly to the ground twenty yards from the boundary boards, beyond which stretched a line of large shade trees. I jerked the stick back sharply, hopped over the boards, and continued across the mercifully flat ground till, with gathering speed, we swept between two of the trees and climbed slowly, ever so slowly, out of danger. Tulsi was full of gratitude for the extra five minutes I gave him for his five rupees.

Our new accountant, George Edwin Pow, occasionally admonished me for my familiarity with the natives. Unlike Scott, his taciturn predecessor, he was inclined to buzz about the office, eager to know what everyone was doing, anxious over whether his demands were being properly executed, constantly on the move, papers waving. In the hottest weather he wore an elegant yellow waistcoat and seldom removed his jacket. Although he entered into the life of our little community with zest, enjoyed gossip and became a diligent club member, he was sensitive and easily hurt. I sensed an underlying loneliness. He carried with him an atmosphere of home remote from the Indian scene and, as a regular church-goer, lived as if he were in an English village.

With Christmas only a week away, Pow told me that he had an invitation to spend the holiday with some friends and trusted all would be well in his absence – a broad hint that I should mind the shop. Kartar Singh and I had already supplied the memsahibs with their peafowl turkey substitute, and I had made the seasonal arrangements at the club, but my heart was not in the preparations. Why didn't we have Christmas at Kotla, I asked Kim, and invite Eric to join us? Eric by this time had a girlfriend, Kitty, who was a secretary in Lahore. 'Why not Kangra?' suggested Kim. 'It's twice as high up. We might even have snow, and it's only another hour's drive.'

'How can I get out of all the club festivities?'

'Tell them you're going up-country on a shoot. They'll forgive anything for sport. After all, you do supply them with their Christmas peafowl.'

Thus, on Christmas Eve, we set out early for Kangra, Kim and I leading the way in the Salmson and Eric following in his more spacious car with Kitty and most of the luggage, which included my shotgun, a Christmas cake and a plum pudding my mother had made and sent out. I had responded with Kashmir shawls, fine silks, carved ivory and Indian objects that I felt would be of interest. As we passed Kotla, a sprinkling of pines appeared on the high ground. Their scent, mingling with the smell of wood fires, seemed like a breath of Christmas already. 'It's wonderful to be here on our own,' I said. 'Why don't more people do it?'

'That's simple,' said Kim, her hair flowing in the breeze. 'At

Christmas the English feel even more isolated from their home folk, so they rally round with nostalgic parties.'

As at Kotla, the Kangra rest-house occupied a fine position with views of the snows. We unloaded the cars and entered. Alas, we were not alone. A hilarious lunch was in progress, and at the centre of the table sat George Edwin Pow, who waved genially. I went over and was introduced to his friends. 'Are you spending Christmas here?' I asked, praying that somehow this invasion might vanish.

'No, no,' Pow replied. 'We're on our way to Kulu. Just breaking the journey for lunch. I see,' he added with a knowing look, 'that you've some game for your shooting trip.'

As I turned back to track down Eric and the girls, who were unpacking, I could hear Pow commencing to regale the club members with accounts of my exploits.

'Gossipy old maid,' said Eric when I told him the news. 'Let's go for a walk.'

By the time we returned, Pow's party had left, and for the moment at least we had the place thankfully to ourselves. Since I had brought along my HMV portable, we listened to records of the *Mikado*, the *Appassionata* and *Kreutzer* sonatas, and, for good measure, 'Lullaby of Broadway'. After a tub and a change we sipped our *chota pegs* round a blazing log fire until we were told by the *khansama* that our Christmas Eve dinner was ready. The table was beautifully decorated with groups of flowers round the four candles, a touch in which I suspected Eric had a hand. We drank to absent friends and ourselves, spoke of other Christmas Eves and wondered where we would be the same time next year. Then we went to bed.

'What on earth's the matter?'

I woke to find Kim shaking me. I was shaking myself. My old nightmare had returned, and I had, as usual, successfully evaded the descending boulder, except that this time, as the chasm opened at the bottom and I needed to stop, it was not the boulder but George Edwin Pow who pushed me into the abyss. After I told Kim about it she said, 'You're worried about the "finger of scorn". You're still a Bangor boy. So Pow goes back and regales the club. What of it?'

'But what about your reputation?'

'I doubt if they could improve on what I've got. I'm only concerned about what I think is right for me.'

'You said we might not be good for each other. What about that?'

'Who knows? I take life as it comes, being a fatalist.'

'But you ought to get married and have someone to look after you, while I'm not at all settled or wanting to marry – not ever, I think.'

'Oh dear,' said Kim. 'Taking advantage of a poor girl. Well, you can forgive yourself freely and stop feeling so guilty. I've got rid of one husband and have no intention of taking on another for a long time yet. When I do, it certainly won't be you, so relax and "simply enjoy" as our Indian assistant advises the dental patients.'

Next morning the ground was a foot deep in snow and it was more like an English Christmas than ever. Everything we could see of India was transformed into a white landscape. 'I told you,' said Kim, 'but the servants won't like it. They hate snow and wrap up in blankets.'

We went out and had a snowball fight as the rest-house staff laughed at the crazy sahibs. Our Christmas dinner was heralded by carols on the HMV. The *khansama* gave us trout from the hatcheries at Kulu, another innovative gift of the British, and four oddly assorted wine glasses were filled with claret and raised to 'absent friends'. A plump peafowl, specially selected from the memsahibs' supply, was proudly carried in on a large willow-pattern plate. The bird was surrounded by tinned sausages and stuffed with sage, onion and breadcrumbs. It smelt wonderful. Roast potatoes, peas and lentils came in well-worn dishes. Finally the plum pudding, borne aloft by Eric, arrived in a pool of flaming brandy. Around the glowing fire we talked of absent friends, of ambitions, of hopes and fears, of the future of India and our own futures. 'Why don't we live here for ever?' I asked. 'What is the point of laying waste our days in getting and spending? Here we have timber for homes and fires, bread, fish, meat, fruit, wool from sheep and goats for home-spun clothes, together with a splendid climate. Up in Hunza, they say, people live for over a hundred years.'

'You'd soon be bored to death,' said Eric. 'Same old daily round.'

'I'm not so sure,' offered Kim. 'Many great men cut themselves off from society. Buddha went into the wilderness. All the Hindu sages and holy men lead lonely lives, and even Gandhi lives simply. Many writers live in remote places.'

'It all depends what you do,' said Kitty. 'They don't need secretaries here.'

'We wouldn't need to work for others,' I explained. 'We'd work for ourselves. All the essentials are here, and we'd live a healthy life in a healthy climate. Good health is the most important aspect of living.'

'Tempting,' said Kim, 'but we live in our minds too, and we need bigger minds than ours to move about in, otherwise we'd all be cabbages.'

'This is too deep for me,' said Eric. 'I'm going to trade myself a large brandy, and may I remind you "getters and spenders" that we'll need to dig the cars out of the snow before we start back to Amritsar tomorrow?'

'Pow sahib wanting to see master,' beamed my twice-born *chaprassi*.

I rose and walked through the office to Pow's crowded desk, and waited patiently as he finished reading a telegram. 'Ah,' he said, 'Barr Pollock and his accountant in Cawnpore have gone down with malaria and been ordered to Nainital. You are to proceed at once to assist A.S.M. Young, who will be temporarily in charge.'

It sounded like good news to me. I hadn't seen Sandy Young since leaving Bombay. I was to leave straight away, so I handed over my duties to Bill Hendrie and Joe Darnley, who wished me luck, and said goodbye to John Reid, who told me to keep up the yoga. Allah Dad, only too delighted, packed my things and his own small bag, summoned a tonga and got us to the station in time for the fast train to Cawnpore. Like all Indians, Allah Dad had friends everywhere and loved a train journey.

'Welcome, Bill,' said Sandy as he met us at Cawnpore station. He was as pawky as ever with his quizzical smile. 'You've timed things well. We've a Hindu-Muslim riot in the bazaar. No work, bank shut, but we'll be inside, guarding the premises.'

Ever since the General Dyer affair, the policy had been not to move in the troops, and the Indian police were powerless to deal with such widespread conflict. I was used to anti-British feeling, but this was something new to me. 'What on earth set this lot off?' I asked Sandy.

'You remember Saunders, who was shot in Lahore? The man who killed him was eventually found to be Bhagat Singh, who threw the bombs in the Legislative Assembly with two others. They became heroes and, as you know, when they were executed in Lahore the local Congress Committee proclaimed a *hartal*. But the Muslims stood aloof and this led to clashes. Both sides are always waiting for the chance to settle old scores. Just listen to them at it.'

I opened a window. From a distance the fearful sound of the mobs carried over the still air. Smoke and flames rose from the area as mosques and temples were fired, homes and shops looted and set alight. The trouble, which had begun on 24 March 1931, took three days to burn itself out. For those three days we remained behind our massive, heavily barred doors. By the fourth day the situation had quietened and I ventured out with my camera.

Mob violence anywhere is frightful, but this Hindu-Muslim conflict was marked by the most terrible brutality. The community remained behind locked doors, frightened to emerge. No one had yet had the courage to start clearing up. Bodies, bloated and fly-ridden, lay in grotesque attitudes. Old and young of both sexes had been hacked to death, arms, legs, hands, feet and heads severed. The Ganges canal, wells and ditches were filled with corpses. A woman hung from a balcony, her stomach slashed, a foetus hanging from her womb. Pariah dogs wandered through the scene, sniffing the dead. Reports of the death toll varied between the official figure of 250 and 1,500, but the former was the count of bodies recovered and did not include those who were burnt along with their houses, or buried, or carried away in the canal and river. Hindu houses and temples in the more predominantly Muslim areas were all destroyed, and vice versa. The following day I set out to visit the Memorial Well, the scene of the previous massacre in Cawnpore when 211 British women and children had been butchered on 15 July 1857. On the way I passed two lorries piled high with corpses. A third had just arrived. On its blood-stained floor lay the hands of a child. I looked more closely and saw that they were both right hands.

I sat in the shade, appalled by the senseless slaughter. How could it be possible for religious beliefs to be worth such carnage? Was it the promise of posthumous glory for the faithful that transformed ordinary mortals into raving homicidal maniacs? I also wondered in retrospect how it was possible, as I had done, for anyone to photograph such scenes. I reached the conclusion that the camera lens had an effect of distancing the photographer from the terrible reality.

Ten days later the manager and accountant returned, pale but able to carry on. Sandy saw me off with the hope that we might meet in London since our furloughs should overlap, all being well. It was strange how our destinies remained in the hands of home staff in head office who were never themselves East of Suez.

Amritsar came like a haven of tranquillity after the horrors of Cawnpore. Lugs and Macwhusky romped around me in a delirium of welcome and Allah Dad was joyfully received by his family. News of the Cawnpore massacre had swept through India and brought renewed criticism of British rule.

John Reid and I still met each morning for our yoga work-out. He had become an adept and was greatly admired by the Indians, though needless to say the club members dismissed it as a ridiculous fad. When I asked him what he felt he had achieved, he replied, 'Peace of mind. I've been able to lose the worries and I'm fit.'

Then John's three-year furlough came round again. He was seen off in a flurry of parties, and I found myself the longest-serving member of the Amritsar staff. John's relief was W.E. Lang, a dapper, slight, reserved man, due to retire after this final job. We got on well and he used to tell me about the lovely cottage he had bought in

Cornwall for his retirement. I wondered whether, as a bachelor, he might not find his retirement lonely, but he never discussed that side of his life, though I suspected a lost love hidden somewhere in his memory. Like my old headmaster Macfarlane, he had a habit of clenching his jaw so that the little muscle on the side of his neck kept twitching.

The Salmson had been an entertaining car to own and drive, but its space was limited and, when an opportunity came, I swapped it for a reliable five-seater Fiat. The new car had stout wooden spoked wheels, a canvas hood and capacious side-pockets, and it could, with room to spare, carry Allah Dad, dogs, bedrolls and ice box. By now the weather was warming up again, the usual unrest commencing. The Gurkhas were transferred from Lahore and I was asked to cooperate in providing diversions. 'Couldn't we play hockey and football with them?' I suggested to Kartar Singh.

'They are very strong people, sahib.'

'So are the Sikhs,' I said.

Matches began, and though we were beaten we enjoyed it, and drank rum in the Gurkhas' sergeants' mess. Later the Gurkhas – a formidable, loyal people – marched through the city, pipes playing, rifles at the slope and kukris swinging from their belts. Before long they would go to their quarters near Dalhousie, but I would still have my faithful Tika Ram.

Each hot weather seemed hotter than that of the previous year, probably because one knew what one was in for and was each time a little less fit to cope. On a night when it seemed hotter than ever, I checked the temperature on the verandah thermometer at midnight. It read 112°F. Waiting for Tika Ram to come round for his usual chat when he found me still awake, I must have dozed off, but reawoke shortly afterwards. Still no Choki. He's making rum or cuckolding someone, I thought. Time passed, and when there was still no sign of the small, neatly clad figure, full of the confidence of his race, I grew anxious. Cautiously raising the mosquito net, I looked around, suddenly aware again of being an easy target, though somehow the mosquito net seemed to offer a kind of cover. I put on my canvas boots and stepped out, taking my Colt and torch from under the grass pillow. Since I would be clearly visible to anyone on the perimeter, I walked carefully round to the back, holding close to the bungalow walls.

I patrolled full circle, making use of the cover of the great mango trees, and as I drew into their shade stumbled on a body. I switched on the torch and there at my feet lay Tika Ram. I bent forwards and shook him. No response. I rolled him over. His eyes were wide open and there was no sign of life. Quickly I switched off the torch and got my back to a tree, then swept the beam round the garden and along our frontage with the road. No one in sight. I shouted for Allah Dad and the boys and the chummery sprang into life.

'Neck is broken, sahib,' said Allah Dad, examining the body. 'He taking mangoes.'

There in Tika Ram's right hand was a cluster of leaves. He had slipped and fallen from a high branch. The mango trees belonged to our landlord, whose fruit they bore.

Tika Ram's widow presented me with his kukri, the one with which he had killed eleven Germans. She seemed composed at his death. I asked if she would like to stay, but she said she wished to go to her own people in Nepal. I gave her money and wished her well. Shortly after this a letter came from the Singer Sewing Machine agent, who asked me for the instalment due on the machine used by Tika Ram, my *chokidar*. I wrote back that I knew nothing of any such transaction, that his widow had returned to her native Nepal and no sewing machine was found in her quarters when the new watchman took over. The agent considered that liability attached to me, and for a long time we exchanged views on the subject. I liked to think that the machine still provided work for Tika's widow in the bazaars of Kathmandu.

Tension in the city increased as the summer drew on. The Freedom Fighters, the National Front, the Congress Volunteers maintained pickets on our godowns and created civil disturbance. On days when the situation seemed dangerous, the DC would send round dispatch riders to warn our small European community not to enter the city. We treated his warnings light-heartedly, remembering the occasion when he paid a visit to the Central Police Station only to have his car stopped by Volunteers lying in the road. More lay down behind the vehicle and, despite the best endeavours of the police, he finally had to undergo the ignominy of getting out and walking.

One morning, when I was at the bank early to decode an unusually large batch of cables, a call came from Lang that the dispatch rider had missed me. A major riot was expected and the King's Own Yorkshire Light Infantry were being sent in. 'Better come out the back way,' suggested Lang.

I locked up and left by the rear exit. All seemed calm as I climbed into the Fiat, placing my Colt in the door pouch before setting off through the narrow back lanes in the direction of the bridge where I expected troops to be guarding the civil lines. The rioters were in the

Hall Bazaar and the lane was almost empty, giving me a clear run. What a bit of luck, I thought, as I swept over a crossing. I could hear the chilling roar of the mob as it bayed for British blood in an unforgettable avalanche of fury. I was on the last lap, and still had an empty road ahead, when a Brahmani bull unexpectedly turned directly into my path and blocked the lane. I just managed to pull up in time and frantically tried to force the beast to one side. Even as I did so, I was spotted. The screaming fringe darted down a side-street and surrounded the car. In an instant I was the centre of a mass of waving arms that tried to drag me out. I thought for a moment of using the Colt, but the notion instantly passed. Instead I struggled to open the door and managed to stand on the running board. Amid screams of 'Death to the British!' I raised my arms and yelled, 'I am an Irishman!'

In the moment's silence that followed a Freedom Fighter shouted, 'What the sahib says is true. He is an Irishman.'

I recognized the man as one of the two who had stopped me on my horse a year before. The mood changed as quickly as it had erupted. Ireland was a blueprint for their struggle, and the screams were transformed into shouts of approval. I got back into the driving seat and the car was pushed and pulled in triumph until we reached the railway bridge, the no man's land between city and cantonments. Here a vast crowd was held by a thin line of police equipped with *lathis*. Ten yards behind them sat Pearson, our magistrate, with the officer in charge of the infantry. The troops were armed with rifles and a machine gun, and in the event of conditions warranting such measures, Pearson was authorized to instruct the officer to order one soldier to fire one shot at a specified man in the crowd.

Prudently my enthusiastic escort dropped back. I drove home wondering if it might not have been more honourable as an Ulster-man to have been torn to pieces upholding the Raj.

8

Ten Thousand Holy Men

There was one bright spot in the wilting heat. As a recognition of almost five years' unbroken service, I was allowed to plan a local holiday in advance. Kim suggested that she hire a houseboat on the Dal Lake for her holiday and I drive up to join her. In the meantime the heat made itself startlingly apparent: pints of cold drinks yielded a trickle of dark-orange urine. I prayed that neither I nor my colleagues would succumb to any of the myriad maladies so generously supplied by Mother India until I could reach Kashmir.

At last, early one Saturday, Allah Dad loaded the Fiat with a well-filled icebox, bedroll, suitcase with warm clothes, his own small bundle, from which he managed to attire himself immaculately, and Macwhusky and Lugs. The car, oiled and greased, its tyres checked and two spares on the back, was as ready as we could make it. We did not stop till we reached Sialkot, where I had a cold beer. Allah Dad drank hot tea from the Thermos, and the dogs, after a rush around and much sniffing of new territory, lapped cold water from the ice melt. There were still 148 miles to go to reach the *dak* bungalow where we would spend the night before going through the Banihal Pass at 9,763 feet into Kashmir.

The road soon reached the foothills and began a long winding climb through sun-struck mountains. Its bad surface slowed us, but the four cylinders beat strongly under the bonnet and eventually we arrived at the *dak* bungalow. The dogs leapt out in a frenzy of excitement. Macwhusky was in his element as he enjoyed this approximation to his Scottish Highlands. It was hard to comprehend how the stench from the steamy drains of Amritsar had so quickly been replaced by the fragrance of flowers, the furnace heat by cool Himalayan breezes. I slept like a log and woke enormously refreshed. If only every night could be like this, I thought, the hot weather wouldn't matter. After breakfast we set off for the pass.

The Banihal tunnel seemed like the entrance to Shangri La. Its shaded entrance was still flanked with walls of packed snow and ice, but there was a glint of sunshine at the far end, and all at once we emerged into a glittering new world. Four thousand feet below us a poplar-lined road stretched in a straight line towards Srinagar. To either side of the road lay a vast checker-board of small fields of light-green paddy, vegetables, yellow rape and areas of still water reflecting blue skies and small white clouds. Beyond the wide flat valley floor, range upon range of mountains rose one above the other in endless splendour.

We approached Srinagar in time for lunch, and I followed Kim's directions, circling the Dal Lake until we came to a turning down a narrow causeway that led to the historic landmark of the old Moghul Bridge. I followed the route with some trepidation, for there seemed no way of turning back, but then the houseboat came into view and Kim was waving from the top deck.

The *Elfin King* was a barge built of unvarnished wood. She comprised a living-cum-dining room, two bedrooms, a bathroom and lavatory. The flat roof was furnished with cane chairs and a table under an awning. Moored at the stern was the cook's *dounga*, a smaller, simpler version of the parent vessel in which the Kashmiri servants lived in ordered confusion. The waters of the lake were covered with lotuses in full bloom, their delicate pink flowers as large as two cupped hands.

After lunch we walked to Nishat Bagh, the 'Garden of Pleasure', which descends in a series of terraces elegantly planted with flowering plants, shrubs and trees. Down the centre a swift stream flowed from the towering mountain backdrop, rippling in white foam down each terrace, with fountains on the level stretches. The flanking flower beds made a blaze of colour with wallflowers, pansies and geraniums, and finally the stream flowed through a pavilion, cooling what was known as the ladies' chamber before plunging into the lake. In the shade of the ancient chenars, families picnicked, the women in gaily coloured saris.

We spoke to an old gardener, who pressed little pokes of seeds into our hands. It was his small private enterprise. I gave him a couple of rupees. Back on the *Elfin King*, we bathed, changed and sat on the top deck, where Allah Dad brought us *chota pegs*. Beyond the lotuses the clear still waters of the lake reflected a mirror image of the mountains, which swam in a purple-blue haze and conveyed a softening sense of peace and ease. Gradually the sun set, brushing the distant snows with pink till colour faded into night and stars lit the sky. 'At five rupees a day, including all food and services, it seems mad not to live here for ever,' I said.

'We've been through that one,' said Kim. 'You've only scratched the surface of living. There's the whole world before you. In a few months you'd start wondering if you weren't missing something else, like the sultan who needed a fresh woman every night, and never had the same one again, no matter how enchanting she was, in case he missed something better!'

Each day that followed revealed a new enchantment. Inspired by the example of a Kashmiri fish-spearer, I tried my hand with his long three-pronged spear. As I stalked my prey, squatting on the platform at the stern of his dug-out canoe and studying the movement of the swirling hypnotic weed, I realized that I should have paid more attention to my physics master on the matter of reflection of light in water. Yet my one success made us a splendid lunch.

One morning we paddled the *shikara* to the city, passing under a rickety bridge that, supported by three stacks of criss-crossed logs, carried the road over the River Jehlum. On either bank wooden houses with balconies lent crazily over the water, their earth-covered roofs thick with grass and wild flowers, their weathered exteriors beautifully carved. The shops bore such strange names as 'Suffering Moses', 'Habiba Joo', 'Ganymede'. The proprietors were distinguished, shrewd, comfortable – descendants of the merchants of the Silk Road. We ventured into the shop of Habiba Joo, who received us in a room with carved panelled walls and an immaculately shining floor that lurched askew, as did every part of the building. We sat and sipped the small cups of sweet tea he offered. 'I will show you everything,' said Habiba Joo.

Soon the floor was covered with carved wooden boxes, trays, papier-mâché trinket boxes, bowls with brass liners standing on three inter-carved folding legs, all with delicate designs painted in glowing colours. There were silk carpets, and silk ring-shawls so fine they could be drawn through a wedding ring. There were amber beads, precious and semi-precious stones. 'What would you like?' I asked Kim.

'I'll just look and think about it,' said Kim.

I chose for myself a fine wooden tobacco jar carved with dragons and a papier-mâché box. 'Where are these made?' I asked.

'Why here, of course,' said Habiba Joo, who promptly piloted us round his workshops.

A row of quiet little boys patiently embroidered silk. Older men carved solid wood. Wet paper was worked into papier-mâché and moulded into various shapes, and jewellery was being cut and polished at special benches. We returned to the shop, the atmosphere heady, and I was hypnotized into buying more of these exquisite products. Habiba Joo was an adept salesman. Money was unnecessary. A chit would do. Infinite credit was thrust upon me. After the customary bargaining, I left well pleased with the price. 'He let you have them cheap because he expects us to come again,' said Kim.

On the way home we stopped to look at one of the floating gardens. These were created by laying long strips of lake weed criss-cross until they were thick enough to support mounds of earth in which plants could grow. The resulting floating mattress was moored at its four corners by poles driven into the shallow bed of the lake shore. Once they were stable, they could be towed from one part of the lake to another, and sometimes the poles took root and the gardens became permanent.

The days flew by in walking the dogs, swimming in the lake, taking photographs, until it came to our last night. 'When will your furlough be through?' asked Kim.

'At the end of December, though I've heard nothing as yet.'

'You must see the Taj Mahal before you go, and Benares for your guru stuff.'

'Will you come?'

'If I can get away.'

'I don't know what I'll do without you,' I said. 'I get an ache under the ribs when you're not with me.'

'You know very well that I only see you at weekends in the cold weather, and not for more than a month of days in the year. You'll find lots of girls in Ireland. This is my home, and though it's new and exciting for you now, in no time you'd tire of it. You've had five hot weathers, but I've had twenty-seven and know what I'm talking about. You're a very small boy still, so don't you forget it.'

Next morning I dropped Kim off at Tanmarg and watched her begin the four-mile climb to Gulmarg on a tough hill pony. She waved once before disappearing among the huge deodar pines.

My journey back to Amritsar was a banishment from Eden. The enchantment of Kashmir ended as I entered the Banihal tunnel. The *dak* bungalow seemed modest and the long road down a descent into an inferno of dust and clangour. The dogs sensed it, and were unusually quiet, but Allah Dad was happy at the prospect of rejoining his family and being able to tell his friends of the sights he had seen.

At the bank I settled back into work as if I had never been away, but I noticed that Macwhusky seemed ill at ease – not eating well and panting a lot. It's the heat, I thought, but the next day he seemed worse and had difficulty in swallowing. Thinking something was stuck in his throat, I probed with my fingers but could discover nothing lodged there. The next day his usually spotless white coat was matted and soiled and he seemed ashamed to look at me. I washed him clean and gave him a *chattie* of water. He lapped thirstily, but to my dismay the level of the water did not decrease. I put him in the car and drove him to the vet. 'Please hold your dog on the table,' the vet instructed.

I lifted Macwhusky on to a zinc-topped table while the vet, a serious-mannered Sikh in his forties, drew on heavy gauntlets and examined Macwhusky's throat with forceps. 'It is my opinion, sir,' he said, 'that your dog has dumb rabies. He must be confined here under observation, and anyone who has been licked or bitten by him must go at once to the Pasteur Institute for urgent treatment.'

I was appalled. When I recovered I said, 'He's a very sensitive dog. He'd be most unhappy away from me. May I keep him at home?'

'You may, provided he is properly isolated and chained.'

'I thought rabid dogs ran wild, biting at random. Why is he so subdued?'

'He has what we describe as dumb rabies. The virus has paralysed his jaw so that now he can neither bark nor bite. But he was infectious before this. You must have been fond of him to risk putting your fingers down his throat.'

'I had no idea what the matter could be. What can I do for him now?'

'Unfortunately nothing. If it is rabies, he will be dead within ten days. I hope for both your sakes it is not.'

We made a doleful couple as we drove home. Macwhusky snuggled up to me and tried to lick my bare knee. I told him to get back in his corner, but he looked so abject that I relented. What was one lick more or less? There was an empty room in the chummery, and there I locked him with food and water. I explained the position to Allah Dad and the servants, but they were all sure they had not been licked or bitten. The club members, however, became terribly upset. They could not remember whether they had played with Macwhusky or not, and they all had prickly heat, which made infection more likely. I telegraphed Kim, but she would have no part of it, her implacably fatalistic nature protecting her from such anxieties.

At the Pasteur Institute in Lahore I completed a card giving my name, address and position, then idly turned it over to see two neatly ruled spaces headed 'RECOVERED' and 'DIED'. In the centre of the treatment room a sterilizer steamed beside a glass-topped table that bore a row of large hypodermic syringes. Round the room sat other patients. It was clear that mad dogs were not particular in their selection of victims: men, women and children of India's many races, even a baby, awaited their turns patiently if nervously. I sat at the end of the queue beside a Hindu with a large paunch. As our turns drew closer, an assistant swabbed a suitable area of our stomachs with iodine. My companion had endured twelve of the fourteen necessary injections, and in all the expanse of his now tender belly could find no spot where he might willingly suffer the thirteenth. Trying to comfort him, I said, 'You are much luckier than me. Where will I find space to put even my third injection?'

'It is well for you, sahib. You can always make joke, but I am frightened man. What to do if all this not working? My friend having all this and dead two years past.'

He was led to the table, and as he went he gave me a mournful backward glance.

As the only European present, I sensed a rustle of interest as to how the sahib would like it. The syringe carried six shots of a thick creamy serum made from the emulsified spinal cords of rabbits killed by the strongest strain of the virus. Between each injection it had its thick needle sterilized in the flame of small burner. The doctor took the syringe in his right hand, pressed out a few drops, pinched my iodined skin between the gloved fingers of his left hand and plunged the needle up to the hilt into the tissue between the skin and the peritoneum. Slowly the serum was injected until the plunger reached the next mark. The withdrawal of the needle left a miniature balloon that gradually subsided. 'Come every day at nine o'clock,' said the doctor, 'and remember, no alcohol or exercise until your treatment is finished.'

The serum had a depressing effect, and I was heartened to find Macwhusky much brighter on my return. We went for a walk in the garden and his interest in familiar places lifted my spirits. Surely this was no rabid dog. Next morning he was still bright and cheerful, though unable to swallow properly. Yet, by putting his head completely under the water, he seemed able to slake his thirst. After these submarine excursions, he would cock an eye at me with a comical look on his face as if to say he didn't approve at all and wasn't it time I did something to help? It made me weep, but he looked a little better and I still hoped he might live to prove the diagnosis wrong. On the ninth day I opened the door to be greeted by a sorry sight. Macwhusky's lower jaw hung disconnectedly like a puppet's when the puppeteer's hand is withdrawn. After watching miserably for a few moments, I went over to him, but even as he tried to drag himself to me, he collapsed, a pitiful little bundle, in death.

After my treatment was completed, I asked the doctor about hydrophobia. He was happy to talk. Most of his patients preferred to know as little as possible. 'The first symptoms are choking sensations,' he said. 'Later there are intense spasms and contortions, face showing extreme terror. Saliva is not swallowed, giving rise to foaming, and though the patient is very thirsty, he is terrified to drink. Any attempt to swallow brings on spasms. Even the sound of running water is sufficient.'

'What can you do for such a patient?' I asked.

'Treatment is only palliative – morphia, cocaine and chloroform. The patient dies from exhaustion in a few days.'

'How does the virus kill?' I asked.

'Once it enters the body from the lick or bite of a rabid animal, it travels along the nerves until it reaches the brain. The time varies from ten days to seven months, depending on the amount of virus which has entered the body and whether or not the infected part is well supplied with nerves. Face and head are the most dangerous areas.'

'My dog was not afraid of water,' I said.

'That is correct. Dogs are not afraid of water, so hydrophobia is a misnomer in their case.'

I thanked him for his treatment and for being so generous with time and information.

'It was a great pleasure, Mr MacQuitty, and you are very welcome to come here whenever you wish, but hopefully not as a patient.'

I had collected Macwhusky's remains from the vet, except for his brain, which was sent to Kasauli for examination. Gopal Das, the *mali*, dug a grave in a corner of the garden and we buried him beneath a red-rose bush.

At the end of September a local holiday enabled me to visit Benares, the most sacred of all India's sacred places, said to combine the virtues of each of the others, besides being the country's oldest city. It lies on a great curve of the Ganges facing the rising sun, which therefore warms the multitudes of pilgrims as they descend the ghat steps to bathe in the healing waters of the Great Mother who gave birth to the Hindu peoples. I hired a boat and drifted slowly past bathers who dipped and bobbed, cupping their hands to drink the precious fluid. Thin saris revealed a startling variety of breasts, their owners oblivious to their crowded circumstances. Farther on the dead, wrapped in white cloth, joined the living in the water before being placed on funeral fires. Round the pyres sat relatives, silent and watching as attendants used long bamboo poles to push cadavers into the hottest part of the blaze. Several bodies were waiting half-awash on the sloping shore, and more arrived as I watched, each carried on a stretcher by four men. Little flags decorated some of the stretchers, but not every corpse received the full treatment, for wood was expensive. Some at convenient moments were slipped partially consumed into the river and nature entrusted with finishing the job.

'Where can I find a guru?' I asked my boatman.

'Sahib, there are 10,000 holy men here. They are everywhere. See them under the umbrellas? Also in houses and temples. Why do you wish to see one?'

'I want to find out about yoga.'

'Ask at the Golden Temple. The high priest will tell you.'

'You're well informed.'

'Of course, sahib. I am qualified official guide.'

'I have two more days. What else should I see?'

You should see Sarnath, where Buddha preached. It is only four miles from here.'

I thanked my knowledgeable boatman and climbed the ghat steps between lines of beggars who exposed dreadful sores and mutilations. Sacred cows littered the narrow street with green pools of ordure. Refuse spilled from dark doorways. I turned into the first temple. A stone lingam stood in the centre of a stone yoni, garlanded with dying marigolds and stained with blood and ghee. In the darkness a faint flame burnt in front of a monstrous figure of Kali strung with skulls. A vermilion tongue flickered out of her dark mouth. I discovered a side courtyard where a white kid was having its neck wedged in a forked wooden post. Once it was secure, the priest beheaded it with a heavy cleaver and a young couple collected the blood and anointed the lingam. The sacrifice, I was told, was to bless the young man's wife with a son.

'Where can I find a guru?' I asked.

The priest pointed across the street to a carved wooden door, which, when I knocked, was opened by a young boy. When I said I had come to see the guru, he led me through a passage and up some stairs that gave on to a large room with a veranda overlooking the Ganges. The guru, a well-built man of about fifty, wore a loose white dhoti and sat in a cane chair. He motioned me to another at his side. 'Why do you come?' he asked.

I explained my efforts to understand yoga and all I felt I had gained from it. But what, I asked, was the ultimate goal? He looked at me in silence. After several minutes, he placed the tips of his fingers together and continued to regard me thoughtfully. 'What you ask is impossible to attain without total devotion over many lives,' he said, speaking, to my surprise, with a cultured English accent. 'I do not wish to appear rude or lacking in understanding, but in terms of yoga you are an infant crawling with difficulty. It will take many incarnations before you can stand, let alone run. The goal is union with absolute reality. The practice of yoga is to by-pass the religious rituals, the worship of our gods and your Creator God, and to become part of the ultimate reality, the deepest self. This is achieved when the dualism of self and Brahma is overcome and all selfhood is lost in the streams of being.' He gave a whimsical smile. 'Have I answered your question?'

'I stand abashed,' I said. 'My Western haste has no place in this quest. I confess I am too critical of the rituals, the squalor, the myriad gods, the sacrifices of animals, the caste system and the violence of the communal riots. I long to build on the good that previous generations have left for me rather than pursue my own salvation.'

'My young friend, I understand your feelings very well. I felt so while I was at Cambridge. My colleagues and I were full of good deeds, but our professors were too deeply engrossed in their subjects to have time for such exercises. As Christ said, "The poor ye have always with you." The great advances in science were made by dedicated men who gradually rolled back the frontiers of ignorance. If I spent my time in political argument and public service I could never achieve my purpose.'

'But isn't this a selfish purpose?'

'I do not think so. The blind cannot lead the blind.'

'But could you not at least persuade the authorities to clean up the city and stop sewers emptying into the sacred waters that people drink?'

'It has been the custom since Benares was built. Hindus believe that the Ganges is so pure that you may safely drink beside her sewers.'

I sensed my time with him was ending. 'Thank you for you patience and kindness,' I said. 'You have opened my eyes, and I will try to understand, though I wonder if, while we are in this world, we would not do better putting it to rights. I think that religion has made people frightened of dying. Would so many people come to Benares if there was no promise of an after-life?'

He rose and, putting an arm round my shoulder, walked with me to the top of the stairs. 'Be content,' he said. 'You have started on the path. You have nothing to fear.'

I walked back to my little hotel, wondering what he meant when he said I had nothing to fear. How did he know I was afraid? What was I afraid of? And which was the 'I' that was afraid?

Next morning I rose at dawn and, after breakfast, hired a tonga to take me to visit Sarnath and the Deer Park where Buddha preached his first sermon after his enlightenment. As we drove out of Benares, my driver, Ram Dut, pointed out the lunatic asylum. 'What do you think of Benares?' I asked Ram Dut.

'Sahib, it is full of mad people.'

'But surely you believe in Mother Ganges who saves all lives.'

'Once I did, sahib, but I was an untouchable, an outcast, working for the Dom Raja – 'King of the Burning Ghats'. I was ill-paid and despised.'

'So what happened?'

'I became a convert to Buddhism and now often driving to Deer Park.'

'You are rich, you own a pony and tonga. Is this what Buddha has done for you?'

'No, sahib, I only *syce*, but is good life.'

The Deer Park was a tranquil place, containing the low ruins of ancient monastic buildings that had housed 1,500 monks when the Chinese traveller Fa-hian visited here in the fifth century. Now it was deserted except for a few figures in orange robes. In the little museum the curator, a short stout man, introduced himself. I could hardly have found a better guide to the principles of Buddhism as he expounded to me the doctrines of the Four Noble Truths and the Eightfold Path. When I said that it sounded like straightforward common sense, he commented, 'Ah, yes, but the difficulty for Westerners is that belief in self is rejected. The "I" for Buddhists does not exist.'

'But here I am talking with you.'

'That of course is true, but it is not the same "I" as yesterday nor will it be the "I" of tomorrow. The point that Buddha makes is that this "I" is not an eternal, unchanging entity living in everlasting immutability somewhere within you. Rather is it a bundle of constantly changing prejudices which make up your personality.'

'I realize that my views undergo change, but this does not lessen the fact that they're mine.'

'And so you become a slave to self. You believe that it is you. Yet you are not the life force that flows through you any more than an electric lamp owns the current that flows through and lights it. The candle flame appears constant, yet it changes from moment to moment. The "I" that cannot do something one day achieves it the next. Where did the first "I" go? It was never there.'

'How can I reason if I reject myself?'

'I see how difficult this is for someone from the West. Let me quote for you what the Buddha actually said. He taught that he who knows the nature of his self and understands how his senses act finds no room for the "I" and thus will attain peace unending. The world holds the thought of "I", and from this arises false apprehensions. "Ye that are slaves to the 'I', that toil in service of self from morning to night, that live in fear of birth, old age, sickness and death, receive the good tiding that your cruel master exists not. Self is an error, an illusion, a dream. Open your eyes and awake. See things as they are and you will be comforted. He who is awake will no longer be afraid of nightmares. He who recognizes the nature of the rope that seemed to be a serpent ceases to tremble. He that has found there is no 'I' will let go all the lusts and desires of egotism." '

We had moved as we talked and now stood before a famous statue of the Buddha preaching. I realized that his position – the legs crossed with the sole of each foot resting upwards on each thigh, the fingers enumerating the Four Noble Truths – was the same as that adopted by my guru. 'Do Buddhists have anything in common with yogis?' I asked.

'Both spring from the Hindu religion and both endeavour to by-pass the complicated rituals of the numerous deities and priests.'

'I find Buddhism refreshing after the frenzy of beliefs at Benares,' I said. 'It seems strange that these religions, with their sacred places so close together, should stand so far apart in their teaching.'

'The teaching of Buddha did not appeal to the Hindus. It is easier to pray than to be "a light unto yourself".'

As I walked slowly back through the ruins, I reflected on how strange it was that this teaching, so popular in Ceylon, Siam, China and Japan, should have been rejected by its country of foundation. At the entrance Ram Dut waited, his pony quietly grazing in the shade of a large fig tree.

In November, Lang, a quiet man not given to parties, invited me to dinner. It was nostalgic to visit the burra sahib's house again. Over dinner he talked about his cottage in Cornwall near St Anthony in Roseland. He had bought it on his last furlough and was looking forward to a peaceful retirement in surroundings he loved. 'Before I leave,' he said, 'I've a small operation that I would like to have done in Lahore. It will mean I'll be away for ten days, but I'm sure you and Pow can carry on.'

'Of course,' I said, 'no problem, but wouldn't it be better to have it done at home?'

'It's very trivial, just a grumbling appendix, but I don't want to break up my homecoming. I'll have all the unpacking and furnishing and I'm anxious to get that out of the way so I can enjoy the spring.'

Lang went into Lahore Hospital on 30 November. On 1 December we had a phone call to say that his condition was critical. He died early the next day. Pow asked me to arrange the funeral for that afternoon. Meanwhile he would advise Lang's friends and suggested we meet at the cemetery. I drove at once to Lahore and saw the parson, who asked, 'What sort of grave do you want?'

'What kinds are there?'

'You can have a first-, second- or third-class grave. I recommend the first class. They are brick-lined and it prevents disturbance by animals.'

'First class, please,' I said, sounding as if I was asking for a railway ticket to heaven.

'Do try to get an oak coffin,' the parson pleaded. 'I'm so tired of burying people in plywood.'

I hurried off to see Ghuram Singh, the coffin-maker. 'Sahib,' he said, 'I have no oak, but can do very nice coffin in teak wood which is much better for lasting and does not mind the wet weather.'

'We will have teak.'

'What size, please?'

Lang was small, but I thought it best to be on the safe side. 'Make it my size,' I said.

'He duly measured me. 'When is funeral, sahib?'

'Today. I will need the coffin and a hearse at the hospital at three o'clock.'

'But sahib, it will take all day to make teak coffin, but have very nice coffin sahib's size all ready.'

He took me into his workshop and showed me a plywood coffin, unvarnished and full of knots. My face fell. 'No one see wood, sahib,' he said reassuringly. 'Is covered with black or white cloth with brass handles and a brass name-plate on top.'

'What is the difference between black and white cloth?' I asked.

'White cloth is for virgins, sahib.'

On the way to the hospital I bought wreaths. In the mortuary a pretty Eurasian nurse reverently drew back the sheet. The body looked small and helpless. I hoped that its former occupant had gone to some even happier place than his beloved Cornwall. Ghuram Singh and his assistant arrived with quite a handsome black coffin that had glittering brass handles and a brass nameplate: 'William Edwin Lang. 2.12.1931.' He removed the lid and he and his assistant stood back. It was bad luck to touch a dead European. The nurse asked, 'Shall I take out his teeth?'

'No, no, just let's get him into the coffin.'

The corspe belched alarmingly as we lifted it. The nurse folded the hands and placed a rose between them. 'I will pray for Mr Lang's soul,' she said.

Ghuram Singh screwed down the lid and, with the assistant, carried the coffin out to the waiting hearse. The hearse was old but the horse young. I told the *syce* to be at the cemetery by five o'clock and to wait outside until the sahibs arrived from Amritsar. As the hearse set off at a spanking trot, I followed in the Fiat. We arrived just as Pow's car showed up, but fortunately the *syce* slowed the moment he saw it. Intelligent chap, I thought, I'll see he gets a good tip.

The parson followed the coffin to a distant part of the cemetery, it being official policy, as I learnt afterwards, to spread interments so as to make the place seem less crowded than it was. Our small group of mourners stood silent and shocked beside the first-class brick-lined grave, but as the parson began to read the burial service, his disappointed eye caught mine over the plywood coffin. 'I am the resurrection and the life, saith the Lord: he that believeth in me though he were dead, yet shall he live: and whosoever liveth and believeth in me shall never die.'

I had a vision of the believers in Benares splashing in the glittering sacred water amid the smoke from the pyres. 'We brought nothing into this world and it is certain that we can carry nothing out. The Lord gave, and the Lord hath taken away; blessed be the name of the Lord.'

The coffin was lowered and we joined the parson in throwing a little parched earth so that it made patterns on the black cloth. I waited till the others had departed and watched the grave diggers place stone slabs across the brick vault and cover all with a mound of earth. Then I laid the large wreaths against the mound and took a photograph for his people. The grave diggers looked at me expectantly and I rewarded them. 'Is the grave safe?' I asked.

'Yes, sahib. Dogs and jackals will dig but cannot reach. This first-class grave.'

Back in Amritsar we drank to Lang's memory and Pow took me aside to make a request. 'I'd be grateful if you'd go through his personal effects and arrange for them to be sent to his family.'

It was strange to return to the empty house. The boys were very upset, wondering about their future. I reassured them that Reid sahib would be back next month and all would be as before. Lang had trunks for most of his gear, but he had bought various things in Amritsar to take home and I thought it best to send the lot. I ordered strong wood crates from the bazaar and had the boys pack everything carefully. Finally I came to his deed box. The keys were in his wallet. Inside the box were documents, a bundle of letters and a faded dance programme in which a dried forget-me-not lay between the leaves and only one girl's name appeared.

Kim was philosophical about Lang's death. She held fast to her belief in the iron law of fate and was equally unimpressed by my new-found enthusiasm for Buddhism. In her view it was cold, selfless stuff. 'When will your furlough come through?' she asked as we drank after-dinner coffee at our Italian restaurant.

'It's due on the day before New Year's Eve. I'll have done exactly five years in India by then, but I shouldn't think they'll let me go before John Reid returns.'

'There something you should see before you go.'

'There must be thousands of things I should see.'

'Yes, but this one's important – the Taj Mahal.'

'I thought it was an over-publicized object, like the Eiffel Tower. Anyway, I'll never be able to have the time off.'

'We could go at Christmas. Two days would be enough.'

In fact getting away proved easier than I anticipated. There were three days free round Christmas, and Pow thought I deserved a rest after dealing with poor Lang's affairs. Kim and I stayed at the Cecil Hotel, discreetly booking in as Mr and Mrs Green. 'We'll see the Taj by moonlight after dinner,' said Kim. 'And wear something warm. It can be chilly.'

The Christmas Eve dinner continued until midnight, and so it was early morning before we got into a Victoria to take us slowly down the Mall, past the polo club and into the Taj road, stopping before the Ganj gate. As we mounted the steps, I could see the moonlit sky through the top of the great arch of the entrance, and with each step a little more of the heavens appeared until, almost dream-like, the white dome of the Taj Mahal rose and the whole building gradually came into view. There it floated, delicate and remote, its exquisite proportions reflected in the still water of the central channel. I stood spellbound, fearing to breathe in case the scene vanished. I held

Kim's hand, and we gazed and gazed, then went quietly forward, absorbing the tiny changes as we moved closer. Christmas Eve had claimed the world and we were alone.

On the other side of the red sandstone watercourse there stretched a row of dark green cypresses, broken by a marble platform before continuing to the tomb. We sat enthralled on a white marble seat as the central dome and four minarets rose before us from their vast marble platform. They were in such perfect harmony that it was hard to believe that this ethereal building had solid dimensions. 'It's superb,' I said to Kim. 'I'd never have believed any building could have such a powerful presence.'

'It has a slender link with us. It was built by Shah Jahan for Mumtaz Mahal, the daughter of Asaf Khan, who was the brother of Nurjahan, the wife of Jahangir whose tomb was our first sanctuary.'

We walked closer. Around the tall entrance were texts from the Koran, the letters growing in proportion as they ascended so that, from the ground, they appeared equal in size. Inside, delicately carved white marble trellis screens surrounded the sarcophagus of Mumtaz Mahal in the place of honour in the centre. That of her husband, who died later, was placed at her side. 'These are empty,' whispered Kim. 'The bodies are in the crypt below.'

We descended a narrow stairway and found ourselves in a small room with coffins in the same position as those above. A hurricane lamp burned softly on a plinth, and beside it lay some jasmine and a duster made of peacock's feathers. The Mumtaz's coffin was small, but the plinth was the same size as her husband's and provided a broad seat. 'Where are the guards?' I wondered aloud.

'They'll be sleeping in one of the rooms. They don't expect anyone to come tonight, otherwise they'd be waiting for baksheesh and telling nonsense tales of the past. I feel sleepy too.'

Kim stretched out and laid her head on my lap and in a moment had done her trick of falling fast asleep. I closed my eyes and thought of the five years that had seemed so long at the outset but which had passed so quickly in retrospect. Where would I be five years from now? The river of life was sweeping me on willy-nilly. If only it could be possible to stop the clock. Maybe Kim was right and we were in the hands of fate. I felt a great sadness that nothing was permanent but everything in a state of change.

'Wake up, wake up, we'll miss the sunrise.'

Kim was tugging at my arm. We ran up the stairs and round to the back of the building where the river curves east so that the first rays strike off the water, throwing the pink dawn light and its reflection on to the eastern side of the tomb. We walked towards the rising sun, whose rays continually changed the shadowings and appearance of the building, highlighting now one feature, now another. Throughout Christmas Day, as it slowly crossed the blue arc of heaven, the sun bathed the tomb in ever-changing angles of light until at last, before night fell, the sunset threw a veil of rose and violet over the shimmering whiteness.

9

Casting a Skin

John Reid came back from furlough shocked to find that the man he had returned to relieve was already relieved by a higher authority. He asked me to dinner so he could hear all the gossip, and as we ate I remarked how it seemed strange that people looked forward to retiring home to a wet cold climate and no servants or the freedom and delights of India.

'My experience of foreign staff,' said John, 'is that they believe home is paradise compared with wherever they've been stationed, but that their average life-span in retirement is very short. My intention is to leave early and see the world. You can live like a lord by going to places off season.'

'I don't want to retire,' I said. 'I took this job to see the world. I want to do a lot of different things and die working. I wouldn't mind staying on here in another job.'

'I'm glad to hear it,' said John, 'because head office are having staff problems and have asked whether you'd be prepared to stay on a few extra months.'

'I'd like that if I could miss the hot weather.'

'I'm sure we can fix it. Anyway, doubtless you'll have your eye on a final fling in Kashmir before you go,' he added, treating me to a quizzical look.'

'Now there's a place where I wouldn't mind spending the rest of my life,' I said.

'Don't be too sure of it,' said John. 'The rest of your life's a long time and bank policy is to send employees to different countries to gain experience. They certainly won't be giving you another posting to India.'

We resumed our yoga sessions and Dr Ram Chandra congratulated us on our progress, especially John for having kept up the exercises on furlough. 'Can you tell me, doctor,' I asked him, 'what the object of life is for the human species? In animals it is survival, so what is it for us?'

'To become one with Brahma, to realize the fallacy of the senses which prevents us reaching nirvana and being absorbed into divine infinity.'

'But the world has so much beauty to offer – music, art, scenery, sunsets, poetry, literature, flowers and animals – all gifts of Brahma. Surely he intended his people to respect and enjoy these treasures?'

'These are of the senses, material things that disappear when the body dies. The delights of nirvana are beyond human expression. They are timeless and cannot fade. They cannot be described, for there are no words for the unknown.'

'But if the whole thing is unknown, how do you know nirvana exists?'

'When you have travelled farther along the path, you will gain glimpses of a glory before which all earthly things fade. This is difficult, I know, for the Western mind, but you are on the way.'

'As an infant I had sudden raptures of serenity, but as I grew older they came less frequently till finally they faded.'

'That experience was possible because your senses were undeveloped. As you progress, you will move closer to reality. You have nothing to fear.'

'People keep tellng me I have nothing to fear, but I am a fearful person.'

'That is why they keep telling you. They perceive your fear. Yet it does not exist, it is a phantom of your senses.'

Head office's instructions for my furlough might arrive at any time. I therefore needed to begin to settle my accounts with India. I had already made arrangements to sell the Fiat when, one morning, Allah Dad came to me with a heavy cloth bag that he held rather nervously. 'Hazur,' he said, 'please do not sell car. Please keep car. I will clean it myself.'

He handed me the bag. 'What is this, Allah Dad?' I asked.

'It is money hazur gave me that I saved.'

'The bag is heavy,' I said.

'There are 228 rupees, hazur.'

'Allah Dad,' I said, 'I am most grateful for your offer, but do not worry, for I will arrange not to deliver my car until I leave.'

'Well spoken, hazur,' he said, bowing his head quickly and turning away.

The account I was most reluctant to face settling concerned Lugs, my faithful companion who had for five years eaten daily from the same dish as Macwhusky. By rights she should have been in quarantine for rabies, but I had undertaken the responsibility of keeping her and now must come to a decision. Lugs was a one-owner dog that had never been sick or unhappy since the time the raw-meat diet saved her life. It was unthinkable to ask anyone else to accept the danger of caring for her, nor did I feel she would be happy in a strange situation. The vet was firm that she ought to be put down, and I felt she would suffer least if I did it myself. One sunny morning I told Gopal Das to dig a grave under a white rose beside Macwhusky's beneath the red rose. I called Lugs and we went round the garden together as we had every day since Macwhusky died, for she was not permitted outside the compound. Finally, as we sat together on the grass, she licked my hand and looked away at someone on the road. It was not hard to place the revolver behind her ear and squeeze the trigger. I was sure she felt nothing. My tears pursued her to the little grave.

In April, John Reid said, 'You ought to take your break now. Your relief may arrive at any time.'

Allah Dad and I packed and made an early start for Banihal, where we spent the night before continuing to Tanmarg. Here we hired tough little mountain ponies and rode the four miles up to Gulmarg, through glades of deodar, blue pine, silver fir, spruce and maple. The air smelt of resin, the source of my amber block with its imprisoned ant, and Kim met us at the top. I paid off the ponies before walking with her through the gently undulating 'Meadow of Flowers'. The plain, three thousand feet above Kashmir, stood high enough for edelweiss and was warm enough for frais due bois and saffron, mauve amaranth, gentians, primulas, anemones, arnica and great masses of the white and blue iris that the Muslims planted on their burial grounds.

'You'll need to be on your best behaviour,' warned Kim. 'The lady who runs the hotel is very strict. Lots of wives come up for the season and her reputation makes their husbands feel safer.'

'What sort of rooms does it have?'

'Oh, not rooms. They're separate huts grouped in a circle with a communal dining room and lounge in front. Your hut's as far from mine as possible. Bachelors are highly suspect.'

The huts were simple and practical, and mine was about eighty yards from Kim's, but directly opposite. It should, I thought, be easy enough to slip across late at night. After lunch we walked round the saucer-shaped valley. My heart sank. Here was no wild, natural beauty spot. The British had taken Gulmarg to their bosom and five different ball games were in progress: golf, cricket, polo, tennis and croquet. 'Is it always like this?' I asked Kim.

'Yes, but we can get away. There's lots of empty space. We should climb Apharwat and fish for snow trout in the mountain streams.'

We had just gone in to dinner.

'I say, you're Bill MacQuitty, aren't you?'

An elderly colonel who had been eyeing me across the dining room came up beside me. I stood, hoping to get rid of him quickly. 'We met in Lahore in 1930,' he reminded me. 'Of course, it's cheek on my part, I'm not in your class, but I do hope you'll give me a game.'

'I'm terribly sorry,' I said. 'I've no clubs.'

'Oh, don't worry about that, there's lots of spare sets at the club house. Now, what about tomorrow morning, nine o'clock on the first tee?'

I looked despairingly at Kim, who gave a little nod.

'It's most kind of you,' I said, 'but I'm afraid I'll only be able to have one round. I'm up here to photograph some of the area and time is short.'

'Jolly sporting of you. Thanks a lot. See you in the morning.'

'Why did you nod?' I asked Kim after he moved away.

'Because I'm working tomorrow but free the rest of the week.'

After dinner we walked again, waiting for the residents to retire, which they stubbornly refused to do. 'We'd best go to our huts,' Kim said. 'Try to slip across later without being seen. If anyone spots you, keep walking.'

'You remind me of Ireland,' I said. 'Where's your famous indifference to public opinion?'

Later I made several attempts, but each time the watchman was doing his rounds, much as Choki used to. I set out to time him, and lay down, hoping that, as the night advanced, he would circle less frequently. I was awakened by a knocking on the door. Allah Dad stood there with my morning tea.

'I'm awfully sorry,' I said to Kim at breakfast. 'I fell fast asleep waiting for the watchman to slow down.'

'Never mind. You were tired. You had a long day. Tonight slip into my hut on our after-dinner walk.'

I went to keep my appointment with the colonel. The golf course was a beauty with thick grass and flowers and tiny rivulets running through to create natural hazards. It was strange to be playing on greens after five years on browns, but I managed to defeat the gallant colonel. After a series of Athol Brose at the clubhouse, he revealed the good news that he was recalled to his regiment.

After dinner Kim and I walked round the huts, and I managed to creep into hers unseen. 'Makes it jolly exciting,' I said, giving her a great hug.

'We'd better set the alarm for five. You'll need to be back in your own bed before it's light.'

As soon as the alarm went, I dressed quickly and slipped out, carefully closing the door behind me. I had expected it to be dark, but it was quite light. The reason and the dilemma lay before me: a blanket of virgin snow. If I went back to Kim we'd be caught; if I crossed to my hut the tracks would tell their own story. Then I remembered the fairy tale of the dog who put crosses on every door. I would make a track to the centre and continue till tracks radiated like spokes of a wheel to every hut. But wouldn't that create too much of a stir? On second thoughts, a spokeless wheel would do the job perfectly. Everyone would think it was the watchman, by now sleeping soundly, I hoped. I walked quickly, leaving footsteps round the entire circle of huts, and the only talk at breakfast was of the dreadful weather making sport impossible.

That day we climbed Apharwat, which was no more than a baby peak compared with its big brothers, Nanga Parbat and Kohlahoi, on the other side of the valley. Even so it had claimed its victims. Only the year before an avalanche had swept down on a skiing hut at Kilenmarg, crushing the stout timbers and killing the occupants. The route up was more of a walk than a climb, and from the top we gained a splendid view over Gulmarg across the valley of Kashmir and the majestic presence of Nanga Parbat, the 'Naked Mountain'. The sun came out and we picnicked on a convenient flat rock.

'Well, most dear, what have you learned from your stay in India?' asked Kim.

I gazed around at the lonely beauty of the mountains. 'Chiefly that I exist only in other people's minds. If I were here alone I would have no way of proving I existed. I would not really be alive. I was taught that the Creator of the universe loved and cared for mankind, but I see no evidence to back it. Nature provides the same treatment for man as it does for other animals. We cannot change it, we can only change ourselves, and that's difficult enough.'

'It's fate, as I said,' said Kim. 'Gods and goddesses are made by man, as are lots of godlings. There weren't any before man came on the scene, and none of man's gods have changed the laws of nature.'

'Dr Ram Chandra teaches me that everything divided into its smallest particles is the same thing, the "breath of an unknowable God". Our salvation depends on refining ourselves until we become part of him.'

'All sounds a bit dreary,' said Kim, 'rather like our corpses being the manure for next year's crop. Where are *you* when you become one with the unknowable? I like being myself.'

'The holy men all seem to thrive on it.'

'Of course they do. They manipulate people for money, like all religions.'

'Well, I like the philosophy of Buddha. He never claimed to be anything more than an ordinary man seeking enlightenment, though his followers insisted he was a god. He dealt in practical terms with living and, like Lao-tzu and Confucius, considered there were enough problems in this world without worrying about the possibility of another.'

'Maybe Old Mother Nature had to have human beings,' Kim suggested, 'because only through them could she discover how the universe worked. The other animals could never have solved its secrets.'

It was a sage pronouncement on which to pack up and start our slippery descent to hot baths and dinner.

Our last night together arrived all too soon. We clung to each other, weeping. I spoke of finding another job, of staying on, but Kim said no job would have anything like the security of the bank. In any case, it was a bad habit to let one person become too important in one's life and I must see my family. She had managed very well before we met and would manage perfectly well after our parting. The next morning there was a dreadful sense of finality as we took a last walk across the meadow. I recalled how I had told her in the past that I could only bring her unhappiness. 'But,' said Kim, 'you brought me a great many things that will remain with me as long as I live. You're part of my heart.'

We walked in silence as far as the path through the wood to Tanmarg. There we stopped and stood silently looking into each other's eyes. I took her in my arms, held her tight, and after a long time kissed her. Finally she gently disengaged herself and walked slowly away until she was hidden by a curve in the road. I stood motionless, filled with misery and indecision, and after an age started down the hill path to Tanmarg. Each step took me farther away from what I most desired. As I stumbled on, I tried to comfort myself that I would return, yet felt it could never be. I was plunging down the bridle path, my eyes filled with tears, when a voice broke through the silent forest: 'Sahib.'

I looked up. Before me stood my *sadhu* and his *chela*.

'We heard from your bearer that you were coming down and hoped we would meet. You are returning to Ireland. We wish you well.'

I gazed at him in despair.

'You are troubled?' he asked.

'I am leaving people I love and a country I have come to love. I am torn between wanting to stay and feeling I have to go home.'

'You do not part from anything in this world. Everything you do, everyone you know, everything you have seen will remain with you for ever,' he said in his soft Irish accent. 'It is because you believe in your senses that you feel loss. Even if you lost your five senses, everything would remain with you. Just as you are part of Brahma, so is he part of you. The world is of a piece and cannot be separated. You have nothing to be troubled about. "Let not your heart be troubled," the nuns used to say.'

'But I am troubled.'

'There is no "I". Everything is in a constant state of change and you have much to do.'

'What have I to do?'

'You have much to learn, and you have nothing to fear. You will not be alone. We will be in your heart.'

He smiled and gave me his hand. I thanked him and his *chela*. He looked at me as if memorizing my face before, followed by the *chela*, he continued up the trail. I stood watching them until they too disappeared into the forest, then I continued slowly to Tanmarg.

Allah Dad waited beside the Fiat. The baggage was packed. We were ready to leave.

The long-awaited news came through: my homeward passage was booked on the P&O SS *Cathay* for 24 June. My relief would arrive two days before I left. Tying up the last loose ends, I persuaded Hendrie to take over the PLH and check the equipment and ammunition at the Fort, which was this time found to be intact. I passed over the Colt .45, two Lewis guns and my carbine, hoping they would never need to be used, along with my two horses, which Hendrie was delighted to have. In the meantime, Darnley had bought a new mare and found her a bit skittish. 'I wonder if you'd give her a gallop for me, take some of the steam out of her,' he asked.

'I'll have a go tomorrow,' I said. 'She seems a sensible animal.'

The mare had a soft mouth and was very willing. As soon as we reached open country I gave her her head and we went away like the wind. There is nothing more exhilarating than a full gallop in the early morning. You feel one with the horse – a veritable centaur. Suddenly I was on my own. The horse had vanished. I had struck the ground but felt no impact. Gathering myself together, I looked around for the mare and saw her some distance behind me, grazing quietly. I walked over, took the reins and examined her. She seemed perfectly unhurt. I seemed all right too, so I mounted and rode home. Half a mile from the chummery I met Allah Dad and the *syce*. 'What happened, hazur?' Allah Dad looked worried to death.

'Nothing,' I said. 'We had a bit of a gallop and she must have caught her hoof in a hole, so off I came, but we're both all right.'

'But where have you been all this time, hazur? It is two hours since you left the bungalow.'

I felt a sudden panic. 'Oh, just riding,' I said as casually as I could muster.

In the bungalow I examined myself carefully, but apart from a bruise on my right forehead there was nothing to show for the experience. Where had I spent the lost time? When I asked Dr Ram Chandra his opinion, he said, 'My dear friend, you are making a habit of leaving your body. This is not advisable at all. Something is worrying you. Tell me.'

I described the last conversation I had held with the *sadhu* and his *chela* in Gulmarg.

'I give you the same advice. You cling to the unreality, you wish to change the world. You have nothing to fear, you are in the hands of Brahma. "When him ye fly, he is the wings," just as your poet says.'

To take my own gear I had zinc boxes made in the bazaar. Each box had two hasps and a bar that slid through them and could be locked with one padlock. Into these, with Allah Dad's help, I packed my books, including a set of the *Encylopaedia Britannica*, my gramophone and records, hot-weather clothes, saddlery, riding boots, sabre, guns, mugs won for various competitions, golf clubs, pictures, everything that might be useful in setting up house afresh elsewhere. The boxes would remain in store until I sent word for them to be forwarded to my next posting, wherever that might be. As each item, carefully wrapped, found its place, I felt a pang of parting. It was like pulling up my roots one by one. I told Allah Dad that he could choose anything he wished.

'If hazur wishes, I would like hazur's bedroll. It will be needed to Bombay, and then I will bring it back with me.'

'Of course,' I said as he turned away, shielding his eyes.

Allah Dad, as I well knew, was an opium eater, though that was a common enough practice in India. Opium, in any case, was the principal ingredient of the chlorodyne that soothed the tortured guts of innumerable victims of dysentery, including my own. Allah Dad took it to gain relief from the state of his teeth, and so I had sent him to Jack Sproull, one of the partners in Kim's clinic, so he could be fitted out with the best upper and lower dentures available. I also gave him his return fare to Mecca to make the pilgrimage every devout Muslim dreams of. Finally I managed to find him a job as cook to the burrah sahib of the National Bank of India – a kindly man with a charming wife. It was a good position, and one that would hopefully continue through each new generation of bank burrah sahibs.

A round of farewell parties commenced. They followed a pattern familiar to me from other people's, the difference being that now they were my own. Pranks were the not unusual endings to such parties, and at one of them the idea grew from nowhere that we should dig a hole in Pow's garden. At three o'clock on a dark Sunday morning, we therefore set out with mattocks and spades and contrived to dig a moderately large hole in his front lawn before silently speeding back to our bungalows. By some miracle – or perhaps because the deputy commissioner of police was one of our party – we escaped un-observed, but I had not anticipated the outcome. Poor Pow arrived at the office, pale, trembling and in a horrible state. It was a signal from the Freedom Fighters; it was his grave. He was a marked man, yet what had he done, what could he do? There would be an uprising; he would be killed. Desperately I searched my mind for a convincing explanation.

'Edwin,' I said, 'you have nothing to worry about. It can't be the work of the Freedom Fighters because they want all the publicity they can get and always use messages. I've received them at the club, as have others. It must be some thief who buried his loot in the security of your garden till he could get back to dig it up again. Maybe he's just out of prison.'

'Do you really think that's it?'

'I'm absolutely certain you've nothing to fear. You'll probably find he's gone off with it, but it might be worth getting your *mali* to dig a bit more just in case.'

Pow was greatly relieved, and the hole did indeed increase in size, though no one ever told him the truth, for that would have worried him even more.

When, on my last day at the bank, I came to say goodbye to the

Indian staff, I took the chance of asking Tulsi Ram what they had thought of me.

'Sir, they all thought you very fine officer, sir dats.'

'But what about me as myself, not as an officer of the bank?'

Tulsi Ram looked sheepish, and then, turning to the others for support, said with a broad grin on his great round face, 'Well, sahib, you were always bounding about dats.'

I thought that just about summed it up.

Back at the chummery in the evening, my ultimate farewell party already in progress, I talked to my relief, a solid Scot of my own age. I tried to convey to him some of my feelings about India, but for better or worse his mind was made up. I do not doubt that he made an excellent officer. Following 'Auld Lang Syne' and everyone else's departure for bed, I wandered alone in the moonlit garden. The call of the *chokidars* reassuring each other that all was well carried across the still air as did the plaintive cry of peafowl, faintly from the far distance. Finally I paused at the little graves of Lugs and Macwhusky under their rose trees. About a year later I was to receive a letter written in the violet ink of a bazaar writer:

Dear Master,

May God grant you long life and many blessings. One white rose tree where bitch is buried now with red and white flowers. This is strange thing. New sahib not caring for garden. I pray daily that old master come back and not forgetting his old *mali*.

Gopal Das

In the furnace heat of the station the morning after my last party, I felt like a man awaiting execution as I exchanged farewells with the group of friends who managed to be there to see me off. Garlands of jasmine, orange blossom and glittering shapes of silver and gold encircled my neck and reached to my knees, the first presented by my *munshi*, Muni Lal. The stationmaster had reserved a first-class carriage for me – 'All to yourself, sahib' – and Allah Dad guarded my two suitcases and bedroll and cabin trunk in which my well-worn stiff shirts and collars awaited release for dinner on the *Cathay*. At last the Punjab Mail arrived. We all shook hands. Kartar Singh held on to me, and I gave him a hug to release him. The stationmaster opened the carriage door, revealing a large block of ice under the fan with a basket of fruit beside it. I thanked him for his many kindnesses. Allah Dad took the luggage, I climbed the steps and stood at the top. Suddenly they were singing 'Will ye no come back again?' as the whistle screamed. The stationmaster slammed the door and, with a great blast of steam, the train slowly pulled away. I leant out and waved until I could see no more.

How on earth, I wondered yet again, did this institution of the Raj of India work? How did this handful of foreigners hold together the divergent millions of India. It could only be a magical illusion, like religion; it worked if you believed in it. As for me, I had left my family to join the bank in 1924. By now it was 1932. How could I expect them to understand the changes that had taken place in me since I left home? My little brother James was a man of twenty, an undergraduate at Oxford reading law. My parents were in their sixties, looking forward hopefully to having their children round them in their old age. To soothe my thoughts, I took out Kim's copy of *The Jungle Book* to read. What a wonderful ability Kipling had to get under the skin of his animals. I felt a kinship with them all, and now, like Mowgli, was returning to my family. ' "It is hard to cast a skin," said Kaa, the Rock-python, as Mowgli sobbed and sobbed.'

Later I slept fitfully as the train roared through the ancient landscape, the rhythm of its wheels echoing my question: *Who am I: Who am I? Who am I?* The wheels carried me revolution by revolution into the future. In the morning Allah Dad woke me with tea, and at Bombay the bank shipping clerk waited to see me on board. We followed him through the familiar throng and drove to the quay where the *Cathay* rose in magnificent splendour above the dock, a towering, gleaming bulwark of efficient Britain. Her look of power and purpose, her hugeness and the bustle of Europeans about her decks, frightened me. It was another world. Did I even want to be a part of it?

The clerk saw my luggage on board and bade me good journey. Allah Dad and I walked the length of the ship. When the 'all ashore' siren sent a shudder through the pier, I shook Allah Dad's hand. He had been father, mother, nurse and comforter to me for five long years, sleeping within ear-shot when I was ill. He had stood between me and the threats and dangers of life in India, never complaining or questioning, his loyalty infinite. Tears streamed down his face and I hugged him cheek to cheek as I blinked back my own. Then I turned and slowly mounted the shining gangway. I walked along the deck until I stood opposite him, and moved to hold him in sight as the ship got under way. I still wept as his lonely figure became indistinguishable from the whole vast receding continent.

Part Two

A Second Skin

10

Furlough

My first task back in London was to report to head office and do the rounds of the managers, who sought news of friends and colleagues and wanted to know what I made of the situation in India. But while most retained a nostalgic affection for the place where they had performed their own first spells of duty, everyone was busy and welcoming parties for the return of a faithful servant were not on the bank's debriefing itinerary. I was told to return next day for an interview with the company secretary, and went to book myself in at the Strand Palace Hotel, where I had stayed in the past with my family. The hotel was full, but luckily Miss Lawson in reception remembered me. The fact that we had always brought her a couple of pounds of Irish butter in the past had touched her Irish heart and she found me a comfortable room.

Next day at the bank the company secretary, Beaky Duncan, greated me warmly and keenly. My reports had been good, he said, but then he added, 'I wonder if you don't have too much interest in life to make a good banker. We need solid, predictable people who run on tramlines and do not deviate until they arrive at the terminus.'

He looked at me closely.

'I don't know about tramlines,' I said, 'but I've very much enjoyed working with the bank.'

'Our problem,' said Beaky, 'is that we don't want to spend a lot of time setting up a chap like you only to have him leave us when we should be getting the best out of him.' He drew some papers towards him. 'Mr Cockburn, one of our inspectors, would like to see you at the Dorchester Hotel tonight at 6.30. Can you make it?'

I nodded.

'Good luck,' he smiled.

I waited to see if Beakey would proffer any advice on how to handle the situation, but he bent over his papers and made it clear he had said all he was going to. In the bus on the way back to the Strand I found myself reading a prominent notice stating where advice about venereal disease might be obtained. Treatment was confidential and free. The more I looked at the notice, the more I thought, why not have a check-up? As far as I knew I had never been exposed to infection, but there were many vague areas in these matters, so why take chances? I got off the bus close to the clinic, where a small group of women at the entrance stared at me curiously. It was only to be expected that a person should feel exposed in such circumstances. Marching in boldly, I asked a stern-looking sister where I must go. 'You can't come in here,' she said. 'This is the hospital for women. The hospital for men is in the next street.'

'I'm sorry,' I stammered, and hurriedly withdrew through the spectators, undoubtedly sharpening their curiosity further.

An ill-omen to start with, I thought, as a small cockney porter in the men's hospital directed me to the fourth room on the right along a corridor painted in standard institutional colours – green walls changing to cream above shoulder height. The room contained rows of wooden benches, on which there sat some thirty silent males. It put me in mind straight away of the Pasteur Institute in Lahore. At one end was a small inquiry window behind which a dour man awaited customers. 'Name?' he demanded.

'I though this was secret,' I said.

'So it is,' he replied, 'but we need your name.'

'If I give you my name, it's not a secret,' I argued.

'It is a secret and it's the rules. We need your age and address too.'

I gave him the details.

'How much do you earn?' he asked.

'What difference does that make?' I asked.

'If it's more than £250 a year, we can't treat you here.'

'Two hundred and ten pounds,' I said quickly, wondering if he would ask for evidence, but he made no further comment and handed me a pink card he had been filling out on my behalf.

I took the card and found a seat on a rear bench. Since the notice in the bus had stressed the confidentiality of the proceedings, I was then shocked to hear the attendant call out, 'Mr Stuart!' Mr Stuart, who had been sitting in front of me, rose and went through the surgery door. Time dragged on, the green and cream walls grew more and more oppressive and I wondered if I had been wise to come in view of my appointment at the Dorchester. Gradually the benches emptied until only I and a large man with a shocking ulcer on his cheek were left. We were summoned together.

The surgery was crowded and noisy, the doctors working away, separated by movable screens. As I walked down a passage between the screens I caught a glimpse of a heavily built man groaning unashamedly as his ulcers were treated. A young doctor beckoned me into his cubicle. 'Drop your trousers,' he commanded in a strong Scots accent, and made a careful examination with his gloved hands. 'When did you expose yourself to infection?'

'I'm not sure,' I said. 'I've been six years in India.'

'Well,' he said, 'no one gets VD off lavatory seats. Have you any symptoms?'

'I don't think so, but I'd like to be on the safe side.'

'I've been a ship's doctor round the Far East and I recommend that you have a blood test.'

I agreed, for this was what I was really there for. He took a sample of blood and handed me another card. 'Take this to the Ablution Room and start treatment. It may encourage you to be more careful in future,' he concluded, clearly unable to resist adding a stiff dose of morality.

The Ablution Room, whose function was the treatment of gonorrhoea, turned out to be like a large underground lavatory. The attendant, a cheerful Dubliner, handed out quarts of permanganate like any good-natured Dublin bar-tender. He gave me a chipped enamel douche can with a red rubber tube ending in a slim nozzle. 'Now,' said he, 'just hang that on the hook above the toilet, put the nozzle up your pipe and let it run in in squirts. Hold it a bit, then let it flow out. It's easy, but don't get it on your clothes. It's a divil for stains.'

Thinking irresistibly of the memsahibs of Amritsar washing their vegetables in the same disinfectant, I hung the douche on a hook above a standard urinal. There were places for fifty, and most of them were occupied by unhappy sufferers. The flow from the douche was regulated by a spring clip on the rubber tube, and I let the permanganate run off down the drain while standing there the same length of time as the others.

'Finished?' asked my cheerful host.

'Yes, thanks,' I replied.

'You'll get to like our little club. Some of our members come back every year. Here's a bottle of Scotch for you. It helps keep down the irritation. And a white cotton bag to keep your dearest member in. It may leak after the irrigation.'

I thanked him again. (A month later a card came to say the tests were negative. Even though I felt sure I was clear of infection, it came as a relief after the drama of the VD clinic. VD must surely rank high on the list of evidences that punishment is no deterrent.)

Back at the Strand Palace I put on my best suit and hurried by foot to the Dorchester in Park Lane to find I was expected. A bellboy escorted me up in the lift to a suite on the Hyde Park side. Banking has some rewards, I thought, as I knocked on the elegant door. A moment later it was opened by a large well-built man. 'Come in,' invited Mr Cockburn in yet another strong Scots accent, and led me into a sitting room with a view of the park and a tray of drinks on a side-table. 'What will you take?' asked the inspector.

'I'd like a Scotch,' I said.

He poured two massive measures into large squat tumblers and added a splash of soda. 'Good health,' he said as we raised our glasses.

I noticed that he consumed a third of his on the first swallow while I only sipped mine. It seemed terribly strong after the diluted *chota pegs* of India.

'You'll be wondering why I wanted to see you,' said Mr Cockburn, looking at me with surprisingly gentle eyes that peered from beneath heavy black eyebrows.

I nodded.

He took another deep draught and stared at my glass. I followed suit. It was obvious that I was expected to keep pace. He turned and looked at the park while he finished his glass. 'Same again?' queried Mr Cockburn.

I nodded again, my throat scorched, and, looking hastily around the room, spotted a large snake plant near the window. We raised our glasses again. He gazed out over the park again. I seized my chance and emptied most of the Scotch and soda into the snake-plant pot.

'We've had good reports of you from three managers, one of whom you buried, but there's been other information as well. It seems you upset some of the European community by mingling with the natives. This we always feel is worrying. It can lead to blackmail.'

Mr Cockburn was obviously embarrassed as he emptied his glass. I did the same, concealing the modest level that remained with my hand. We raised full glasses again. I had by now positioned myself beside the snake plant and could effect a quick off-loading whenever the chance occurred.

'There is also a clause in your agreement which precludes the possibility of marriage until you reach the status of accountant. We understand you may have some entanglement in this direction?'

He finished his whisky and reached for my glass, by now fortunately empty again. Again we raised our glasses. Again he took a deep pull. It was clear that he did not care for his task. It was also clear that the more he drank the less he cared for it. He watched me sympathetically, I thought, and waited. I explained that I had arrived in a new country and been interested in all its aspects. The bank had instructed me to learn the language so as to understand what our customers were saying. I studied yoga, as did John Reid, my manager, and enjoyed the friendship of many Indians. After all, wasn't our staff and weren't many of our doctors Indian? The police, the army, the whole country was run by Indians with only a handful of British.

As he replenished our glasses Mr Cockburn began to smile.

'So far as marriage goes,' I said, 'I've always been terrified of being tied down. I've spent six years in one particular hot, unhealthy, mosquito-ridden area, and without the support of love and affection it would have been impossible. During that time I saw my colleagues replaced several times over.'

By the next refill the inspector was smiling hugely. He spilled a little of my drink as he handed it to me, then swayed slightly as he stood and looked at the tiny figures walking in the park below. 'You're an Ulsterman,' he said. 'You're all right. I'm sorry to have to question you. We're all servants of the bank. Go home, take a good holiday. No doubt we'll meet again in the Far East.'

Mr Cockburn shook me convivially by the hand as he saw me out.

The grimy wet poverty of London had, as I gazed from the passing boat train's windows at the rows of dank backyards, seemed more hopeless than the sunny squalor of India. I realized too that there was a price to pay for my long absence: I was a stranger in my own land. The London I had so greatly loved seemed to hold no place for me. Six years was a long time. In the meantime, my cousins, uncle and aunt were fascinated by me. How well I looked. How grown-up I was. They could hardly have been more welcoming or kind, but their interest was in my homecoming and it was impossible to convey to them my life in India. I visited the Toc H, Mark 1, and found the house the same but my friends moved on. I wandered down Portobello Road to the Venture Club. The premises were again borded up and empty, and when I asked passers-by what had happened, no one knew.

On the Heysham boat home I asked for an early call so I would see Bangor as we steamed up Belfast Lough. It was a fine sunny morning and the blue sea sparkled in Bangor Bay. Soon I glimpsed Craigavad, with its unhappy memories of my first day at Rockport school, and then the channel narrowed as we passed the stocks where the ill-fated *Titanic* was built. The moment we were docked, there was my brother Jim springing up the gangway to greet me. We shook hands a little shyly. 'Pop's waiting in the car,' said Jim. 'He's taken the day off. Mother's at home making the welcoming dinner.'

Father, standing beside a new Wolseley car, seemed smaller. His hair was grey. He was as carefully dressed as usual and wore his customary black-striped shirt with open wing collar and immaculate bow tie. With a big hug he told me how well I looked, and blew his nose several times as we waited for Jim to fetch the luggage. We drove down to Bangor, and as we turned up the steep drive to No. 89 I saw the trident that marked the roof ridge – the emblem of Siva. Now, I thought, I'd never have known that if I hadn't been to India. Mother wept, making small noises as she clung to me. I held her tightly and told her how much I had missed her, how lovely it was to be home.

Unpacked and back in my own room, I decided to explore the boxroom and found it unchanged. The boxes and bedsteads of my ancestors were untouched. I opened the black deed box, and there lay the ant preserved in amber and the little Indian carvings that had spurred me into seeing the world and but for which I might never have left. Downstairs I gave my presents and was plied with questions covering every aspect of my life – except for girls, still regarded as a dangerous topic by a mother with two sons. My letters home had kept them in touch with my day-to-day life in India, and in a surprisingly short time all their queries were answered. Then it was my turn to listen, and I heard how well Jim had done at Cambridge reading law, after graduating at Oxford. 'We bask in his reflected glory,' said Father.

Mother had prepared my favourite lunch: mushroom soup; a great roast of Irish beef, underdone and served with mashed potatoes and brussels sprouts; apple pie with thick Irish cream. The house still overflowed with love, and gradually the long separation faded and we were together again.

Next day Harry Kerr and I went for a long walk round the coast. He told me he enjoyed working for the *Belfast Telegraph* in the job once held for me. Since he was due a week's holiday, he suggested we hike round Donegal.

'I'd like that,' I said.

Kathleen Bell, the girl next door, had married. My friends at the swimming pool wondered why I couldn't have got a job at home. 'Too bad you had to go away,' they said. There was little interest in what life in India was like, and as the days passed I realized that I had indeed become, as my old headmaster put it, 'a luxury tramp'.

As soon as Harry's holiday came we set off by way of Letterkenny to climb Mount Erigal. At night we put up at a cottage and next day walked to the coast. Donegal, in the north-western corner of Ireland, has its shores washed by the clear waters of the Arctic Circle but fortunately warmed by the Gulf Stream. We swam and sunbathed while our feet recovered, and in the evenings drank creamy, black Guinness, sang Irish songs round the pub piano and danced with the local girls. There was drinking, singing and dancing wherever one went in Donegal. To round off the week, we walked south along the coast and climbed Slieve League, where we balanced ourselves across the One Man Pass, the highest cliff in Europe – barely two feet wide at the top and dropping a sheer 2,000 feet to the sea and equally steep for some distance down the landward side. Then Harry, his week up, left me at Killybegs, and I continued alone to Galway.

It was extraordinary how this contact with nature comforted me in my sense of loss for India: the simple reality of mountains and seas, the green grass and the thatched, white-washed cottages whose owners were always willing to give you a bed. The little pubs and shops, the weaving cottage industries, the churches, but above all the friendliness of the people, captivated me. One day I took a short cut across a moor, deciding to walk until sunset, but without warning the sky grew overcast, a sea mist blew in and all landmarks were obliterated. I struggled across the uneven ground in search of a friendly cottage. After an hour's hard-going the fog lifted and I spied a solitary homestead about a mile off. I walked quickly towards it, hoping the fog would hold back till I got there. When I knocked a woman opened the door.

'Could you please let me have a bed for the night?' I asked.

She hesitated, said, 'I'll ask my husband', and went inside.

The husband came out and said, 'Will five shillings with your tea be all right?'

'Yes,' I said.

There was a fire burning in an open hearth and the woman had been baking on a griddle hung from an iron hook. I was heaving off my rucksack when the man said, 'Your room's not ready yet. Will you take your tea first?'

'Of course, thank you,' I said.

They sat me by the table next to the fire and we ate hot soda-bread and butter with boiled eggs. Like all Irish people they were interested in strangers, and by the time we finished talking it was nearly midnight. They gave me a candle and showed me up some narrow stairs to a small bedroom beneath the thatch. I undressed and slipped into the soft feather bed and was asleep in an instant. Just before dawn I awoke gasping for breath. My childhood asthma had returned with a vengeance. I struggled to a tiny window in the gable, managed to get it open, thrust my head out as far as I could and gulped deep breaths of the cold morning air. Gradually the fearful spasms subsided and I managed to dress as I continued to swallow draughts of air. It must have been the feathers, I thought. By now the sun had risen, but the house was silent. I decided not to go down until I heard someone stirring.

The room was sparsely furnished except for one very large wardrobe that ran along the length of the wall opposite the bed. I opened the door, thinking it might have a mirror. It did not, but several items of female clothing hung from hooks and in the bottom was an odd bundle of blankets. Curious, I lifted a corner of one of the blankets and exposed some grey hair. Lifting the corner further revealed that a little old woman half-lay, half-sat in the nest of blankets and was obviously dead. Here was the cause of the delay for my room, and doubtless she was the mother of either the husband or the wife. Death had been a constant companion in India, and so the initial shock quickly subsided, but as I reflected on the tradition of Irish hospitality I wondered if my hosts would mention the matter. After a time I heard movements downstairs and the wife called up that breakfast was ready. A bright fire burned in the hearth and I took my previous seat.

'Did you sleep all right?' asked the husband, looking at me speculatively.

'Yes, indeed,' I said, 'very well, and what a lovely comfortable bed.'

They exchanged glances but said nothing more. I paid my 5s. (25p), bade them farewell and set off for the town of Galway, taking lifts and buses to shorten the journey.

In Galway town I was invited to a poteen party. It all began with a pub conversation that resulted in five merry chaps in a battered car setting out for a distant farmhouse on a nightmare ride along country lanes and finally down a rutted farm track. The farmhouse was in darkness, but Patrick, our leader, knocked and a window opened above the door.

'Kathleen, it's Patrick. We've come for a drink.'

The window closed, a light appeared, and after a few mintues the door opened and we were let into a large living room. The daughter of the house, a dark, slender beauty with a delicate grace that one didn't expect to find on a rough farm, held an oil lamp which she placed on a table. 'I won't be a minit getting the goat's milk,' she said in a soft brogue.

'Why do you need goat's milk?' I asked.

'It has to be warm from the goat, and that settles the poteen,' she said. ''Tis like fire without it, 'tis all fresh from the still.'

Kathleen returned with the goat's milk and soon the poteen was flowing.

'How is your father?' Patrick asked.

'He's busy dying of the decline,' she said, using the vernacular term for tuberculosis, 'but if I give him a sup he might sing for us.'

We trooped upstairs to a large bedroom where an old man lay, gaunt and white. Kathleen raised him on the pillows and gave him poteen and milk to sip. It was like a sacrament. Gradually he returned to life. 'Will ye sing for us, father?' she requested.

We stood silent around the bed. Then softly, with infinite clarity, he commenced:

'Oft in the stilly night
Ere Slumber's chain has bound me,
Fond Memory brings the light
Of other days around me . . .'

One of Tom Moore's *National Airs*. His spirits seemed to soar with the song. When the others went down to continue with the poteen, I remained behind in the room. The old man smiled at me.

'What gave you the most pleasure in life?' I asked.

'Ah,' he whispered, 'to be behind two good harses with the swing plough. I ploughed the straightest furrow in the county.'

'Is there anything you want?' I asked.

'If ye could get me one of them rubber rings that blow up. My bones are cutting through my backside.'

I sent him the best rubber ring I could buy in Galway town.

The train returned me by way of dear dirty Dublin to dirty hard-working Belfast whose tall factory chimneys belched poison into the pure Irish air. I bought a Wolseley Hornet, a six-cylinder cabriolet. It had a bench seat in front which I asked the garage to hinge so it would lie flat to form a bed, then I asked my mother to be my first passenger and drive round Ireland with me. She was only too delighted. 'I have the very book for us,' she said. 'It's by a grand writer, H.V. Morton, and it's called *In Search of Ireland*. He made a necklace of the best bits.'

Our first stop was Dublin, where she used to take me as a child and we often spent Christmas at the Shelbourne Hotel and each day fed the ducks on St Steven's Green. We went to the Gate Theatre, run at that time by the illustrious duo of Hilton Edwards and Micheál Mac Liammóir, and saw a production of *The Playboy of the Western World.* We visited the Guinness Brewery, where we drank in the sampling room. We went to St Michan's Church, whose vaults contained the mummified remains of three Crusaders. My mother was reluctant to descend to view the grizzly corpses, but the verger shamed her into it by saying, 'Sure the little childer keep running down to play ther. A grown woman like you shouldn't be afeared.'

The leathery skins of the antique travellers were still supple and, as was the custom, we shook hands with one of them for luck. In Killarney we saw Mrs Bryce's Island, Ilnacullin, and at Castle Blarney we kissed the famous stone. So we continued until we reached home via the Glens of Antrim. My father had made the same trip in 1911, driving one of the first Wolseley cars. A photograph of him and his companions on the road hangs today in the Ulster Folk Museum.

I had been two months at home when Father took us all to Canada, whither he was invited by the Canadian Pacific Railway Company. We sailed on the *Duchess of Atholl*, known as the 'Drunken Duchess' from her constant roll, and stayed at the Château Fontenac in Quebec and the Royal York in Toronto. The latter had a telephone in every room – a great and novel luxury after the laborious message system of India. My parents and I held conversations with each other from the comfort of our respective beds. Our high point was a visit to Niagara Falls, where we walked under the mighty cascade and wondered how anyone could find the courage to go over the edge in a barrel. After the family returned home, I continued to New York. The Empire State Building, the tallest building in the world, was just opened, and I had formed an ambition to see the city from its summit.

Despite bread queues, soup kitchens and down-and-outs, the vitality of New York struck me as unbounded. The mixture of races must have represented every country in the world, and all had come there for the same reasons: freedom from oppression in their own countries; freedom for men and women to work as they wished; freedom to start a new life. This was how the world began, I thought: the survival of the fittest, using every device and enticement to get to the top. It also meant freedom for rackets. Prohibition was handing the Mafia a lucrative unofficial licence to do business.

I found a room in a small hotel and set out to explore. In Times Square a glittering electric sign proclaimed: A HUNDRED OF AMERICA'S MOST BEAUTIFUL HOSTESSES, TEN CENTS A DANCE. I crossed to the entrance and bought a dollar's worth of tickets from a sallow man in a shabby dinner jacket. Steep stairs led to a large dimly lit room, in the centre of which a tangle of dancers was swaying slowly in locked embrace. Round the walls hostesses sat on low divans in the red glow of heavily shaded lights. They wore alluring outfits – Cleopatras, señoritas, see-through baby-doll nighties, clothes of many nationalities. I chose a demure Virginian lady who said she was a colonel's daughter earning money for her university studies and was reading history. After dancing for ten minutes, she drew me into a dark alcove with a soft divan. Here we snuggled together until interrupted by a thick-set man in a dinner jacket who demanded tickets. I tore one from by bunch and gave it to him. 'Hey, what's the big idea?' he grated.

'I've been dancing with the lady,' I said, 'and this is in payment.'

It took some time for the situation to clarify. Briefly there were two bands, and though the music was continuous, it changed from one band to the other every minute. Sitting out was charged at the same rate. My bill amounted to two dollars. 'Go on, give him the money, honey. Ain't I worth it?' said Miss Virginia.

I handed him the tickets and a dollar. 'Why don't we meet outside and you can show me the town and keep the money for yourself?' I suggested to Miss Virginia.

'Fine,' she said. 'You wait outside.'

I went downstairs and waited in the square, admiring the brightest lights in the world. After half an hour I bought another dollar's worth of tickets and went back inside. The colonel's daughter was looking scared. As we danced she said her boss wouldn't let her leave, so after sixty seconds I swapped her for Cleopatra. Gradually I spent all my tickets and must have been the most unpopular man in the room. I bade the bouncer good night and rejoined the throng in the square, walking away through the swirling mixture of heteros and homos, drunks and drug addicts, rich and poor, old women and young girls, some timid, some aggressive, and everywhere a sense of excitement and danger. A bus stood on a corner, A TOUR OF CHINATOWN – ONE DOLLAR emblazoned on its side. 'Room for one more,' yelled the conductor.

I paid my dollar and got aboard. The bus was full. What a lucky break, I thought. Then to my astonishment two men got up and left. 'Last two seats,' the conductor bellowed, and so it went on as each new customer got on. The bus had been packed with decoys.

Eventually we set off. The bus being roofless, we had a good view of the elevated railway and the dilapidated houses along our route. Whenever we stopped at the lights or in traffic children on the sidewalk screamed, 'Rubbers!' meaning 'rubbernecks'. After twenty minutes we turned down a dimly lit side-street and disembarked. 'Keep together,' warned the conductor. 'This is a tough neighbourhood.'

We stayed in a huddle as we followed him through the stage door of a shabby theatre. From the stage we gazed down on the woebegone homeless of the great city sprawling in the stalls while our guide launched into a passionate talk on their plight and requested funds for the refuge. There was one old man who was in rags, but who had a fine face and a distinguished air, with snowy white hair and beautifully tended beard. I carried the image of him away with me as our guide led us next through a narrow passage into the courtyard of a Chinese temple. Here we reluctantly made contributions to temple funds under the pressing demands of a half-caste Sino-American priest. At the temple shrine we paid for lucky pieces of paper drawn from a tall vase by a pretty Chinese girl, but even as we were engaged in reading our fortunes our guardian conductor disappeared. We went out to get on the bus, but no bus stood there. We held together in our tight group, wondering what to do next as ragged children screaming 'Rubbers!' surrounded us. After about a quarter of an hour, to our great relief a bus drove up and charged us $2 each to take us back to Times Square. Such rackets proliferated.

Prohibition may have reigned, but the one thing not prohibited was hospitality, and no sooner did I call in on the Chartered Bank in Wall Street than I was invited to lunch. From then on it was a round of parties, meeting new people and being warmly invited to stay in their homes. I was also made a member of the bank's speakeasy, Jack and Charlie's, today the prestigious '21' Club. As I soon came to realize, my friends were paying for protection at every turn. Anything delivered – milk, newspapers, laundry – required protection. If a car needed a wheel changing, a breakdown van must be called, self-help not being tolerated. Parkers who declined to tip some vagrant watcher would return to find slashed tyres. The rackets were a spin-off from Prohibition, the bootleggers having the support of the drinkers and there being few Americans who did not drink. A hip-flask, the mark of maturity, was worn by all smart young men. There was illicit distilling, but much alcohol arrived from abroad in bogus drums of paint or mixtures that could easily be separated. Customers bought it by the gallon from bootleggers and made up their own drinks with flavours from the local drug store: Scotch, Bourbon, rye, brandy, cherry brandy, everything available and legal in non-alcoholic essences. All the consumer needed to do was dilute the alcohol with water and add the preferred essence; and sugar in the case of liqueurs.

Walking round the city I found myself being stopped by men with watches for sale. They would walk alongside you in a quiet street, thrust a watch into your hand, extol its value, explain how it was one over from a delivery and only half-price, until, as they edged you into a wall or doorway, their patter culminated in threats. Nights were certainly dangerous and I was always glad to reach the sanctuary of Jack and Charlie's. One evening I sat beside a tall fair girl who was with a rather tipsy man who seemed on the verge of passing out. I ordered an old-fashioned, but before I finished it the man slipped quietly into oblivion. 'Can I help?' I asked the girl.

'Thank you,' she said. 'It's OK.' She beckoned and two waiters helped him into a back room. 'Where do you come from?' she asked. 'I haven't seen you around before.'

I told her.

'What would you like to do in New York?' she asked.

'I'd most like to see the view from the top of the Empire State Building,' I said.

'Let's go. I've got my car outside.'

'What about your friend?' I asked.

'He'll be fine. It's happened before.'

The view from the top was staggering: a forest of sky-scrapers and twinkling lights that flashed and reflected in the river all the way down to Long Island. There was a stiff breeze, and couples watching the scene clung to each other. Beatrice, for that was her name, put an arm round me.

'What can we do next?' I asked.

'Let's go down to Blue Point,' she laughed above the wind.

Distance never being a problem in the United States, we arrived in Blue Point in time to see the sun rise out of the eastern sea. Then we had an enormous breakfast of coffee, waffles with maple syrup, and bacon and eggs with sliced peaches. When I said to the waitress, 'I wonder if I could have a tomato juice?' she looked at me in amazement and responded, 'Why not?'

'In America you don't wonder,' said Beatrice, 'you ask.'

I told her about the time when I said to a paper-boy that I wanted to go to East 67th Street and he shouted back at me, 'Why the hell don't-cha!'

Beatrice took me home and introduced me to her folks, who shook some of their own specials, not so lethal as certain others I had sampled since they were all made from the same alcohol. The friendliness of Americans far surpassed that of any other country I had been to, including Ireland. Maybe, I surmised, it descended from the early pioneers who had no choice but to cling together.

When the time came to leave America, I had to tear myself away. My new friends came down to the quay and we held a farewell party on the Cunard ship. America seemed to me to be a great big warm-hearted country, and one I would gladly return to. Whereas in Britain there was envy combined with a shockingly rigid caste system, America had little enviousness of riches, the attitude of every American being, 'If he can make it, so can I.' The voyage home passed uneventfully and soon I was back at No. 89, my furlough half-over.

Life at No. 89 proceeded at a slow and steady pace. I helped my mother with her gardening and ran her into Bangor on shopping expeditions. John the gardener, a thin, gaunt, hardy man who worked and drank with a will, showed up once a week, having wheeled his barrow and tools three miles from his cottage in the country. He was part of our close-knit family and got on particularly well with Father. They often joked about which of them would outlive the other.

I had long talks with Father, who remained secure in his philosophy that all was for the best: Dr Campbell knew about health, his bank manager and stockbroker about finance, the government about running the country. His modesty had led him to refuse a knighthood. It would only make living more expensive in his view, and besides, he said, look at the people who got them. For similar reasons he refused to run a Rolls-Royce. It would only invite people to charge him more. He turned down increases in salary, saying he was paid enough already.

In that era of masters and men in the printing industry, Father became famous for his 'Q' Betterment Scheme, which led to the formation of the Joint Industrial Councils composed of employers and employees and finally to the Whitley Councils. All of these aimed at bringing workers and management closer together in friendship and understanding, and settling practical costs for printing work to avoid price-cutting at the expense of wages. Father did, however, tend to see life in terms of black or white, right or wrong, with few grey areas, and to require a direct 'yes or no' to any query. Among the many stories told of him was one about a new apprentice to whom he said, 'What's your name boy, Yes or No?' Whenever one of the huge printing machines of the paper broke down, he would demand of the foreman, 'Can you fix it? Yes or no?' Alas, this rigidity of mind rebounded on him in later years. As he grew into his old age, he began to suffer from anxiety and had a slight nervous breakdown. Molehills became mountains and all his fun and laughter was transformed into worry. He could not stand arguments and would raise his hand to end them.

I got on well with my brother Jim, though I never cared for his subject of law. 'It's more fun than you think,' he told me, and dragged me along to one of his lectures. The subject was a lady who pulled a lavatory chain while sitting on the loo, whereat the cistern, having grown loose over the years, crashed down on her head and killed her. Who was to blame? The students all seemed to be having fun, and it made me wonder whether I ought to take a shot at a university degree to make up for my lack of education. I went to see the Dean of Pembroke College, who listened attentively to my life story. After tea and a very warm discussion he said, 'You should stay where you are. You will learn more in the outside world. Academic studies, after the experiences you have had, would not help you as much as your present situation. You should see more of the world. That will be your university.'

I thanked the dean for his advice and left, thinking he was right.

Since I had enjoyed following H.V.Morton's footsteps round Ireland, I decided to follow him round Scotland and England too. My Baird cousins were Bobby and his two sisters, Pat and Jean. They were the children of Major Baird, who looked after the smart horses and traps that delivered the *Belfast Telegraph*, and would eventually inherit the company since Sir Robert Baird had no children of his own. Bobby decided to come with me to Scotland, and we took the car over on the Larne-Stranraer ferry and drove through the Highlands to Ben Nevis, which he wanted to climb. When we were a short way up, it began to rain, and Bobby's heavy leather coat became saturated, but, always full of go and enthusiasm, he kept on leading the way. After the climb we ate an enormous dinner, starting with a Scots broth thick enough to stand a spoon in. That night we slept like logs. In the morning when I went into Bobby's room to call him, to my astonishment I found him lying under a quilt of grey ash. His final cigarette had set the coverlet smouldering, but fortunately the smoke had drifted away from him and out of the window, and miraculously the possibly damp blankets had not caught fire.

Scotland struck me as cold and hard. No wonder, I thought, the bank recruited most of its staff from among this sturdy, serious breed. John Reid's Aberdeen was a grey granite mass; Edinburgh claimed to be 'no mean city', but its slums were as bad as Dublin's. The clear seas and islands were magnificent, yet I found no temptation to linger. I dropped Bobby back at Stranraer and crossed the border into England.

England had a different flavour, its little villages bright with flowers, each village green marked by a friendly pub. The people were polite and kind, interested in preserving their own independence and yours along with it. There were no quick friendships or instant hospitality as in the United States, and no matter how full the bar, each customer remained a little England, making his own judgements and decisions. A formidable race, it seemed to me: cool, logical and sentimental, hard to sway and easily underestimated.

I drove south, heading for the West Country and the house in which my old manager Lang had so looked forward to spending his retirement. I felt I ought to offer to tell his people about his death in Lahore, but arrived at what turned out to be an old farmhouse, the garden banked with roses and no one at all about. I inquired at the local pub. The great wooden boxes that I dispatched from Amritsar had been the talk of the village, but they arrived too late for his parents, for his father and mother died a few months after hearing of their son's death. Relatives had come to take the boxes away. I wondered whether the girl on the dance programme had ever heard what happened. I thought of Kim and wondered if we should ever meet again. We had agreed we would not write. She had insisted we must both have time to think, time to be free.

Visiting head office again, I had news of my next appointment: Colombo in Ceylon, one of the most sought-after postings on a lovely tropical island surrounded by warm seas and coral strands. My heart warmed with joy at the fact I would be close to India. The ship, the P&O SS *Rapurna*, was due to sail on 9 February from Marseilles, and instructions were sent to Amritsar for all my boxes to be forwarded to Colombo. I passed a happy Christmas and New Year with my family, and then, in January, heard from 'Uncle' and 'Auntie' MacCulloch, a hospitable couple who had been my burra sahib and his wife on the occasion of John Reid's first furlough. The invitation, promptly accepted, was to join a fortnight's skiing party in Switzerland with seven or so others in a small family hotel in Lenzerheide. Elsi, the daughter of the hotelier, was great fun and kept us all in high spirits. After a few days on the nursery slopes under Elsi's tuition, we took packed lunches and, strapping seal-skins under our skis, climbed to the top of the local mountain through deep virgin snow. After lunch we climbed higher, then took off the skins and made a slow descent with frequent falls. Only the toe of the boot was anchored to the long wooden ski, and turning was achieved by advancing one foot as far as possible in front of the other and following it round in a telemark. The pines and sparkling air had me thinking wistfully of the Himalayas.

The last two weeks of my furlough I spent at home. My parents had been delighted to hear of my posting to Ceylon, which they thought sounded far more civilized than Amritsar. I suggested they might come out and have a holiday with me to split the long five-year absence, and Father, who was a great traveller, said they would certainly consider it.

Five years! Father would be seventy-three, Mother sixty-eight. Maybe I would never see them again. The thought must have been in their minds too, but they concealed it as we talked about the wonderful experience it would be for me to see this exotic country, famous for its tea and well known to my Uncle Robert, who worked at one time with the Mazawattie Tea Company. They were all great tea drinkers, and I promised they would be sent supplies of the best leaf the island could produce. I wondered one last time what I could possibly do that would make me happy to live at home, but still could think of nothing. To live and work in Belfast would, I knew, have me reduced in no time to feeling trapped. Our farewells were brave. We waved goodbye at the Heysham boat, knowing now what five years implied, and that this time it could be for ever.

11

Isle of Spicy Breezes

'No time for breakfast,' said Robert Johnson, a stern Scot I had met previously at head office, sent now to greet me on the SS *Rapurna* at the end of its uneventful voyage. 'The clerk will see to your baggage and car. We must get back quickly. There's a lot of work on and the chap you're relieving sails this afternoon!'

The bank, a new building of red sandstone with a colonnade of pillars surmounted by large pink elephant heads, stood in a commanding position opposite the Colombo Clocktower. I was swiftly introduced to Wemyss, the manager, Buckley, his No. 2, and Mildren, the accountant, who mopped his brow with an eau-de-Cologne-cooled handkerchief. Fans stirred the drenched air above the marble floor. I was aware of spreading damp patches on my smart white suit. Being in Ceylon seemed very like visiting the Tropical House at Kew Gardens.

My area of responsibility turned out to be current accounts, of which there were about 5,000 in thirty-two huge ledgers. The signature on every cheque had to be verified and initialled as it was cancelled in red ink. Obviously it was impossible for me to know so many signatures, and therefore the clerks were my first line of defence. The cashiers too would report anyone they thought suspicious. I made the decision to check only items over 200 rupees, working on the calculation that no forger would operate for less and that I could make up any lesser loss myself. There were, in fact, two forgeries during my first week – trying it out on the new man. Both times I was able to keep the perpetrator engaged until the police arrived.

The bank arranged for me to stay at the Galle Face Hotel until I could find a billet for myself. The hotel was a large red building at the end of the Galle Face Green, a long stretch of grass that ran for about a mile beside the sea. There was a constant breeze, and in the evening people strolled, waiting for the sun to sink with a final flash of green below the rim of the Indian Ocean. I had a large room overlooking the sea, and was regularly lulled to sleep by the roar of the long swell as it broke unceasingly on the reefs surrounding the island. Jackdaws and crows regarded the hotel as their home and brazenly hopped or flew through the open windows, helping themselves to food or any glittering object that took their fancy.

By contrast with Amritsar, Colombo struck me as stiff and formal. The naval base at Trincomalee reinforced government and social protocol with a preference for the image of London's high society over the freedom of a tropical paradise. The missionaries had long since put a stop to any exposure of breasts among the Sinhalese, and women's sarongs were topped with white bodices. The Colombo brothels had been closed despite the frustration this induced among the large number of sailors using the port, a final lever in the campaign having been the discovery by the Ladies' Vigilante Committee of the Governor's green Raleigh bicycle outside one of the pleasure houses. When I arrived Ceylon was known as 'the island of the four Ss': sunshine, sodomy and sexual starvation. As Reginald Heber, the Anglican Bishop of Calcutta, wrote after losing his luggage in Colombo:

> What though the spicy breezes
> Blow soft o'er Ceylon's isle;
> Though every prospect pleases,
> And only man is vile.

Many 'old Ceylon' British families had been there for generations and formed a county class. They certainly had no wish to be importuned by birds of passage. The usual card dropping was augmented by the signing of visitors' books and the making of calls on Government House, the bishop and the heads of the armed services. The card disclosed its owner's position, firm or rank, and thus enabled island society to embrace or reject at will. Multiple caste levels existed among the Europeans, but for every stratum the colour bar was absolute. One English professor was reprimanded for walking

with a Sinhalese student on the Galle Face Green. The colour bar
also applied to the Burghers, the descendants of the Portuguese who
arrived in 1505 and of the Dutch who dispossessed them in 1658.
Their interbreeding with Sinhalese and Tamils had produced beautiful, intelligent people, but, as in India, they were outcasts.

As a member of the bank I was expected to show social muscle, but
I felt lonely and unhappy and spent my evenings walking along the
Galle Face Green and the beautiful palm-fringed sandy beaches,
listening to the comforting sound of my beloved sea. Then, soon after
my arrival, I had a call from the police. They had caught a man
smuggling opium into Ceylon who claimed to know me. I asked his
name. 'Allah Dad Khan,' they said. I hurried round to the police
station and there, indeed, found poor Allah Dad. When I explained
that he was my bearer and was allowed opium pills for pain, they
agreed to release him if I accepted total responsibility for his conduct
and recognized that he would need to find a substitute for opium in
Ceylon. To this I readily agreed, signed a paper and, to their
astonishment, embraced the vagrant. I placed his scanty luggage in
the car and we set off for the hotel.

'Allah Dad,' I asked, 'how on earth did you get here?'

'Hazur, we heard you were to go to Ceylon. Word came for your
boxes to be sent, so I came.'

'But your wife and children, your job!'

'Hazur, I asked for leave so I could see that hazur was not wanting
for anything, and then, when hazur is settled, I can return or stay as
hazur wishes.'

He had travelled more than 2,000 miles down the length of India
before boarding the ferry to Jaffna, where he had been caught. He
then managed to get himself transferred to Colombo and eventually
persuaded the authorities to contact me. Fortunately the Galle Face
Hotel had quarters for 'boys' and there was no difficulty in finding
him a place. The next morning I was woken by a familiar soft voice
saying, 'Half-past six gone,' and found my tea at my bedside. For an
instant I thought I was back in Amritsar until the roar of the surf and
the chattering crows shattered the illusion. 'How are you getting on?'
I asked Allah Dad.

'These are strange people, hazur,' he said. 'There are Hindu
Tamils and Sinhalese Buddhists, and Muslims who are called Moors
and also some Afghan money-lenders.'

'Do they upset you?'

'No, hazur, they could not upset a Pathan.'

'We will see how things work out. Meantime have a little holiday.
The hotel people are looking after my needs, but I hope to move into

a chummery soon and then it will be like the old days.'

The people, the climate, the way of life could not have been more different from life in the Punjab, and it became daily more evident that Allah Dad was homesick. At the end of a month I put it to him that he had seen me safely settled. I was well cared for in the luxurious hotel and soon would have the opportunity of joining friends in a chummery. It was clear that he was relieved. I gave him his fares both ways and three months' salary, and once more we parted with great sadness. I was later overjoyed when a letter from him arrived confirming that his job had been kept open for him.

Allah Dad's departure left me feeling more lonely than ever in this palm-filled paradise. I though of Kim a great deal and wondered whether she could fit into Ceylon's colonial scene. Again I cursed myself for ever leaving the Punjab and the Himalayas. There was more substance to life in the vast solitude of the mountains with someone who loved and understood the country than could ever exist in Colombo's artificial social round. Kashmir had been my Garden of Eden. I should have stayed. It was as if an innocence then part of me had silently slipped away.

Kim and I now wrote constantly, and I would take her letters up to read on an empty terrace on the top floor of the bank overlooking the busy city. Before long a new note became apparent in the writing. She was getting on and a nice chap wanted to marry her. Her friends advised her to accept. I sent her the return fare to Colombo so we could talk it over. My cheque reached her the day after her wedding to an English businessman I had never met. Doubtless she realized that I was not mature enough for such a tie. I felt a vast hurt but also, I had to admit, a glimmer of relief. My fear of losing my freedom was still very great, and now, for better or worse, I really was alone. I went down to the shore and watched the sun sink till it vanished in its bright-green flash.

I had picked up a little Sinhalese and could talk to people I met on my walks: old men mending nets, younger men fishing with long lines or hand-flung nets in the shallows, children playing on the sand or splashing about in the surf. The young men were graceful with slender hips, broad shoulders, large eyes, gleaming teeth, and long black hair shining with coconut oil. The girls were equally graceful, with nubile figures and well-formed breasts. An extraordinary feature of their lives was that the boys and girls seemed totally unaware of one another. The boys walked about in couples, holding hands, while the girls busied themselves with household chores, carrying water pots on their attractive heads, their waist-long hair hanging in shining tresses. They swept floors, fetched firewood, cooked, and hung out washing as if the boys did not exist.

There was little privacy. I could only suppose they were all waiting for the cover of night. I wondered if there were some taboo, or whether it was because of the religious element that was so strong in the island, what with the Roman Catholics and the Buddhists. As for the sex-starved Europeans, they lived, as in India, in a goldfish bowl of exposure. Chattering servants and inquisitive watchmen regaled each other and their employers with the latest indiscretions. Life seemed easiest for homosexuals. The local boys could move about freely without attracting attention. Nor did sexual starvation apply to young European tea-planters in the cool hills. They could always find relief and comfort among the girls in their labour force, the custom being to maintain your courtesan in a discreet but recognized liaison. Should the planter in due course make a suitable marriage, the girl was usually willing to accept compensation and leave with any children that might have followed from the union. I never heard of any breath of scandal from that source.

The fact that Ceylon's Europeans were sports mad could partly, I imagined, be put down to sexual starvation. At the Garden Club, the hub of activities for the European community, there were tennis courts and squash courts. There was a cricket club, a golf club and a sailing club. The Colombo Hockey and Football Club supported soccer, rugby, hockey and a great sports week that was almost a junior Olympics, with shot, javelin and discus events, high and long jump, sprints and hurdles, a half-mile race and a gymnastic display. Oddly enough, except for a tiny sea-water pool at the Galle Face Hotel, there were no swimming pools, for swimming was not as popular then as it became in post-war years.

Eventually I achieved my ambition of setting up a new chummery and having a home of my own again. Derek Spearman, who worked for Steel Brothers, came in with me, and we rented Storm Lodge, a splendid house on the sea front. Derek was a charming, thoughtful man whom I had met several times at the club, and we asked Pat Wayman and Willoughby Park, who also worked in Colombo, to join us. Storm Lodge, sited magnificently about half a mile south of the Galle Face Hotel and within easy reach of the Garden Club, was well named. Its rear lawn ran down to a sea that crashed and thundered on the reef. In stormy weather, spume swept at the long low building and turned all the brass fittings green. The front lawn was surrounded with flowers, frangipani, cana lillies, oleander and a multitude of other tropical plants. Two brass cannon guarded the massive porch.

Inside, a lofty lounge ran to the left, and on the right was a great mahogany-panelled dining room. Both rooms were well furnished with expensive carpets and heavy mahogany chairs and tables. Upstairs were four huge bedrooms, mine being on the extreme right and facing the sea.

At the hotel I had found a new boy called Ram, an Afro-haired Tamil, young, inquisitive, intelligent and eager to learn. Within a few weeks he was driving my car round from the garage, paying no heed to my protests that he had no licence. 'It is my job to look after master,' he said, 'and I am not driving on the road so no one can catch.'

In no time he knew all my engagements and could tell me who was going to be at any party I was invited to. Furthermore he would warn me of any traps that might be laid by mamas with daughters of marriageable age. I must remain a bachelor, he insisted. His last master married and the new mistress had no time for poor Ram. He was a rebel who cut the pooh-bah social scene down to sensible proportions, and as a result we got along together very well. Ram was ever enterprising and every day worked hard on some new project to surprise me and gain points.

Shortly after settling into my new luxurious home, I received a call from the secretary of the local Toc H. Would I join the branch and do something for them in Colombo? I agreed and ran a gym class for the Deaf and Blind Institute near Mount Lavinia. There were eighty very keen boys. I obtained a springboard and an athletics horse, and soon the deaf boys were jumping over the horse while I caught them as they landed. Eventually some of the blind boys grew envious and asked if they might jump too. At first I was reluctant to expose them to the risk, but soon found that, guided by my voice, they became as expert as their sighted friends.

I played squash and tennis at the Garden Club with Maurice Murdoch, brother of the famous comedian 'Stinker' Murdoch of *Much Binding in the Marsh* fame. I also found myself playing left-wing three-quarter for the rugby team. Since Harry Greer, a distant cousin whose father had been ADC to the previous Governor and ran a tea estate at Kerimetia, played inside me and gave me many excellent unselfish passes, I scored a lot of tries. The *Times of Ceylon* used a picture of me in the act of performing a vigorous hand-off to head their weekly rugby column. Another photograph in the *Times of Ceylon* showed me shaking hands with the Governor before the Low Country *versus* Up Country match. It all went to enhance my social acceptability.

Trade, it was interesting to note, was socially acceptable in Ceylon, for the prosperity of the island depended on the economic production of tea, rubber, copra and, to a lesser extent, plumbago and semi-precious stones. Brokers were not looked down on in the way that the box-wallahs were in India, but went about in snow-white tunics, taking open cars or rickshaws to pursue deals of magnitude. Their work was similar to that of their counterparts in London, and I detected that they liked to equate Colombo with the City. After a hard-working day they would join in a few rounds of drinks at the club and stay on until it was time for dinner or a party. The fact that they lived in an entrancing tropical paradise never apparently occurred to them. The natives were taboo and there were enough Europeans to go round. To add to their interest, numerous ships brought friends for holidays as well as a sprinkling of visiting celebrities.

I began to suspect that the true key to the island lay with the Burghers. They knew where to find the best things, they spoke the language, they were thoroughly integrated with island life. They were able and intelligent and held top positions in medicine and law. Many of their young women were extremely beautiful and would have sent hearts racing anywhere in Europe, but in their own country they were sadly, like their Eurasian equivalents in India, ostracized by the whites.

My life in Colombo took on a rhythm. Breakfast at seven with fresh pineapple, coffee, bacon and eggs, toast and marmalade. Car to the bank, lunch at the Grand Oriental Hotel (known as the 'GOH'), end work about five, and so to the Garden Club for tennis or squash. Or, in the rainy season, to the Colombo Hockey and Football Club for the Saturday match, or to the Royal Colombo Yacht Club for races round the harbour in their fourteen-foot Dublin Bay wags. After sport a shower, drinks in the bar or with the ladies on the Garden Club lawn, then a cocktail or dinner party or simply back to Storm Lodge for a quiet meal.

Giving parties was a way of life for the Colombo ladies. Hostesses constantly tried to dream up new ideas for enlivening their hospitality. One invitation requested guests to bring a non-human living creature with them. I and Tony Humphreys, another Colombo merchant, decided to take from the beach a couple of small crabs safely confined in jam jars, but as we passed the Governor's Residence I spotted his pet pelicans wandering about on the well-kept lawn. Ambition fired, I stopped the car and, in the semi-darkness, scaled the low ornamental wall and captured the nearest bird. It seemed drowsy and offered no resistance, but as I was making my way back I was surprised by the guard. I explained that the bird was required for an important function and would be returned before morning. The guard saluted and helped me back over the wall with my sleepy prize. The white bird, with its enormous beak, set off my evening dress to perfection. The reception was held in a magnificent apartment in Galle Face Court. It was reached by a lift – an unusual feature in Colombo buildings – and in the lift the pelican seemed enormous, though fortunately it remained quietly in my arms, as if sitting on its favourite perch. We were conducted into the large reception room, in the middle of which stretched a magnificent blue Persian carpet of the royal peacock design. I walked to its elegent centre to show off my trophy to best advantage. The pelican took a dignified look at the well-dressed throng, then, with an almost imperceptible hiccup, spilled a horrible mixture of half-digested rotten fish and slime on to the exquisite centrepiece. During the awful silence that followed I rushed out headlong, holding the bird's beak down on my best jacket to try to prevent any recurrence. The bird, by now thoroughly upset, continued to vomit despite my efforts to clamp its beak shut. Tony, crouched against the door, was deluged, but manfully he drove me back to return the pelican to its rightful home. The guard, joined this time by his sergeant, helped me to lift the bird with its voided stomach across the wall. They both saluted and the sergeant said in the curiously penetrating accent of the Sinhalese, 'I hope pelican being helpful to your function?'

'I don't know what I would have done without it,' I said. 'Thank you very much.'

I had been working late after the close of business one pay day when Pereira, my junior ledger clerk, approached me and asked, 'May I speak to you privately, sir?'

'Why, of course,' I replied.

Apart from ourselves the office was empty.

'I am going to kill myself,' he announced.

Pereira, a pale slight young man of about nineteen, was a Burgher and one of my best clerks. He it was who had indicated the forgeries to me during my first week. 'Why do you want to kill yourself?' I asked.

'I am hopelessly in debt, sir,' he said, 'and the Afghan money-lenders are in wait for me outside. If I do not pay them something they will beat me, and I have no money to pay.'

He looked down in tears, and it was indeed a most serious admission. The rigid rule of employment in the bank's service required the instant dismissal of any clerk found to be in debt. 'Are there other clerks in your position?' I asked.

'Yes, sir, at least three. I know because I have seen them pay the Afghans.'

I had a shrewd idea that this was a conservative estimate, and so I said, 'I will come with you now and speak to the Afghans. Tomorrow I will talk to the manager and see what can be done.'

'Oh, please don't do that, sir,' he wailed. 'I shall surely be dismissed.'

'I think we can avoid it. In any case, it is not a matter that should lead you to contemplate suicide. If everyone who was in debt killed themselves, there would be no customers left in the world, never mind the bank.'

Pereira promptly cheered up and we went out together through the massive porch. Outside on the pavement two burly Afghans stood leaning on stout sticks. They wore the traditional baggy white trousers, loose white shirts, embroidered waistcoats and neatly wound turbans. They looked surprised to see a European walking with a Sinhalese. Speaking in Urdu I asked, 'To which of you does Mr Pereira owe money?'

One of the men stood forward. 'It is to me, sahib,' he said.

'How much does he owe?'

'First there is the sum that I lent, 150 rupees, and then there is the interest, 45 rupees.'

'Are you not a Muslim?' I asked.

'Yes, sahib.'

'And does not the law of Islam prohibit usury?'

'That is so, sahib, but this is not a Muslim country and we abide by the laws of this country.'

'Come to the bank on this day week and I will see that you are paid the correct amount of your loan. In the meantime if I hear any word of you molesting our staff I will place the matter in the hands of the police.'

He looked at me curiously and salaamed. I saw Pereira safely on his way and told him not to worry.

On Monday I had a word with the chief cashier, and told him that anything he said would be treated in strictest confidence. He confirmed Pereira's account, and also told me that the Afghans charged an illicit 18 per cent, getting round the legal limit of 6 per cent by making the borrower sign a promissory note for three times the amount of the loan. 'If I can persuade the manager to agree,' I suggested, 'would it be possible to call in all these promissory notes and buy them at the proper rate from a fund to be paid off by deductions from the salaries of the clerks involved?'

'If you can succeed in this, sir, it would be a godsend for us.'

The manager was reluctant to grant a condition of confidence until I pointed out that a situation had been going on unnoticed by the foreign staff and was one that implicated all of us. It was also a situation which could fortunately be corrected, whereas the matter would, if it proved widespread, reflect badly on our management position. It was arranged that all outstanding promissory notes must be presented that Friday, vetted by the chief cashier and the money-lenders paid off to the amounts of the original loans. The Afghans were naturally thoroughly put out by this turn of events and their spokesman protested, 'Sahib, you are destroying our business. We serve a useful purpose and have traded like this many years.'

'You know very well it is a rule of the bank that no clerk may borrow,' I said, 'and you have used this knowledge to blackmail these people into submission. You have also got them to sign promissory notes for money you did not lend. This too is against the law. If you do not accept this arrangement today, I will institute proceedings which will lead to deportation to your own country where your excesses will certainly be rewarded with prison if not execution.'

I had no idea if deportation was a practical possibility, but so far as the bank was concerned, the debts were settled.

The most frustrating work for me continued to be coding and decoding telegrams. It had been bad enough in Amritsar, but in Colombo the unceasing flow of cables often grew to a torrent. We worked a six-day week and sometimes Sundays, yet there were certain sub-accountants who seemed to have a knack of keeping their desks piled high with papers which miraculously vanished at the end of the day and left them free to make a fast getaway for the club. Since there was a fair amount of movement of bank personnel between responsibilities, I tried to keep my desk clear, and even indulged in reading the *Times of Ceylon* to give the impression that my work load was light in the hope someone might covet it, especially the telegrams.

The moment I did have any free time, I would try to distance myself from the bank and Colombo.

Bentota was a small fishing village on a river of the same name, thirty-seven miles south of Colombo. Its rest-house sat on a low rise overlooking the sea. There was a large fresh-water lagoon divided from the sea by a spit of sand, and an immense sand beach fringed by palms. The river contained, where it reached the sea, beds of small delicious oysters. They were not part of the local diet, but we persuaded an ancient pearl diver to gather them for us. His only equipment was a bamboo nose clip and bamboo goggles, a cross-section fitted with glass cemented in place with gum. Soon these weekends became treasured breaks and three friends often joined me: Tony Humphreys, David Ewen and Surgeon Commander. Tommy Hunt of the Royal Navy, commonly known as 'Tunt'.

At daybreak in Bentota a light breeze would rustle the palms and send a flow of cool air through the rest-house. Slowly the grey tones of the landscape took on colour as the sun rose above the lagoon, the air cool and clear and the sea and sky a pale loveliness of greens and blues. Already fishermen with their nets waded in the shallows, dark silhouettes against the surf. Gradually the chill departed, the villagers and their dogs awoke, girls, grave and graceful, walked down to the fresh-water lagoon to bathe and fill their waterpots. As the sun moved up the sky, the colours intensified, the sand became a white glare, the sky deep blue and the sea a translucent green ridged with foaming breakers.

The sea was the great attraction. Surf riding had not yet reached Ceylon and we experimented with surf boards of various sizes. After breakfast we would walk down to the beach with our boards and wade through the shallows to the long slow swell that reared itself up before curling forward to break with thunderous power. With practice we learnt to launch ourselves on top of a wave before it broke, then to toboggan down the steep slope with great licks of foaming water curling round us till its spent force deposited us on the hot sand.

Time passed quickly. Morning merged into midday and *mahouts* led their elephants down to the lagoon, where they sank into the cool water, blowing great sprays of water over themselves and trumpeting with pleasure. The *mahouts*, who stayed with their elephants for their lifetime, scrubbed them carefully, cleaning eyes and ears and making sure their huge charges were comfortable. Soon we followed the elephants' example and returned to the rest-house to sluice ourselves down before lunch. After a siesta on the veranda we returned to the surf.

At other times it was not so peaceful. Occasionally there were storms and giant waves created dangerous undertows. Hurled to the bottom we were ground there in a revolving torrent of sand and small stones that seemed never-ending. All you could do was hold your breath and hope you would surface quickly. Other hazards were jellyfish, and dainty Portuguese men-of-war trailing twenty-foot threads of sapphire flame, every inch armed with vicious stings. The slightest touch raised livid white and excruciatingly painful weals. Fortunately a poultice made from a local plant provided relief.

In the evenings, after washing off the salt with dippers of cool fresh water from Shanghai jars, we sat on the veranda and sipped long whisky and sodas while the rest-house cook prepared the evening

The old Moghul bridge, Dal Lake, Kashmir

Cottage of Maggie Dirane, star of Robert
Flaherty's *Man of Aran*, on the island of Inishmore

Maggie Dirane in her cottage

1936. The Chartered Bank, Bangkok; we slept above the banking hall. Tom Hobbs, myself and Leslie Thom of Steel Brothers *(left to right)* in the front garden which is now the site of the swimming pool of the famous Oriental Hotel where Somerset Maugham wrote one of his novels

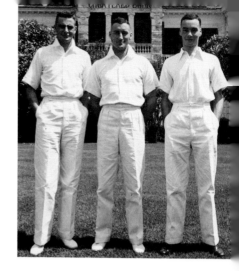

1933. J.C. MacPherson, a Chartered Bank colleague, and I climb the great rock fortress of Sigiriya, Ceylon

Outrigger sailing canoes in Negombo harbour. These fast and flexible craft are stitched together with coconut fibre and sail out of sight of land in search of good fishing grounds

View from the Chartered Bank of the busy Chao Phya River

The converted junk *Stormalong* which I sailed in the Gulf of Siam

Sunrise at Angkor Wat, Cambodia

alvoes fired by the Japanese flagship *Itzumo* explode beyond the International Settlement, Shanghai

Shanghai. Looters and other offenders are summarily executed

1943. I direct *Nineteen-Metre Band*, a film about the BBC service to India. Sir William Beveridge, Wickham Steed and Kingsley Martin *(left to right)*

My first commercial production was for Lucky Strike. The team in Merton Park Studios: *(left to right)* myself, Geraldo, in front of his orchestra, and Ray Elton, director *(centre)*.

Paul Nash sketching at the Cowley Dump where he painted his famous picture *Totes Mere* showing a dead sea of enemy aircraft washed up on our shores

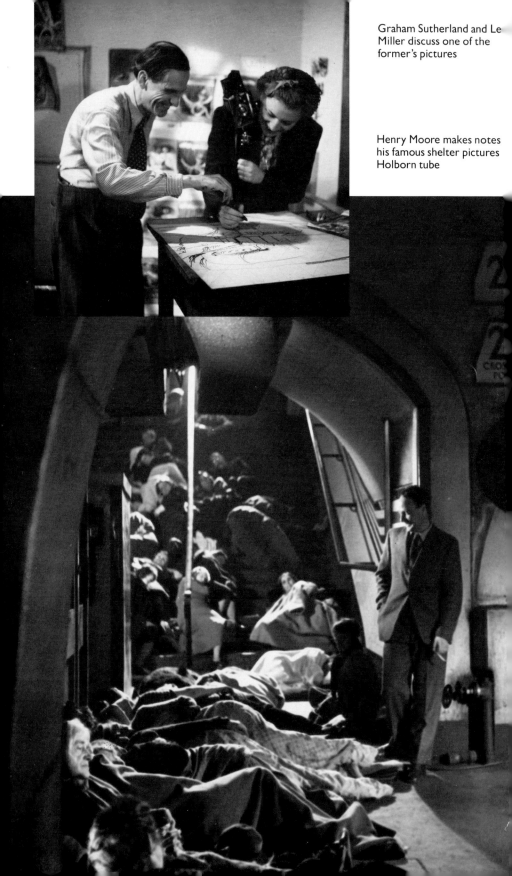

Graham Sutherland and Le
Miller discuss one of the
former's pictures

Henry Moore makes notes
his famous shelter pictures
Holborn tube

meal. The Sinhalese are excellent cooks. The first dish to arrive would be great platters of the tiny oysters flanked with fresh limes cut in two. Following these came a magnificent seer fish cooked in coconut milk and surrounded with mounds of pink prawns. Then there was curried chicken with brown ceylon rice and a host of small dishes of mango chutney, lime pickle, grated coconut, green peppers, sliced onions and tomatoes. Chilled beer was our drink. For desert we had mangoes, mangosteens, lichees and the delicious but evil-smelling durian. Finally it was back to the veranda for coffee, liqueurs, cigars and talk. The extraordinary thing was that this Gauguinesque paradise, so close to Colombo, was always deserted apart from ourselves. Our freedom invariably ended too soon, and on Sundays we reluctantly drove slowly back to civilization through the scented night.

A frequent and welcome visitor to Storm Lodge was Vivian Berkbeck, JP and unofficial magistrate, who lived at Moneragalla, the 'Place of the Rocks'. He was an authority on elephants and responsible for the huge game sanctuary where Ceylon's wild elephants roamed freely. Whenever an elephant went *must* – that is to say, into a kind of mad state of frenzy – it was Vivian's task to dispatch it. He also had to protect the villagers and their crops from the ravages of rogue elephants. All the heavy work in Ceylon was done by elephants, and from time to time wild elephants would be herded by armies of beaters into stout stockades in the jungle. Each wild elephant was then tied to a tree with the help of the tame elephants, and after a period of discipline, comforted and protected by their life-long *mahouts*, they became reconciled to their new circumstances. Whenever visiting admirals, generals and other important personages expressed the wish to bag an elephant, Vivian would be approached by the Governor to make the necessary arrangements. This, of course, was only possible if there was one needing to be dispatched. If these 'sportsmen' failed to kill their huge target, Vivian was on hand to see that death was as pain-free as possible.

As soon as I had the chance, I accepted Vivian's warm invitation to pay him a visit and set off on the five stages of the journey to Moneragalla. First there were main roads, then minor roads and next a dirt track that petered out at a place where Vivian's *syce* awaited the visitor with a pony. Half a mile on horseback led to the base of a rocky outcrop, up which one scrambled on foot. Vivian's bungalow perched on a small flat area on top of the rock. Around its tiny lawn, elephants' skulls served as flower pots for exotic orchids. In the bungalow their huge empty feet were receptacles for walking sticks, umbrellas and other flower containers. Golf clubs rested in a golf bag made from an elephant's penis.

The lounge was comfortably furnished with wide armchairs and elegant cabinets of china that vied for attention with rare animal heads staring from the walls. My bedroom had a fine view over the green jungle. In the outposts of Ceylon, as in those of India, dressing for dinner kept up morale, and so I changed into my white linen mess jacket that had at the outset scandalized Colombo's hostesses, accustomed as they were to gentlemen wearing formal black dinner suits of wool. (I was given to pointing out that my white mess jacket was washed after every use whereas the homeside jackets, heavy with sweat, became steadily less hygenic with each occasion.) Suitably clothed, I joined Vivian on the veranda for sundowners served in cut-glass tumblers by boys in white starched uniforms.

Vivian was an excellent host, and we could as well have been in the Dorchester admiring Hyde Park as a tropical wilderness miles from civilization. The long dining table shone with polish, reflecting Nell Gwynn candles and carefully written menus. The seven-course dinner was served with appropriate wines, the only Oriental intrusion being a crystal vase holding long green capsicums, which Vivian munched with relish, as if they were celery. I put a tooth into one and my mouth was scorched. Above us an elephant's head, complete with tusks, silently witnessed the meal. Skins of lesser animals covered the floor, and in the corner a four-foot elephant phallus supported a lamp in its pink meatus. I remarked on its originality, which pleased my host.

Vivian was lord of all he surveyed, a contented bachelor in nature's kingdom. Near by the Veddas, Ceylon's aborigines, lived nomadic lives, eating wild honey and killing small game with bows and arrows. Here too were found the tiny loris monkeys with their large bright eyes, their tears supposedly a cure for gonorrhoea. These unfortunate creatures would be held close to smoking fires and their tears collected in small bottles for sale in the bazaars. An even more pitiless industry was tortoiseshell, to gain which the wretched tortoise was held over a low fire until the heat blistered the flesh from the carapace. High-caste Sinhalese men were given to doing their hair up in buns and, like Spanish señoritas, wearing tortoiseshell combs stuck in the top, thus proclaiming their importance and the fact that they did not carry burdens on their heads.

When I asked Vivian what his views were on the colour bar, he said he saw it as unfortunate, but, he added, there were relatively so few Europeans: 'Only 9,000 in a population of around six million made up of seventy different races. If we intermarried we would find ourselves trapped into family intrigues and subjected to all sorts of pressures.'

Ceylon had three and a half million Buddhists, Buddhism having been brought to the island in 270 BC by Mahendra, reputedly the son of Ashoka. This made the Buddhists the majority, but their peaceful faith did not seem to stop them murdering each other over trivial quarrels and the local murder rate was abnormally high. Then there were the Tamils, imported from south India to work on the tea estates. They spoke Tamil, were adherents of Hinduism and were considered by the Buddhists to be inferior. The Buddhists and the million and a half Tamils were continually at each other's throats, only uniting in their hatred of the half-million Muslims.

'And don't forget the Burghers,' Vivian continued, 'about 32,000 of them. They keep themselves very much to themselves and were, of course, rulers here for about 140 years, as the Portuguese were before them. Oddly enough, we've been here the same length of time. Naturally we'll be giving the island independence in due course, but meanwhile it makes my life a lot easier if there's some distance between me and the people I administer.'

'Seems jolly arrogant to me,' I said, 'to come and conquer people and then make them second-class citizens and complain about the "white man's burden". After all, China, Siam and Japan manage very well.'

Vivian grinned. 'There are lots of planters who have native girls, but if I lived with one here I'd be kicked out. The government magic would fail. We're accepted because we're supposedly incorruptible.'

'So what *will* happen when the British leave?' I asked. 'We've failed to train the local people to take over. Whatever the pressures, we'll leave them trying to cope with a situation for which they've not been prepared. Intermarriage and treating them as equals would at least be a start.'

Our stimulating discussion continued into the early hours and I was sorry to leave next day for Colombo, though Storm Lodge had by now developed a reputation as a popular chummery. Its four members knew between them many people on the island, not to mention visiting voyagers on the P&O and Bibby lines, both of which called at Colombo. One evening ten guests arrived unexpectedly from a passing P&O boat, including among them a young lady called Heather Lyon and her charming mother. I summoned the cook. 'Sir,' he exclaimed, 'there is no meat in the house. What to do?'

'What about the turkeys?' I asked.

A couple had been given to us at Christmas, but they looked so attractive in the garden that we had not the heart to eat them and christened them Hector and Lysander.

'Sir, gardener going home and we Buddhists cannot kill.'

I called Ram, who promptly said he could not think of killing the birds. He was a vegetarian and terrified of blood.

'Put Hector on the front lawn and Lysander in the back garden and fetch me my sabre,' I commanded.

I had never used this handsome weapon for anything other than drill and tent-pegging, but I reckoned that, if it could kill a man, it should be effective with a turkey. The birds were accustomed to us and I had no difficulty in getting into a good position with Hector. A quick swipe lifted his head twenty feet away. Lysander, possibly having caught some faint warning signal from his departing friend, was more difficult to corner, and finally I had to persuade the cook to hold the head and Ram the body while I made a swift down-stroke, whereupon Ram fainted.

Dinner started an hour late but was declared a great success. Heather, a large and beautiful girl who was full of confidence, eventually founded the Heather Jenner Marriage Bureau and was responsible for thousands of happy wedlocks. She may therefore be seen as a worthy beneficiary of the sacrifice of Hector and Lysander.

The following week a visiting naval commander and his pretty wife came to stay for a few days. He was a traditional officer with a high sense of service and honour. On the last night of their visit I awoke at three in the morning with a feeling that something odd was happening. I sat up and watched my bedroom door gradually open. In the half-light a form in white slowly advanced across the room, and as it came nearer I saw it was the commander's wife in her nightdress. I held my breath. She moved in a rather stately manner and finally got into bed beside me. Feeling duly flattered, I nevertheless looked at her closely. Her eyes were open and fixed. The woman was sleep-walking. If I woke her, she would probably scream. If I didn't wake her, who would ever believe my story? For half an hour I lay in a sweat of apprehension until she began to move again, got out of bed and retraced her steps. Quickly I bolted the door.

Over breakfast the commander said, 'My wife's a sleep-walker. I hope no one was disturbed during the night, but there's no need to worry. She always finds her way back to bed.'

Shortly after this event Vivian turned up with a large parcel.

'Just a little something for the chummery,' he beamed. 'Always gives a good start to conversation at mixed parties.'

It was the elephant-phallus lamp-stand.

12

Lione

One morning I found in my mail a pale-blue envelope bearing a Ceylon stamp. It was sealed with a little blob of red wax and bore my name in a firm, well-defined hand. It gave off a faint and unfamiliar perfume as I opened it and I was aware that my *peon*, personal office servant, was observing me with interest. I put the letter in my pocket, deciding to read it later. My *peon* was fully capable of deciphering even the most complex documents upside down, and it was a part of the Sinhalese temperament to show an intense interest in anything and everything. I did not open the letter until I was secure in the privacy of the top terrace. The letter read:

> Dear Mr MacQuitty,
>   You do not know me, but I have seen you many times and have watched you playing rugby football. I very much want to meet you as I have fallen in love with you. I will be at the Buddhist shrine near Gregory's Road at eight o'clock next Friday evening. I know your car, just stop and I will get in. I am eighteen and rather small. If you are not there I will understand, but I will try again.
>
> Lione

Was this a trap; was she a decoy? Blackmail was a speciality of the island, which also had one of the highest robbery with murder rates in the world. Could it be the revenge of the forgers now out of prison; or of the Afghans deprived of their victims? There was always the possibility that it was genuine. Burgher girls were as carefully guarded as their sisters in Holland. A sense of adventure decided me.

That Friday evening I pulled up under the bo-tree, switched off the engine and opened the door. Apart from oil lamps on the shrine, the road was in darkness. Suddenly, as quietly as honey flowing from a jar, Lione slipped into the passenger seat. She held out a hand. As I took it she opened it and left in mine a temple flower. 'Let us go,' she said in a whisper.

'Where to?' I whispered back.

'Towards Mount Lavinia,' she said.

Mount Lavinia was seven miles south of Colombo. At this time of night the road was empty except for a few bullock carts. About two miles short of Mount Lavinia, she directed me down a narrow lane that led through a coconut plantation, and as we neared the bottom said, 'Turn left here. It is rather bumpy. Drive carefully.'

Another fifty yards and we came to a small rise overlooking the sea. It was a place of secluded beauty where the light of the full moon shone through the palm fronds and gleamed on the water. For the first time I looked at my determined seductress. Moonlight mingling with swaying palm-frond shadows showed me the slight slim figure of a young woman dressed in white. Her dark hair, drawn back from an oval face, hung down her back in a thick plait. Her large eyes stared calmly back at me. 'Do I please you?' she asked.

'Yes,' I whispered, 'very much.'

We sat in silence, contemplating the distant breakers on the reef.

'You think me bold?' she asked.

'Too beautiful to be bold,' I said.

'It is very difficult for me to go out at night. I said I was going to see friends with my brother. We must leave here in an hour.'

I slipped an arm around her tiny waist.

'I told you I was small, but I am quite strong,' she said, and held me close.

I unhooked the straps to the car seats and we lay down. Her dress, which hung in pleats from a low neck, was gathered at the waist by a thin gold belt. When I undid the belt's clasp the dress fell away to become the cloth on which she lay. It was her only garment. Her skin was as pale and smooth as ivory. Her lips and breasts were full. I thought at once of reproductions I had seen of the paintings of the ladies of the king on the gallery wall at Sigiriya.

'Do I please you?' she asked again.

'More than I can say.'

In a trice her mood changed, her shyness slipped away. Now she was the huntress, I the prey. I lay still, hardly daring to breathe, and soon was equally naked. As her hands, lips and tongue made exploratory moves, I closed my eyes. When I resurfaced to the outside world – the roar of the surf, the rustle of palm fronds, the croaking of frogs, the sharp noises of insects – I found myself lying under a cataract of waist-long hair that had escaped from its loose plait and fallen about us. I parted it to reveal her rounded breasts and a smooth belly descending to perfectly moulded thighs. We lay a long time in a still embrace before I opened my eyes again and again lifted the curtain of hair. Framed by the side window of the car, and watching us with startling intensity, was a pair of gleaming eyes.

'Time to go,' I said.

To my relief the eyes promptly disappeared. We dressed quickly. I started the engine and switched on the headlamps. There was no one in sight.

'When can we meet again?' I asked.

'I can see you only once a month. If you wish I will meet you at the shrine at the same time on the same day four weeks from now.'

'I'd like that very much,' I said, 'but what if for some reason one of us can't make it?'

'If I cannot I will write, and if you cannot then, on the day we are to meet, leave a newspaper on the driving seat when you park your car at the bank. I will see it there.'

'Can't I get in touch with you?'

'That is impossible.'

At the bo-tree she slipped away as silently as she had arrived, leaving me to ponder on the strangeness, the secrecy, the almost predestined inevitability of this encounter. And the face at the window? There was no privacy in Ceylon, but, whatever the outcome, I had been a willing victim.

My desk clerk said, 'There is a gentleman to see you, sir.'

'Show him in,' I said.

The young man, a Burgher, seemed a shade nervous.

'How can I help you?' I asked.

'Sir, it is a private matter. May I speak to you alone?'

I motioned to my clerk to leave us.

'Sir, I think you have a car, number X 3379?'

'Yes,' I said, with a nasty feeling that I knew what was coming.

'Some time ago you were seen trespassing on my uncle's property and thereon you committed an immorality.'

My heart began to pound. Any involvement in blackmail would terminate my banking career. I said nothing and did my best to remain calm.

After a few moments he continued, 'My uncle is a reasonable man. He says that if you will give him 1,000 rupees he will take no further action in the matter.'

I looked at him with all the sternness I could muster and asked, 'What is your name and what is the name of your uncle?'

He gave me his name, but refused to give me that of his uncle.

'Now,' I said, 'I want you to understand that you have committed a criminal offence. You have tried to blackmail me and I intend to inform the police.'

As I reached for the telephone his pale face grew paler and he began to protest, 'Sir, this is not my affair. I am only trying to help you with my uncle.'

'Tell your uncle,' I said, 'that if ever I hear from you or him again, I will immediately place the matter in the hands of the police. I am recording your demand in my bank diary and this will be used as evidence.'

He had begun to sweat and his hands to tremble as he rose from his chair. He looked at me as if he was going to say something more, but remained silent a moment and then left.

It was only another week until my next assignation with Lione, and when the time came I repeated the arrangement for our first meeting. Lione slipped into the passenger seat with the same ease as before, and again she held out her hand. This time it held a small pigeon orchid.

'Where shall we go?' I asked.

'There is a better place, nearer to Mount Lavinia,' she said.

We drove in silence, and once more she told me where to turn down towards the sea. Again a narrow lane ran through a plantation of coconut palms, but with this one there were no signs of habitation. As I switched off the headlamps Lione said, 'I was afraid you might not come.'

'Why?' I asked.

'Well, after being accused of immorality I thought you might have been put off.'

'How do you know about that?' I asked.

'Colombo's a small place.'

'But won't this disturb your secrecy?' I asked.

'Oh, no, they have no idea whom you were with. Anyway, you frightened them, just as you frightened the money-lenders. I don't think they will do anything more.'

Scandal was the life-blood of Colombo and the jungle telegraph operated ceaselessly. One unfortunate banker with a weakness for voyeurism had been caught watching a girl undress through the window of her lighted room. Her Burgher brothers had handed him over to the police.

'What makes this place better than the last one?' I asked. 'Isn't someone just as likely to turn up?'

'No one will come here. It is supposed to be haunted by the souls of an old couple who were murdered here for their money. Witch-doctors were called in to cleanse it, but people are still afraid to come here after dark.'

'Surely you don't believe such nonsense?' I said.

'But I do. We have witchcraft and witch-doctors here who can cure people when Western medicine fails. They can cast spells too. Haven't you noticed those small objects – sometimes miniature houses – placed on the walls or pillars of offices and buildings. They are there because someone inside believes that another of the staff is doing him an injustice. This sign, created by the witch-doctors, will cause the guilty one to confess. The people of Ceylon are supersti-tious. But we have talked enough. Tonight it is your turn to make love.'

She unhooked the seat straps and lay back. My heart beat faster. She lay perfectly still as we began our love-making. I tried to prolong the sensation, but the urgency of nature took over.

'You are too abrupt,' she chided me. 'I did not come to be ravished!'

'I thought I was doing rather well,' I said.

'Have you studied biology?' she asked.

'No.'

'Well, I will give you a brief lesson. The human heart at rest pumps a gallon of blood every minute through sixty miles of arteries, veins and capillaries. These channels, if opened up and spread out, would cover a field of an acre and a half. The senses we so much enjoy have 9,000 taste buds and 13,000 million nerve cells to distinguish between heat and cold, pain and pleasure. You should try to realize this when you make love, to use a little more imagination and have respect for this biological miracle.'

'Lione, you have never had a more willing pupil.'

Finally we lay at peace.

'Perhaps you're a witch?' I whispered. 'I certainly think you've bewitched me.'

'Perhaps I am,' she replied, 'but you must not fall in love with me.'

'Why not?'

'What we are about has nothing to do with love.'

'But you said in your letter that you'd fallen in love with me.'

'It was the only word you'd have understood.'

'What is it about then?'

'It is the worship of nature. A taste of honey.'

'Listen,' I said, 'there is someone there.'

'I know,' she replied, 'but he will say nothing. He is deaf and dumb.'

'How can you know that?' I asked.

'I have been here before. He is the watchman.'

Back at the bo-tree I asked when we could next meet.

'Do you want to see me again?'

'Very much.'

'My people go to Anuradhapura on the last day of the month, which is a Saturday. You could take the weekend and see me there? Stay at the rest-house and meet me at the shrine at sunset. When I leave I will be alone. Follow me at a distance. Do you understand?'

'But why all the mystery?' I asked.

'One day I will tell you,' Lione said as she slipped away.

When R.R. Johnson, who had welcomed me on my arrival, fell in love with Moira, a pretty nurse at the Colombo Hospital, he ran into the usual problem of finding somewhere secluded to pursue his courtship. Finally and ingeniously he settled on the centre of the football pitch. For several months darkness concealed his trysting place from the European population, until, one Saturday night, a torrential rain-storm flooded the field. The ancient car refused to start. The couple waded home. The car remained, a silent witness for Sunday-morning church-goers.

Some months later Robert asked me to be his best man, an honour I happily accepted. He was very correct and very nervous. It was to be a Scots wedding in kilts and with a piper, and I managed to find a piper and full regalia, even an Argyle Sutherland kilt for myself. On the wedding morning I made a dash to the church to check that all was well, but ran into a police trap on the way. No amount of explanation could dent the Sinhalese officer's devotion to duty. Precious minutes ticked away as he made his notes. By the time I had escaped and rushed back to Storm Lodge, Robert was in a terrible state, fearing we would be late. I suggested a stiff Scotch.

'You wouldn't expect me to go to my bride with whisky on my breath,' he growled.

'I thought we were having a proper Scots wedding,' I said, suddenly wondering where on earth I had left the ring.

In the event, the wedding went smoothly. Rice, our new manager, turned up immaculate in a grey topper and tails, his wife in a flowing flowered silk gown. Moira's wedding dress was a dazzling creation in white with a splendid train that, when it came to the wedding photograph, obliged me to stand on one side to avoid treading on it. As usual with such occasions, every detail of London custom was followed to the letter. No wonder the British Empire was a success.

Two weeks later I was hauled before the magistrate. 'Have you anything to say to this charge?' he asked.

I explained about the wedding and added that, since the road was empty at the time, I thought that the sooner I got off it and left it empty for the next car, the safer the road would be.

'I was in the following car,' said the magistrate. 'The fine is 50 rupees.'

At the end of that same month I drove the 126 miles to meet Lione at Anuradhapura, by the bo-tree reputedly originating from a cutting from the Buddha's original, sent by Ashoka to Ceylon in 250 BC. Having found the rest-house and left my bag, I set out to explore. The most famous object in the town is the Moonstone, which is not a jewel but a semi-circular slab of stone, carved in concentric rings with processions of animals and floral designs, and set at the foot of a flight of steps. An old Sinhalese sat on a low wall beside the stone. He had a roguish look to his wrinkled face and, imagining him to be a watchman, I asked him if he had gained harmony and wisdom through living in this sacred place. 'Women are the only mystery in life,' he told me. 'Solve them and you have the secret of living.'

'How do you do it?' I asked.

'Ah,' he said, 'it is very difficult, but little by little you learn.'

Eager to talk, he told me that there was in his village a maiden of great beauty whom he had guarded and befriended after her parents died. He had grown obsessed with her, but restrained his passion on account of her youth and waited patiently as she slowly ripened. Even after the maiden was willing, he still waited, savouring his anticipation. Finally, no more than a month ago, she had led him into the darkness of one of the old temples and at last he enjoyed the rapture of possessing a nymph as rare as those that appeared on the walls of Sigiriya. Too late he discovered that, despite all his care, he was not the first. The maiden of his dreams moreover gave him gonorrhoea.

'Will you now abandon the lusts of the flesh?' I asked.

'Oh, no,' he said. 'I have a witch-doctor who has cured me before.'

'What about the maiden?' I asked.

'I will not use her again.'

'But you'll send her to your doctor to be cured,' I said.

'No,' he replied. 'She is giving favours to my enemy.'

The air was still with reverence. Worshippers knelt and prayed in silence. The roots of the bo-tree fell in a curtain around the shrine, and altars in little stone shelters were covered with flowers and offerings of food that tree rats ate even as priests half-heartedly shooed them away. The branches were festooned with pieces of cloth tied there by suppliants for favours sought or received: pleas from barren women, from the sick and those in trouble. Slowly I paced out the perimeter of the huge tree. There was no sign of Lione. Then, just as the last rays of the sun dissolved into night, she arrived through the entrance. She wore a Sinhalese sari and a close-fitting white bodice, and until our eyes met I was not sure it really was her. After a pause before the altar, she walked slowly through a side-gate. I followed discreetly as she continued through the ruins, and was barely able to make out her white bodice in the gathering darkness. When she turned the corner of a building and vanished, I hurried forward and looked round the corner. The darkness was absolute. I moved too fast and stumbled. A small hand gripped me and led me through a doorway. 'No one will come here,' she whispered.

We stood pressed against each other, the top of her head just reaching my chin. I had not realized she was so small.

'There is a stone bench here,' she said, and guided me to a low slab.

'How long have you got?' I asked.

'Less than an hour. I am being picked up at a friend's house, and it will take me some time to get there.'

'Can't I give you a lift?' I suggested.

'That is impossible.'

The stone slab was narrow, hard and cold. After a while she said, 'You're not very good in temples. You must lie down on your back, so.'

She arranged me in a position that forcibly reminded me of the knights on their tombs in Exeter Cathedral.

'Do I cross my legs?' I asked.

'Of course not. Lie perfectly still.'

I lay in the eerie darkness, aware of faint night sounds outside.

'Keep still,' she whispered.

Time after time I reached the brink, and time after time she held me back. At long last I was overcome.

'You *are* impatient,' she whispered, 'but you are improving.'

'When shall I see you again?' I asked.

'Tomorrow morning I will be at the shrine at eight. Park your car on the road outside and we will drive round the ruins together.'

'But you will be seen,' I said.

'I am all right here,' she said. 'My people will not move till noon, and before then you will be on your way back to Colombo,' and she kissed me goodbye.

I sat on the stone slab a long time, the great ruined city, more than 250 square miles in area, around me. I thought of its kings and its magnificence, of its millions of inhabitants, of its suffering under Tamil attacks until finally deserted in the ninth century. There was little sense of the life of its former glory, with the notable exception of the green and flourishing bo-tree and the faith it inspired.

Next morning for the first time I saw Lione in daylight. She wore a white skirt and blouse, and her hair, tied up in a white silk square, was not black but dark brown. Her eyes were hazel. She *was* beautiful. As she got in beside me she held out her hand. It contained a shimmering moonstone. 'To remind you of the moonstone of Anuradhapura,' she said.

'You are very beautiful,' I said. 'Like the moonstone, you have a pale translucent quality and a shimmering centre about which I know nothing.'

'It is a centre I keep for myself. I have Venetian blinds in my mind, and I keep out thoughts that I do not need, especially when I am with you. And now,' she said, 'I have a bone to pick with you. Take this direction and I will show you the eight sacred places of the Buddha.'

I drove slowly along the narrow road.

'I am a jealous person,' she continued, 'and you have other girlfriends. You need not shake your head. You go sailing with one – the tall Miss Whittow at the Yacht Club.'

'Yes,' I said, 'but nothing more.'

'Do you like tall girls? Heather Lyon is also tall.'

'But she only came to dinner once at Storm Lodge. We were all there.'

'Then there is Mrs Murdoch, who is very pretty.'

'I play squash and rugger with her husband. He is a great sportsman.'

'I know. I watched you both at the athletic meeting. Overall he came first, and you came second, but he entered for all events and you did not. If you had done them all, you would have won. You are ungainly but strong. Anyway, promise me that as long as you are in Ceylon you will have no other girls but me.'

'I will meet them, but that will be all.'

'I'm glad, but if I ever find out you have been unfaithful, I will put a spell on you.'

I laughed.

'What are you laughing at?'

I told her about the pelican that had been such an unexpected feature of a party – given by Miss Whittow, as it happened.

'I have one more question,' she concluded. 'Do you like boys?'

'What do you mean?'

'Well, Sinhalese boys are beautiful and there is a lot of sodomy in the island. Are you bi-sexual?'

'No,' I replied.

'Then why do you go to the Deaf and Blind Institute and play with the boys?'

I told her about Toc H and how I had agreed to give physical training to the boys.

'Is that all?' Lione asked sceptically.

'But of course,' I said.

'The boys love you,' she said. 'I have seen the blind ones leap from the springboard and fly over the horse to be caught by you.'

'Blind people don't find many things as difficult as you might think. I like the boys and they seem to like me, but that's all there is to it.'

'Well,' she said with what I thought was an amused twinkle in her eye, 'I don't mind you carrying on with the boys. I think you are only a boy yourself.'

We parted by the vast bell-shaped dagoba begun by King Mahasena in the third century AD and about half the size of the Great Pyramid of Giza. I was glad to leave the ruins, for I was beginning to find the place oppressive. The dank green jungle was never-endingly at its work of reclamation. Whichever way the eye looked, stone and plaster were stained with lichen and black fungi, the roots of trees burst walls asunder and the granite colums that had once supported palaces leaned awry.

I continued to urge my parents to visit me, but the long voyage, four weeks each way, was a daunting prospect for Mother. She had never got over a trip to Marseilles in 1913, when we ran into a gale in the Gulf of Lions. I could remember how the ship had rolled as if it would never right itself, then stopped with a great shudder before rolling the other way to repeat the frightening performance. With each roll I had watched fascinated as my father's braces, hanging on the door hook, swung almost to the horizontal. Father said that after that ordeal the smell of a tarred rope was enough to send Mother off, but eventually family affection overcame her terror and in February 1935 they arrived together in Colombo harbour on the P&O SS *Chitral*.

I met them with the pinnace and drove them straight to Storm

Lodge, where Ram took their baggage and established them in my room. They had had a good voyage. My mother had soon gained her sea legs and enjoyed the new experience, and my father, a seasoned traveller, was fascinated by the East, which he had never seen before. They had played deck games during the day and bridge every evening.

In Colombo, friends rallied round and invited them to parties. Since it was the cool season, Father wore a tropical suit and waistcoat with his open wing collar and bow tie and, occasionally, a topi he had bought in Port Said. Mother wore pretty cotton print dresses that were cool and suited her well. I took them up to Kandy, where she was overwhelmed by the Royal Botanic Gardens. Rare orchids dripped in swathes around us and the palms, tropical trees, shrubs and flowers were beautifully spectacular. 'I never thought I'd see such plants except in a hothouse,' said Mother. 'It's like the Garden of Eden, and all my spices that I have in little jars, nutmeg, cinnamon, pepper, vanilla, cloves, are growing around us!'

The Muslims, I told her, also regard Ceylon as the Garden of Eden, and on a later trip to Kandy we visited the Temple of the Tooth. The building itself is not impressive, but inside the famous Sacred Tooth rests on a lotus leaf fashioned from pure gold and protected by seven bell-shaped caskets nesting within each other and increasing in richness with each decrease in size. The Sacred Tooth itself gave the impression of being some five inches long, but this we learnt was a boar's tusk originally used as a hiding place for the real tooth at a time when the Catholic Portuguese were intent on its destruction. According to the guardians, the original tooth is still inside.

I pointed out to Mother the road along which the sacred relic was carried in the July-August Esala Perahera procession, the most magnificent religious spectacle in the world when sixty of the island's largest elephants, gorgeously apparalled, are led by Kandian dancers through the town to the temple. Musicians bang drums and blow shrill trumpets as they gyrate with the dancers. At night the scene is lit by flaring torches. It seems a far cry from the actual teachings of Buddha, but certain Christian pageantry is as colourful and perhaps as far removed from the Sermon on the Mount.

It gave me pleasure to point out to my parents all the things that had a special appeal for me: the palm-fringed lagoons, the coconuts being gathered and husked, the fish market, the outrigger canoes, the paddy fields and the great Lion Rock at Sigiriya, which thrust high above the green jungle like a huge rock rising out of the sea. But what they liked best was to be safe with me in my home. They were overcome by Ram's devotion to their needs: the fresh orange juice and pineapple, the early-morning tea, evening dinner at the chummery. They felt they were truly a part of my life.

On their last evening we gave a special dinner to include friends from up-country who had entertained them. At the end of it Mother, to my great surprise, for I had never before known her to do such a thing, swept aside her natural shyness, stood up and made a simple speech to thank everyone for all the kindnesses that had filled their holiday with happiness. Next morning I took them on board and saw them safely into their cabin. When the call for 'friends ashore' sounded, I gave Mother a big hug and many kisses as she tried to hold back her tears. Father followed me down the companionway and stepped on to the flat deck of the lighter, where he promptly did his little corkscrew dance while Mother waved from the rail. I followed the ship out to the breakwater and waved a final farewell. Part of my life was departing with them. They had grown older.

One place I never had time to show them was Adam's Peak, which casts its 7,000-foot shadow across the island at every sunrise. On the summit is a flat area, 150 feet square, where Buddhist monks live beside the imprint of the sacred foot, which is five feet in length. I had always wanted to climb Adam's Peak and jumped at the chance when some tea-planter friends of Tony Humphreys invited us to stay the night with them and climb the peak in the morning.

We set off in Tony's car, a venerable wooden-spoked Pontiac with a canvas hood, not unlike my old Fiat in Amritsar. The excellent road ran through beautiful country, but as we climbed to the high land surrounding the peak, it became rough, narrow and tortuous. When a tropical downpour suddenly engulfed us, the road turned into a river. Rounding a sharp corner, the front off-side wheel slipped over the edge, where the car hesitated a moment before starting to slide down the steep slope. With great presence of mind Tony steered for a stout tree, which fortunately held and brought us to rest twenty feet below the road. We got out gingerly, fearing to dislodge the car, and after twenty minutes of wondering whether to walk on and get help, were relieved to see an elephant approaching with a road gang. In no time they attached ropes to the car and pulled us out. We rewarded our helpers and continued the journey, relieved to be back on the road. After some minutes I felt a pricking sensation in the groin. Pulling up my shorts I exposed a black slug-like creature. It was a leech. 'Don't pull it off,' warned Tony. 'Light a cigarette and burn it. It'll drop off then.'

He stopped the car. We were covered. We lit cigarettes and searched one another for the squirming vampires, and after all the delays it was night before we reached the lane leading to our host's bungalow. We were thankful to see boys waiting to guide us in with hurricane lamps, and after stiff whiskies and hot baths stained with still-oozing wounds, we enjoyed an excellent dinner. Next morning, at 4 a.m., we set out to begin the slow climb of the cone-shaped mountain. Soon we found ourselves among pilgrims devoutly praying at each station and bearing offerings for the shrine. There was no doubting the sincerity and faith that shone in the eyes of the worshippers, but had not prayer and witless euphoria been condemned by the Buddha? 'This only do I teach, suffering and the release from suffering. Be ye lamps unto yourselves.' How did the giant tooth and footprint benefit the teaching any more than the millions of words amplified from the Four Noble Truths in the Pali Canon? One day, I vowed as we climbed, I would try to meet the Dalai Lama himself and learn what he thought about it.

I was returning home late from the bank one Friday evening when I noticed thousands of lights flickering in the cemetery. Attaching myself to a group of people at the entrance, I followed them between the candle-lit graves. They came to a stop at an open grave, and, too late to turn back, I stood embarrassed among the mourners. A white-haired man, bending over an elaborate coffin that rested on two trestles, opened a small lid on the coffin's top and, one by one, the mourners filed past, each in turn sprinkling liquid from a crystal bottle that he handed them. Finally I was left alone. He motioned me forward. I took the bottle. In the opening I saw the pale face of a girl, framed in long dark hair. I sprinkled a little of the bottle's contents, which ran down her cheeks like tears. I looked more closely at the tranquil features, so fine, so beautiful. They reminded of Lione. I wondered if this could be some sort of omen.

I had arranged to meet Lione that weekend at Sigiriya, where she was staying with friends. Knowing of my interest in Anuradhapura, she had suggested I ought to climb the Lion Rock, 'her' rock, and that she would meet me on the summit at eight o'clock on Sunday morning. As it happened, I found myself travelling with sad tidings. A cable from head office, received on the Saturday morning, instructed me to proceed to Bangkok by the first available steamer. A Danish ship was to leave in five days and I must sail on her.

Sigiriya made a natural fortress. Even with the help of iron railings and ladders it was difficult to climb. Half-way up was a small refuge covered with wire gauze in which climbers could shelter if attacked by wild bees. I broke the climb to look at the famous life-size frescoes of maidens bearing dishes for the king, which I had before seen only in illustrations. Their diaphanous garments revealed the tiny waists and perfect breasts that are the abiding heritage of young Sinhalese women.

The final ascent was made with some trepidation. The ladder, loosely fastened to the vertical rock, swayed under my weight. Eventually I scrambled to the top and saw Lione some distance away, seated on part of the old palace wall. I sat beside her, took her hand and waited for it to open with whatever gift it contained. Her hand remained clenched.

'What have you brought me?' I asked.

She opened her hand. It was empty. She looked out over the green jungle stretching to the horizon.

'What's the matter?' I asked.

She looked at me. 'I have always given you something because I have always taken something from you,' she said. 'In this way I do not owe you anything, neither do you owe me anything. I will not be taking anything from you again, so do not need to give you anything.'

'I don't understand.'

'That is what you say, but deep down you know that this is true. You have not told me that you are leaving Ceylon and this will be our last meeting.'

I protested that I had only just received the news myself and was going to tell her that very morning.

'I believe you,' she replied, 'but it makes no difference. Like your body, your mind is ungainly, but like your body, it is strong. You are greedy for life and experience. You have finished here for the moment, but one day you will return. When you do, I shall have gone.'

We sat in silence. A large frog emerged from a green pool and sunned itself. As we watched, a *tic polonga*, a Russell viper, glided from a crevice in the ancient wall. I half-rose, but Lione restrained me. 'Like us they are natural creatures. Leave them to nature.'

The frog froze. The viper moved slowly until, with a sudden strike, it clamped its jaws on the frog's leg. The terrified frog struggled wildly. The snake's jaws were small compared to the size of the frog, but gradually they engulfed the victim until only the back legs protruded, kicking desperately until they too finally disappeared. 'You think nature is cruel?' Lione asked.

'It is terrible for the frog,' I said.

'The poison numbed its senses. It struggled but did not feel pain. Man's inhumanity is worse.'

'Tell me why you have always been so secretive? Are you a witch?'

'I am a white witch, but this is another matter. I worship nature and use it for my needs. I only lied to you once when I told you I was eighteen. I am twenty-five, but people say I look younger.'

'Much younger,' I agreed. 'If you had told me you were seventeen I wouldn't have doubted it.'

'I please you?' She looked serious.

'You've always delighted me,' I said, 'but *why* so much secrecy?'

'I will tell you now because I will leave this rock before you and shall never speak to you again. I come from a strict family and my husband's a jealous man.'

We sat again in silence. The snake had disappeared. 'It's time for me to leave,' she said. 'Do not speak or watch me go.'

Leaning towards me, she kissed me slowly on the mouth. I remained there a long time afterwards in this place where King Kasyapa had sought refuge after killing his father, Dhatu Sena, fifteen centuries before. From here he reigned for eighteen years to avoid the vengeance of his brother. I wondered why he had killed his father or, come to that, why he had not killed his brother. I wondered why it was Lione's rock. Then it came to me: add 'ss' to her name and it gave you 'Lioness'.

All too soon I was having to leave this island and start afresh with a new language among an unconquered people in whose country there was no colour bar, but who, like the Sinhalese, were Buddhists. During the next week there were farewell parties for me, but it was the last time, my Ceylon friends said with one voice, that they'd make friends with birds of passage. It was all too upsetting when they left. They came to see me off on the Danish cargo ship, the SS *Lalandia*, which carried ten passengers and was bound for Penang, whence I would proceed by train to Bangkok. The ever-attentive, ever-resourceful Ram meanwhile fixed himself up with a job driving a bus on the strength of having practised bringing my car round to the front door.

13

Real Bangkok

The SS *Lalandia* steamed out of Colombo harbour and headed south past the Galle Face Green where I had spent so many lonely evenings watching the sun vanish into the Indian Ocean. That evening the passengers dined at the Danish captain's table. When he sat down in his shirt sleeves, we thankfully followed suit. The absence of social ritual was a welcome relief after the P&O's tyrannies. The only other passenger going to Bangkok was Prince Purachatra, who regaled me with a wealth of light-hearted stories about his country.

'I think you will like us. We find the Irish sympathetic, though we are not so celebrated for fighting.' He looked at me with a broad smile. 'We had only one war, long, long ago with Burma. We are a free people – *thai* as we say. You'll love our girls. Everyone does. They are like flowers, pretty, feminine and very clever. They run the businesses while the men enjoy themselves.'

'Are they so different from other girls?' I asked.

'Unique. For one thing, there is no illegitimacy in Siam, despite the efforts of missionaries to introduce it. We have a land of smiles and plenty. A child means only, as we say, another handful of rice in the pot. We love children. To us they are all legitimate. In fact each one gets a new name all to itself.'

'It all sounds too good to be true,' I said.

'There's an even more amusing custom. Leading families angle to have their daughters invited to the Royal Palace. Siamese monarchs have very large families and add another wife whenever they see a girl they like. It gives the girl a permanent status, and if she is lucky enough to have a son whom the king likes, he may even become the next monarch. You might say that the king is a real father to his people.'

Next morning after breakfast I joined the prince for a walk around the deck. We settled ourselves in comfortable long-chairs and watched the clear blue Indian Ocean divide before the heavily laden ship. Penang was three days' away, and from there the Bangkok Express made its 900-mile journey up the Kra Isthmus to the Siamese capital.

'We are devout Buddhists,' explained the prince, 'but we also have a leaning towards Brahmanism. In fact all our marriage ceremonies are Brahman in origin and Brahmans preside over various court rituals. We also have a tendency to placate nature spirits, *pi*, rather like your Irish fairies. You will find little houses put up for them all over the place. But Buddhism comes first, and our young men all spend some months in a monastery before starting work. Girls also join the order and, with their shaven heads and yellow robes, look like beautiful boys. We hold to the Theravada tradition, as do Ceylon and Burma.'

'This interpretation of the teaching of Buddha seems to me,' I said, 'pretty far from the original Four Noble Truths in the way that it turns Buddha into a god and preaches an after-life that he never proclaimed.'

'True,' said the prince, 'but you have to remember that, as the number of followers grew, all sorts of rules and regulations needed to be introduced to allow them to live together peaceably. You have exactly the same thing in Christianity. Christ was against building temples and blessed the meek, but people demand spectacular worship and in Siam they are well supplied. You'll be amazed by the joyful architecture of our temples. Even our funerals are famous for feasting and fun.'

Yet I thought, as he said this, that a sad expression ran across his features.

The voyage continued happily and uneventfully. I rested and took the opportunity to read up on our Bangkok branch. It had been opened in March 1894. Its present office was on the river front between the French Legation and the Oriental Hotel, where Somerset Maugham once stayed and wrote a book. The Menam Chao Phya, 'Mother of Waters', flowed at the bottom of the bank's garden and was the main highway. It could take ships drawing twelve feet of water up to Bangkok. Stemming from it were innumerable *klongs* or canals. They spread out like branches from a tree and ships' cargoes could be unloaded and transported anywhere in the city or farther afield. Bangkok was known as the 'Venice of the East'.

On the evening of our fourth day after leaving Ceylon, we sailed into Penang. I was given no time to explore, but was whisked to my sleeper on the train by two clerks from our Penang office. When I awoke next morning the train was puffing through a sea of paddy fields from among which little attap-thatched houses rose on stilts. At Bangkok I was met by Ian Pemberton. Pem, as he was known, was a courteous, reserved Scot of about my own age, and once again I was rushed straight to the bank, my predecessor, Shepherd, having already departed. There I met my seniors. The manager was George Grant, a red-haired Scot famous for having once given one of his Calcutta sweepstake tickets to his *ayah*, whereupon it won an enormous sum. He had sought a portion for his generosity, but the *ayah* kept the lot. Grant was a big, jovial, sociable man, terse but full of fun. Our chief accountant was James Stuart, a tough, self-centred Scot whom I had first met in Amritsar. The senior sub-accountant, Joe Miller, was a heavy, dour, taciturn Scot, nicknamed 'Hong Kong Joe' from the fact that he found nothing quite right and never as shipshape as it had been in Hong Kong.

The bank, magnificently situated, was a large square building with massive stone arches. Its banking floor was white marble, and the mess above had marble-paved verandas. At each corner was a room protected from insects by gauze screens. Our quarters at the top were divided by wooden partitions that rose to within a few feet of the ceiling and allowed for ample ventilation if little privacy. I was allocated a corner room facing the river on the Oriental Hotel side, and an inside bedroom.

The garden ran down to the river and a little landing stage. Its green lawn was flanked with hibiscus, frangipani and canna lilies. A large jacaranda tree stood in the southern corner next to the river, which bustled with ocean-going steamers, ferries, tugs, lighters, barges, launches and canoes of various sizes. The large canoes, about forty feet long, had flat sterns, not unlike Venetian gondolas, from which a rower propelled them with a single oar. He kept both hands and one leg on the oar while standing on the other leg. It seemed an impossible balancing act, and I never tired of watching it.

Sometimes our garden became flooded with brackish tidal water, but the ebb and flow achieved the basic drainage. The *klongs* and river fronts were lined with houses built on stilts, and the Siamese used the all-embracing waters to fish, wash, clean teeth and pots and pans and empty bowels and bladders. Whenever there was an epidemic of cholera, it swept through the population like wildfire, but while thousands died, many more were immunized by the excellent hospitals.

After my first evening of drinks at the club and dinner at the mess, I went to my room, aware of a strong sense of the curious challenge of sleeping in a strange place for the first time. Ah Lee, my new 'boy', had laid out my things, it being the custom for servants attached to the mess to carry on from one *nai*, or 'Mr', to the next. I thanked Ah Lee and said goodnight. I cleaned my teeth, had a shower and went to my bedroom. Ever since Amritsar, I had given up wearing pyjamas, and the light was off to avoid attracting the myriads of insects that were Bangkok's greatest scourge. I raised the mosquito net and slipped into bed, only to realize it was occupied. Hurriedly I switched on the light. The occupant was a pretty Siamese girl. Cooly appraising eyes peered at me from behind dainty fingers that held a tiny lace handkerchief. 'Me Hua,' she announced. 'I take care of Nai Shepherd. Now I take care of you.'

'I don't know that I want to take on Mr Shepherd's arrangements just yet,' I said.

'Me no arrangement, me very good,' she grinned.

'You go home now,' I said, feeling at something of a disadvantage in my nudity. 'One day perhaps we meet again.'

'OK,' said Hua. 'Your boy know where find me.'

She got out of bed and pulled on a pair of black silk Chinese trousers, skilfully wrapping the wide top round her slender waist and tucking it in. Then she put on a white blouse over her well-shaped breasts, tossed her black hair and slipped her feet into sandals. She was tiny. 'Me pretty?' she queried.

'Very. How old are you?'

'Seventeen,' she replied. 'Why you no want me now?'

'I like to find my own,' I said.

'Me too,' said Hua, 'and I catch *you*.'

'Well, not tonight you don't,' I said.

'You come and see my hat shop,' said Hua. 'No far.'

'How much did Mr Shepherd pay you?' I asked.

'He no pay,' said Hua indignantly. 'Thai girls free. No take money. Like loving for love.'

She ran from the room. My new home was silent except for slight sounds of movement and tiny suppressed chuckles that seemed to spread across the common ceiling and harmonize with the soft splash of the Menam Chao Phya as it flowed on its way to the gulf.

The club bore the prefix 'Royal', which seemed odd outside the confines of the British Empire. It so happened that the King of Siam had donated it to the European community. The club, the sports centre of the city, covered every activity, barring polo and sailing. It had a relaxed, friendly atmosphere in which people of different nationalities and sexes mingled happily. After the social claustrophobia of India and Ceylon, it took me some time to get used to such freedoms. On Saturdays, during the wet season, we played rugby, sometimes against Malaya, and water polo on Sundays. Our rugby captain was Silverthorne, known as 'Long John Silver' but a stocky, dapper, cheerful professor of mathematics at the King Chulalonkorn University. He lived by himself in a little house surrounded by paddy fields. We became friends and I frequently dined with him and played chess. He introduced me to Madame Schlepianoff, a Russian pianist who gave musical evenings at her home. These made me feel that I have never really listened to music before, and I sat at her feet entranced.

Pem introduced me to Louise Wood, professor of English literature at the same university, and her sister Amelia. Their father, W.A.R. Wood, the British consul-general in Chengmai, had written books on the country, including the vivid *Land of Smiles*. Their mother, Boon, had been a young Chengmai girl when their father met her when he first came out in the service. He fell in love with her and married her. When the British ladies of Bangkok gibbed at having a Siamese as a potential first lady at the embassy, the Foreign Office counter-attacked by promoting Mr Wood to a superior position in Chengmai.

In the dry season there was polo. The Polo Club had started when Phya Gadaharabodi, a lowly stable boy who rose to be Master of the Royal Stables and to play for Siam, helped a few enthusiastic Europeans to obtain ten acres of an old mulberry garden from the king. A Danish engineer, Sorensen, then dealt with the problems of levelling the area and flooding it nightly to preserve the grass in the dry season. A club house and stables were built, and what was possibly the most economical polo club in the world was born. Phya Gadha, as he was known, was a gifted, natural player, cool, controlled and cheerful. He was the core of the club, and since not many people played polo, he gave me a warm welcome. He was, just then, recovering from disfavour at the palace. Sent to Australia to buy 200 horses for the Siamese cavalry, he had arrived to a tremendous banquet put on by the dealers. Not to let the king's reputation be outdone, Phya Gadah threw an even grander party; and so the junketing continued until only enough funds were left to buy four horses.

One Sunday morning I stood with him, R.P. Jones and G. Watts, who made up the Siam team, to inspect six ponies that the club had ordered from Australia, trained to stick and ball. They were in the charge of an immensely strong, thick-set Australian aborigine called Joe. The ponies looked ragged and wild after their long sea journey, and Joe's job was to convince us that the club was getting what it had ordered. On to the first pony Joe strapped a big Australian saddle with curving knee holds, double girths, surcingle and horns for ropes and halters. Suddenly he seized the pony by its lower lip, pulled its head round to the girth and was securely in the saddle before the animal had time to protest. A few spectacular bucks, a mad gallop round the field on a loose rein, and then he asked for stick and ball. He worked the animal through a full rage of polo strokes before doing the same with the remaining five ponies. It was clear that with him in the saddle they could handle the game. When he finished I asked him if he could stop the horse at a gallop. Away he went and turned, to come thundering straight at our little group. Twenty feet from us he shouted 'Hup!' and the pony stopped dead.

'How on earth did you train it to do that?' I asked.

'Just I gallop him down deep trench we have and say "Hup!" 'fore he hit earth wall. He no hit twice.'

I asked him about the fodder we were using. He took a handful, chewed it thoughtfully, then said, 'Good.'

I bought a black pony and called him Gungha Din, and later bought a second pony, Galloping Gold. The latter had a curious history, having been a frequent race winner until she pulled a tendon, when her owner turned her over to a farmer. She came to me in a parlous state. Her coat was torn and ragged from barbed-wire fences and she had thrush in all her hooves from standing in wet or flooded fields. R.P. Jones advised, as a vet, a course of Stockholm tar, and every day I scraped out the infected hooves and packed them with tar and tow. Fed and groomed, she soon had a fine glossy coat and the thrush gradually vanished. She was a gentle ride and moved well once the tendon had healed.

John Silverthorne, an inveterate gambler, knew the horse well. He had always had an ambition to ride in a race, but had never learnt to ride, though he was light, strong and nimble – good jockey material. I said I could have him and Galloping Gold ready to race in the autumn meeting. She wouldn't win, I said, but I didn't think she'd come last.

'Impossible,' he said. 'I was never on a horse in my life.'

'You're a gambler,' I challenged him. 'If you can't do it, I'll give you the horse.'

Galloping requires more nerve than skill, and John soon gained confidence. At the autumn meeting the horse was entered for a short handicap event, and when she and John appeared, the old favourite received a tremendous cheer. 'I only hope they don't bet on her,' said John as he rode to the starting post.

Galloping Gold was away like an arrow. John gave her her head and held on grimly. In a few moments the race was over. The old favourite came in third.

Further pupils included Tom Hobbs, a tall pawky Scot on his first appointment to the East who relieved Pem. Another was Leslie Thom, a cheerful new recruit for Steel Brothers. The three of us became friends, did yoga exercises together, persuaded the club to stock fruit drinks and generally revelled in the life of Siam.

The polo field lay between two water-filled ditches and, at certain times in the rainy season, hundreds of 'climbing perch' would lever themselves across the grass, using their well-developed gills to get from one ditch to the next. It was an amazing sight, and when it happened the stable hands would rush out with buckets to collect them. Siam swarmed with fish and reptiles. Flood a dry field; the next day it teemed with fish that had been sheltering in the dried mud waiting for the rains. In many gardens small pools were sunk in which 'grass fish', a species of carp, were fed on lawn cuttings. These fish were eaten raw in thin slices, like smoked salmon, and dressed with sugar and vinegar.

Siam was a land of plenty with no taboos about food. Anything that moved was eaten. Frogs, alas, were skinned alive while customers waited. Small frogs, skin and all, were thrown into hot pans and fried to a delicious crispness. Mud turtles, terrapins, tiny squid the size of a little finger, dried shredded pork skin – all these and many stranger dishes were eaten with gusto in booths, street markets and restaurants. Snakes were considered a great delicacy and were, in addition to being a valuable food, renowned for their medicinal properties. Their convoluted bodies floated in large glass jars that lined the shelves of chemists' shops, and prescriptions were made up from doses of liquid from the various jars. Live snakes were kept in cages, and portions of their livers and gall bladders were cut out and prepared while the customer watched carefully to make sure he was getting the real thing. Snakes were big business in Siam, the sale of their skins a major export.

Apart from being a major source of food, fish were also in demand for gambling and hence were another of Silverthorne's enthusiasms. He took me to where matches were held in a shed about the size of a tennis court. At eleven o'clock in the morning it was already crowded and several bouts were in progress. It was a much quieter contest than cock fighting, but just as deadly, the fish concerned being the tiny *Beta pugnax*, a heavily finned minnow that attacks other males with unbounded ferocity. All round the shed on shelves stood rows of sealed glass jars, each jar containing its owner's fish. When two owners thought they had a suitable match, they took them to the ring-master, who stood before a tall glass vase half-full of water. The spectators crowded round and laid their bets. The seals of the jars were broken by the ring-master, who then tipped the fish into the vase and placed a numbered card on top.

To begin with the fish circle each other, remaining pale and frequently coming to the surface for air. Before long brilliant colours suffuse their fins and gills, which stand out like large ruffs, doubling their size and creating a dazzling display of iridescence. Moving in intricate circling convolutions, they seem to dazzle each other, till suddenly one strikes and with a savage snap tears a strip from a glowing fin. The tiny membrane, still glowing, sinks slowly to the floor of the jar. The fish continue to tear and snap, and all at once one fish has the other by its lower jaw. Locked face to face, they writhe and twist, but then, unable to swim, sink slowly to the bottom. After a minute they break away and the favourite redoubles his efforts. His opponent turns pale. Fins and ruff no longer erect, he streaks away. The fight is over. The ring-master scoops up the fish in a small net and returns them to their jars.

Assuming this sport to be so popular because it must be so incorruptible, I said as much to Silverthorne. He swiftly disabused me. Some jars had optical glass to make fish seem smaller. A drop of opium slipped unobserved into an opponent's jar could make a fish drowsy. A smear of snake gall on the fins could make them obnoxious to biters. I bought two fighting fish and took them home. In the morning one of the jars was empty and there was no sign of its fish anywhere. When I asked Ah Lee, he explained that the *chin choc*, a small lizard that runs all over the walls, fishes them out with his tail. The minnow snaps at the tail, is pulled out and eaten. Having learnt this I covered the jars with gauze.

Bangkok's night life centred round the Hoi Tien Lao, a complex of restaurants with a dance hall on the top floor. Here Siamese and chinese hostesses, 'golden flowers' dressed in clinging silk, danced and flirted outrageously with the customers. They were alluring, dainty and pretty, with slender bodies and tiny hands and feet. Their dark eyes smiled from behind fluttering wisps of lace. Natural and uninhibited, they suggested to Western Protestant man what he might have enjoyed if original sin had never barred him from the Garden of Eden. As I watched one night at the dance hall, having driven there in a second-hand Singer I had recently bought, a small hand slipped into mine. I looked round and there was Hua. 'You dance with me?' she grinned, leading me on to the floor.

'What are you doing here?' I asked.

'I come here often,' she said. 'I like dancing.'

'Are you a hostess?' I asked.

'No, I am hat-shop girl.' She tossed her bobbed hair indignantly. 'I told you before.'

Hua was a lovely dancer, light as a feather but with a firm contact where it mattered. We danced, then sat out talking at a secluded table over a Tiger beer and an orange squash.

'You like see real Bangkok?' she asked.

'Isn't this real?'

'No, this pretending.'

Outside we got into the Singer and drove through busy city streets and then through the old quarter till we came to a rough track shaded with trees.

'Leave car here, OK,' she said, and led me by the hand down a narrow path to a little landing stage where a boat, not unlike a punt, was moored. When she called out in Siamese, an old man emerged from a small wooden house. She spoke to him and he went back to the house and returned with cushions which he put in the boat. Hua helped me in. 'You sit here,' she said and sat beside me.

The old man picked up a pole and pushed the boat slowly into the *klong*. All was quiet. The moon came up and shone on us through the branches of trees and clumps of bamboo. We passed little homes on stilts, their soft lights gleaming through the open doors and windows. Occasionally a lamp glimmered on a waterside shrine or from a *pi* house, the tiny homes built for the nature spirits to ensure protection for the real houses.

'You like real Bangkok?' asked Hua.

'Very much,' I said.

There was a genuine magic in the warm air, a sense of timeless security as we floated silently through the night.

'Next time I take you to Sunday Fair,' promised Hua.

And so she did. The fair spread out around a large open space beneath the Golden Mount Wat. The mount was artificial, made from mud that came from digging the *klongs*. From the top we had a wide view of the city and its innumerable wats, as the temple shrines were called. It seemed that rich people often wanted to leave a wat as a memorial to themselves. Then after they died, no one was interested in their upkeep, and as a result many wats became derelict and finally disappeared. The more important wats, dedicated to members of the royal family, became centres for monks and not only survived but were embellished with countless gifts from worshippers, who thus acquired merit. Gold leaf was a popular way of showing devotion, and those who could afford it dabbed bits on to their favourite shrines and images. Soldiers did it to protect themselves in battle, even though war was most unlikely.

The narrow steps leading to the summit were crowded with people, including many young boys with various designs shaved on their closely cropped heads. Some had crosses, others circles. They bent their heads so I could take photographs.

'Why do they have these funny haircuts?' I asked Hua.

'They do this short hair until they can make love, then have long hair.'

'Girls too?' I asked.

'Girls earlier,' she said.

As I put my arms round her to stop her being buffeted as we descended, she turned and said half-seriously, 'You like my hair?' and I said I did, for its bobbed style seemed to suit her tempestuous nature.

The series of booths making up the fair extended round the flat field at the foot of the mount. There were side-shows of jugglers, of fat or thin people, of dwarfs, of Siamese dancers with whitened faces and delicate slim hands who could bend their fingers back until their elongated finger stalls touched their forearms. Hua gave a little shudder as we looked at Siamese twins in a basin of formaldehyde under a glass plate. Like the original Siamese twins, Chang and Eng, they were united at the sternum.

From a walled enclosure on the far side of the fair came sounds of music and merriment. Hua led me through the gate, and inside were booths of sweetmeats, stalls of food and fruit, bottles of soft drinks.

'What's all this for?' I asked as we were offered various delicacies.

'Is for dead people,' Hua explained, pointing to three elaborate gaily decorated platforms at the far end of the enclosure. 'Come see.'

There were steps up to where a coffin rested on supports above a small fire. Relatives and friends from time to time placed a short stick of wood on top of the fire, and an attendant stood with iron tongs. I mounted the steps and peered nervously into the coffin. The bottom was an iron grid on the centre of which rested a pair of wizzened feet facing an equally wizzened head. As I gazed in astonishment, a violent spark shot out of the head and, to the spectators' delight, I jumped backwards. Hua, who had come up behind me, said, 'You no 'fraid dead man?'

'No,' I said, still shaking, 'but why only head and feet?'

'Rest all burnt up, so fireman push close.'

'Why is the body so dry?'

'Keep many years in wat store. When dry no smell.'

The atmosphere was festive. I could see no mournful faces. After dark an open-air cinema added to the excitement. The early Western movie it was showing captivated the cheerful mourners.

In another enclosure a mass Chinese funeral was taking place. At the centre was a tall catafalque containing a huge gaily painted urn. Around its base rows of skulls rested on piles of bones. Household goods fashioned in paper waited with pyramids of 'gold' coins for the conflagration to send this 'worldly wealth' into the ancestral heaven. Chinese men and women lit joss sticks before their ancient gods. Fire crackers and Catherine wheels were ready in position to deter evil spirits from the ceremony. In an upright glass case hung the dried mummy of a woman, its mouth hanging open. Beside it was a spiky tree on which mourners were impaling money.

When I asked Hua why they did this, she, in turn, asked a woman who had just impaled a note. The woman explained, 'When find body like this, it holy and they ask blessing.'

I took a photograph of the mummy, and then we waited as the pyre was lit. Catherine wheels whirled and blazed, crackers banged and fire engulfed the scene. Gradually the flames subsided. The dead had joined their ancestors.

'You like real Bangkok?' asked Hua, looking at me seriously.

'Very much,' I said.

The photograph I took that night appeared in the Bangkok press. A week later it appeared again under the heading, MUMMY IS A DUMMY. The police had discovered the body to be a fake and the mountebank responsible was under arrest.

Prince Purachatra, my first source of information about Siam, had died. Sadly I waited with the crowds of spectators for the funeral procession in which the ceremonial urn containing the body would be carried to the cremation ground. His cortège was led by musicians playing drums and horns, followed by priests, retainers and soldiers. Surrounding the urn was a bodyguard in ancient livery. It seemed odd that a large urn should be used instead of a coffin, and I asked Louise Wood how they managed to get the body inside it.

'They truss it up like a chicken,' she said, 'but first the body is washed and dressed and family and important people pay their respects. When this is finished, the corpse's knees are brought up to the chin, the thighs are tied to the stomach and the arms are bound, encircling the legs.'

'But what about the smell?' I asked.

'The urn is lined with silver and has a sealed lid. The body rests on a perforated base on a bed of salt, through which its fluids drain into a pot beneath. This pot has a tap and the priest draws off the fluid every day until the body is dry. All this takes place while the urn sits in state until the day appointed for the cremation.'

'How do you come by this arcane knowledge?' I asked. 'It seems a bit gruesome for a girl.'

'It's my country, and as a professor in King Chulalongkorn's University and having the consul-general for a father, I'm asked to functions and meet top people. They've no secrets from me. If you like, I'll take you one day to see an even more curious method.'

Meanwhile, at the cremation wat, the urn containing Prince Purachatra's body was placed on top of a tall pagoda-like structure glistening with gold. Tiered seats ran round the square and the central pyre, raised on a platform, was reached by two flights of stairs. In single file the mourners mounted the stairs and each placed a small stick of sandalwood under the urn. After the last mourner had placed his stick, the Regent lit the fire and the ceremony drew to a close. It was a moving, elegant affair, the culmination of a series of carefully planned rituals. My mind went back to the *Lalandia*, to the prince's sudden sad expression. No doubt he had known he was returning home to die.

The following week Louise told me that she had arranged for our visit to a different form of cremation. We dined first at the Oriental Hotel, where Somerset Maugham's room was still preserved with some pictures of the period. As we sat at a table overlooking the busy river and talked about him, I said, 'I've always wanted to write. What books should I read? How should I start?'

'What do you wish to write about?' she asked.

'For one thing, about Siam, about the curious customs and the happy way of life.'

'I'll do a deal with you,' said Louise. 'I'll teach you to write if you teach me to ride. I think your task will be the harder one. To begin with, you'd better start reading Sir Thomas Browne's *Urn Burial*.'

Later on at the wat we were met by a friendly Buddhist priest and taken to a large storehouse stacked from floor to ceiling with heavy wooden coffins. On the coffin ends, painted in white, were the names of occupants and their dates of death. Four men, whom I took to be undertakers, stood patiently waiting. 'You wish to see the whole operation?' the priest queried.

'Yes, please,' I said.

'It is the first time Europeans have come. It is not pleasant.'

He looked at us questioningly. Louise reassured him. The men lifted a heavy wooden coffin from its place in the stack and carried it outside to a corner of the courtyard surrounded by screens. Here they lowered it beside a zinc-topped table. A hurricane lamp cast shadows over the scene as they prised off the lid. As soon as the lid was removed, a strong smell of creosote was noticeable. On top of the corpse lay several neatly folded garments. These were perquisites of the undertakers. The corpse itself, wrapped in blankets, was lifted on to the table and the blankets removed. The white winding sheet beneath the blankets were stained and gave off a smell of decay. At the bottom of the coffin a deep layer of dried tea leaves had adsorbed the moisture and retarded decomposition. When the sheet was unwound from the head, it revealed recognizable features of a woman with black hair.

The relatives, who had been waiting outside the screens, were then admitted, and sprinkled perfume on the face and made the graceful *wai* gesture, bringing the hands together as if in prayer and bowing over them. They were quiet, respectful and apparently undismayed by the gruesome sight. They left almost at once, and the undertakers, using short knives, skilfully removed the flesh from the bones, which they then placed on a clean white cloth together with the head. The separated flesh was gathered up in the original wrappings and burnt in a secluded corner. The bones and head were to be cremated in another wat with everyone present.

'Why don't they wait until the body has completely dried out?' I asked the priest.

It was because of family reasons, he explained, and also because a geomancer had given the family an auspicious date for the cremation. Sometimes, he added, a priest would ask his pupils to sit round a corpse and observe its decay, so that they might learn the futility of all earthly things and the impermanence of life. 'It would take the conceit out of you,' as my mother said when she saw the dried corpses of the Capucine monks hanging on the walls of the catacombs at Palermo.

'So when do I get my riding lesson?' asked Louise.

'Would Sunday be all right?'

'Yes, and that'll be much more frightening for me than anything we've seen tonight.'

The half-year balance was over, but when Tom Hobbs and I checked the adjusting we found that it incorrectly showed a profit instead of a loss. We debated whether to tell our superiors or let them suffer the wrath of head office, but finally we revealed our secret. It was not well received by Stuart, the chief accountant, who had no idea that anyone other than himself and the chief clerk were venturing into his preserves. Eventually he softened and, as a reward, granted us a long weekend's leave at Hua Hin, a small fishing village a four-hour train journey south from Bangkok, on the western side of the Gulf of Siam. Harry Tudor of the Hong Kong and Shanghai bank joined us and we set out with great enthusiasm. Like Tom, Harry had charge of the safe keys, and similarly needed special permission to leave the capital.

Hua Hin had a warm sea and a beautiful sandy beach. We relaxed, sunbathed and swam to the amusement of the local fishermen. Along the coast, and far out in the shallow sea, stood circular stockades with mile-long avenues of stakes leading into them – fish traps for the *pla tu*, fat little silvery fish that swam in shoals like mackerel. The fishermen's lives were hard. The traps were owned by syndicates of merchants, who paid the government licence fee. They gave the fishermen a small wage and a percentage of the catch.

The first evening, as a full moon shone through nets drying on tall scaffolds and made delicate patterns on the sand, I joined one of the fishing boats. The skipper took me out to it in his dugout canoe. Once on board, he summoned his crew with blasts on a conch shell. They swam out with their clothes tied in bundles on top of their heads, and one after another slipped over the side until we numbered eight. Then the anchor was raised and the sail hoisted.

Outside the shelter of the land a fair breeze heeled us over and we made good progress. A shimmer of phosphorescence crossed the water like shot silk and flecked our bow wave with green fire. I fell asleep on a comfortable pile of nets, only to be woken as the sail was lowered. The boat stood alongside a circular palisade of heavy stakes. After securing the boat to the stakes, the crew went to sleep.

'When do we fish?' I asked the captain.

'When *pla tu* come,' he replied, and fell asleep himself.

It was cold and dark when I next awoke. Clouds hid the moon and, by the light of several torches, the boat was drawn through the narrow entrance to the trap. One end of a deep net was fastened to the entrance stake. The rest was gradually lowered and taken round the interior of the stockade until the ends overlapped. The top of the net carried floats and the bottom heavy rings through which there ran a draw-rope. By pulling on this rope the bottom of the net was closed and the *pla tu* had only one way of escape left: over the top of the net.

As the crew pulled in the net, the *pla tu* streaked through the water in tight shoals. Some leapt over the top like silver tiddly-winks, but hit the net as it rose higher and fell back. Soon the net was boiling with fish as they were scooped into the boat with long-handled landing nets. Eventually the net was empty, except for a tangle of spiny blue crabs clustered in the bottom. These were carefully removed and placed in a box by themselves. As we turned for the shore, the wind dropped and the men pulled on the heavy oars. I sat in the bow, looking down at the clear sea, a mat of weed spreading ahead. The weed as we approached resolved itself into a writhing cauldron of black-and-yellow banded sea snakes. The crew paid no attention, but rowed through them, spilling the short wriggling bodies off the oars.

'Are they dangerous?' I asked the captain.

'They poisonous,' he confirmed, 'but mouths too small to bite people.'

'Why don't the *pla tu* swim through the stake gaps? They're three feet wide in the avenue and six inches in the stockade.'

'It is their nature, for which we thankful. We make prayers and *pi* houses for getting fish.'

We spent our last day swimming and sunbathing. Our train was due at 4 a.m. next morning, and we needed to be on the platform ready to board, for it did not stop unless there were passengers. As we stood on the platform in the pre-dawn chill, the train puffed towards us from the distance and, as it approached the straight to Hua Hin, gathered speed. We waved frantically in vain. It tore past with a roar of smoke and steam and vanished down the line. In a panic, we rushed to the stationmaster. 'No need for worry,' he said. 'There will be another train at noon.'

'But it stops at every station.'

'You should have taken the express.'

'But it didn't stop!' we cried.

'Sometimes in hurry. Important person from palace on board no let stop.'

'What about the bank safes?' asked Harry Tudor.

'That's all right,' I said. 'Your bank has a spare set of keys for ours and we've a spare set for yours.'

'But yours are locked in our safe,' said Harry, 'and your accountant won't be able to get them because I have the key.'

'My God,' said Tom, 'it's the same with us.'

'Well,' I said, 'they can always borrow cash from the Bank of Siam for today.'

'That's the end of holidays for me,' said Harry miserably. 'They're terribly strict on the safe routine and this is my first job.'

'I'll take full responsibility,' I said. 'I'm the senior chap, and it wasn't our fault.'

When we did get back, I told the manager, Grant, that it had been a question of protocol and there was no way we could have stopped the train.

'Don't let it happen again,' he said sternly, but added, 'Thanks for the adjusting.'

Stuart recommended Tom to stay away from me. I was, it seemed, a bad influence.

When George Grant was transferred to Ipoh, his relief was Malcolm Oliver, a liberal manager who enjoyed the local society and, more importantly, gave me ten days' leave to visit Indo-China and our branch at Saigon, where my old friend Sandy Young was stationed. Since Silverthorne was in the middle of the summer recess, we set off together in his Rover, heading for Angkor Wat. We entered Indo-China through the French customs post made famous by the painter Henri 'Douanier' Rousseau, and reached Angkor at nightfall. Our lodgings were the Bungalow des Ruines, a rambling wooden building with thin walls. A French couple in the next room kept me awake with the regular creaking of their bed and the lady's ecstatic cries of, '*Non, non!*'

Next morning, after a French breakfast of coffee, croissants and black cherry jam, we set out to the ruins in bicycle-rickshaws, light wheelchairs towed by bicycles that were much faster than the bicycle trishaws of Bangkok. After a couple of miles the jungle gave way to open ground and there we saw Angkor Wat and its surrounding temples rising grey and timeless beyond a wide moat. We walked slowly down the broad causeway across the moat, silenced by the spectacle and feeling we were being watched. Indeed, we were. As we drew closer we saw on every tower four huge faces of Siva. They smiled with ironic humour at our pigmy approach. 'We will remain,' they said, 'but you will be scattered on the wind.'

The causeway balustrades ended in seven-headed cobras. *Apsaras*, lovely damsels with slim waists and full breasts, smiled from the walls, their clinging garments so delicately carved that they seemed naked. On the high stone walls bas-reliefs showed the activities of the forgotten citizens who mysteriously vanished eight centuries ago. On the sides of the temples more reliefs told the story of the *Ramayana*, that epic of the early men of Asia who were our ancestors.

Wishing to live for ever, the gods and demons gathered potent herbs from the forest and cast them into the sea. Then, using a mountain for a churn and the holy serpent Vasuki as a rope, they churned unceasingly until from the swirling waters rose the *apsaras*, the celestial dancers and courtesans of incredible beauty we had seen carved on the walls. Finally the liquor which was to give them eternal life formed on the surface. The gods and demons, forgetting their previous cooperation, began to fight for the precious elixir, and after an age of conflict the gods won. Such, in brief, was the story of the *Ramayana.*

The temple interiors were divided into long corridors and tiny rooms, their size governed by the fact that, like the ancient Egyptians, the Khmers never learnt to build an arch. Ceilings were limited to the length of the longest stone they could quarry. Windows were few and barred with slender stone columns. The floor was deep in dry bat droppings, which crumbled beneath our feet and filled the air with a heavy, musky smell. On the ceilings the bats clustered thickly. Along the corridors and in the rooms, statues of Buddha patiently awaited the return of their ancient worshippers, but the atmosphere was forbidding and I was glad to return to the sunshine and fresh green of the surrounding forest.

Silverthorne and I sat in the shade to enjoy the packed lunch and cold beer we had brought from the hotel. Several naked children peered at us from the shelter of the trees, then ran off, only to return later with bunches of wild flowers. Two of the older boys had cross-bows, which they loaded by standing on the bow and pulling the string back to the trigger latch with both hands. We gave them food, and they showed their skill by sinking the bolts deep into a tree trunk through a two-inch square of paper from our lunch box.

Next morning we drove to Saigon, the 'Paris of the East', a large modern city with tree-lined boulevards, cafés, fine buildings and vice in abundance. Walking along the rue Catinat, we were stalked by rickshaw coolies who whispered in sibilant tones, '*Madame Française Missou?' 'Madame Metisse?' 'Madame Annamite?' 'Boy Français?' 'Boy Annamite?'* 'Very hopefully Lussian schoolgirl?' And finally, '*Fume?'* Opium smoking was popular in Indo-China, and smoking parties were given in much the same way as cocktail parties, though the lights were lower and the guests closer to the floor. I heard various opinions about the effects. It was said to be an aphrodisiac for women, but to have the opposite effect on men. It made dull conversation seem brilliant. It brought happiness and calm to the worried mind.

Sandy Young escorted us to a local den, a wooden building with small dark rooms. Here we lay on hard couches while Annamite girls prepared the pipes. Opium for smoking was like thick black treacle. A bead of it was picked up on a steel needle and dipped and twirled until it was about the size of a small pea. This was toasted over a vegetable-oil lamp until it burnt with a bluish flame. The needle was then thrust through a small hole in the base of an inverted clay bowl fixed to a short, thick bamboo tube. The glowing bead adhered to the clay, the needle was withdrawn and the smoker placed his mouth over the end of the tube and inhaled deeply. Two or three lungfuls were sufficient to consume the bead. We smoked three pipes each, but try as I might I could discover no sensation. To draw in the smoke it was necessary to open the mouth as wide as the tube, this ensuring that the smoke passed directly into the lungs, not merely into the mouth, as in cigarette smoking. I had expected to splutter and cough at first, but the smoke, though slightly sickly and smelling of mimosa, had no irritant effect. It was more like scented steam.

We drove through a forest of tall trees to visit Dalat, the hill station for Saigon. Periodically clouds of white butterflies covered the windscreen and blocked the radiator, forcing us to stop from time to time and laboriously winkle out their dead bodies with a bent wire. Farther on we were held up by a fallen tree, which was being removed by Moi tribespeople with primitive axes. The women, naked above the waist, used baskets strapped to their backs to carry away debris from the road, while younger girls brought water for the men from the forest. It looked as if we would be there a couple of hours, so I left Long John with the car and wandered into the forest, where I came across the Moi's rough shelters near a small stream. Here girls were gathering water in earthenware pots while others bathed gleefully. Some wore a brief cloth skirt, but others went naked and seemed little embarrassed by my photography. As I discovered later, the French held beauty competitions for them in Saigon.

One evening after dinner we attended a *son et lumière* performance at the Bayon where a silhouette of enormous heads stood against the darkening sky. We sat in the front row and waited. After a time the silence was broken by tinkling Cambodian music. Suddenly arc lights threw shadows across the grey stone flags of the forecourt and picked out the doorways and pillars in sharp relief. The music grew quiet and mysterious. From the blackness of the centre doorway a fantastic creature sprang into the foreground: Hanuman, the monkey god. Moments later he was followed by an *apsara* looking as if she has just descended from her place in the temple of Angkor. Slowly she pivoted and made signs of appeal towards the door, from where two more identical and fascinating creatures sprang out lightly. All three held hands and again made anxious gestures towards the door, whereupon, like a river of gold and jewels, five, ten then twenty more streamed from the darkness as if all the treasures of Angkor were being released from centuries of immobility to reenact a fragment of the *Ramayana*. Undulating across the courtyard with scarcely visible steps, they went through the stylized movements of their ancient dance. Finally the music died away, the *apsaras* vanished and darkness reasserted itself. I still felt a sense of foreboding. How was it that this civilization had ended so suddenly eight centuries before while something very similar to it still flourished in Siam?

Loy Krathong, the 'Festival of Light', coincided with the news that I was to do a spell of relief duty in Ipoh before going on furlough. Loy Krathong was the most moving of all the country's festivals, *loy* meaning 'float' and a *krathong* being a small lotus-shaped boat made from a plantain leaf. In this was placed a candle, a stick of incense, a flower and a coin. The candles and incense were lit and the Siamese made a wish as they launched each tiny craft. Hua insisted that we should launch our *krathongs* together, and as we drove down to our *klong* we could see the moonlit waterways already dotted with flickering lights, each carrying the hopes and fears of its owner. The water spirits were honoured as the *krathongs* disappeared into the distance, bearing away the sins of the past year.

Our boatman was waiting and Hua had brought along two *krathongs*. We waited until we came to an empty stretch on the *klong* before lighting the candles and incense. Hua was unusually serious as she lowered her boat into the water. 'You go as *krathong* go,' she said, 'but I no forget you.'

I launched my frail craft and we watched in silence until the two drifted beyond our vision. 'Will you find another *nai* when I'm gone?' I asked.

'No, I work my hat shop. Is busy now.'

'Will you marry?' I asked.

'One day, maybe.'

I told her I was being sent to Ipoh.

'Yes, I known, then home to family. You will not forget real Bangkok?'

'I shall not forget you,' I said, 'and I hope you have great happiness in your life.'

'Hua always happy,' she said, giving me a hug and tossing her head back to look at me.

I shall miss real Bangkok very much, I thought. Hua had a strange aura, a natural warmth like sunshine, an undemanding acceptance of nature. She was practical. Her hat shop always came first.

Gunga Din I left to Tom, and Galloping Gold to Louise. Louise was to be courted by Pem, and would in due course marry him. I said goodbye to the Polo Club, and presented them with a brass foot rail for the bar. Little did I guess how Japanese jackboots would find it a convenient foot-rest in the not-far-distant future. I also said goodbye to the Japanese photographic shop at the bottom of the bank lane. Its genial proprietor, who had sold me my cameras and printed my pictures, would turn out to be a high-ranking Japanese who established his headquarters in my bank the moment the Japanese invaded. The interned Europeans were to come under the fatherly care of the consul-general, W.A.R. Wood, who happily survived the war and lived to be ninety-six in his beloved adopted land. Tom Hobbs was to make a daring escape by boat on the Mother of Waters to join the British troops in Burma. 'Long John' Silverthorne, alas, was destined to die.

14

Portentous Shadows

The KLM Dakota flew high above the glittering wats and followed the great river down to the Gulf of Siam where the giant fish traps looked from the air like hearts and arrows. It followed the palm-girt coastline of Malaya until we landed at Penang, where one of the bank's clerks was waiting to see me through customs. In no time we were speeding down a clean asphalt road on our way to Ipoh, the neat plantations of rubber trees and little villages of stilted houses looking fresh and trim after the friendly confusion, dirt and disarray of Bangkok.

At Ipoh George Grant welcomed me warmly. I had a feeling that he might have asked for me. He introduced me to the chief accountant, who asked me to take over cash so that the sub-accountant in charge could catch a boat that sailed the very next morning. 'How much is in the safe?' I asked.

'Over half a million Straits dollars.'

I felt uneasy. 'Don't you think I should check it?' I said.

'Oh, it gets surprise checks all the time,' said the chief accountant. 'It's OK. Other reliefs have accepted it.'

Recalling the empty ammunition boxes in the fort at Amritsar, I still felt uneasy. 'In that case, would you take over first and let me take over from you?' I asked.

The chief accountant went red in the face. 'I'm giving an order,' he said.

But by that stage I'd done twelve years on one leave and did not feel like taking risks at the last minute. All bank officers had identical powers of attorney for the bank. Mine was as good as his. 'In that case we'll have to cable London for authority,' I said.

'What do you mean?' he stuttered.

'I mean that I'm not taking over until I've checked the contents of the safe.'

The cashier was a pleasant, intelligent man, and we worked together quickly. I checked random bundles of notes and found nothing amiss, but still had an odd feeling that all was not well. Finally we came to the coin. The Straits dollar pieces were rolled in brown-paper tubes in hundreds. Unrolling the tight packages was tiresome, and then, of course, they had to be rerolled. I could see the cashier was unhappy. 'I'll only do random checks,' I promised.

We slit the paper tubes and the silver dollars spilled on to the table. After a while, I simply opened one end, content to see the silver dollar; but then my qualms returned and I went back a roll and tore off all the paper. Neatly packed in the middle between silver dollars at either end were copper coins. There was nothing else for it. The cashier and I had to go back to the beginning and open every roll of coin and check every bundle of notes. Afterwards I had the coins rerolled in clear cellophane.

During my six months at Ipoh, A.E. Evans of the Shell Company invited me to share his bungalow. He was known as 'Educated' Evans because he possessed a BA. He also had a dry sense of humour and was an admirable antidote to the colour-conscious European community, who lived in Malaya, I discovered, much as their counterparts did in Ceylon. But at least Ipoh had a flying club where I could spend many happy hours doing aerobatics; and I was to play my last game of rugby in a match between Perak and Penang.

Opium and sex were dispensed by government-controlled sources, and there was no romance in either. The European doctor who inspected the Ipoh brothel invited me to accompany him on one of his tours of duty. The girls 'worked' in small wooden cubicles, furnished with chair and bed and with ventilation slats reaching to the ceiling. Madame was a buxom Malay, who ran her establishment with a firm hand and a total absence of erotic frills. She produced her book and advised the doctor that all the girls were well and that a new girl had arrived. After she directed him to her cubicle, the doctor promptly went in, sat the girl on his knee and advised me to find one for myself. I had gone there hoping to learn what tests were carried out and what qualifications the girls required for the job, but the good doctor was caught up in his own experiment. I asked Madame whether people did not find the abrupt approach off-putting. 'No, no,' she said. 'Men only come for girl and that what gets.'

She beamed and offered me a cold beer from her ice-box. Eventually the doctor reappeared, but unfortunately slipped and grazed his shin on an open concrete sewer. Madame rushed to his aid and, quickly raising his trouser-leg above the torn skin, applied spittle.

Some miles away at Taiping there was, I discovered, a museum devoted to the Sakai aborigines, about whom I immediately wanted to know something more. I went to see the director, a Mr Noone (whose widow after his death married a man called Good and hence became known as 'Good Afternoon'). Mr Noone kindly arranged for me to visit as guest a Sakai encampment where a tribe of some forty members lived in a long communal shelter raised from the ground on five-foot piles. Each family had a partition to itself, and each kept a fire burning on an earthern hearth. Treasured possessions hung from the thatched roof – skins, hornbill skulls, dried fish, jawbones of animals, bamboo sections used as containers and cooking pots. The men wore loin-cloths and some had feathers or flowers stuck in their hair. The women wore brief skirts of a felt-like material made by beating the bark of the ipoh tree. The children went naked and were much loved, as indeed were the tribe's domestic animals. The first thing I saw when I arrived was a young woman suckling a child at one breast and a baby piglet at the other.

Around the camp rose the dual world of the jungle: above, in the tree-tops, a sunny sanctuary of chattering, singing life; below a silent world, dark and forbidding, where animals moved with stealthy caution, weaving their way through thick vegetation which threatened to suffocate everything by its rapid growth. Survival for the Sakai had been the discovery of the blow-pipe and poison dart. This simple but sophisticated weapon made them masters of their hazardous environ-ment. The seven- to eight-foot pipe was fashioned from a hollow, node-free species of bamboo to which nature had given a natural taper, like the choke in a shotgun barrel, which made for accuracy of aim. The eight- to eleven-inch dart was made from the stiff leaf-rib of the bertam palm, its point sharp and fire-hardened. The butt of the dart, which steadied it in flight, was made of the wood of the same palm. A small nick made below the point ensured that, if the shaft was broken off by a frantic animal, the poisoned point remained in the wound. A wad of palm down was placed behind the dart in the blow-pipe to prevent loss of air, and the dart was propelled by discharging the full capacity of the user's lungs into the breech of the blow-pipe. This gave a maximum range of some eighty yards, though most targets would be little more than thirty yards away. The poison was made from the sap of the ipoh tree, *Antiaris toxicaria*, or the ipoh creeper, *Strychnos tieute*, to which was added snake venom, scorpion stings, poisonous fish spines and other animal poisons. The ingredients were simmered to a treacly consistency and the dart points dipped in the brew and dried. Dipping was repeated until the desired strength was attained, the relative virulence then needing to be marked on the butt with dots, for too strong a dose in a small animal rendered it unfit for consumption. As it was, the area around a wound needed to be cut out immediately. Provided the skin was penetrated, the poison was deadly, and thick-skinned beasts could be killed by shooting them in the lip or eye. Small animals and birds died almost instantly, but larger animals took several minutes, according to the dose. In man, I was told, at first no pain was felt other than the wound. Then muscular spasms began, followed by vomiting and death, all in the space of a few minutes. The darts were carried in hollow reeds stowed in bamboo quivers, which also contained the down. The blow-pipe was carried for protection in a larger length of bamboo.

The chief and four members of the tribe led me into the jungle, slipping through the heavy undergrowth with uncanny silence and motioning to me to follow their example. I followed as silently as I could for about a mile, when all at once my guides vanished. I stopped and listened, utterly alone. There was no sound save for a chattering in the treetops. I looked down and saw, to my horror, a small snake looking at me, its tongue flickering, and at my feet a swarm of black leeches undulating towards my unprotected ankles. I had started to back away when I heard a sharp *ping*, like an airgun. The Sakai chief appeared, followed by the others, and I realized they had only ever been a few yards away from me. They pointed upwards. A monkey with her baby clinging to her swung from a high branch; another swing and her hold loosened. She fell to the ground, her baby still clinging but miraculously unhurt. The dart point was cut from the dying mother and the baby wrapped in a cloth to be taken back to camp.

After some minutes, another monkey appeared on a high branch. The chief squatted on his haunches, drawing in his breath until his ribs stood out. Placing his loaded blow-pipe to his mouth, he encircled the butt with his lips and took aim. His chest suddenly collapsed as the pent-up air rushed along the pipe; there was the same hollow *ping* and the monkey disappeared. We waited in silence until the chattering stopped; another minute and there was a dull thud to our right. The chief followed the sound and reappeared triumphantly holding a large male. Back at camp the baby was nursed by the children while the monkey carcases were cut up and cooked, hands and feet being regarded as special delicacies. Singed in the fire, they provided much joyful chewing.

Bamboo supplied almost everything that the tribe needed. I watched a comely mother sitting on the bamboo floor of her section of the long-house, heating a bamboo section on a fire of bamboo twigs. Steaming in the pot were bamboo shoots. That evening a tribal ritual was held: a calling up of their familiar spirits. The women sat at one end of the shelter, drumming out hollow disturbing sounds from wooden cylinders. The men moved round in a circle, beating themselves with bunches of leaves and making whistling noises by forcing air from their lips against their shoulders. Each Sakai had a familiar spirit, a thing of the jungle. It could be a tree, a bird, an animal that protected and guided him. After an hour, the men began to rotate as well as moving in a circle. Their movements grew faster and became blurred in the firelight. A man collapsed and lay motionless where he fell. One by one the others fell until the floor was covered with silent forms, except for two who failed to get a response and sat alone and withdrawn.

Another twenty minutes and one of the fallen men stirred and moved to his family hearth. Gradually the others woke, and soon the camp fell quiet. By morning, decisions would be made. Perhaps it would be a move to a new site. I had no idea what was going on in their minds, but their way of life struck me as remarkable. They enjoyed freedom, fraternity, equality, and were in tune with nature. Their poison also enabled them to take fish from the streams, including the trout with which Europeans had stocked the rivers for sport. Though they could kill with a scratch, murder was almost unknown among them. If there was a transgression of tribal law, such as a man going off with another man's wife, suitable recompense was agreed according to the length of time the wife was absent. It was considered a sin to mock animals, but not humans, since they could answer back.

Back at Ipoh my chief clerk asked me why I spent so much time with these low people, who were so stupid that they could not tell a lie.

That January in China, the Japanese made Pu Yi, the last Emperor of the Manchu Dynasty, the Emperor of Manchoukuo, which they had taken and occupied. War in the East was beginning to look a distinct possibility and the government gave notice that all British subjects suspected of being homosexual must return home. Homosexuals had been blackmailed during the First World War and were therefore considered a security risk in any potential conflict. About a hundred and fifty were involved, of whom only two fought their cases, and they both won. The remainder left, except for the bank's lawyer, who hanged himself from his ceiling fan. A month after this my leave came through and several eyebrows were raised as I bade farewell to the European community.

I had decided to fly home this time, and to break my journey in India to visit Kim. The KLM Dakota refuelled at Bangkok and Rangoon, and so brought me to Calcutta. Nostalgia engulfed me as I wandered through the bazaars with their familiar smells and sounds and the sacred cattle ruminating in the busy streets. In the evenings I was taken to the Saturday Club or dined at Firpos, where new bottles of Johnny Walker Black Label whisky and Napoleon brandy were left on each table for the diners to help themselves.

After a couple of days I caught the train to Lahore, and since I was on leave and could ignore the bank's edict of first-class travel, I travelled second. My fellow travellers were a retired American engine driver, a mullah and a Hindu businessman. The American was enjoying a life-long ambition to travel round the world on trains, and was delighted by the fact that the Indian Railways had given him a free pass on all their lines. The mullah was famous, and at each stop his followers brought him baskets of fruit and garlands of flowers, until the carriage overflowed. At midday the Hindu produced a hamper and offered us chapatties, curries and sweetmeats, while the mullah loaded us with fruit. In our closed compartment, all racial and spiritual differences were temporarily annulled and we ate together with goodwill.

The American said that his great wish was to see the Indian rope trick, and was disappointed when we confessed we had none of us witnessed it. I told him, however, that I did have with me a magic Indian key that might interest him. It was a very simple trick that, under oath never to reveal the secret, I had bought in Amritsar from a magician. I handed the American the key and told him to put his ring on its stem. He tried for some time and then said, 'It's impossible. I'm an engineer, and there's no way you can get that ring on the key.'

My other companions were equally unsuccessful. I took the key and instantly returned it to them with the ring on the stem. Now they tried to get it off, but this they also found impossible.

'It's my wedding ring,' said the burly American anxiously. 'I'll get killed by my wife if you can't get it off again.'

I took the key and handed him his ring released.

'Have you any more magic?' they asked.

Only the magic of India, I said, which teaches that all things divided into their smallest particles are the same thing, the Breath of God. We are all part of life, of our Creator – the train, the fruit, the food, ourselves. The mullah was silent, then he said, 'There is but one God, and one day all mankind will acknowledge this as you do.'

As the journey proceeded, I had been watching the familiar country scenes and was, with increasing anxiety, asking myself the old questions. Why had I not married Kim and stayed on? What fear stopped me? Now I wondered too if I was wise to be seeing her again. Next day, when we came to Amritsar and I saw that the station was unchanged, tears came to my eyes. As we drew into Lahore, Kim was waiting on the platform. She was wearing a pretty white dress and had put on a little weight. She gave me a big hug and a kiss. 'Oh, it's good to see you,' she said, 'but how thin you are. We must feed you up.'

Outside, she ushered me into a huge, gleaming American Buick. 'Now *I* can drive,' she laughed.

She and her husband had a suite in Faletti's Hotel and had booked a room for me, but her husband was on tour and so we had the place to ourselves. In her lounge I noticed a picture of myself on the piano. The next morning Allah Dad presented himself with his eldest son, having travelled from Amritsar to pay his respects. He wore a fine new *pugaree* and a new scarlet waistcoat. He looked healthy and vigorous. His false teeth were immaculate and I suspected that his spell in gaol in Ceylon might have weaned him off opium. We talked of the old days and once again parted sadly.

That evening Kim and I had dinner at our little Italian restaurant, which had grown by now to be rather grand. The proprietor remembered us and refused to take payment. 'You were my first customers,' he said. 'You brought me good fortune.'

We drove to Shahdara and entered through the side-gate to Jahangir's tomb. Around us roses and jasmine filled the air with perfume. We sat on the sarcophagus and clung to each other. On the marble I read again:

BE NOT DISAPPOINTED OF GOD'S MERCY.
HE SHALL FORGIVE YOUR SINS.
THE LIFE OF THIS WORLD IS BUT A BUBBLE OF VANITY.

The next day Kim saw me off on the train for Karachi. We had visited our old haunts, and remembered our joys and sorrows, but we had moved on, we were not the same people. Why was it so impossible to go back? What had changed in us? The answer came with the rhythm of the train's wheels. 'Too late, too late, too late,' they seemed to say. 'Time does not wait. There is no life save the present.' We could not turn back the clock, but I knew that we would always be a part of one another – that was something nothing could destroy.

The Dakota from Karachi carried thirty-four people but could not accept miscellaneous luggage. To make the best use of its limited space, each passenger was issued with two tough blue fibre suitcases. (I still have mine.) The small one fitted behind the seat and the large one was carried in the hold. The plane averaged 150 m.p.h. and covered about 600 miles between stops for fuel. Our first landing was at Djask, a village on the Persian Gulf, where Iranian officials stood in a row of bright uniforms to check our papers. Then, in the rest-house, we ate sweet pancakes and fish done in batter. After refuelling we flew over the gulf to Basra, below us the secret bays where pirates formerly hid their schooners. Soon the bays gave way to oil refineries. Surplus gas flared in the sand from depressions sited at safe distances from the gleaming storage tanks. The airport hotel was a modern glass and steel structure that contrasted sharply with the old city of Basra's narrow streets and date palms.

Next stop was Baghdad, a dream of golden domes and shining minarets, and after that we passed over the Dead Sea, the pilot flying low to give us a glimpse of the River Jordan and the Mount of Olives. In the waiting room at Lydda, I drank fresh orange juice at a table with Noël Coward and a young army officer with a neat moustache. They did not join our plane to Alexandria, where we were served strawberries and cream before crossing the Mediterranean at 14,000 feet to gain us a greater chance of making landfall should the engines fail. Small oxygen cylinders were brought round for passengers who had breathing problems at that altitude.

I was determined not to miss the chance of seeing Athens, but at once ran into trouble. I had no visa. 'You cannot land in Greece without a visa,' said the immigration official. 'You must continue your flight.'

As good fortune would have it, the plane had already left. They seized my passport but allowed me to go to a hotel late that night. No food was available and I could change no travellers' cheques until the banks opened the next day. I slept fitfully, but next morning, though breakfastless, was lucky to meet up with a small dapper American, John R. Reinhard, professor of literature at the University of

Philadelphia. He was just setting out for Delphi, and invited me to share his car. My host sat in front with the driver while I took a seat in the back. We drove towards Mount Parnassus, but by this point I felt overcome with hunger. I had noticed a small package in the corner, and opened it to reveal lettuce sandwiches in brown bread. Supposing it to be the driver's lunch packet, I ate one. It was delicious. I'll buy him a proper lunch, I said to myself, and finished the package. On Mount Parnassus I picked up a handful of snow, the first I had seen in six years. Then John said, 'I think I'll have my sandwiches now. I have a weak stomach and can't stand Greek food.'

What had I done, I agonized. How could I make recompense? I came out with the truth.

'But why did you eat my sandwiches?' John protested. 'Why did you do it? You seemed such a nice man.'

He was still perplexed by my behaviour when we arrived in Delphi. Our driver took us to a *taverna*, producing from the boot a guitar that he played with exuberance. Gradually John relaxed, and I persuaded him to join me in a bottle of retsina and a harmless lunch of bread and olives. The result was catastrophic. We both suffered intolerable cramps on the return journey. Fortunately our fellowship in disaster made him more sympathetic and, after guiding me round his favourite haunts in Athens, he presented me with a large volume he had written on medieval life. The sights he showed me included the cell where, according to legend, Socrates drank the hemlock and requested his friend Crito to sacrifice a white cock at the temple of Jupiter as a thanks offering for his recovery from the long disease of living.

Having decided to complete my journey home overland across Europe, I took the steamer *Andros* to Brindisi and the train to Rome. The Eternal City was agog for the Führer's historic visit to Il Duce, and the streets through which he was to pass were lined with braziers and flag poles. The houses had been repainted, and even the street surfaces were given a cobbled effect. It was a photographer's paradise. I took photograph after photograph, ending up with Mussolini's wedding-cake palace, whose guards had the new small rifles with short bayonets. A moment later three men in macintoshes surrounded me and demanded my papers.

'Who are you?' I asked.

'Special police,' they replied.

'Please show me your authority,' I countered.

They looked incredulous, but after some argument called over a policeman on point duty, who confirmed their identity. I told them that my passport was at my hotel, but they bundled me into a waiting black Fiat and took me to police HQ. In this gloomy building I was placed in a whitewashed cell with barred windows and given forms to fill in which required full family names going back for two generations as well as full details of my occupation and my reasons for being here. Eight hours later I was taken before the prefect. He was a dignified kindly man who, after a brief conversation, ordered my release.

Anxiously awaiting me at my hotel was Raftopoulos, a Greek whom I had met on the train from Brindisi. We had dinner together and he offered to show me the sights of Rome the following morning, and to protect me from the attentions of the plain-clothes branch. The next morning was cold, but a clear sky made it ideal for photography. While I waited for Raftopoulos I stood in a patch of sunlight alongside the hotel and began to feel warmer and glad to be alive on such a beautiful morning. Then a voice said, 'Your papers, please.'

Once again I found myself hemmed in by three macintoshed figures, but this time I had my passport ready.

'Why do you stand in one place?' they asked.

'I was warming myself in the sun and waiting for a friend who will be here at any moment.'

'You must come with us now,' said the leader.

An identical black Fiat drew up and, protesting loudly, I was taken to a different headquarters and asked to fill in the same forms as the day before. Six hours later I was taken to the district prefect, and to my relief it was the same man, who upbraided my captors and apologized. I returned to the hotel, where Raftopoulos was once again anxiously waiting, and although he did in the end show me the sights, they had lost much of their ancient majesty amid the nervous flutterings that heralded Hitler's visit.

Next day I took a train to Zürich. In Switzerland the officials were jolly, the sun shone and I boarded a train to Lenzerheide, where I had enjoyed my first winter sports with Uncle and Auntie MacCulloch. Elsi, the daughter of the house, who was keenly admired by the Chartered Bank boys, made up my room, which had a sunny balcony. The following day we walked together up through fields of gentians and crocuses until we reached the steep snow slopes. Then, using seal skins, we climbed to a level space where we opened our rucksacks and had a lunch of *Bunderfleisch*, garlic sausage, hard-boiled eggs and crunchy bread and butter washed down with red wine, followed by hot coffee from the Thermos.

It was hot in the sun and I stripped to the waist. The crisp bracing air flowed over my skin and the scent of pine filled my nostrils. I lay back on the warm rock and wondered why on earth I should ever return to the humid, sticky, disease-ridden Orient when I could stay here, run a *pension* and live like a king. I looked at Elsi, small, sturdy, flaxen-haired and apparently without a care in the world: a creature of the freedom of the mountain, lakes and valley, her own mistress, as good a skier as any man. Perhaps one day she would own the family hotel. 'I know what you're thinking,' said Elsi.

'What?' I asked, returning from my vision of the future.

'You're thinking, why don't I marry this nice Swiss girl and live here and run the hotel?' She laughed at the expression on my face. 'Lots of men come here who think the same. Tomorrow one comes. He is an advocate and very persistent, but I am not sure about him.'

'Why?' I asked.

'He's infatuated about me and terribly jealous, but he has some problems.'

'What sort of problems?' I asked.

'He's a fetishist. He can't make love unless I give him my panties so he can hold them over his face.'

'Well, that doesn't seem too difficult. They have to come off anyway.'

'Yes, but Freud says it is dangerous. His affections could easily turn away.'

'Why bother with him? There are plenty more men.'

'He showers me with gifts. He's very rich and important, and my parents think I should settle down.' She paused. 'I've had a very free life, you know,' she said, looking at me, 'and maybe they're right. He's coming tomorrow and he'll be terribly upset to find you here, but I'd like to know what you make of him.'

'I can easily put up in the village,' I offered. 'I wouldn't want to spoil anything.'

'No, I want you to stay, and so do my parents. We all want to see how he'll handle the situation.'

On Sunday morning I was breakfasting on the terrace: coffee, croissants and my favourite jam, black cherry. I had forgotten about the advocate when the terrace door swung sharply open and a heavily built, serious-looking man, about ten years my senior and with closely cropped hair, approached the table, stopped, clicked his heels and said, 'I have the honour to address Herr William MacQuitty?'

'Yes,' I said, offering him a seat.

'I have something to ask of you,' he said, sitting down heavily. 'I want you to leave at once. I am going to marry Fraüline Elsi and I do not wish her to be persecuted by the attentions of others.'

He trembled with emotion. Maybe it was hard for him to speak to me at all, I thought, but probably not. I did not reply. It seemed obvious that, as a welcome guest of the family and an old friend, I was hardly persecuting anyone.

'Your silence betrays you,' he declared. 'You must leave now or give me your word of honour that you will marry Elsi.'

In the background I could sense the family listening. 'I am sorry to disappoint you,' I said, 'but I have come here for a holiday, as I have done in the past. Whatever Elsi wishes to do is her affair.'

'Then we must fight a duel.'

'I am sorry to disappoint you again,' I said, 'but I am a Buddhist and am not allowed to fight duels, or for that matter anything else.'

'Then you are a coward,' he said.

'Yes,' I said, 'a coward, and a frightened one at that, though my fear is not of you, but of life.'

He gave me a bitter look. 'I will write to the directors of your bank and tell them the type of man you are,' he said before rising and striding indoors.

I went skiing alone, wondering what would happen next. The solitude of the mountains had grown less enjoyable. There were problems, it seemed, even in this orderly land. By the time I got back, the advocate had departed.

'What did you make of him?' asked Elsi. 'My family thought you were wonderful.'

'I thought he was difficult, but maybe all lawyers are. It's part of their profession. He doesn't have much of a sense of humour.'

'Swiss men don't have a sense of humour about marriage. A match is a question of position and wealth, and he has both. Of course, it is flattering to have a man of his standing infatuated with one.'

'Or perhaps,' I grinned, 'with one's panties.'

At the end of the week Elsi saw me off on my last lap for home.

The family were overjoyed at my return. My brother, now twenty-six, seemed closer to me. Father had weathered well, but Mother was looking tired. She was getting some help in the house from Sarah Collins, a warm-hearted girl from Ballina, County Mayo. Sarah, who was now one of the family, talked about Mayo, which I had walked through on my previous leave, and said I should see the Aran Isles, which had the finest scenery on the coast. It took me two weeks to bring my family up to date and visit all my old friends. The gap between them and myself had grown even wider. All were married and settled. I packed a rucksack and set off alone.

In Galway I took the ferry to Inishmore, the largest of the Aran Islands, and at the little harbour got a lift in a sidecar from Pat Mullen, father of Barbara, who later became the famous housekeeper Janet in the TV series, *Doctor Finlay's Casebook*. Pat took me straight to the cottage of Maggie Dirane, star of Robert Flaherty's film *Man of Aran*. 'The only place ye can stay,' he said.

Maggie, unspoiled by her film success, continued to live as she always had done. Food was cooked on the open hearth and the vegetables were from her garden, the loam for which was a mixture of seaweed and earth laid out on the hard rock. My bed seemed equally hard. Maggie was a strong, direct woman with a Madonna-like face. She woke me in the morning by pulling the bed-clothes off with a majestic gesture, only to reveal me stark naked. Startled, she covered her face and burst out laughing.

After breakfast I walked round the island to the cliff-top fort of Dun Aengus. On the overhanging cliff a boy sat with his feet dangling over the edge, fishing in the sea two hundred feet below. As I watched, he caught a big ling and nearly tumbled from his perilous perch in his effort to haul up the long line before the jerking fish dislodged the hook.

A mile farther on I came to a cottage that bore the inscription:

COME AND CONSULT THE GREAT ALCHEMIST
GOD BLESS DE VALERA. GOD SAVE IRELAND

Beneath the crude lettering, a bright green shamrock and a harp were painted on the uneven whitewashed wall. I knocked. A thin old man came to the door and looked up at me shrewdly.

'I want to know the secret of life,' I said. 'It seems to me that you may have the answer, living here amid the simple realities of nature.'

'Ah,' he replied, looking at me sharply, 'I am an alchemist. Give me silver and I will change it into gold.'

I handed him a silver florin (a two-shilling piece, or 20p in today's money). He took it carefully and placed it in a small earthenware pot that he sealed with some putty. 'You must return next year, when it will be ready,' he said, watching me closely.

'Can't you do it today?' I asked.

'No, no,' he said. 'There's a secret substance in the pot which cannot be disturbed. It would be most unlucky, terribly misfortunate for you and your family.'

Only nine more like me, I calculated, and he'll have a gold sovereign.

That night neighbours arrived with a fiddler and we sang old Irish songs. Then a dark-haired beauty danced 'The Blackbird', arms, head and shoulders still while her feet twinkled in intricate patterns. In the morning I had to waken myself. Maggie had gone down to the rocky shore to collect seaweed for her vegetable patch. Seaweed was used to eke out the small amounts of soil on the island and also burnt for iodine. The tiny community sold seed potatoes, livestock and knitted sweaters to pay for their tea and sugar. Those who wanted more from life departed for England or America.

In the bay I watched curraghs pulling out for the day's fishing. There were four or five men to a boat, three pulling two oars each and the others baiting and preparing the lines. The boats were made of tarred canvas skins stretched over a light wooden frame with a high prow for protection against the heavy Atlantic breakers. The fishermen never learnt to swim. 'The sea would not give up her fish to those who took advantage of her,' they said. They wore pampooties, soft shoes made of cow hide with the hair left on the outside to give them a better purchase on the slippery rocks.

I left Aran refreshed, my cares blown away by the Atlantic breezes. Aboard the SS *Dun Aengus*, steaming back to Galway Town, I found myself sitting beside de Valera's daughter. Unlike her famous father, she said little, perhaps worried about the terrible troubles brewing on the mainland.

Returned to Belfast, I exchanged the simple life for a new Ford V8. In this my brother James and I made a trip to the South of France, driving down the route Napoléon, staying at little hotels and enjoying the food and wine. I mentioned to him my periodic idea of finding a job at home. 'What about medicine?' he suggested. 'You've always been interested.'

'It takes seven years and I haven't your sort of brain. I'd be no good at all those examinations.'

We left it at that.

At Juan-les-Pins we met Hugh, a bronzed Englishman and an enthusiastic water-skier who was practising for a water-skiing tournament to be held the following week. James had to return to Oxford before the great day, but I stayed on to see Hugh make the best jump, whereupon, for some reason, he was disqualified. He promptly accused the judge, who had given the first prize to his own wife, of cheating. The furious judge as promptly challenged Hugh to a duel, which Hugh as promptly accepted, naming me to be his second. I was horrified. The judge's second, a swarthy lawyer, took my name and address and said he would call on me in the morning to arrange details.

Hugh turned out to be the black sheep of a family from whom he received a monthly allowance provided he stayed out of England. He was a splendid specimen, but had no knowledge of duelling. He had spent eleven years in France, his sole interest being to get the most for his allowance, at which he was remarkably skilful. He could barely read or write, but he spoke French fluently.

'You must write a letter to Madame apologizing for your behaviour and we will leave immediately,' I said.

'I can't do that,' he said. 'I have been insulted. I was the winner. I jumped farther.'

'There's no justice,' I said, 'but if you don't come now you may be killed, and in any case, I think there is a French law against duelling, so they will catch you either way, and then your happy life in France will be at an end.'

Eventually he gave in. 'You'll have to write the letter,' he said.

As soon as it was done we paid our bills, packed the car and, with some apprehension at the chance sighting of any *gendarme*, drove steadily westward. Hugh was an entertaining companion, his years in France having given him not only enormous knowledge of the country but an ability to find the best bargains. I asked him about his ambitions.

'I have only one,' he said. 'It is to find the girl of my dreams and marry her.'

'Tell me about her,' I said.

'She is petite, beautifully built, with long black hair, blue eyes, small breasts, but above all very strong and supple.'

'What about her mind?'

'She must be clever and wise. I have cunning, but I'm out of my depth with clever people. Apart from that, she must be passionately interested in food, wine and love-making.'

'Did you ever come close to finding her?'

'No. Once or twice I thought I had, but either something was missing or else they didn't like me.'

'Where do you look for her?'

'In the *maisons de plaisir*.'

I looked at him in astonishment. 'Surely you don't expect to find a wife in a whorehouse?'

'Why not? The girls are experienced and most of them want to settle down. They have to be good psychologists.'

'But won't they have had enough of sex? Why should they be passionate?'

'Ah,' he said knowingly, 'that's why they become prostitutes in the first place.'

'But people will look down on her,' I protested.

'I don't think so,' he said, looking serious. 'Mary Magdalen was a whore. People don't look down on her.'

Equipped with the official list of the 'Houses of Pleasure', we searched methodically through each establishment along our route –

'only looking', much to the annoyance of the Madames, but Hugh knew his rights.

We passed through Lourdes where, in 1858, the fourteen-year-old Bernadette Soubirous had visions of the Virgin Mary in the grotto with its underground spring; and where thousands of pilgrims had left their crutches as testimony to the miraculous healing powers of the waters. From there we went to Bordeaux, where Hugh took me to the famous Châpeau Fin restaurant and ordered a bottle of Haut Brion 1905.

'The year of your birth, Bill. This is a little thank-you dinner for being so kind to me.'

The wine was an excellent vintage and I tried to imagine the people who had harvested my birthday grapes. After dinner we went to see a travelling circus, whose main attraction was a Russian flying trapeze act. As the Russians entered the ring, Hugh grasped my arm. 'That's my girl,' he whispered.

A slender dark-haired girl stood between two muscular men. Her white leotard revealed a small but perfectly proportioned figure. After a brief bow, the three swarmed up the rope ladder leading to the platform.

'She may not have blue eyes,' I said.

'I know she has, and she has small breasts too. It's my girl.'

'You'll have to learn Russian,' I said.

Hugh paid no attention. His eyes never left the girl. The act was well done if not outstanding. No risks were taken, though the smooth precision of the trio brought rounds of applause. The act ended with the girl performing a double somersault and landing in the safety net.

'I'm going round to see her,' said Hugh, getting up out of his seat.

'Wait till after the Grand Finale,' I urged.

'No. I'm going now.'

'She's probably married to the catcher,' I said, trailing helplessly behind.

'She's my girl,' said Hugh. 'Wait here. I want to do this by myself.'

Fifteen minutes later he returned. 'She has got blue eyes,' he said.

'And the catcher?'

'The catcher is her father and the young man's her brother.'

'And the mother?'

'The mother died last year. They said if I liked I could help with their equipment. The man who did it had a row and left.'

'What happens next?'

'I'll stay with them. I will never leave her.'

We celebrated far into the night. Hugh was a changed man. It was a miracle, like those of Lourdes.

My mother was still tired. I asked our family doctor, Dr Campbell, what should be done. He recommended that I take her to Dr Abrahamson of Dublin, who was a fine diagnostician. Mother liked the idea. It would give her a holiday and she loved Dublin. Dr Abrahamson said it would be necessary for her to stay in the Portobello Nursing Home for a few days while he carried out several tests. Remembering my happy days at the Venture Club in London's Portobello Road, I hoped this was a good omen. After four days, Mother came out of the nursing home, but Dr Abrahamson asked me to see him first. 'I'm afraid I have bad news for you,' he said from behind the large desk in his consulting room. 'Your mother has an inoperable carcinoma of the oesophagus. She has less than a year to live, and it is likely to be an unpleasant death. The gullet becomes obstructed. She will need a good doctor and eventually a nurse.'

I looked at him, not knowing what to say. Eventually I asked, 'Are you going to tell my mother?'

'No,' he replied. 'That is why I asked you in first.'

'Should I tell her?'

'I recommend that she be left in ignorance. Do not deprive her of hope.'

Mother came in and stood very still. 'I hope I've been a good patient,' she said.

'Very good,' smiled Abrahamson.

'What are you prescribing for me?' she asked.

'No medicine, but you should take things more easily and avoid tiring yourself. We are all getting older.'

'Is there any special diet?'

'No,' he said. 'You will be glad to hear that you may eat anything you wish, anything that you enjoy and that agrees with you.'

Mother thanked him for all his care and consideration, and then we drove to St Steven's Green and walked to the little lake where she had taken me as a child to feed the ducks. A new generation of children were feeding them as we stood and watched in the autumn sunshine.

'What a kindly man he was,' she said. 'Isn't it wonderful that I don't have to do anything difficult or take some horrible medicine?'

I said yes, and had to make every effort to hold back the tears as we strolled to the little stone bridge where, as a child, I had thrown pennies into the water to ensure my return one day.

When we arrived home I told my brother, but we decided against telling Father for the time being. He was closest to her and would have the most difficulty in playing a part. The time had come for me to return to the East. My posting was to Shanghai, so at last I would see China. I sought out Beaky Duncan to make a point of explaining to him the family circumstances, and he said he saw no problem about the bank allowing compassionate leave for me to be with my mother at the end. I arranged with Dr Campbell that he would cable me in good time.

'I feel much better since we went to Dublin,' said Mother as she kissed me goodbye.

'I'll see you again soon,' I said. 'It won't be so long as the last time,' and hurried to the waiting car.

15

April Fool?

I stood in my favourite place on the boat, looking down at the white bow waves as the SS *Chitral* thrust her way through the China Sea. All at once the cascading white was stained with yellow. Seventy miles from its mouth, the Yangtze River had come to meet us.

In 1842, Shanghai, the largest city in China, had been opened to foreign trade by the Treaty of Nanking. Fourteen years later, the Chartered Bank was built on the bund of the Whangpoo, a tributary of the Yangtze up which the *Chitral* now steamed before anchoring in mid-stream. Ian Pemberton, there as if fated to meet me, whisked me through customs. Along the quay from the *Chitral* another ship was unloading Jewish refugees from Germany.

'Thousands arrive every month,' said Pem. 'Shanghai is bursting with European refugees quite apart from Chinese fleeing the war and Chiang Kai-shek's "scorched earth" policy. The poverty's terrible. Distinguished foreign doctors give consultations for a few dollars. The Jews are crammed into empty schools and are given two bowls of soup a day. The Chinese are worse off, living in makeshift shelters. Hundreds die each day and are picked up by municipal trucks and cremated.'

We drove along the bund, passing rolls of barbed wire and soldiers with rifles and then the ornate entrance to the Chartered Bank, known locally as the 'Mac-ka-lee' bank after its first manager, John Mackeller. Only a few hundred yards off, the Japanese flagship

Idzumo lay at anchor. We left the International Settlement, crossed into the French Concession and finally turned into a large house, No. 7 Tunsin Road. 'Once it was in the country,' said Pem, 'but Shanghai has expanded.'

Chinese servants opened the massive front door, revealing a large hall leading to a comfortable lounge where a coal fire blazed in an open hearth. We went through to the back where, on a well-tended lawn, a Saluki coursed, his long hair streaming in the wind. 'That's Ali Baba,' explained Pem, and the dog, at the sound of his name, stopped his whirlwind circling and nuzzled his long cold nose into my hand.

The other members of the mess followed us into the garden, and so I met Francis Warburton, a jolly chartered accountant who played squash and had a twenty-five-ton yacht anchored near the *Idzumo*; John Rudgard, an MA of Pembroke, Cambridge, a scratch golfer and a mining engineer who had been blind in one eye from birth; and a Yorkshireman, Frank Iken, an exchange broker and violinist. It was to make a pleasant change from my usual chummeries, which had tended to contain only bank members and shop talk. My Chinese boy – all male servants in China being called 'boys' even by the Chinese – skilfully introduced me to my new country. In China you belonged to your possessions. I belong to No. 7 Tunsin and whatever things I had there. Nothing belonged to me. Suits were given numbers, No. 1 being evening dress and so on. The International Settlement (formerly the British and American Concessions) and the French Concession formed a multinational, sophisticated society isolated in a war that the Japanese waged without mercy.

At the time when I arrived, Shanghai contained about four million Chinese, 60,000 foreigners and more than 300,000 well-equipped troops of the Japanese forces of occupation. The Japanese had installed puppet authorities to control the city, but many Chinese who accepted these positions were assassinated by loyalists. Few lord mayors lived longer than their inaugural banquets, and one who had hoped to avoid such a fate by arriving incognito, failed even to alight. He had been knifed through the rickshaw's canvas back. Japanese barricades hemmed in the Westerners' areas, with the exception of the waterfront, which was kept open by British, American and French naval units. This created intolerable frustrations for the Japanese, who watched rich trade passing beyond their control while they were bombarded by streams of criticism from the free local and international press.

It might have been thought that the Japanese, with the reporters of the world on their doorstep, would have sought to present themselves in as good a light as possible. No such concern seemed to trouble them; or perhaps they thought their behaviour exemplary. The catalogue of atrocities was endless. One revelation was that Japanese officers were ordering young recruits to bayonet the unarmed Chinese prisoners who wandered 'free range' within the confines of Shanghai prison yard: 'Good bayonet practice on live targets.' Japanese soldiers flung people from the Garden Bridge into the Soo Chow Creek while soldiers of the Seaforth Highlanders watched in helpless fury from the International Settlement end. Other Chinese were lashed to trees with barbed wire and left to die. The foreigners were outraged, but had no power to intervene (and eventually, of course, were to suffer in their turn). It perplexed me that such a cultivated race as the Japanese could be so barbaric. Much of it seemed to lie in their contempt for prisoners, for they regarded suicide as preferable to being taken alive.

Meanwhile Chinese execution squads roamed the streets, and looters or anyone who broke regulations received summary justice. Men were beheaded kneeling, a thin noose being passed round the victim's head and between his teeth. Two assistants then held his arms back while a third pulled on the rope, stretching his neck for the executioner's heavy chopper. It looked dreadful, but at least it was quick and was said to be painless. Sometimes as many as twenty men were lined up waiting. Women were garrotted sitting on the ground, their backs to a wooden post with a hole in it. A loop of cord was passed through the hole and round the woman's neck, and the executioner inserted a stick through the other end of the loop and twisted it until the victim was strangled. Payment by a relative or friend ensured a more rapid dispatch. A common sentence, however, involved a far slower death. The offender was placed in a tall wooden cage and suspended from a wooden collar that fitted round the neck. With his hands manacled behind his back, his only relief was to stand on tip-toe on flat floor slats to reduce the weigh on his chin and skull and ease his breathing. After a day or two, as the body stretched, an official would remove a slat, thus maintaining the tension. A notice attached to the cage described the crime, but the felons themselves could not speak. Only their eyes showed they were still alive.

Despite the surrounding horrors – or perhaps because of them – life in Shanghai was a succession of sports, parties, dances, night clubs and riotous living. It had become the world's most sinful city. The atmosphere was electric. There was no time to lose. It was later than we thought. White Russian refugees provided talented musicians and glorious hostesses for the innumerable night clubs, among which my personal favourite was DD's, which had a brilliant pianist and excellent food. Its speciality was a cube of steak impaled on a sabre, broiled over a charcoal fire, *flambé*ed with brandy and brought to the table with enormous panache by a Cossack in full uniform. The Sun Ya, in Nanking Road, served some of the finest food in China. At the Del Monte, a large dance-hall, clients were kept happy by taxi-dancers till dawn summoned them back to work.

At my first dinner party I found myself sitting between an attractive American woman and a pretty Russian girl with stars sparkling in her fair hair. The American talked about painting, and I asked if she did any painting herself. 'Sure do,' she said, 'but I use human canvases.'

'What?' I asked.

'I'm an embalmer,' she explained. 'I worked in the cosmetic section at Forest Lawn in Los Angeles, but I can make much more here. None of the Chinese want their dear departed burnt, so they have them embalmed, and those who can afford it have them sent to relatives abroad.'

'How's it done?' I asked.

'Promise not to tell. The Chinese copy everything, but I think I'm safe because they don't like touching corpses.' As she continued, it was clear she was an enthusiast for her vocation. 'I make people look twenty years younger. I inject paraffin wax under the skin and smooth away the wrinkles. Wadding fills the sunken cheeks and make-up does the rest.'

'But what about preservation for the long journey to Europe or the States?'

'Simple. I introduce embalming fluid into a vein under the left arm and the body fluids are driven out through an artery opened under the right arm.'

At this stage the pretty Russian, whose name was Sonya, asked what we were talking about. 'Painting,' I said. 'You have splendid collections in Leningrad at the Hermitage.'

Instantly her eyes filled with tears. 'I shall never see Russia again,' she said. And then, as instantly, her face lit up again and she was filled with high spirits and animation.

After dinner we crowded into a taxi, ninepence for any journey – distances were short inside the perimeter. Sonya sat herself on my knee and lost not a moment in kissing me passionately in the darkness. When we got to DD's she apologized. 'My fiancée was killed a year ago. Now I am trapped here, and when the Japanese take Shanghai, I am doomed, like all other people with no passport.'

On Sunday she took me to the Russian Orthodox church, whose impressive ritual with gorgeous vestments and magnificent chants still seemed an oasis of faith. Outside I noticed a small parcel done up in matting, and curiously undid the string. Inside lay the body of a little girl. 'Leave it,' said Sonya. 'The truck will come tonight.'

I also joined some of the establishment clubs, and at the Shanghai Club drank at the longest bar in the world. I rode with the Shanghai Hunt on a stocky Mongolian pony called Flocky, which had a large identity mark cut out of one ear. Members turned out in full hunting gear to follow a paper trail across all sorts of obstacles. Sometimes they took short cuts over carefully tended vegetable patches, to the rage of Chinese farmers, who retaliated by hurling dippers of human fertilizer at any rider who came within range. The following day the hunt secretary would pay up compensation for any damage.

Whenever I could get away, I rode Flocky into the unoccupied countryside, which was grey, flat and featureless except for thousands of huge wooden coffins sprinkled across its surface. Some were enclosed in little houses with gaily coloured tile roofs; others had collapsed, revealing the skeleton occupant. Farther on, a pillar of smoke rose from a walled compound, and whenever I drew close to it I was aware of a smell that was distinctly reminiscent of the ghats at Benares. It was the cremation ground for Shanghai. In more ordered times, burial sites had been carefully chosen by geomancers. Now mass cremation was the only solution to the terrible harvest of mortality.

Inside the cremation ground a stack of bodies, five hundred or more at a time, would be piled in a rectangle of rough coffins, though most corpses arrived uncoffined. Some were half-clothed, and many small children were naked. A burly Chinese foreman encouraged his conflagration to get going with ladles of kerosene oil, replacing fallen bodies with a sturdy pitchfork. As the flames rose, the half-frozen bodies produced alarming movements and sounds as gasses expanded by the heat forced a passage through their throats. From time to time the dead moved and an arm or a leg made a sudden gesture. Even more dramatic was the emergence of a white skull as the wind whipped off a blackened mask of burnt skin.

Once he was sure the pyre was well alight, the foreman sat and ate his bowl of rice, protected from the bitter weather by the warmth of the human bonfire.

In 1938 the Japanese gave the Federal Reserve Bank of North China the sole right to issue banknotes, intending by this ruse to raid the foreign exchange reserves of the Chinese government. The Chinese government promptly devalued the national dollar from 1s. 2d. (about 6p) to 8d. (just under 3½p). The courageous printer of the new issue designed a figure of Confucius making a rude gesture with his fingers, which went unnoticed by the Japanese but served as a warning for the Chinese. As soon as the Japanese realized what had happened, they cut off the brave printer's head.

My first job with my colleagues each morning was to sign several hundred of our own Chartered Bank notes. These were legal tender, and eagerly sought by the Chinese, who hoarded them against the day when the Japanese left. Another task was to take over the P&O Bank, which the Chartered Bank had bought, and to try to persuade its customers to transfer their accounts to us. The Chinese clerks were helpful, but terrified at the prospect of losing their employment. Two of the European staff came to join us.

'Face' is the most important single issue in China, and no one should be allowed to lose it. The direct rebukes that Europeans levelled at each other and their servants struck the Chinese as deeply shocking. My desk servant in the bank was hopelessly slow, the simplest task too much for him. At last I decided to make a change and sacked him. The chief clerk came to me at once. 'Please keep Wang Fu,' he said. 'I will go in his place.'

Such altruism was not uncommon in China. Even a condemned man could sometimes be reprieved if another was willing to be executed in his place.

'But you are first class,' I told the chief clerk, 'and Wang is unable to carry out the simplest duty. Why should I keep him and lose you?'

'Sir, if you break his rice bowl he will never replace it, while I can find other work.'

'Perhaps,' I suggested, 'you could arrange for his transfer to some other position.'

'This I can do,' he said, 'and if you will be so kind, it will appear to be promotion.'

During my walks I noticed that most shops had humble exteriors. This was done deliberately to assure customers that their money was not being wasted on inessentials that increased the price of merchandise. Every available vacant space between the shops and housing was occupied by Chinese refugees who built crude shelters out of old mats and discarded timber. Here they lived with their families and, like Irish tinkers, tried to produce something to sell. Metal advertising signs were stolen and cut and hammered into trays, boxes and roofing. Paper was used for insulating slippers, tunic padding or, if plain on one side, for writing paper. Cartons, wrapping paper and newspapers helped to keep out the bitter cold. In the midst of battle the thrifty Chinese collected everything left over: empty shell cases, ammo boxes, anything unguarded. There was no waste. The Sino-

Japanese war must have left the least litter in history. Boy Scouts charged a dollar a head to retrieve the wounded, and sampan coolies made even more ferrying people across the Soo Chow Creek to the safety of the International Settlement.

I used the bank launch to explore the Whangpoo. Past the creek the *Idzumo* loomed grey and menacing, her guns trained across the International Settlement. In 1937 she had been attacked by a Chinese plane carrying a huge bomb. Heavy anti-aircraft fire unfortunately deflected the bomber's aim and the 800-pound bomb fell short, exploding amid the crowd who came to watch the spectacle and killing and wounding 6,000.

Soon I left the tall buildings behind and arrived at the Ordure Quay, where the meticulously collected night soil of the city was loaded into barges for distribution to outlying farms. There were no containers. The excrement was sloshed in from the carts and smelt to high heaven. This splendid product had enabled Chinese farmers to grow rice crops from the same fields for thousands of years – the finest land conservation scheme known to history, everything returned to the good earth.

Beyond the Ordure Quay, the city water works were sited a few feet above the filthy river. Farther on still lay ice farms, small squares of land, flooded in winter, from which blocks of ice were cut and stored in straw-lined pits for summer.

St Patrick's Day being widely celebrated in Shanghai, I invited friends to join me for dinner at the French Club. I ordered Bushmills whiskey and the French chef offered to make Irish stew. I had white carnations dyed green for the centre-piece and was looking forward to a jolly evening. On St Patrick's morn, I was woken by my boy holding a telegram. It was from Dr Campbell to say that my mother had only a few weeks to live. At once I cabled Beaky Duncan to request my compassionate leave and, to make doubly sure, I got 'Hoppy' Hopkins, our manager, to add that he could spare me as he now had additional staff from the P&O bank.

The party was a great success, and although I was saddened by the news, I felt relieved that I would soon be home again. Next morning a reply arrived from head office: 'Re. your telegram no. 5 regret cannot accede to request re. W.B. MacQuitty.'

'I'm very sorry, Bill,' said Hoppy. 'There's no way round the board's decision.'

'I need to think about this,' I said.

I went out of the bank, stood on the bund and gazed down into the brown flood that linked me with Bangor Bay. Fearful but in no doubt, I went back to Hoppy. 'I've decided to resign,' I said.

He tried to dissuade me. 'Don't be hasty. Sleep on it.'

'I've made up my mind,' I said.

'You're absolutely determined?' he asked.

'Yes,' I said, 'absolutely.'

He summoned the chief clerk. 'Arrange for Mr MacQuitty to catch the first steamer to Dairen and book him on the Trans-Siberian Express for London.'

I thanked Hoppy and walked out with the chief clerk. 'Last time we spoke it was about Wang Fu leaving the bank. Now I am the one to leave.'

He looked at me with his usual serious expression. 'A person's treasure is where his heart lies,' he said.

My friends thought I had overreacted. I could tell from their expressions that I had diminished the importance of my job, and by inference theirs as well. Pem was sympathetic and helpful, taking charge of my possessions, which he would send on by steamer. I said goodbye to the staff, who were also clearly concerned at a resignation that, with a pension due in only four years, cast doubts on the value of sixteen years' service in the bank.

The SS *Tsingtao Maru* was to sail from Whangpoo dock. The following morning I gave Ali Baba a final pat, the rest of the chummery having already left for work. With only two suitcases for luggage, I settled into my taxi and the boys bowed politely. At the Garden Bridge a Seaforth sergeant said, 'The Japs'll no' allow a Chinese to cross today.'

'What'll I do?'

'Put him under the back seat and drive over yersel', man.'

'Can you get back to the Settlement all right?' I asked the driver.

'OK, sir,' he grinned.

At the dock I paid my driver and added danger money. He seemed happy as he left me. In spite of the war, gay streamers linked the *Tsingtao Maru*'s passengers with friends on the shore. The siren screamed, the streamers lengthened and broke as we headed towards the Yangtze. Our first port of call was Tsingtao, where 900 men and women labourers were herded on to the foredeck. Among the throng were babies and children whose mothers struggled to prevent them being crushed. The deck was soon crowded, but still they came, clutching pathetically small bundles, until packed in a solid mass, bulwark to bulwark, unable to sit or even move. Mercifully the twenty-four-hour voyage to Dairen was completed in a flat calm.

At Dairen I passed through the first of the eight customs posts separating me from Ireland. A heavily braided official requested, 'Exposure of tobacco,' and rolled each of my ten cigarettes across his bright-violet customs stamps. From the customs I went to the Manchoukuo Foreign Office, where a serious Japanese young woman clerk helped me to fill in visa forms. Since the Asia Express for Manchuli did not leave until the following morning, I got a room at the Yamato Hotel and, after dinner, hired a taxi to show me the sights. The city turned out to be deserted, and the glare of the taxi's strong cab light made it difficult to see out of the windows. I asked the driver to switch the light off, but, he explained, it was police orders – to prevent immoralities. The contrast with Shanghai was total.

Next day, on the Asia Express, the pride of Manchoukuo, I managed to get a seat in the observation car. It contained an elaborate writing desk with pens, paper and unspillable ink, though the jolting of the train made writing impossible, and so I confined myself to watching Manchoukuo unfold before me. We passed Mukden and Hainking, the new capital, crossed the Sungari River and pulled into Harbin as night fell. The station was crowded with Japanese soldiers and sailors, the latter looking absurdly young, with round shining faces and spick and span uniforms. The soldiers, by contrast, were dirty, exhausted and unhappy. They combated the bitter cold with fur caps and coats, balaclava helmets and heavy gloves. Socks protected the muzzles of their rifles.

I pushed my way through the hostile steaming mass and gradually reached the passport office where, no aid forthcoming from antagonistic officials, I struggled through an incomprehensible maze of inquiries and filled up complicated forms in triplicate. After a frustrating two-hour wait, an official pompously condescended to stamp the forms and I was able to escape to a heavily ornate hotel. Here I was given slippers, a kimono and a hot tub, for which ceremony at least the Japanese were to be warmly congratulated.

Harbin was the last opportunity to stock up for the journey, but all I was able to buy was some dried fruit and two bottles of Johnny Walker Black Label. From Harbin to Manchuli, where we would join the Trans-Siberian Express, took another twenty-four hours. The barren steppes we passed through were brightened from time to time by herds of wild ponies. Stocky, shaggy animals like Flocky, they galloped beside the train for miles at a time. I wondered how they survived. The ground was covered with frozen snow and there was not a blade of grass in sight.

Manchuli lay lonely and deserted, lifeless in the cold grey dawn amid a tangle of railway lines. We waited in our warm carriage for something to happen. Eventually a door in one of the station buildings opened and a stream of shivering porters emerged to carry our luggage to the customs shed. The Chinese have a saying: when it is hot, everyone is hot, but when it is cold, only the poor are cold. Now it was our turn to stamp our feet on the snow-covered tracks and slap our sides to try to keep our circulations going. At length the customs officials arrived. Everything was opened, books were examined. My negatives were taken out of their envelopes and held up to the light. Finally our luggage was put aboard the Trans-Siberian Express, which awaited us on the other side of the station.

Imagining that the broadest gauge in the world would carry a truly majestic locomotive with matching rolling stock, I was disappointed to see that the train consisted of eight dilapidated coaches drawn by a wood-burning locomotive with a big smoke stack. My coach was an ancient Cook's wagon-lit, with its brass boxes for oil lamps still intact, though the lamps themselves had been replaced by electric bulbs. There were eight two-berth compartments and one small hand-basin to every two compartments. At either end of the coach was a lavatory. There was also a boiler to heat the carriages, and a small shower.

The *provodnik*, our car attendant, handed us brown-paper forms containing the regulations for passengers proceeding through the USSR with transit visas. Stays caused by calamities were, we read, permitted for twenty-four hours, but after that passengers must report to the OGPU. Gradually we sorted ourselves out and carefully stowed our belongings. I took a final stroll to stretch my legs before the ten-day journey started, but just as I reached the end of the platform, the whistle blew and, with clouds of steam hissing from the engine, the train began to move. Taking no chances. I hopped into the first open carriage and laboriously made my way back to my compartment through a sprawling jumble of hard-class travellers clustered on wooden benches. I had just seated myself exhausted when the train stopped at Otpor and gruff Russians in heavy boots and tunics burst in, seized our carefully placed luggage and triumphantly carried it to the Russian customs at eightpence a piece, irrespective of size. Hastily I gathered up my briefcase, rug and coat, narrowly forestalling the intentions of a bearded giant.

The customs hall was large and well lit. The walls had a pair of life-sized pictures of Lenin and Stalin and an abundance of red flags. My typewriter and camera caused the officials consternation, and four of them quickly crowded around. Time was no object. Everything was opened and questioned, books were read. Currency, travellers' cheques, valuables were all entered in a large ledger. Baggage not wanted on the journey was sealed, my passport, typewriter and camera taken away. They would, I was assured, be returned to me when I left Russia. My photographs intrigued the inspector, who asked politely if I'd allow him to have one. I said I'd be delighted, and with no hesitation he chose Maggie Dirane bending over a kettle on her open fire in Inishmore, Aran. It will be used for propaganda, I thought: how the poor live under their capitalist masters.

Hours later, the fatiguing ordeal over, we returned to the relative comfort of our compartments, only to find that the porters, unable to read the labels, had dumped the baggage indiscriminately. As we gazed in dismay at the confusion, the whistle blew and the train jolted into movement, an event accompanied by a sudden outburst of wild Caucasian music. The music swelled ever louder until the carriage vibrated with sound, and thereafter, ingeniously piped along the train, it continued every day from morning till night.

My compartment, at the end of the coach, contained upper and lower bunks, a small table at the window, and a facing chair on which sat my travelling companion, Captain Croft, a China coast pilot. The captain had, as an old China hand, done the journey many times. He suggested we ought to be prompt about going to the dining car at the rear of the train. 'Best to get in early before the good dishes vanish,' he advised.

The head waiter was a buxom girl in her twenties, her No. 2 a cheerful balding man of about fifty, who did not seem to resent being bossed by a girl. I was not surprised when I noticed him fondling her bottom in the galley. Neither of them spoke English. As the captain had foretold, many items were *nyet*, but we made a good meal of black bread, strong borsch with sausage and sour cream, and a Caucasian mutton *shashlyk*. The beer was good, though stocks soon ran dry, and the champagne cheap if frequently flat, for cork was scarce in the USSR and the corks to the bottles less than an inch long. There was also caviare, fresh and pressed, at five and six roubles respectively. The most expensive main dish was our *shashlyk* at seven roubles. As a matter of historical interest, including sleepers, meals coupons for Russia, two sea passages, the whole journey lasting from 18 March to 1 April, came to £39 16s. 2d. (£39.81).

Our first stop after the customs was Karimskaya, where the line from Vladivostok joined the main Siberian route. We descended the high steps of the carriage on to the low wooden platform, thankful to stretch our legs. The main feature of the station, as with every station along the route, were the innumerable statues, busts, paintings and photographs of Lenin and Stalin. No room was too humble to miss their presence. Even the engine driver's cab had two stoutly framed photographs. Next in popularity came the Red Flag, which, worn and faded, fluttered bravely from every vantage point.

Everyone headed for the large buffet, unheated except for its heavily muffled humans and great steaming samovar. Food was scarce. Black bread and a few slices of fat pork rested on the stained counter. 'In the old days,' Croft told me, 'the peasants brought food to the train – roast chickens, hard-boiled eggs, ham, different kinds of bread and cake. It was good business for them.'

Two gong strokes warned us to look sharp and get aboard, for Russian engine drivers were punished for unpunctuality and invariably departed on time. One elderly American lady had great difficulty in climbing the high steps and stood helplessly as the train began to move. Before we could do anything to assist, a Russian colonel leapt down and swept her on board with gallant efficiency.

On the third day I explored the train. After the first category compartments came soft class: four berths, well upholstered and roomy but without bedding or toilets. No separation was made for the sexes, and a missionary lady returning to Scotland after thirty years in China conducted a long battle with the *provodnik* to find her a carriage without men. Hard class was bare boards, but bedding could be hired for one rouble and another rouble for each time it was changed. All class distinctions vanished in the dining room, where the same food was served to everyone.

From time to time the Intourist official asked if we had any complaints, and whatever comment we made received stock answers combined with straight denials.

'This butter is rancid.'

'It is excellent butter. Russian farmers produce the finest dairy produce in the world.'

'The train is very slow' – we averaged 22 m.p.h.

'It is very rapid, the finest train in Russian and the longest railway in the world. Moreover, it carries four times more traffic than European railways.'

'Why is it so cold? Why does the *provodnik* allow the fire to go out?' – we engaged in a constant row with the man to get him to do his job.

'The train is warm.'

In fact the Intourist official had no control over the *provodnik*, but then no one seemed to have any direct control over anything in Russia. Everything must be passed to a higher authority.

As the days of the journey passed, the Russian colonel who had rescued the American lady invited me to a game of chess. Although we had no language communication, we enjoyed playing and drank one another's health in champagne. We were pretty evenly matched, though I could see he thought some of my moves strange. Another person whom I met was a Dr Johanna Brandt, a cancer specialist from South Africa. When I told her about my mother she said, 'We are experimenting at the moment with a diet of grapes or grape-juice. We believe that it inhibits the wild cells while nourishing the normal cells. It is obviously too late to cure your mother, but it might give her some relief.'

I thanked her and said I would try it, though privately wondered whether this mightn't be some sort of promotion for the South African grape trade.

At Novosibirsk, the youngest city in Siberia, founded in 1893 with the construction of the railway, we came to a stop alongside a long freight train of box cars. Each car had a small heavily barred window cut out of the top section, and, as I gazed, a jumble of pallid faces rose behind the bars. When they saw me smoking, they made gestures. I passed across a packet of cigarettes that was swiftly and skilfully drawn through the bars. Suddenly there were loud shouts of, '*Nyet, nyet, nyet!*' Between the trains heavily muffled guards ran towards me, rifles with fixed bayonets at the ready. I slammed the window shut and took refuge in the next compartment, the sole occupant of which was the American consul, F.R. Engdahl, who had been observing the scene. Within a few moments a man dressed in black furs and ostentatiously carrying a pair of handcuffs mounted guard outside the door and did not leave his post until we reached the next station.

We passed many of these trains, which, Engdahl explained, were transporting prisoners to vast camps in Siberia, where several millions worked on sparse rations until they died. Many in fact, he said, died in the unheated trains on the journeys to the camps, which could take weeks. When we asked the Intourist official what he thought of this, he replied, 'The prisoners are well treated. They have plenty of food and sufficient heating, but also they are wicked men and deserve punishment.'

As we approached Omsk, other long trains dragged past us, this time hauling flat-cars of tractors, reapers and binders, harvesters and other equipment for the vast communal farms. Your peasant, the Intourist official explained, was a lazy fellow, and new legislation required each district to be self-supporting. After Omsk we came to the fertile black-soil belt where patches of snow lay like cotton wool on a carpet of coal dust. Soon we were climbing the eastern slopes of the Urals, the scent of pine and wood fires reminding me of the Himalayas. At Kirov we purchased well-finished boxes made of burl, a growth on the trees of the district, and full of delightful whorls. Russian passengers crowded round and bought presents for their children. Shortly after midday we entered the drab, muddy outskirts of Moscow and twenty minutes later drew into Severni Station, where Thomas Cook's agent told us we had until midnight to explore the city. Meanwhile our train would proceed to Smolenski Station where we would rejoin it for our journey to Stolpce on the Polish border. I enjoyed a much-needed bath at the Hotel Metropole, and when I went down to the lounge found a pretty Intourist girl of about twenty, wearing a grey dress and a green beret, waiting for me. 'I have been appointed to show you our great city,' she announced with an attractive accent. 'My name is Olga.'

First we walked across Red Square. It was larger than I had expected, and the Church of St Basil with its onion-shaped domes looked tiny in the distance. On the right a queue a mile long waited to enter Lenin's mausoleum. 'I'd love to have seen Lenin,' I said.

'So you shall,' said Olga, and without more ado or a 'thank you' pushed me to the front of the patient Russians.

The entrance was guarded by smart soldiers, and more guards lined the descending staircase to the main chamber. There, in the centre, lay the remains of Lenin in a large glass case, only his head and hands visible. The eyes were closed in a pale calm face with a sprinkling of reddish hair on the cheeks, thickening to a small pointed beard. Having heard the rumour that, because of decomposition, the body had been replaced by a wax replica, I looked closely for evidence until sharply moved on by a guard. The cadaver had seemed genuine. The Russian doctors responsible for the preservation of the body claimed it would keep for centuries. Why not, I thought. After all, the mummy of Ramesses the Great had kept for more than 3,000 years.

After a brief visit to St Basil's and the Kremlin, we went by metro to a high point overlooking the city and its tall new buildings. Here we caught up with the rest of our party, who had been visiting churches transformed into museums where the Creation, as portrayed in the Bible, was trounced by the findings of modern science. Not all superstitious believers were convinced by this demonstration, Olga told us, but with proper education their children would be protected from the 'opiate of the people'.

We returned by metro, each station of which had been planned by a different architect and was now kept spotlessly clean by old women who continually mopped up the mud brought in from the dirty streets. There was an impression of a series of museums filled with mosaics, carvings, sculptures and paintings. Stainless-steel sliding doors hid the rails and tunnels. They did not open until the trains stopped, and at that point train and platform doors opened simultaneously, as in a lift. The effect induced claustrophobia.

On one platform I spotted a dozen gaily dressed girls, quite unlike their drab sisters. 'Who are they?' I asked Olga.

'Oh, they are ballet dancers,' she said, a shade petulantly.

'Why don't you wear pretty dresses as they do?'

'Men and women are equal in Russia. We do not have to dress to please men. We are liberated.'

'Wouldn't you like pretty dresses for yourself?' I asked, for all the world as if I had strayed into the script of *Ninotchka*.

'Why should I? My work is more important than vanity.'

Two stations later we got out and, in the street, picked our way through the muddy slush. Queues waited at closed shops. 'What are they waiting for at this late hour?' I asked.

'They wish to have a good place in the morning. I have seen photographs of people in London doing the same. Sometimes, the article said, they had queued for days.'

'That's only once a year for big sales,' I said, 'when they sell your lovely sable furs for half-price, and surely they are worth queuing for!'

Olga looked gratified.

I had been told it was important to exchange gifts with Russians, and therefore, back at the hotel, gave her a Chinese silk square, which overwhelmed her. She gave me a guidebook to Moscow and we shook hands politely and parted. Our train was waiting and we rejoined our familiar coach.

As we travelled onwards to the West, I asked the missionary lady what prospects Christianity had in Russia. 'Very good,' she replied briskly. 'Better than in China.'

'Why should that be?'

'In China we have too many brands of Protestant Christianity and no persecution. Christianity thrives on persecution. The Roman Catholics do better. Their missionaries are well educated and they started three centuries ago. Today they have around three million converts.

'How many do you have?'

'About half a million communicants and as many more baptized. The problem is that although we have been in China for a century, we have such a variety of competing sects that we have confused the Chinese. We have Anglican, Baptist, Presbyterian, Methodist, Lutheran, Reformed Presbyterian, Quakers, Apostolic Faith, Advent Christian, Pentecostal Assemblies of the World, United Brethren, Bethel Mission, Hephzibah Faith, Mennonites, United Church of the Nazarene, Seventh Day Adventists, Church of God, Holiness Movement and many others.' She laughed. 'You didn't think I could remember so many, but I've met all of them in my thirty years. It's a Tower of Babel for the Chinese, who are logical people and, indeed, hold the strong moral principles of Buddha, Confucius and Lao-tse. Their ancestor worship venerates age and the Chinese care for the old and infirm much more than we do.'

'I've always felt we are too arrogant about proselytizing,' I said. 'We should study local faiths before we try overturning them in favour of ours. There are many Buddhists in China, and fine Buddhist temples even in sinful Shanghai, and the teaching of Buddha is similar to that of Christ, though he never claimed to be a god.'

'I'm sorry, but I can't agree with you. The message from God and the Bible is that we must spread the true faith.'

The next afternoon we arrived at Niegoreloye for our final bout with the USSR customs. My sealed luggage was returned with my passport, typewriter and camera, but everything I had with me was examined once again, in case, I supposed, I had received some improper object or literature along the way. Engdahl was subjected to the same treatment and, furious at his diplomatic immunity being violated, took up all the books that the Russians demanded to see and flung them from the window on to the platform. They were brought back by an angry official while, outside the window, armed soldiers took up positions. Engdahl waited until we were on the move again and then, to my terror that the train might be recalled, thrust his books down the wide lavatory shaft on to the track.

A few minutes later we arrived at the frontier. A wide swathe, cut through the forests, was lined on both sides with high barbed-wire fences and watch-towers. As we reached the Polish side, the sun cast the shadow of a great wooden cross across the train's path. Polish officials jovially stamped our passports and the customs inspection was a mere formality. Soon we were in a buffet filled with eager waiters and a wonderful selection of food and drink. The contrasts with Russia were so marked that I concluded that the Poles delighted in accentuating them.

Our new coach was a dream of pastel greens, with soft cushions, concealed lighting and spotless windows. Each compartment had a complete toilet, individual heating and two bell-pushes to attract instant service from attentive stewards. Most reassuring of all was a small metal plate bearing the inscription 'Made in Birmingham'.

We passed through Warsaw at night, were briefly awoken by the German customs at the frontier and glided into Berlin on the morning of the fourteenth day. A seven-hour stop allowed for a tour of the capital. The Berliners looked well and cheerful. The shops were crammed with merchandise, but the sky overhead was busy with ominous aerial activity. People to whom I spoke regarding the likelihood of war were cheerfully incredulous, but at the Dutch frontier despondent groups of Jewish families were herded away from our train by Storm Troopers. They awaited a train to take them out of Germany but apparently ours was not the one. My thoughts went back to the refugee Jews in Shanghai and I wondered what their fate would be if or when the Japanese annexed the foreign concessions.

At midnight, on 31 May, we reached the Hook of Holland, I boarded the ferry for Harwich, and in the morning hurried ashore to get on the waiting boat-train. In the breakfast car I sat at a table with a jovial, red-faced man who wished me a jolly good morning. 'What do you do in Manchester?' he asked.

'I'm afraid I've never been to Manchester. I'm going to London,' I said.

'Well, you're going a long way round. This is the special express to Manchester. There's a big convention and they've laid on a special train.'

Fifteen day's non-stop travelling, and then to have got on the wrong train in my own country! Evidently I looked appalled.

'April fool,' he chortled. 'April fool. Got you that time!'

'You certainly did,' I said, still shaking with tremors of dismay.

Was I indeed an April fool, I wondered. Had I over-reacted in resigning? How would I cope with unadulterated Ulster? What could I do with my life? Banking qualified one for no other job. Would the bank give me my provident fund, formed by taking part of my salary each month, to which the bank added a similar sum to provide a nest-egg for a faithful servant on retirement?

Beaky Duncan received me at head office with his usual Scots directness.

'I'm sorry the board didn't take my advice. They've lost a good man, but you're well out of it, you can do better. Call on me any time if I can be of help – a reference or whatever. They're giving you your provident fund, less what the bank put into it, and they're subtracting the cost of your passages to and from Shanghai.' He got up and put an arm round my shoulder as we walked to the door. 'Good luck,' said Beaky.

I went down the stairs and out through the banking hall that I had first entered so timidly sixteen years before. No one spoke to me. I turned into Bishopsgate and found myself surrounded by all the bustle of the financial capital of the world, though I was no longer a part of it. Sadly I walked slowly away, and continued walking through London until I reached Piccadilly Circus, where I sat on the fountain steps and watched the traffic swirl around the little God of Love on his high pedestal. Finally I took a taxi back to Liverpool Street to collect my suitcases, and then, with a sinking heart, went to Euston to catch the boat-train to Ireland.

Part Three

Chairman of Talents

16

Death and the Inner Life

At home in Belfast I found there was a far from gloomy atmosphere. Mother looked pale and worn, yet still ran the house cheerfully and was full of joy at my return. She had been kept in ignorance of her terminal condition and I wondered whether telling her the truth might not have been better, for she felt she was being a poor patient and a disappointment to her doctors. Within the month she grew too weak to get up, but still refused to have a nurse. A quiet woman of great natural wisdom and courage, she clearly sensed that her life was drawing to its close. We talked long about her childhood, of the trip to Ceylon and our journey round Ireland. The ease with which she recalled events of the past and the intense pleasure it gave her to relive them astonished me. As she grew weaker, she agreed to the district nurse coming in each morning to help me bathe her. Gradually I became more efficient at making her comfortable. Fortunately the tumour had not reached the point of blocking the gullet and she could still eat. Remembering Dr Johanna Brandt's advice, I asked Mother if she fancied grapes or grape juice. 'That would be lovely,' she said, 'except they're so expensive.'

'I can get us a barrel from the market wholesale. They're in season and quite cheap.'

The grapes and grape juice did indeed make her seem more like her old self. I took the courage to pray the disease might go into reverse and burn itself out. I bought a sun lamp and gave her small doses to make up a little for her inability to be in her cherished garden. At the end of the month Dr Campbell brought in two consultants, who set about putting her through a lengthy examination.

'How am I getting on?' she asked them.

'You're doing very well,' they replied.

But now, for the first time, there was an impatience in her voice as she said, 'I'm a dying woman, and you three wise men can neither cure me nor put me out of my suffering. I have to go on to the end, a nuisance to myself and everyone else.'

Although they looked abashed, they continued with hopeful platitudes, but as I saw them out they told me there was nothing more they could do and the end was close.

Mother invited an old friend, Fanny Whitehouse, to stay. They had once worked together in Belfast and were at one time both in the running for my father's affections. Fanny had visited us on several occasions with her daughter, Peggy Mundy-Castle, a poet whose work greatly appealed to my mother. Fanny was a widow, and perhaps it was in my mother's mind that she might, after her death, provide a comfort for my father. She was a charming, gentle person who lightened the atmosphere of the house as she talked of the old days.

When Mother and I were alone together one afternoon, she suddenly said, 'I would like to be buried in Bangor cemetery, high up where there's a good view of the sea.'

'No need to talk of this,' I said. 'You're improving all the time – getting more and more like your old self.'

She placed a hand beside mine on the coverlet. 'Look,' she said, and the hand, as it lay between my tanned fingers, could have been made of white wax. 'Just a small Celtic cross with one word, RESTING,' she continued insistently. 'I saw one in the cemetery in Ceylon and liked it very much. No flowers, except a few from the garden. Don't take any buds, only those in full bloom.'

The parson called several times, but gently, firmly she declined to see him. She did not wish to be disturbed in her final thoughts. Besides the grapes she sometimes fancied ice cream or, occasionally, oysters; it was almost like the whims of pregnancy. It seemed to me that she really was regaining some of her strength. In fact, one day she invited several old friends in for tea. The party was a great success, and after the guests left we had a long talk about the part each one of them had played in her life.

But the next morning, when I went into her room, she said, 'Something terrible has happened.'

I rolled back the bedclothes and saw a pool of blood. The tumour had ruptured an artery and her life was draining away. Dr Campbell came immediately, but by then she was already unconscious. Father pleaded with the doctor to rouse her so we could say a last goodbye, but he advised it was better to leave her in peace. Gradually her breathing slowed and finally we awaited a breath that never came. The date was 21 July 1939.

When the district nurse arrived, she and I together cleaned up the bed, which was protected by the rubber undersheet, washed the body, packed the openings with cotton wool, bandaged the sagging jaw, changed the sheets and put on a clean nightdress. Against the smooth fresh pillow my mother's features were calm and distant, but it was as it had been with my old manager Lang: the presence had departed. I found I was unemotional about the death and much involved in filling in forms, ordering the coffin, arranging for the grave on the site she wanted. On the fourth day, undertakers brought in a plain coffin and carried it in a blanket up the difficult stairs. I went out into the garden to collect the flowers, and as I plucked the full blooms, avoiding the buds, was suddenly overwhelmed with grief. I sobbed over each bloom until I could no longer see what I was picking. It seemed unthinkable that this quiet, unassuming woman of natural wisdom, who had devoted her life to the care of her family, should have suffered such an end. Jim and I had been brought up with enormous love, but never spoilt. She would have died for us ten times over, and the only thing to make her cross was if we flouted local custom or good manners.

Shortly after the funeral I had her room repapered. The paper-hanger remarked, 'You know, there's a peculiar smell in here.'

'I know,' I replied. 'We've noticed it for some time. My mother, before she died of cancer, used to worry, thinking it was the disease.'

'No,' he said. 'I work a lot in hospitals. It's not that sort of smell. This is something under the floor.'

'A dead mouse?' I suggested.

'Do you mind if I take up a floorboard?'

'Not at all. We'd like to know.'

A slow leak in a gas-pipe joint had produced a tarry evil-smelling deposit.

Fanny Whitehouse left a week after the funeral. It was clear that my father wished to be on his own. The idea of his living in a hotel was discussed, but he decided he would be happier at home, where Sarah Collins, our housekeeper, could continue to take care of him. As for me, my purpose in resigning my job and returning home had been fulfilled, and where should I go now; whatever should I do? Having talked things over with my brother, I decided to return to London, where friends had offered me a small flat in Victoria Road, Kensington. Barely had I unpacked my bags before I was aware that I had brought with me an unexpected companion. I stared in consternation as several flat, white segments cruised around the lavatory bowl. Pulling myself together, I collected samples and took them to a pathology laboratory near Harley Street. The pretty receptionist asked my name and, a moment later, introduced me to the lab technician as Dr MacQuitty.

'It's the beef tapeworm, *Tinia saginata*,' he pronounced.

I paid a fee of 5s. (25p) and went round to Boots, where the pharmacist, after consulting the British Pharmacopoeia, advised male fern in a solution of camomile: no food for twenty-four hours, then two ounces of castor oil followed by the male fern extract and, after a further two hours, another two ounces of castor oil.

The next day, empty except for the companion of my bowels, whom I had christened 'Oscar', and already beginning to feel like a murderer, I took the castor oil. The male fern's menacing smell of iron filings put me in mind of Socrates and hemlock. Supposing I was allergic to it and had a violent reaction? I was alone in the flat; no one would come until morning. I picked up the glass. The smell was terrible. Taking a deep breath I swallowed the lot. Its metallic taste was shocking. I broke into a cold sweat, which gradually subsided, and after two hours took the remaining two ounces of castor oil. There was not long to wait. Ready in the bathroom, on thickly spread papers, I had placed a large basin of warm water, and into this, in a steady flow Oscar descended tail first. After fifteen feet his progress stopped, and though I was afraid to pull in case he broke, it was impossible to remain squatting over the basin. In the end I pulled very gently. He broke. That's torn it, I thought. The head's still inside and he'll grow another tail in no time.

A few moments later another spasm seized me, and this time Oscar could hold out no longer. Spread out on newspapers he measured twenty-nine feet from the tiny head that had clung to the stomach wall to the last segment grown all the way through the intestine. I arranged a decent interment in a jar of pure alcohol and presented him to the Queen's University, Belfast, where, for all I know, he still adorns the medical specimens room. I felt no different for the loss of my fellow traveller and eating companion, except that my weight increased. When I wondered where he and I could have met, I decided he must have arrived in one of the flaming cubes of nearly raw steak so dramatically thrust on to my plate by a Cossack sabre in DD's night club in Shanghai.

I was not long in London before Fanny Whitehouse's daughter, Peggy Mundy-Castle, invited me to spend a weekend at her home in Tonbridge, Kent. I had first met Peggy twenty years previously when she and her family stayed in Bangor, and now she and her three children gave me a warm welcome.

'We have another visitor,' said Peggy. 'The psychologist Wilhelm Stekel. He escaped from Vienna after Hitler's Anschluss.'

I went into the garden and saw a small grey-haired man in a grey suit hoeing weeds out of the gravel drive. As I approached, he stopped his work and held out a hand. 'I have been told about you,' he smiled. 'You are an old friend of Peggy's and, like me, a William.'

His eyes were deep set in a heavily lined face and his chin carried a neatly trimmed beard. He regarded me with a look that was friendly but strikingly penetrating. The instant flow of conversation that sprang up between us was stemmed only by Peggy summoning us for tea.

'I can see you've found some ground in common,' said Peggy.

'Yes,' replied Stekel. 'Neither of us likes the army, yet we both joined, and both became corporals. William left Shanghai under the Japanese invasion and I left Germany when the Nazis took over. William has studied yoga and the philosophy of Buddha, which has done so much to enlighten the world, and I have studied psychoanalysis.'

Peggy, it emerged, was helping Stekel to write his autobiography. Originally one of the group associated with Freud in the pioneering days of psychoanalysis in Vienna, he later, like Jung and Adler, broke away to become an apostate in the eyes of orthodox Freudians and to develop his own line of active analysis. In his view, all neuroses, whether to do with sex, power, ambition or whatever, sprang from mental conflicts, whereas Freud saw in neuroses the consequence of undischarged libido. Stekel also disapproved of Freud's long-term approach, considering that an analysis extending over several years could actually be detrimental to the patient. His own approach was to seek to arrive at the patient's enlightenment through an independent exploration of the material and an intuitive grasp of the patient's character. It was a matter of using intuition to slip past the patient's resistance to being freed or cured. In discovering the cause of an individual neurosis, he used dream interpretation as his chief instrument.

That evening, when I asked him what he considered to be the best training for a psychoanalyst, he replied, 'I am sorry to say there is no training that is suitable. Either you are born a psychologist or you will never become one.'

The thought flashed through my mind that, if Buddha had found enlightenment in the shade of the Bodi tree, perhaps I would discover it in the shade of Wilhelm Stekel.

The following day John Gunther, the American journalist and author, called to visit Stekel, bearing with him a copy of his latest book, *Inside Asia*, inscribed 'To the man who gave me eyes and wings'. Stekel had previously reviewed Gunther's *Inside Europe* in which the writer's uncomplimentary opinions on Hitler and Mussolini had earned him an honourable place on the Nazi black-list. Later on Gunther was to write in *Look* magazine, in the issue of 7 May 1940:

> The ten most interesting people I have ever met are, Archibald MacLeish, Leon Trotsky, Sinclair Lewis, Mahatma Gandhi, Winston Churchill, The Duchess of Windsor, Madame Chiang Kai-shek, Eamon de Valera, H.G. Wells, and Dr Wilhelm Stekel, who possesses the most subtle, the most closely packed, the most flashingly intuitive mind I have ever had the good fortune to meet.

Stekel expressed to me his conviction that Britain would be caught up in the war with Germany, and he was proved correct on 3 September 1939. I promptly returned to Belfast, where I had a talk with my old headmaster, 'Duffy' Gibbon, now chairman of the Recruiting Board of Northern Ireland; for did I not have my pilot's 'A' licence to offer, not to mention six years' experience in the Punjab Light Horse?

'MacQuitty,' said Gibbon, 'the maximum age for pilots is twenty-eight, and you are thirty-five. You could get a ground job, but in my opinion you are not cut out for soldiering. You weren't when you were at Campbell, and you haven't changed. You should do something in communications or training.'

When I told him about Stekel, he commented, 'Psychology has an important part to play in this war. It is a war about the dictator *versus* democracy. Go back to London and get on with it.'

My father was apprehensive about the idea of my working in London, and said prophetically, 'It will be a prime target for the German air force. Our navy may still rule the seas, but that won't stop Germany ruling the air.'

The weekend I returned to London, Stekel invited me to visit him at his rooms in the Pembridge Court Hotel in Notting Hill, where he had resumed work now the autobiography was finished and Peggy was busy typing it out. Again I expressed my interest in psychotherapy, and he said at once, 'Come and work with me.'

I felt overwhelmed.

'We start tomorrow morning at nine o'clock,' he said.

When I arrived on Monday morning I found Stekel sitting in a comfortable armchair by a gas fire that had a gas-ring attached on which he was making strong black coffe in a copper pot. As soon as it was ready, he invited me to join him, and drank the unsweetened coffee with enjoyment as he helped himself to a short black cheroot from a box at his elbow, then carefully wrapped a travelling rug round his legs, for he suffered badly from diabetes and the circulation in his feet was poor.

'First,' he instructed me, 'you will take out a subscription with Lewis's Medical Library and read the books I prescribe. You will then go to the Tavistock Clinic and listen to the lectures – Hadfield and Bennett are good. Tomorrow you bring me your dreams and we start to go through your analysis together.'

'But,' I protested, 'I'm quite normal. Is it necessary to do my analysis?'

'It is essential. First, it is the only way in which you can appreciate the method, and secondly, everyone has a blind spot, a scotoma. In the analyst, this means he is blind to any complex he shares with his patient.'

'Perhaps,' I ventured, 'some of the shortcomings you find in Freud, Jung and Adler are because they have never been analysed?'

'MacQuitty,' he said nodding, 'you are greatly gifted.'

Thenceforward, every morning at nine, I read Stekel my dreams. To begin with I feared I might not dream at all, or that, if I did, I would forget what I dreamed. Nevertheless, with a pencil and pad beside my bed, I was soon recording all manner of strange situations in which, at first, I could discern no meaning. It seemed obvious that my unconscious mind had no problem with keeping its affairs under wraps. Yet Stekel's interpretations, conveyed with a delicate clarity, gradually brought me face to face with myself. The phrase, 'Know thyself and to thine own self be true,' began to take on a telling significance.

In the second week of my analysis, I developed physical symptoms of unease, my pulse racing and my breathing becoming laboured. One morning I offered a dream in which I was climbing stairs, and suddenly stopped, unable to move. On either side of me the solid walls melted away and I stood alone on a skeleton stairway that reached into the heavens. Feeling that something terrible was about to happen, I woke trembling and in a sweat.

'What is your earliest recollection of stairs?' asked Wilhelm Stekel.

'Going up to my cot,' I said.

'What so terrified you about the stairs?'

After a long pause, I answered, 'Death.'

'Your own death?' queried Wilhelm.

'No, I don't think so.'

'Was there a pet that died?'

'I can't remember,' I said, though my pulse began to race.

'How did it die?' he asked.

But, probe as we might, nothing further emerged.

The next day I brought a particularly vivid dream. I was asleep and felt in my sleep that I was being observed. I was afraid to open my eyes, but even though I kept them shut tight, a pair of eyes stared into mine. Again I woke up sweating and trembling, my pulse racing away.

'Were these eyes human?' asked Wilhelm.

'I don't think so.'

'Where they the eyes of an animal?'

After another long pause: 'Yes.'

'A dog perhaps?'

My pulse rate shot up. 'Yes.'

'You had a dog as a child?'

The eyes flashed back into my memory. The scene was clear before me. 'My dog Jap,' I whispered, 'killed in an accident. My father had him stuffed and placed on the landing half-way up the stairs. Every night, as I passed him on my way to bed, his eyes flickered at me in the gaslight.'

'How old were you when this accident happened?'

'A little more than two.'

Stekel's eventual summing up of my analysis revealed feelings of guilt from early childhood, though the source remained unclear. There was a strong religious strain emphasizing punishment, which led to an extraordinary ability to control emotion. This, in turn, created a contrast between outward calm and a turbulent inner emotional life: every action under control, the head ruling the heart, the result a state of tension. This may have come partly from my father, who not only gave my dog continuity after death, but also constantly voiced strong religious convictions and asserted that his sons must be 'souls of honour'. During the nervous breakdown he suffered, he could not tolerate contradictions of any kind. Mother was also prone to anxiety in case we did something to cause the 'finger of scorn' to be pointed at us – a phenomenon my brother and I thought of as a signpost pointed by neighbours.

After analysis came a brief period of reconditioning the psyche to enable life to be lived fully and freely. First, I must forgive myself. The dictum, 'Judge not that ye be not judged,' certainly included not sitting in self-judgement. Finally Stekel said, 'Continue to work with me or find some other congenial occupation. There is nothing to be afraid of.'

There it was again: the phrase that all my gurus used. I felt at once that a long-carried burden had been lifted from my shoulders, that my fears were paper tigers. It was quite remarkable how this stricken old man, driven into exile and sitting by his fire drinking black coffee and smoking black cheroots, had been able to guide me through dark labyrinths of despair into sunlight. He now began to give me some of his patients' dreams to interpret, and, to my surprise, I found them relatively easy to understand and realized how clever my subconscious had been in choosing dream language obscure to me. Before long I was given patients to work with therapeutically, and found myself entering into a happy and rewarding period that lasted in all about a year. Whenever I came upon a situation that I did not understand, Wilhelm would use it to illustrate his method.

Most patients with worries seemed only too glad to talk about them. They could reveal things to a stranger that they would never for a moment consider telling their friends. Sometimes the cause of the trouble could be instantly evident to the analyst, but the problem then was to lead the patient to discover the truth for himself in his inner heart. The patient's initial account was a cover story, and after that, like peeling an onion, the analyst gradually took him to the centre of his neurosis. Dream analysis provided a short cut through the onion skins and could, to the intuition of a man like Stekel, quickly reveal the source. The guiding of the patient required a therapeutic bond with the analyst that should, after resolution, be dissolved to enable the patient to stand on his own feet.

In the spring of 1940, Wilhelm began to lose his long fight against illness. Besides arteriosclerosis and prostatic disorders, he suffered great pain from diabetic gangrene in his foot and was unable to walk, walking having been one of his greatest pleasures. He was still an avid reader, and every day I brought him books from Boots Library. He loved music and spent many hours playing the piano. When I asked him what he had found most rewarding in life, he replied, 'Work is the joy of life, and it is all done by love.'

In May he handed me a letter.

'What is this?' I asked.

'It is the highest award I can give you,' he said.

It was a diploma written on the paper of his Institut for Psychotherapy:

INSTITUT FÜR PSYCHOTHERAPIE

Leiter: Dr Wilhelm Stekel

This is to certify that William Baird MacQuitty has worked with me in 1939 and 1940, during which time he studied my active method of Psycho Therapy and Psycho Analysis.

I consider that he is gifted in this science and that he is capable of dealing with any cases he may encounter.

In view of his exceptional abilities I trust that those members of the Medical Profession with whom he comes in contact will assist him in his work.

He carries with him my best wishes for his future.

3rd May 1940
Wilhelm Stekel

Spezialarzt für
Psychotherapie und
Nervenleiden

He also gave me for safe keeping a copy of his autobiography, for he was afraid that it might be destroyed in those days when the German air raids were continuous and bombs fell nightly on London. On 24 June, he told the hotel staff that, because of his diabetes, his doctor had ordered him to take nothing to eat after his tea and that he did not wish to be disturbed. On the following morning the manager, getting no response, forced open the door and found him dead in bed.

Wilhelm's suicide did not surprise me. He was a practical physician. He knew the agonies Freud had suffered and that the future held no joy for him. Above all, he had no wish to end up in a hospital where he would have no control over his life. I believe he had decided long ago that he would make a dignified exit. When the time came, an overdose of aspirin was sufficient.

In less than a year I had lost two people who meant much to me, but their presence remained with me and, as I returned to Belfast, I found myself in good heart.

17

Simple Silage

Feeling it would be wrong for me to pursue a career in any kind of psychotherapy without a medical degree, I started work with a retired schoolmaster to prepare for the pre-medical examination for the Queen's University. My heart sank at the syllabus: heat, light, sound, electricity, magnetism and chemistry, not to mention Latin, my most feared subject at school. Since a seven-year course lay before me, I felt the need for a second string and used my provident fund to buy Prospect Farm, which lay on high ground and commanded a fine view over Belfast and the lough. It was only three miles from Stormont, the Northern Ireland Houses of Parliament, of which I took advantage to ask the Minister of Agriculture how I should tackle farming. 'Make silage,' he said, and referred me to one of his experts for help.

With Jack Kernohan I walked my eighty acres as he lucidly revealed the most effective way of turning my small farm into a practical venture. Under his guidance I acquired Robert Dunn, a taciturn Ulsterman, and his small shrewd wife. They were to live in the house and run the farm on a sharing basis. Among other equipment, I purchased a Ford Ferguson tractor and a concrete tub silo for making silage. Already inherited from Willie Price, the former owner, were twelve Friesian cows, a milk contract and milk churns, a selection of pigs, ducks, hens, a strong six-year-old farm horse, a heavy County Down farm cart and a huge unused manure mountain which, when we carted it to spread on the land, turned out to contain several cattle rotting in its vast interior.

'Willie dealt in cattle,' said Jack, 'and never tilled the land, but you'll soon have it in good shape.'

Slowly I began to appreciate the logic and labour of farming as a relief from the academic grind. Our water supply came from a small sweet well, sixty yards downhill from the byre. At dawn, before milking, each cow drank about three gallons of water, and having to carry it up left me aching before the day's work started. Piped water therefore became my first priority. On our eastern boundary a small stream ran through a pretty glen, and here I installed a ram that pumped water through 1,500 feet of pipe to a 1,000-gallon tank that we built in the field above the farmhouse. Under cover of darkness, Robert, Paddy the hired hand and I then dug a channel across the county road to carry a pipe to the cold-water tank in the house, where I had installed bathroom and lavatory. Next morning, the connection to the partly filled tank being made, I raced up to the roof to await the arrival of my new water supply. There was not the faintest gurgle. My God, I thought, we've positioned the tank too low on the hill. Down by the road the explanation became plain: a steam thresher had passed in the early hours and fractured the pipe. That night we buried a new pipe deeper and were rewarded with noisy splashes and water flowing into the cistern.

Ulster was a strange close-knit community, which, out of a population of just over a million, produced six of the eight field-marshals who led the British forces during the war: Alanbrooke, Alexander, Auchenleck, Templer, Dill and Montgomery. Ulster people, I found, were warm, curious and full of 'the repartee', which meant taking each other down a peg or two. I could hardly have received a warmer welcome among them. I became a member of the Royal Ulster Yacht Club, played polo and was invited to join the County Down Stag Hounds, which made a change after the paper chases of Shanghai.

Every winter de-antlered stags were hunted over the little fields of County Down, known as the 'basket of eggs' country from its hilly nature. The stags were all called by name and, having no antlers to catch in the thick hedges, could run very fast. Some of the stronger ones would lead us into the Mountains of Mourne. A stag brought to bay was never molested by the hounds, which simply surrounded it and patiently waited until the first huntsman arrived and held his arms round its neck until the stag cart arrived to return it to the deer park. Sometimes stag and hounds felt equally that they had had enough and trotted home together, knowing a good meal awaited them. The Irish hunters were mostly ridden on broken snaffles and, left to their own devices, took their riders safely over the daunting country of double-banked lanes, wide ditches and thick thorn hedges with blind drops on the far side, sometimes into quarry, bog or boulders.

Occasionally we were joined by members of an English hunt, and once I helped an Englishman who had had a bad fall into a nearby cottage for a rest. The lady of the house brought him a bowl of warm milk. As he gratefully sipped it, a little pig came and sat beside him. 'I see your little pig has taken a fancy to me,' he said.

'Oh, no,' the woman replied, 'it's his own wee bowl, he knows.'

It was a 'cuppy' pig, the one too many in a litter which is brought up on a cup.

In the area of the arts, Alfred Arnold, a senior civil servant, introduced me to the Group Theatre in Belfast and its talented actors, including Harold Goldblatt, Joseph Tomelty, J.G. Devlin, Bee Duffell and Richard Hayward. Sydney Smith, a gifted painter, painted my portrait between doing vast *trompe-l'oeil* murals for the interiors of Harland & Wolff ships. Maurice Harding made a sculpture of my head. Nevertheless, though I fitted into the life of the province and anticipated a medical degree, I began to feel trapped. Even as I pondered, Jack Kernohan phoned to say that the Minister would like to bring some farmers to see my silage. I was, it seemed, to be held up as an example of the province, Ulster farmers being notoriously conservative in their ways. Silage, of course, is simply young grass fermented with water and molasses in a pit or silo: a kind of grass jam. It does not require the dry weather needed to make hay and contains more protein. Saving money on imported feed was seen as an essential part of the war effort.

After the farmers had departed, duly impressed, I think, by the simplicity of the process, I suggested to the Minister that his department might make a film about silage and show it to the farmers in the winter when they were not so busy. He shook his head. 'We don't believe in films,' he said.

I felt a sudden annoyance at this negative response and heard myself say, 'I'll make a film, and if the Ministry doesn't like it, they needn't buy it.'

'How much will it cost?' he asked.

I had no idea about movies, but reckoned, from my still camera experience, that it could not be more than 10s. (50p) a foot. I added threepence for luck.

'I'll look at it when you've made it,' he said, smiling broadly.

Jack gazed at me in disbelief. I had committed the unforgivable

Ulster sin: opened my big mouth, knowing nothing about the subject, and undertaken to teach the Minister his business. There was set to be long laughter at the Ministry and the 'finger of scorn' would undoubtedly be pointed in my direction. I had little sleep that night, but felt better in the morning. As my father frequently said, all his worst fears were never realized. I got in touch with Richard Hayward, who had acted in some of the Paramount quickies, and found him full of enthusiasm. His friend, Louis Morrison, a wedding photographer, had a movie camera, a 100-foot clockwork Eymo that he loaded from 1,000-foot cans of professional film.

'What about sound?' I asked Louis when we met.

'I've a sound system that I put together myself,' he said.

And thus the film *Simple Silage* was born.

We held a brief conference and agreed that Richard would direct, that I would produce and supply the farm and finance, and that Louis would be responsible for camera and sound. Profits, if any, would be divided equally between us and I was to bear any loss. Richard had a friend in London, Germain 'Jimmy' Berger, a Belgian film director, who agreed to look after our 'rushes', the exposed film, and send them back to us daily so we could monitor our progress.

The results were beautiful and made the making of silage look truly simple. Most of the film was shot silent with a commentary over, though we did need about ten minutes of direct sound, and for this the Eymo was inadequate. I hired a Vinten camera from London Studios, the running speed of which was shown on a tachometer. When the tachometer on Louis's bootleg sound outfit and the Vinten both showed twenty-four frames a second, we shot Richard in conversation with farmers. Although we had to run sound and vision separately at the rushes, we felt delighted with the results.

A few weeks later, shooting ended, I went to London to Kays Laboratories, where I rented a cutting room with a Moviola and started to edit the film with one of the lab assistants. All went well until I came to the direct sound. Despite lining up the tracks exactly on their clapper-board marks, Richard's lips continually went in and out of synchronization. Finally the penny dropped. Without a lock between the sound and picture cameras, they were bound to vary. Yet all was not lost and, by cutting away from the worst lapses, I was able to produce a creditable result. Opticals, fades, mixes and dissolves smoothed my path; Irish music bought by the yard blended with the round tower and shamrocks of the title.

Filled with mixed feelings of achievement and anxiety, we arranged with George Lodge, the manager of the Classic, Belfast, to give the film a first showing at his cinema. Invitations were sent out, and for the opening night we had a full house including the Minister of Agriculture, the Lord Mayor of Belfast, members of the Cabinet, the Senate, the Commons, the Corporation, the Chamber of Commerce and Trade, the Ulster Farmers' Union Executive Committee and my delighted father. The evening was a huge success and the next day the *Belfast Telegraph* gave us a notice:

> This film, which deals with silage in all its aspects, is a brilliant example of the local film talent which is in our midst and of which very few of us are aware. It is one of the best documentaries so far and Ulster should be proud of an excellent effort. We look forward to many more.

There was still the question of finance. The film had cost £805 11s. 7d. (£805.58). My 10s. 3 d. (51p) price to the Minister worked out at £1,031 4s. 6d. (£1,031.22½), giving us a payment of £75 4s. 4d. (£75.22) each for a great deal of very hard work and, for me, considerable financial risk. Yet no one had so far mentioned money. I approached the Ministry. With true Ulster caution they said, 'We know nothing about films,' and sent my application on to the Ministry of Information in London for advice. Three weeks later I received a letter requesting my presence in the capital.

After a tiresome journey through security controls and crowded quarters in a blacked-out steamer to Liverpool and a blacked-out train to London, I presented myself at the office of Jack Beddington, head of the Film Division of the Ministry of Information. Beddington, who had been in charge of Shell advertising and created the famous slogan, 'That was Shell that was!' had a melancholy face that reminded me of the actor Adolphe Menjou. He called in Lord Arthur Elton, supervisor of films, a large, genial personality with a red beard and sandalled feet. Both men were very relaxed and congratulated me. They had produced two films on silage and thought mine better. 'So what is your next film to be?' Beddington asked. and thought mine better. 'So what is your next film to be?' Beddington asked.

I explained that I had no notion of making films, but had landed myself with this one and was really learning to farm and hoping to obtain a medical degree. They looked at me in some astonishment, surrounded, as they were, by eager film-makers eyeing the large government grant they had at their disposal. After a pause Beddington asked, 'Are there any films you could suggest for Northern Ireland?'

'Yes,' I said. 'Why not make one about the American troops flooding into Ulster and how they're setting down in their training camps – something for their wives and families, their sweethearts and friends in the US?'

Beddington turned to Elton, who nodded.

'Excellent idea. Go and do it,' said Beddington. 'We'll put you on reserved occupation.'

'What about the money?' I asked.

'Do as you did with *Simple Silage*.'

'But that was my money and I still haven't been paid.'

'I'll write to your Minister,' Beddington said. 'It's a good film.'

They were still looking perplexed as we shook hands.

Back in Bangor, I redoubled my studies and got several modern books on physics and chemistry. They were more advanced and differed from those my tutor had chosen. When I broached this with him, he said, 'The books I gave you are the set books for examinations. Of course they're out of date, but so are all the professors. It's impossible for them to keep up with the rapid scientific advances being made today. It you want to pass, for God's sake stick to the answers they're after.'

Suddenly I felt as if I were back at school, trapped in the academic straightjacket from which I thought I had long since freed myself. The next day, as I was picking up swill for the pigs from Crawfordsburn Inn, beautifully restored by its owner, Paddy Falloon, I mentioned my qualms.

'I'm going south for a couple of weeks,' said Paddy. 'I want to buy a castle. Why not come along? They're going for nothing just now. Maybe I'll start another inn in the south.'

In Dublin there was little evidence of war or rationing. We ate huge steaks at the Dolphin and gourmet meals at Jamet's. We drank in the Palace bar with the talented painter Harry Kernoff; with Micheál Mac Liammóir and Hilton Edwards of the Gate Theatre; with Maurice Walsh, a retired excise officer who was the author of novels including *The Key Above the Door* and *The Small Dark Man* and drank Red Hackle whiskey. Through Victor Waddington, the art dealer, I also met the architect, Michael Scott, the sculptress, Hilary Heron, and the painter, Jack Yeats, the younger brother of W.B. Talk was stimulating and drink flowed gracefully. I had entered a world of saints and scholars, of Synge, Joyce, Michael Collins and de Valera, in which the war was never mentioned.

From Victor I bought a small painting by Jack Yeats, 'The Sailor's Last Return', which showed an old sailor walking away from his boat with a sack over his shoulder and the sunset giving way to darkness behind him. It moved me greatly, but Paddy could not imagine what I saw in it. Despite Victor's enthusiasm, the cynical Dubliners for the most part regarded Yeats as a 'dauber', though they revered his brother. Victor himself was full of dry wit, compassion and good humour and maintained a stable of young Irish artists, encouraging and guiding them to success. He also had a private life, never discussed and only emerging much later, for he was responsible for saving many Jewish children from the Nazi extermination camps and was said to have organized from time to time secret rescue missions into Germany.

On the subject of castles, Paddy consulted the Dublin estate agents. They told us there were two castles then on the market: Killarney Castle at £4,000 and Castle Freeke at £11,000. At Killarney Castle, the home of the McGillycuddy of the Reeks, we arrived late. It was 9 p.m. when I pulled on the bell chain. Nothing happened. I pulled again. A light went on in a third-floor room of the grey turreted castle, a window was thrown open and the white nightcapped head of the McGillycuddy poked out.

'I'm sorry we are late, sir,' I called up. 'There was an accident on the road.

'What d'ye want?' a stentorian voice demanded.

'We've come to buy your castle, sir,' I said in my best brogue.

'I'm not selling,' roared the McGillycuddy.

'Your agents in Dublin sent us to see you, sir,' I called back.

'Damn the Dublin agents and you along with them,' barked the voice, and the white nightcap withdrew and the window slammed down.

'I don't like the place, anyway,' Paddy whispered as we drove away.

We stayed at a small hotel in the town and in the morning had bacon and eggs for breakfast. The bacon was home cured and lay on the plate in two thick slices, Paddy's portion including the sow's teat and a few hairs. Being a fastidious eater, he pushed the plate away. I offered him mine, but all he could stomach was tea and toast.

Castle Freeke was an immense, stone-built mansion with enough lead on the roof to sink a battleship. It was surrounded by 11,000 acres and had a mile of coast with rights of salvage. There was a forest, a huge kitchen garden with twenty-foot beech hedges and a 50,000-gallon water tank at its centre. Everything was in first class condition, and the steward showed us round. Suddenly he shouted in a high-pitched Kerry accent, 'Ou blackguard ou!'

A boy fled from the shadow of the vast tank, from which a six-inch jet of water shot thirty feet across the gravel path. The steward, still swearing, hastily turned off the big valve.

Had we bought Castle Freeke, we would have been wealthy men later, though even at £1 an acre it would have been a hazardous undertaking. Today a huge caravan site lines the shore and the land is worth many millions, but the grand castle lies in melancholy ruin, its roof long since sacrificed for the lead.

The trip to the Republic cleared my head. A seven-year slog at the university was going to be beyond my powers of concentration. The talk and meetings in the Palace bar had given me a glimpse of other worlds. I made my apologies to the university and retreated to the farm. There was plenty to be done, even on my small acreage: crops rotated, animals cared for, sowing and reaping, building a new open barn to protect the hay and straw, keeping the books. The tractor I kept fully employed by undertaking work for other farmers. It was a demanding non-stop life, but it had the great advantage that I was dealing with nature, a hard but honest adversary.

I kept up with my photography and writing. Richard was keen to do more films, but I could not see how we would sell them. Without distribution, we would have been at the mercy of a cynical trade. I walked over my land with a growing satisfaction. I vowed to settle down quietly and continue learning practical farming, and once I knew more about it, to buy a better farm, one that ran down to the sea with a tiny harbour big enough for a couple of boats. I would set crab and lobster pots, go fishing, perhaps sail round Ireland, enjoy the company of gifted friends and perhaps marry and raise a family here, among my own people. It seemed a prospect of heaven after the hell of Shanghai, yet still something else was beckoning. It was another version of the dream of life in Kashmir that I had often talked about with Kim and to which she had always responded that I should get back into the world, commenting shrewdly, 'You'd be lost without the challenge of new things. Once you know how something works, you tire of it.'

A year after meeting Beddington I had a call from Ian Dalrymple, head of the Crown Film Unit, which came under the Ministry of Information, inviting me to work as assistant director on a film about American troops in Ulster. Brian Hurst, director of *Dangerous Moonlight*, was to direct, and the script was by Terence Young, later director of the '007' films. I was dazzled: a government-backed film for my idea and a weekly salary of £5 11s. 9d. (about £5.58), less deductions.

My first task was to arrange accommodation for the eleven-strong unit, and this I achieved at the Grand Central Hotel, Belfast. They

1945. A statue of Drake looks down on American sailors dancing on the Hoe

8 May 1945. VE Day, Piccadilly, London

1950. *Street Corner*, a film about policewomen, brings Commissioner Sir Harold Scott to Pinewood Studios. Barbara Murray sits between us and Peggy Cummins pours tea. This film was produced by our own company, London Independent Film Producers, and directed by Muriel Box

1945. I discuss the filming of *The Way We Live* with Lady Astor and Sir Patrick Abercrombie in Lady Astor's Plymouth home

d-of-picture still. Ralph Thomas and I surrounded by many of the cast and crew who ⎪rked on *Above Us the Waves*. It turned out to be Winston Churchill's favourite film

53. The authors of *Above ⎪the Waves*, Jimmy ⎪nson and C.E.T. Warren, ⎪scuss the script. *(Left to ⎪ht)* C.E.T. Warren, ⎪self, our adviser ⎪mmander Donald ⎪ameron VC, RN, (who ⎪d the famous X Craft ⎪d on the German ⎪ttleship *Tirpitz*), Jimmy ⎪enson and Ralph Thomas, ⎪e director, holding ⎪e script

The producer works on difficult sequence with t underwater unit

John Mills stands on Submarine XI during the filming of *Above Us the Waves*

4. The première of *Above Us the* *...res* was held in Malta. Here Betty ...l are being congratulated by Prince ...ip. The proceeds went to his ...ing Fields Fund.

...g George VI with the Home Fleet. ...otain W.H. Fell OBE, DSO, RN ...plains the rig worn by 'human ...pedo' crews

1963. *The Informers*, Pinewood. I join our stills man to shoot. *(Left to right)* Catherine Woodville, Nigel Patrick, Reg Wyer, my resourceful cameraman, and Ken Annakin, the director

1989. Arthur C. Clarke on his terrace in Colombo

...a, The Immortal Kingdom.
...mperial Majesty
...ammed Reza Shah Pahlavi
...his Empress Farah Diba
...e steps of their palace
...hran

...nmy of Ramesses the Great, Cairo Museum; the subject of *Abu Simbel*

1963. The family with Robert Graves

Our second home, Mote Mount, Nan Clarke's Lane, Mill Hill, London

Betty in the South of France on our honeymoon

arrived in time for dinner and I went to bed feeling I had got off to a good start. At seven the next morning the production manager, a pretty, dark-haired girl called Norah Dawson, burst into my room. 'The call was 6.30. Anything wrong with you?' she blazed, obviously furious.

'I'm terribly sorry,' I said. 'I didn't know when you were starting.'

'It's on the call sheet on the notice board.'

'I'll be down in a minute,' I said.

I found the unit in a large room on the first floor and was introduced to Micky McCarthy, first assistant director. He looked up momentarily from a pile of script that he was breaking down into scenes which took place in the same location. Camera and sound crews were busily checking equipment and the continuity girl was typing out location sheets for Norah. As I watched the frantic scene, I realized with growing horror that I was an amateur gate-crashing a highly professional band of documentary enthusiasts. I asked Norah if there was anything I could do. 'Yes,' she said. 'I need transport to take the unit to the American Camp Tynan on Sir Norman Strong's estate in Enniskillen.'

'What sort of transport?' I asked humbly.

She looked at me in astonishment, and I could read her thoughts: *An assitant director who can't work out the necessary transport!* 'Three cars and a large van,' she said as she turned to the camera crew.

Fortunately I knew a transport firm, and we arrived at Camp Tynan late that afternoon. The surly sergeant on the gate had not been forewarned to expect this equipment-festooned bunch, some with long hair, sandals and safari jackets. 'Bunch of bloody draft-dodgers,' he growled. 'Hope I'm the hell out of here before you start messing around.'

'I'll arrange for that,' said the director, Brian Hurst, in his high-pitched voice, adding a baleful stare for good measure.

Brian was reputed to be gifted with extrasensory perception and was thought by some to possess the evil eye.

Inside the camp we received a cordial welcome from Colonel Sylvester, who had charge of the 25-pounder battery. We were assigned bunks in Nissen huts and fed in the canteen on steak, fried eggs, potatoes, peas and pineapple, all dished up on the same plate. Jars of relishes and bottles of sauce lined the tables. The orderly punched holes in a five-gallon drum of tomato juice and dextrously filled a large jug to offer us. Fresh-baked bread and American butter completed the meal. All the food was brought over from the States, including the vegetables, which were dried.

Morning call was for six as we were scheduled to shoot the eight o'clock parade. I awoke on time to a strangely silent camp. Lucky chaps, I thought, they probably don't get up till seven. I made my way to the bathhouse. No one was about, and neither, I noticed, were any of the 25-pounders, half-tracks or jeeps. I scurried about the camp. It was empty. In the sick bay I discovered the truculent sergeant, apparently awaiting examination for suspected appendicitis. I asked the medical orderly where everyone had got to. 'On a secret exercise,' he said.

'When will they be back?'

'Dunno. It's top secret.'

Four days later the battery returned, weary and mud-spattered, from the boggy exercise area. The following morning Brian picked his cast from the paraded men. The story of *Letter from Ulster* was simple. Two soldiers complain they never get any home mail. The colonel discovers they have never written home and orders them to write ten pages each. My job finally crystalized into finding people to play the Ulster parts, including singers and suitable locations. I came up with railway trains whose staff did our bidding, border roads with country policemen who were not too sure where the border lay, and Denis Martin, an Irish singer with a beautiful voice. Gradually the unit came to accept me, but I was struck by the way they were slowed down by internal restrictions, such as who should touch what. They seemed over-equipped and over-manned for such a simple film, and wherever they went an aura of self-importance formed a sacred pool around them. Union meetings came before the film in order of importance, except, of course, in the eyes of the producer and director.

For me the three weeks of shooting were over all too soon. We bade farewell to Colonel Sylvester and our two actors, Sergeant Don Prill, a twenty-year-old student from Minneapolis, and Private Wally Newfield, twenty-three, from the same city. Micky McCarthy had already left, and the unit was set to sail for England on Saturday night. Then came an unexpected reprieve. Brian suddenly realized that although he had recorded a Protestant service in camp, he had left out the Roman Catholics. 'Fix it, Willie,' he said to me.

I got agreement from St Mary's Church, Belfast, and asked Colonel Sylvester for men. 'They're off-duty,' he said, 'except for ten prisoners. You can have them.'

Norah and I hauled the half-ton velocilater that carried the camera and cameramen for tracking shots through Belfast's cobbled streets and installed it in St Mary's. Lamps and tracks were brought ashore, and on Sunday morning all was ready for the service. I placed the prisoners among Madonna-like girls in long black shawls. It was to be filmed in one take, a tilt down to the priest giving the Benediction and then a slow pan to the congregation and a track down the aisle. Finally I whispered to Brian, kneeling in the front row, that all was ready. 'You direct,' he said, 'I'm praying,' and closed his eyes.

He was a Protestant who was equally devoted to the Roman Catholic Church and its high ritual. Trying to control my trembling knees, I called, 'Action,' in a low voice. Chick Fowle, the cameraman, got the whole complicated shot on the first take. When I saw the rushes I had a shock. Seated in the third row was my father, beaming among the stony-faced prisoners at his much-loved first born. My first piece of direction was promptly christened 'MacQuitty's waxworks'.

A week earlier Brian had received a telegram from the noted producer Sydney Box, inviting him to direct a film version of the Frederick Lonsdale comedy *On Approval*. He asked my advice and I said, 'Do it. It's an excellent comedy and you've a good cast – Clive Brook, Beatrice Lillie, Roland Culver and Googie Withers.'

'Will you come with me?'

'Of course I will, if they'll have me.'

There was an extended postscript to the making of *Letter from Ulster*. In return for the Americans' three weeks of hospitality, I bought them a case of whiskey as a parting gift. This expense outraged the British Treasury and for three years a battle raged as to who was responsible and who should pay. Finally Jack Beddington settled the matter by pronouncing that, if it was for the men, it was too little, and if it was for the colonel, it was too much. For some reason this formula seemed to satisfy the Treasury, and in the fulness of time I came to hear no more about it.

18

The War and the Artists

Brian took me to meet Sydney Box in his office at Guild House,
Upper St Martin's Lane. Sydney was a large, fat, balding, jolly man
who wore glasses and reminded me instantly of the Laughing
Buddha, Mi-lo-fo. *On Approval* was his first venture into the feature
market with his production company, Verity Films, and once again I
found myself hired as an assistant, this time to the producer. My
salary again was £5 a week, but there were no deductions. Shooting
was to start in six weeks, and meanwhile I had to find accommodation. I walked north through Soho, and at Soho Square was aware
of being followed. I turned to see a tall, thin, elegantly dressed man,
who asked in courteous English, 'May I be of assistance to you?'

'I'm looking for somewhere to live.'

'Follow me,' he said, and turned into a side-door to No. 21, the
Manor House. Up we went in a small lift to the top floor, where he
had his office. 'I only need one room,' he announced, 'and if you like
you can have the rest of the flat. The rent will be £12 a month.'

I could hardly believe my good fortune. There was a large
bathroom, a small kitchen and two rooms, one overlooking Soho
Square and the other giving on to a flat roof with a parapet. 'May I
move in today?' I asked.

'Why, of course,' replied Mr Ripley, for that was his name.

In his office Walt Disney greeting cards bedecked the shelves. Mr
Ripley was Disney's London agent.

I settled quickly into Soho, where small documentary companies and huge film organizations jostled one another in and around Wardour Street. Facing me from across the square was the formidable Association of Cinema Technicians, led by George Elvin, which ran a closed shop, and woe betide anyone who dared to make a film in conditions that did not comply with their regulations. Below me the vaults of No. 21 were packed with thousands of feet of highly explosive nitrate film. My only escape route lay down the stairs that wound round the lift shaft. I had to take care over opening my door. It was set in a cosy recess and formed a perfect shelter for the street ladies of Soho to conduct their assignations. Once, in a hurry, I burst out and received a beating from a lady with her skirts up and a sailor with his trousers down.

In the basement was a large garage with a glass roof covering the well that separated the Manor House from Cross & Blackwell's offices next door. In the basement the caretaker, Cyril Brookfield, lived with his wife and young daughter and their cat Tommy. They took to coming up to my flat during air raids, convinced that their 'lucky' Irishman was not going to be blown to smithereens. One night they were just opening my door when a bomb went off a few hundred yards away in Tottenham Court Road. We were perfectly safe, and not even a pane of glass was cracked, but Tommy raced across the roof, jumped the parapet and fell into the well with a horrid sound of shattering glass. We rushed down but could find him nowhere, though a hole showed where he had fallen through. Next morning we discovered him draped across the starting handle of a truck. By some miracle he was still alive, and after three weeks of careful nursing he made a full recovery.

Jimmy Berger, then directing *The Rose of Tralee* with Diana Sheridan and John Longden at Riverside Studios, arranged for me to be on the floor from time to time. The studios, on the Thames beside Hammersmith Bridge, were on the outside a square unattractive brick building, but inside a magic world of Irish scenes. Nothing seemed beyond the art department: cottages, castles, moors, gardens, streams, skies and oceans could all be created within the sound-proofed boxes; the huge sound-proofed cameras never had to leave the comfortable security of their artificial world. I was astounded by the speed and skill of carpenters, plasterers, property men, painters, paper-hangers and make-up and costume personnel. Complicated sets were constructed in hours, torn down in minutes. Money ran like sand through an hour glass, and any stoppage was agony for both producer and backers.

As I came to learn more about film production, I saw that the writer made the most important contribution, then the director, and then the cast, but that the work of none of these could reach fruition without the producer. The successful producer needed to be a chairman of talents – a leader not a driver. Working as an assitant producer taught me a lot, but I realized that, if I did not help myself, no one else would do so; there was no school for film producers. With John Hooper, my accountant, I therefore formed a company with Jimmy Berger, Berger & MacQuitty Films Ltd, rented another room in No. 21 for £80 a year and made it into a cutting room with a Moviola and all the necessary equipment. For £250 I bought a Newman Sinclair clockwork camera that ran 200 feet of film at one winding, while three captured German Arriflex cameras with sophisticated through-lens viewing – three lenses mounted in a turret and driven by an electric motor – cost me £100 each. I was then able to hire out the cutting room for £5 a week and the Newman Sinclair to the Rank Organization for £10 a week and so generate a small income for the company. I bought a 1939 grey Vauxhall saloon for £205 and garage space at 8s. 6d. (42½p) a week. All I needed thereafter was financial backing for my ideas.

The Highlander Pub was the watering hole of the documentary film makers. Here I met Arthur Elton again, and John Grierson, who set the documentary movement going with *Drifters*, a story of the Scottish herring fleet. (Some said that the documentary makers had been drifting in his wake ever since.) I also met Edgar Anstey, Basil Wright, Paul Rotha, Humphrey Jennings and his Scots editor McAlister, who claimed that all he needed was whisky to lubricate him while he extracted wonderful sequences from the thousands of feet shot by Humphrey. All were friendly and helpful, but were attached to film companies and felt I had jumped the gun in setting up on my own. Jack Beddington felt the same, and years later he told me that he greatly regretted not backing me in those days.

The Two Brewers was the Verity pub, and here Sydney Box worked out ideas for films on the backs of envelopes with a stubby pencil and passed them to his accountant, Alfie Burlinson, to check the costing. He never seemed to have problems in setting up films, and could, like a skilful juggler, keep some thirty documentaries on the go at any one time. His output was stupendous, and he never seemed happier than when he was in the thick of complicated negotiations sandwiched between writing scripts and doctoring other people's.

One day Sydney asked me to help on a film about the Thames water system. The cameraman-director, Ray Elton – no relation to Arthur – was a tough, practical film-maker with a quick if sometimes caustic wit. Our equipment was a Newman Sinclair camera, a heavy tripod with an even heavier hydraulic pan and tilt head. I carried the tripod and held the clapperboard. The opening shot was the sewage outfall neart Southall. Ray shot everything: the churning spiked wheels that lifted disgusting debris from the untreated sewage; the men with long rakes and forks removing objects that would not break down in the settling tanks; and finally the dubious outflow as it mingled with the tidal waters. It was an uninviting subject, but at least it put me in the swim, so to speak, as an accepted London film-maker.

By now *On Approval* was due to be shot at Denham, the largest studios in Europe, but a week's delay caused by another picture over-running meant we had to start in a small studio at Merton Park. My first step was to apply for membership of the Association of Cinema Technicians, without which my film career would have ground to an abrupt halt. The Edwardian set was the vast kitchen of a gloomy Scottish castle where Bea Lillie, Googie Withers, Clive Brook and Roly Culver were to try living together before marriage. The cameraman, Gunther Kramph, a German with a high reputation, spent three days placing and spacing the lights in position for Clive to walk, candle in hand, through a door on the left to sit on the kitchen table and then cross to the sink to talk to Googie.

Merton Park was ill-equipped for sophisticated work and it was extremely difficult for the technicians to arrange the lighting to Kramph's satisfaction. As a candle was carried across the room, electricians with rheostats lowered the lights behind it and increased the lights in front. Each lamp was shielded with a lead snood that had to be bent to the exact pattern to match the candle-light. The kitchen ceiling was supposed to leak in several places, and this effect was accomplished by suspending buckets from the gantries, each bucket punctured with a pinhole to allow water to drip slowly into a variety of vessels placed on the kitchen floor. These vessels of various sizes emitted musical notes as the drops fell. Because of the low-key lighting, the shadows of the vessels did not appear and had to be painted on the floor. Never in the history of filming can so much trouble have been taken over such a small scene, but since it was the first in the schedule I assumed the meticulous approach would gradually moderate.

Meanwhile Brian sat in his director's chair, sick of rehearsing his frustrated actors and fuming at the delay; and Clive and Sydney spent anxious hours in the office watching the costs mount without an inch of film in the can. Clive was especially anxious since he was financing the film, but Brian promised to do one long take of eight minutes to bring things back on schedule. On the fourth day, the great moment came. The clapperboy held up the board: 'ON APPROVAL. Castle kitchen, Take 1.' Sound and picture cameras were running to speed, the boom operator held the microphone over the door. 'Action,' called Brian in a quiet though urgent voice.

Clive entered from the door on the left, as he had done throughout the interminable rehearsals, and looked superb in a polka-dot silk dressing gown and matching scarf. He moved to the table. The light rose and fell as the electricians worked their rheostats; the water dripped melodiously into the vessels. Clive sat on the kitchen table, an elegant leg swinging languidly, his long conversation with Googie about to begin. Suddenly he looked straight at Brian. 'Brian,' he said in a surprised tone, 'this is the wrong side of my face. I shall have to come in from the door on the right and exit left.'

For a moment Brian looked at him thoughtfully as if digesting the situation, and then said very slowly in his high-pitched voice, 'Go and fuck yourself.'

In the stunned silence that followed, Clive walked off the set, through the passage and out into Merton Park High Street.

'You shouldn't have said that,' I said to Brian.

'Willie,' he said, 'I can't stand his clacking teeth in the love scenes.'

Clive was brought back and went silently to his dressing room, where Sydney joined him. After a long wait he returned whistling to the set and the scene was shot as rehearsed. I discovered that he had suffered a facial injury as a pilot in the First World War, though he had gone through rehearsals up till then without mentioning it.

At the end of the week we moved to Denham, a great barracks of a place where a main corridor ran like a street down the whole length of the complex, the huge stages to one side and the facilities to the other. At the end of each day's work I drove Brian back to his studio flat in Kinnerton Street, where Carl Mayer, the great German scriptwriter, was staying with him. Here they would go through the script together. Carl, a small, dark, quiet man, close to the end of his life, was ill and without work. Times must have been hard for him in the midst of the war. All his writing had been for the movies and his scripts had laid the foundation of the German Expressionist school of film-making, including, as they did, *The Cabinet of Dr Caligari* and *The Last Laugh*. It was from an idea in one of his scripts that the notion of the tracking shot was developed, achieved by pulling the camera in a pram, hence the term 'dolly shot'. Carl was very likeable, but neither he nor Gunther Kramph seemed appropriate figures to be working on a fluffy Lonsdale comedy.

Within a few days Brian was summoned to the office and told, with all Sydney's compassion, that the picture could not go ahead with him and Gunther. Their talent was for dramatic subjects; it was an error of judgement for which no one was to blame. It was a bitter blow to Sydney to lose his key men only ten days into his first feature, and since there was no money to employ a new director, he and Clive decided to direct themselves and managed for cameraman to prise Claude Friese-Greene, son of England's pioneer of the movie camera, away from a picture he was just finishing on the neighbouring stage.

That evening Brian was holding a party in honour of the American director, John Ford, and had invited Norah Dawson, who was working at Denham. As I drove them to Kinnerton Street, he said he was leaving the picture because he disagreed with the way they wanted it shot, but Norah took him up sharply, 'You've been fired, Brian.'

'Quite right,' he chuckled. 'It doesn't pay to resign.'

'I'll leave too,' I offered.

'On no account,' said Brian. 'It has nothing to do with you. One day we'll make a picture together.'

When we arrived at the flat and Brian told John Ford he had been fired, Ford asked, 'Did you get the money? That's where it hurts.'

'Yes,' Brian grinned. 'All of it.'

Brian wore an old blue shirt outside a pair of flannel trousers and put everyone instantly at ease. Celebrities at the party included Cecil Beaton, who designed the costumes for *On Approval*, and Noël Coward, who was called 'a silly old bitch' by a good-looking fair-haired boy who immediately burst into tears. Otto Lucas, the hat man, was there, as were Douglas Fairbanks Jnr, Doisha and Terence Young and Denis Martin, my singer in *Letter from Ulster*, whose voice won from John Ford fulsome appreciation and a promise of work. There were also several guardsmen, and the wine and spirits were unlimited even though our ration was something like a bottle a month. Friendly police, previously engaged by Brian, brought the party to an end at 3.30, whereat many slept where they fell; but towards the end of the party I had been sitting between Brian and Norah on a large settee when Cecil Beaton came up, sat on the floor at Brian's feet, turned to me and asked me to go home with him. I said I was taking Norah home, but he continued in a charming persuasive voice until Brian said, 'Oh, go on, Willie, don't be so Dundonald.'

Since my farm was in the suburb of Belfast called Dundonald, Brian's remark, which puzzled Cecil, was explicit to me. I was being too suburban. I took Norah home.

After its faltering start, the production of *On Approval* moved rapidly ahead. One of my jobs was to bring Beatrice Lillie to the studio in time for her lengthy hair-dressing, make-up and costume. Each day at 6 a.m. I called for her at 55 Park Lane, and each day she was ready. Friends of Bea's would call to see her at the studio, and on one occasion the Duchess of Kent arrived with her party incognito until Bea gave her a graceful curtsey. As I was talking to the duchess, the tea boy came up and said, 'Here's a cuppa for you and your girl friend.' I also often took Bea back to Park Lane after filming was over.

Her flat on the roof was a joyful place despite the blackout. Her door was always open and people drifted in until the small hours and slept on the floor if there was an air raid. Bea was popular and there was a never-ending stream of such people as Noël Coward, Martha Raye, Leslie Henson, Isabel Jeans, the Baroness D'Erlanger, Lady Caroline Paget and her aunt Bridget, Lillie Palmer and her sister, known as 'Cuddly' Palmer. One evening, when I had taken my brother along, Bea was asked how she kept so fit. 'Why, standing on my head,' she said, and gave us a demonstration, revealing her bright red bloomers. Baroness D'Erlanger then said, 'That's easy,' and followed suit, her dress tumbling over her head to reveal a shapely but unadorned bottom.

Beneath Bea's jolly exterior, however, lay a deep sadness. Her only child, Bobby, had been killed on Easter Sunday six months earlier when a Japanese plane dropped a 500-pound bomb on the frigate *Tenedos* in Colombo harbour. The explosion had blown off the end of the ship and killed fifteen sailors, her son among them. 'It seems silly making a funny picture when my heart is broken,' she said to me, yet she never faltered.

One day she received an invitation from a famous medium to attend a séance. Bobby had apparently been trying to get through to her. When she asked me to go with her, I agreed, provided she did not reveal my identity. We were asked to arrive at eight and not to eat beforehand. The medium seated our little group round a table and instructed us not to cross our legs. The lights were switched off and in total darkness we listened to music. After about an hour a little girl's voice came through. She asked Bea to sing a duet with her, and this they did, very charmingly. Then a message came for me from Sir John Martin Harvey, who had died a few days previously, wishing me luck and urging me to carry on with the job and look after his ring. I concluded that the medium caught the 'Mac' part of my name as we arrived and thought I was the actor Max Adrian, Sir John's protégé. I therefore remained silent, and after that the voice of Micky, an irrepressible cockney boy of nine, told us how, on the other side, they all lived in houses and led just the same lives as ourselves and there was nothing to worry about. He also sang songs with Bea, but still there was no word from Bobby. It was on the whole a happy experience. Others in the group talked to their dear ones, but, like religion, it seemed a matter of faith. We left unconvinced.

On 1 November there was an air raid at Denham. Everyone was rushed into the shelters situated beneath the studio floors in narrow passages designed to carry the water mains, gas pipes and electric cables. The effects of a direct hit were unimaginable, and there was only one narrow exit. I vowed that never again would I let myself be jammed in an underground shelter, and sat and held Bea's hand while Flanagan, her maid, stood beside us, making nervous conversation. The place was packed as we heard the first bombs in the distance. The second stick fell closer and hitherto silent people began to talk in loud voices. Then there was a terrific *crumph* and the lights went out. After a few minutes they came on again, and then went on and off several times to convey the all-clear. We emerged slowly and gratefully to resume work.

Once the shooting of *On Approval* was finished, the general opinion was that the picture was a problem. But with some skilful editing and a witty opening commentary it gained critical praise. Eventually it settled down to being seen as a minor classic of its kind.

Sydney asked me to be temporary production manager until Betty Box, his sister, was able to take over. The job was to service the documentary units (microcosms of the big features) with transport, cameras, film, sound, studio space, accounts and so forth. It involved a checker board of moves and decisions to keep film flowing through the cameras from early morning till late at night. A couple of weeks in I was elected shop steward, though I do not remember ever calling a meeting. There was too much to be done to stop for arguments. As Churchill said of the Mulberry Harbour, 'Don't ask me about the difficulties, they will speak for themselves.' By turn I directed, acted, carried the camera, drove the unit, found locations, food and shelter. It never occurred to me that one day these jobs would be departmentalized to such an extent that in one of our pictures, *Miranda*, starring Glynis Johns as a captured mermaid, production would stop for a day while shop stewards wrestled with the question of whether seaweed came under props as dead matter or the garden section as living vegetation.

My stint as production manager ended when Betty took over and I was asked to rescue a film for the British Council. Entitled *The Bridge Builders*, it was designed to show that East and West had common ground and improve relations with India for the war effort. The picture was overdue, no filming had taken place and a lot of the budget had been spent on an unsuccessful script and research. Since the BBC broadcast to India on the 19-metre band, I decided that *Nineteen-Metre Band* should be its title while calculating that their programmes would supply all the material we needed. With a great friend and splendid cameraman, Reg Wyer, I set out for the BBC studios, where Z.A. Bokhari, the head of the department, let us loose in the studio.

The first thing I thought would make a good mix was Eastern and Western Music, and so we shot Leon Goossens playing South Indian classical music on the oboe accompanied by Narayana Menon (the future head of Indian radio, and then television) playing the veena, a long, stringed instrument with large sounding bowls at each end. Next John Wills at the harpsichord played Brahms, accompanied by Narayana on the veena. It was the first occasion on which Eastern and Western musical instruments were united in harmony, and the press made quite a fuss about it.

On the lighter side, the film showed the adventures of two mice travelling about England in the pocket of an Indian boy and asking all kinds of questions to do with the British way of life; and on the more serious side were discussions with Sir William Beveridge, Wickham Steed, Kingsley Martin and Edith Summerskill. None of the cast were paid or under control, and at one point Edith said she must get back to the House of Commons since her scene would not be ready for an hour. I took her straight to make-up and whispered to the girl to take an hour over it. Edith came on the set an hour later looking marvellous and gave me an enormous smile. But my greatest *coup* was to direct T.S. Eliot reciting 'Little Gidding', which is, I believe, the only filmed record of him reading his poetry in existence.

While *On Approval* was still having problems, Sydney became involved with producing another feature, *The Flemish Farm*, for Filippo Del Giudice's Two Cities company. The film, directed by Jeffrey Dell, ran into trouble in the middle when Clifford Evans, playing the hero, was summoned before a tribunal for conscientious objectors. 'You've got to get him off till he's finished work,' said Sydney, 'or we've no picture.'

It was a tricky situation: a conscientious objector making a film about a Flemish farm where gallant Allied troops were hidden and helped to escape from the Germans. The tribunal were a difficult bunch, representing the Church, the trade unions, the law, medicine and the armed forces. In the end they reluctantly granted him time to complete the film.

Jeffrey Dell and his wife Jill lived in Malcolm MacDonald's house in Frognal, Hampstead, next to General De Gaulle. Jill was a writer and had worked on Jeffrey's script for the picture under her maiden name of Craigie. She was eager to direct and was writing a script about the war artists and their role in recording events. I liked the idea and mentioned it to Sydney, who said we might fit it in later, but for the moment he had undertaken a project for the Co-op on the theme of the Tolpuddle Martyrs. He wanted me to take charge of production and Bob Compton Bennett would direct.

The studio for *Men of Rochdale*, as the film was called, was a converted church in Marylebone Road, and Bob was a first-class director. Quiet and meticulous, he would write down everything in minute handwriting, his face seemingly always sad and serious. Sydney felt, however, that shooting was taking rather long and said I could have anything I wished if only I brought it in on budget. 'I'll settle for your trench coat,' I said.

The final scene, shot in the church hall, showed the men of Rochdale being exhorted to stand up for themselves as the camera tracked down the aisle of poverty-striken faces. I arranged for a spare take to end in a big close-up on a shawl-covered woman in the back row. As the camera moved in, the woman threw back the shawl to reveal Bea Lillie, glittering with jewels and offering her famous artificial smile. It was so well received that I thought I'd leave it in for our first screening for the Co-op, who were not amused. Nevertheless the picture came in on budget and I wore the trench coat for years.

Often when I walked back from Bea's flat in Park Lane to Soho Square by way of Piccadilly, I stopped off at the Players Theatre, then in Albemarle Street, where the excellent show was compèred by Leonard Sachs. He and his brother Hymie had given Denis Martin, the talented young Ulster singer, coaching and encouragement which proved so successful that years later he ran the theatre himself. One of my favourite artists was Hedli Anderson, a lovely redhead who married Louis MacNiece, the Ulster poet. On one wall of the small theatre Feliks Topolski had painted a grand mural of the royal coach, with horses, footmen and outriders, his inimitable swirling strokes carrying the Royal Family towards the stage. Unfortunately this magnificent spectacle disappeared during a spring cleaning when industrious Mrs Mops washed down the wall.

Professor Joad, one of the regulars at the Players, told me how he used in his youth to roam Piccadilly with 10s. in his hand, but could make little impression with the ladies. 'Now,' he said, 'as a popular philosopher with grey hairs on my chest and sprouting out of my ears, I can't keep young women out of my bed.' The bombs did not apparently deter the ladies of Piccadilly. A six-footer in a huge picture hat regularly used to tip it sideways and whisper to me, 'Would you like to come home with a naughty little girl?'

One became used to the sirens, the drone of enemy aircraft, the searchlights and barrage balloons, the thump of the bombs, the thunder of the anti-aircraft batteries, the showers of spent ammunition, the bulging hoses snaking across the streets, the clatter of fire teams and rescue squads transporting heavy equipment. Many found the situation exhilarating, and I confess that I did too during the raids. But the aftermath was dreadful: the search for the dead and wounded, the seas of broken glass, the shattered buildings, the smouldering fires and an awful smell of charred wood and plaster that hung in the air for days. Small wonder if many sought safety abroad, but many who could have done so stayed and did what they could to help.

Yet, if we were having problems, those in the Far East were much worse off. By this stage the foreign staffs of the Chartered Bank and many of my friends had been imprisoned, civilians having been advised by their embassies to obey the Japanese and go quietly. Pemberton and Lousie, who had married, were in the Shanghai gaol and Louise's father, W.A.R. Wood, was in Bangkok gaol, as was Long John Silver. I went to see Beaky Duncan and suggested that, since I was entitled to an Irish passport, I might go round the East as a neutral observer and try to keep in contact with the captured staff. The idea was appreciated but not considered practicable. In any case, the Swiss and other neutral embassies were doing all that they could.

Filippo Del Giudice, a voluble Italian lawyer turned film producer, was persuaded by Sydney that Jill Craigie's idea for a film on the war artists would be worth backing. The respective cities of this Two Cities company were London and Rome, and he had been released from internment as an alien on the Isle of Man after helping to control a riot among the camp's inmates and declaring his intention of producing pro-British films. The promise was amply kept. He raised the finance for Laurence Olivier's *Henry V* and produced Carol Reed's *The Way Ahead* among many others. He was full of warmth and enthusiasm for 'his talents', as he called the British writers, directors and artists who worked for him.

The war-artist movie was to be called *Out of Chaos*. It would be the first film to put contemporary paintings and painters on the screen. Jill would direct her own script and I would produce. The modest budget was a little over £7,000. We would have only a week in the studio; the rest would be on location with a cameraman and assistant. Del was taking a risk with an untried woman director (women directors then being almost unheard-of) and a subject that lacked mass appeal. The British Council and the Arts Council, from whom we hoped for more backing, both turned the project down.

Jill was small, dark, pretty and determined – very determined. Her script was to answer those questions that arose in the minds of the public when they saw their money being spent on artists whose work they regarded with suspicion or ridicule. The first step was to get Kenneth Clark, director of the National Gallery, and some of the war artists to agree to be filmed; then to take the artists to suitable locations where we could film them at work. They would be shot silent with a commentary over, except in the studio and National Gallery, where we would have direct sound. The unit consisted of Jill and myself, the cameraman Pennington 'Penny' Richards, who had been invalided out of the Army Film Unit suffering from shell shock, and our loader-clapper boy, Leslie Hughes, who was still under military age.

First, we filmed Paul Nash at the Cowley dump of crashed and burnt-out aircraft, mostly grievously our own. The relics of death and disaster lay in orderly rows of twisted metal as terrible momentoes of the airmen's desperate efforts to survive. It was all too easy to visualize those last searing moments. Engines had smashed through air-frames already riddled with bullets and grotesquely melted seats nestled in the wreckage so that you half expected to see human fragments amid the horror. Paul, as he guided us through this cemetery of aeroplanes, frequently stopped to use his inhaler, for he suffered from severe asthma. He was, at forty-three, an impressive, withdrawn man with penetrating eyes and wit. From time to time he spoke vividly of his reactions to the dreadful spectacle. His vision of it, conveyed in his great canvas in the Tate Gallery, was of a 'Totes Mere', a dead sea of wave after wave of wrecked planes breaking on the shore. As a keen photographer, he took an interest in Penny's light-meter. Jill was ever-eager to shoot, but Penny would refuse until the sun shone or the light was constant for a sequence. When Jill said, 'I can't see any difference,' Paul looked at her with admiration and said, 'Not even with those beautiful eyes?'

Our next subject was Graham Sutherland at the Imperial Chemical Industries limestone quarries at Hindlow, Buxton. Graham was thirty-eight, small, dapper and forceful and, like all the war artists, totally dedicated to his work. He saw inside his subjects to a degree that made his later portraits of Somerset Maugham, Helena Rubinstein and Winston Churchill strikingly illuminating (too much so for

Lady Churchill, who destroyed the one of her husband). We also filmed him in his studio and a replica of it we built in Merton Park on the site of the Clive Brook incident. Graham worked in gouache on a sheet of paper placed flat on a table, often dropping cigarette ash on to the wet surface. When I queried this, he said that art had no boundaries.

Stanley Spencer had to be filmed working with the ship-builders at Port Glasgow. He arrived early at Victoria Station, where we found him waiting patiently for us with Daphne Charlton, a pretty girl who sported what was known as a 'peek-a-boo' bang, a wave of hair that hid one eye. He had met her in 1939, and they had been friends ever since, but Stanley took me on one side and said, 'You mustn't let Daphne come with us. She is stronger than I am and every afternoon when I was painting in Exeter she would carry me off to bed.'

It was a near thing, but we waved her goodbye as the train pulled out and took our seats opposite a young naval officer and his bride, still shedding confetti. Stanley immediately began to talk about his marriage with Patricia. He had been very nervous on his wedding night, he said, and made sure he got into bed first, where he felt safer.

Patricia meanwhile went into the bathroom and stayed there a long time while Stanley grew more and more tense. Finally she came out wearing a 'see-through' black lace nightie and scarlet lipstick. 'I was so shocked,' Stanley said, 'that I couldn't do anything and our marriage was never consummated.'

The young couple were hanging on every word. From the girl's expression I judged she could well have a black lace nightie in her suitcase.

The only accommodation I could find for us in Port Glasgow was the Glencairn, a boarding house run by a large, dark, no-nonsense Glaswegian woman who said she had two double beds and a single. Jill took the single, and Penny and I, being tall, shared one double, while Leslie and Stanley, being short, shared the other. We descended to supper past white marble statues of nude Italian ladies and found a dining room with a heavy mahogany table, solid mahogany chairs and thick green velvet curtains falling in swathes from heavy brass curtain rails. During supper Stanley announced, 'I never have any trouble getting to sleep. I always wear my pyjamas under my clothes. This saves a lot of time going to bed and getting up, and of course it doesn't disturb the little people under my arms.'

Leslie give him a look of horror.

That evening I sat up working out the next day's schedule, and by the time I retired Penny was already in bed and asleep. He had a fine black beard that twitched as his lower jaw moved from time to time and made his teeth click. The barbiturates he was on for his shell shock gradually took effect, and very slowly he commenced to snore. Then, with a quiet, smooth movement, he rolled himself and the bedclothes into a cosy cocoon around himself and left me uncovered.

I got out of bed and went to explore the house to see if I could discover a blanket. Downstairs in the dining room I found Leslie lying on the sofa, wrapped in one of the landlady's velvet curtains. I shook him. 'What do you think you're doing?' I hissed.

'I couldn't sleep with that man. I've been bitten all over.'

'Nonsense,' I said, 'it's only your imagination.'

'Anyway, I'm not getting into bed with him again.'

'It's not every day a clapper boy gets the chance to sleep with a famous artist. It's an incident you'll remember with pride. Don't forget to put everything back where you got it.'

I went to look in Stanley's room. It was empty, but in a cupboard I found some spare blankets, and took a couple. On the way back I passed the lavatory. The door was ajar and there sat Stanley, reading. 'What on earth are you doing?' I asked.

'I'm just reading. I found a wonderful book and it's nice and quiet in here.'

'Well, go back to bed now and get some sleep. We can't have our star with bags under his eyes.'

'How I envy you, Bill,' he said. 'You manage everything so easily. I wish you could take care of me. I find life terribly difficult. I don't understand money, I'm always in debt and my life is completely mixed up. Now, why don't you take me under your wing? I'll let you arrange everything and I'll be free to get on with my painting.'

Stanley was very appealing. We talked a long time, and finally I got him back to his bed. Penny was still snoring when I returned to my own.

Next day at the yard Stanley received a warm welcome from his ship-builders, among whom he was immensely popular. The giant cranes, cradles, slipways, gantrys, girders and plates with their riveters and welders provided him with magnificent material. He sketched scene after scene in rapid bursts on a roll of strong white toilet paper that made me think of the papyrus scrolls of ancient scribes. Yard after yard became covered with details of his concentration. Here and there he made notes: 'Remember the woman welder', 'Don't forget the finished ship.'

'Why do you use toilet paper?' I asked.

'Because it is cheap and doesn't end. It gives me continuity, and if I don't like the sketch I don't have to waste the paper!' he said with a joyful grin.

Filming continued with reassuring speed and *Picture Post* sent Jeanne Heal to do a feature with the photographer Leonard McCombe. Stanley was in his element. One evening I suggested that we all relax at a movie. Stanley had never been to a cinema before, and the film, a Western, had him enthralled. As the unsuspecting hero rode down the gulch, an Indian brave lay in wait behind a rock. The rider drew nearer and nearer, the suspense increased. Suddenly Stanley stood up and yelled, 'He's waiting for you behind the rock!'

There was a stir in the house, then silence. The Indian leapt out, the fight was on. More Indians appeared, but our hero, his Colt blazing, drove them off, their dead left behind them. Stanley's voice rang out again: 'He fired eight shots and it's only a six-shooter!'

At Stanley's home in Cookham in Berkshire we filmed him working on his long narrow canvas 'Welders' that hangs today in the Tate. Stanley had given the house to Patricia, who allowed him to occupy only his bedroom, reached by a back stairway. In this bedroom-studio, which measured twelve feet by sixteen, Stanley had tacked the canvas round the walls from the window to the door, where the surplus canvas was rolled up and fastened. Once he had finished one section, he pulled out all the tacks and moved the canvas along to its next position. He was delighted to show us everything and to chatter about his extraordinary domestic circumstances, about which books have since been written.

Our next location was Henry Moore's studio at Much Hadham in Hertfordshire. Henry was forty-three, a strong, quiet man with a simple, natural way of explaining what he was doing. When I asked why he carved human beings in such odd shapes, he said that the human figure interested him deeply, but that abstract qualities of design were essential and the psychological element must not be neglected. I mentioned that I had worked with Stekel, and as he was showing me various sculptures, he paused before a large egg-like shape with a hole through its centre in which rested three small eggs. He said, 'I suppose Stekel would have had some theory about this.'

'What do you think about it yourself?' I asked, feeling the answer was obvious enough, for he and his charming wife Irina had not so far had any children.

'I don't know,' he said. 'I carve figures out of stone and the material excercises a force of its own. When I carved this, I was not thinking that it represented food or life or that the eggs might hatch into birds.'

I asked him how he painted his famous tube-shelter scenes.

'First I use a wax crayon to put highlights on the white paper. These don't show up until I cover the paper with a grey wash, which is the colour of the tube shelters. Having established the situation, I fill in the detail with Indian ink. I came upon this idea by accident when I was doing a drawing to amuse a young niece. She had some wax crayons, and when I added a wash of watercolour I found, of course, that the watercolour did not take on the wax.'

In London we filmed Henry drawing people sheltering in Holborn Underground Station, where they came every evening and had their regular pitches on the platform, safe from the exploding world above ground. Penny managed a long tracking shot from a train supplied after hours and Henry moved among the sleeping figures, making notes and sketches.

Finally, we repaired to the National Gallery. Here, for the opening sequence, Kenneth Clark, architect of the War Artists Advisory Committee, said, 'The committee was set up to choose artists to make a record of the war, not simply a record of the facts but a record of what the war felt like.'

Since he was nervous, Jill suggested that he sat on the edge of a table and used his hands to illustrate his points. (Many years on, he was still using his hands in the same way when he made his famous TV series, *Civilization*.) Afterwards, when I asked him to autograph a still I had taken, he inscribed it, 'From your most incompetent and overpaid stand-in, Kenneth Clark.' Our final scene, also shot in the National Gallery, had a group of 'ordinary' people looking at Graham Sutherland's 'Limestone Quarry' and arguing in the way of the public, 'If that's a painting, my small son's a genius,' and so on. Eric Newton, the art critic, then joined the group to deal with their bewilderment. In response to the final question, 'After all, suppose I do get to understand pictures, what will it do for me?' Eric lifted his drawn and tortured face and declared, 'It makes life so much more enjoyable.'

The editing and dubbing went smoothly and the finished picture received first-class reviews but no release in any cinema. Rank, the distributors, were adamant that there was no room for such a film in houses where the public had to pay. This moved Ernest Betts, writing in the *Sunday Express* of 10 December 1944, to give it a three-star rating and say:

Some of our most famous artists have been set to work to paint the war, and this is a film showing how it was done. Artists like Henry Moore and Paul Nash went into shelters, shipyards, air raids, hospitals, quarries and put down what they saw. But can you understand it when you see it? Well the subject is sharply debated on the screen. It tries something new and advances the cause of the cinema as an intelligent medium. It is so good. In fact it isn't being shown anywhere! No release has been set, but it will be and the sooner the better.

We also received publicity from the photographer Lee Miller, who worked for *Vogue*, and Dave Scherman, her colleague on *Life*. They had both spent a day with us at Much Hadham and were most enthusiastic about Henry. As time went on, the film began to be shown in art houses, but still it received no general distribution and thus, after all the hard work, all the hopes and fears, all the wonderful notices, remained on the distributor's shelves. On the positive side, it had all been a wonderful experience. Stanley Spencer became a firm personal friend and the war artists' pictures were acknowledged as national treasures.

19

'Never Pay Cash'

One evening in June 1944, as I sat enjoying an after-dinner brandy in the garden of my friend Manny Lederman's cottage at Chobham, Surrey, a light appeared in the sky and came directly towards us. It moved quite slowly beneath the barrage balloons. There were erratic bursts of engine noise and flames shot from the fuselage. My God, I thought, a plane in trouble. Still stuttering and spouting flame, the first flying bomb – which is what it was – passed overhead and disappeared towards London.

The V1s or 'doodle-bugs' soon became a part of London life. Many were shot down or tipped off course by courageous pilots manoeuvring a wing under the missile, but enough got through to wreak havoc, for they carried almost a ton of high explosive. Everyone had their flying-bomb story before long. Mine came as I was driving across Vauxhall Bridge. I heard the ominous noise, stopped the car and saw a bomb coming directly towards me. Government instructions were to lie in the gutter, hands over eyes and stomach clear of the ground, but I only just managed to drop to the ground before a vast explosion shook everything. It had landed two hundred yards beyond, behind a row of shops that protected me from the blast.

I drove quickly to the scene, where two lorries had been reduced to tangled metal and people were already trying to pull the drivers free. About thirty small houses lay in rubble and a large area around them had suffered blast damage with windows, doors and roofs blown off. Rescue teams were on the scene within minutes. No fires were started, but firemen commenced hosing blood off the road where civilians and a pair of dray horses had been killed. A priest appeared and seemed to know at once to whom to give the last rites; and, within five minutes of the explosion, the first stretcher came out, carrying a woman and her baby. The baby's head was crushed flat, but the mother would not let the body go. Both were blackened, bleeding and covered with dirt. Soon there were too many helpers and the area was roped off. Householders who were more irritated than scared, to judge by their faces, began to sweep glass and debris into the gutters, though here and there a frantic mother searched wildly for a child.

I drove three walking cases to a nearby hospital – already hit itself that morning, though with only one fatality. The windows had been blown out, but the sister, a Dublin woman, carried on as if the situation was quite normal. In the ward lay men, women and children engrained with explosion grime and criss-crossed with plaster where they had been cut by flying glass. Dust and grit from their hair dirtied the pillows. As I stood there, another alert sounded. The hospital was full, the bed cases could not be moved and the sense of helplessness was total. The tension was agonizing, yet no one said a word or panicked. Minutes later we heard the explosion in the distance. By the time I got back to Vauxhall Bridge, all casualties had been removed and mobile canteens were serving tea.

In the film world, Sydney Box had meanwhile perceived that, to get a fair return on all the risks and hardships involved in production, it was essential to own a film rather than produce on others' behalf. He therefore rented Riverside Studios from Jack Buchanan and bought the rights in *29 Acacia Avenue*, a lightweight comedy play by Mabel and Denis Constanduros about a suburban family in which the parents go on holiday, leaving their engaged daughter to take care of the home. In their absence, she is persuaded into a pre-marital romp with her fiancée, but at the crucial moment the unexpected return of the father and mother prevent the couple getting together. Henry Cass was directing and the cast included Gordon Harker, Betty Balfour, Henry Kendall, Hubert Gregg and Jimmy Handley and his wife Diana Sheridan. The budget was £45,000, £30,000 of which was to come from Barclays Bank, whose friendly manager guaranteed that the loan would be sanctioned at the next board meeting, a week after we started shooting. We weren't to worry, he said; it was a mere formality.

Henry brought in amusing rushes and inspired everyone with confidence. On Thursday afternoon our bank manager phoned in dismay. His directors had turned down the loan and he was abject in his apologies. Sydney, always at his best in such situations, talked to Gordon Harker, who put in £2,000, while I took a £5,000 piece. Alfred Shipman of the Shipman & King cinema chain, who had always been flirting with the idea of backing films, was then given an ultimatum by Sydney to put his money in now or he would never have the chance again. He put up the balance with the proviso that his money came out first.

The completed film looked very good, but no distribution had been arranged in advance and no distributor seemed in a hurry to take it. Month succeeded month, and our position grew desperate. At last J. Arthur Rank agreed to see it at the Odeon, Edgware Road, where it was slipped into a programme in place of the second feature. There we sat apprehensively with Arthur Rank and John Davis, Arthur's *alter ego*, and the Rank distributors. To our great relief, the film produced abundant laughter and, at the end, applause. Arthur and his entourage retired for twenty minutes to the manager's office. When they emerged, Arthur, a moderator of the Methodist Church, pronounced the film immoral and pinpointed this as the cause of the immoderate laughter. He offered to pay our costs to leave the film on the shelf. In fact the story that shocked Rank was mild compared to many shown on his circuit, and while his offer was generous, it was not one we could accept. It would, apart from damaging the careers of artists and director, have undermined our ability to make other films. It was two years before the film went out on the ABC circuit, and when it did long queues lined up to see it everywhere that it ran.

I often spoke to Sydney of my time with Wilhelm Stekel and the influence he had on his patients, and the idea of using the unconscious mind for a film appealed to him and his wife Muriel. Together they wrote a script about a guardian and his ward, a girl in love with music. Bob Compton Bennett was chosen to direct and James Mason played the psychoanalytic guardian, Ann Todd the girl. The resulting film, *The Seventh Veil*, gained Oscars for Sydney and Muriel for the best original screenplay for 1945, the year in which peace finally broke out. It had only cost £92,000, but surpassed all box-office records wherever it was shown. Arthur Rank promptly invited Sydney to take over Gainsborough Studios at Shepherds Bush on a contract to produce ten to twelve pictures a year with budgets of £150,000 to £200,000 apiece.

In the meantime, Jill Craigie and I had been looking for a subject to follow *Out of Chaos*, and settled on *The Way We Live*, a film about the rebuilding of a blitzed city. We discussed the project with Clough Williams-Ellis, Professor Patrick Abercrombie and the distinguished town-planner, Sir Charles Reilly, famous for his plan for Birkenhead, who was full of enthusiasm and helpful ideas. Del gave us the backing of Two Cities and we set off to find a suitable city. Our short-list eventually narrowed down to Hull, Coventry and Plymouth, and since Abercrombie's plan for Plymouth struck us as far-sighted and practical, that became our final choice. J.D.M. Harvey, a brilliant artist of architects' plans, provided wonderfully realized views of Plymouth reborn. The lord mayor, Alderman H.G. Mason, and his committee accepted the idea and from then on the city in all its aspects was ours.

Having warned the aldermen to wear the same clothes each day for continuity, we spent three days filming them in the council chamber. Suddenly I was recalled by Arthur Rank. He had received a complaint from Lady Astor that we had left out her husband, the prime mover in the House of Lords for getting the plan accepted. She was insisting that the film be stopped forthwith. I drove up to London through the night and next morning took the cuttings from local papers about our filming in the council chamber into Arthur's office. He looked at the clippings, summoned John Davis from the adjoining room and said, with what was I suspected a note of relief, 'Look at these, John. We're too late.'

Awaiting my return to Plymouth was a telegram from Del congratulating us on the council-chamber material, but I was still apprehensive that Nancy Astor, a splendid fighter who virtually was Plymouth, would find a spoke to put in our wheel. Having met her several times on my first visit to the city, I knew she was fierce but approachable, and decided I must see her at once. I arrived at her house at 12.30, to be told by the butler that she was entertaining guests over pre-luncheon cocktails. Upstairs, I spotted Abercrombie and Paton Watson, the city engineer, in a corner. It looked very much as if the film were being discussed. Nancy Astor, turning and seeing me, said in frosty tones, 'You have not been invited.'

'I know that, Lady Astor. I'm only here to show you the scene in the script where Lord Astor addresses the House of Lords – the key scene in the picture.'

I held the script in my hand, but she ignored it and swept away among her distinguished guests. A little later, when the butler announced that luncheon was served, I screwed up courage to follow the gathering downstairs and take up a position just to the right of Lady Astor's chair. She continued to ignore me and lunch proceeded as if I were invisible. Soup was served, then lobster thermidor, then chicken Maryland. At last, as she helped herself to the chicken, she asked, 'Well, what is it?'

I opened the script at the section where Lord Astor addressed the House of Lords. She gave the pages a rapid glance and declaimed, 'What is that bitch up to?'

'Lady Astor,' I said, 'Jill Craigie's given your husband the best scene in the picture, and the most expensive one. We've made sure he has full recognition for his part in the Plymouth plan.'

'Sit down and have some lunch,' she said.

'Lady Astor,' I replied, 'I didn't come for lunch, but I will take a drumstick,' and lifted one from the dish in front of her.

Suddenly she laughed. I withdrew, clutching my drumstick.

Plymouth being a seafaring city, I arranged to spend an afternoon on a trawler to see how we might weave this element into the picture. It was a hot sunny day and I wore an open-neck shirt and cotton trousers. Our skipper was a small, dark Cornishman who wrote and recited bawdy poetry, and his crew on this occasion consisted of one old man with a massive hernia. The skipper started the single-cylinder diesel engine by heating the cylinder head red-hot with a blow-lamp and then turning over the heavy flywheel with an iron bar, whereupon the engine thumped into life. Fifteen miles out, the trawl was lowered and towed for two hours; and when it was hauled up, the bag bulged with an unexpected catch of prime fish. The old man pulled the slip knot and the fish spilled across the deck. The knot was retied, the trawl relowered.

It was expected that I should make myself useful in return for their hospitality. I was handed a small knife and we set about gutting the fish. The scene was tumultuous: large skate with curved mouths, fat brill, sole, plaice, some whiting, hundreds of queen scallops and spider crabs. We worked quickly, sharpening our knives on the iron edge of the hatch. Struggling fish are difficult to hold, and soon my hands were full of spines, but it was exciting work and the sunshine and fresh air were wonderfully stimulating. 'When do we turn back?' I asked.

'Not while we're catching prime fish,' laughed the skipper.

Two days later we thumped into harbour. We had trawled through the night and I was cold and exhausted from lack of sleep. I was also covered in blood, slime and fish scales. As we rounded the headland, the old man said as he nursed his hernia, 'I know a heap of folk 'oud change places with 'ou.'

'Where are they?' I asked, my teeth chattering.

'Thar,' he said, pointing to the cemetery.

The film's première was held at the Plymouth Odeon on 29 July 1946. That September, as the first documentary film to be shown at the Cannes Film Festival, it received outstanding praise, and the notices in general were wildly enthusiastic – even better than those for *Out of Chaos*. The finale to the film showed a great march through the city by 3,000 youngsters carrying banners that read: 'POOLS FOR SCHOOLS', 'PREMISES NOT PROMISES' and so on. At their head were the bands of the Boys Brigade and the Army Cadet Force, and the march ended in the Guildhall Square, where nineteen-year-old Doris Sergeant, a telephone operator and chairman of the Council of Youth, declared, 'Let us have the plan as soon as the labour and materials are available. We in our turn will do our best to be worthy of the great traditions of our ancient city.'

In another scene, Michael Foot, the Labour parliamentary candidate for Plymouth, was talking to the fishermen. He spoke passionately of the new city that would rise from the ruins, of the new schools, the great shopping arcade, the broad avenue that would lead through the city to the Hoe. We had also asked Hore-Belisha, defending what was regarded as a staunchly traditional Liberal seat, what he thought about it. Hore-Belisha said, 'Plymouth has no need for a plan. It is ideally situated with the sea in front and the moors behind. Plenty of room for expansion.' In the general election of July 1945 the people of Plymouth voted overwhelmingly for Michael Foot.

For our part, flushed with success, Jill and I set about tackling another topical subject, the nationalizing of the coal mines.

There was by now a slump in the film industry. The Berger & MacQuitty partnership had closed down from lack of work. Our previous success had lulled me into a sense of security, however, and I was determined to make *Blue Scar* with my own new company, Outlook Films, whose logo was a small owl. Jill agreed to write a feature script for £1,000, half of this being promised by John Sutro, who was also keen to put money into the film itself. I produced the other £500. When the script was duly completed, John found he was unable to help further, but the Coal Board liked the story and agreed to pay half the costs, which I estimated at £45,000, though this figure contained nothing for Jill or myself. I had not attempted to get a distribution guarantee. In the back of my mind I knew it was an unlikely probability, but I also had absolute faith in the film we were capable of producing. Even so I must, if we were to proceed, both guarantee completion and find the remaining £22,500.

Backing a film without distribution needs almost suicidal courage, but the alternative was to lose the progress already made. We could, I calculated, shoot on location and save studio costs. I would buy a van and save transport charges, and perhaps, considering the slump in film production, my friend George Elvin of the Association of Cinema Technicians would allow me to employ his members on a profit-sharing basis. 'Not likely, Bill,' was his response. 'My job is to see that my members get paid their full salaries.'

'I'm a member too,' I said, 'and without producers there wouldn't be any salaries. Wouldn't your members be better off working, even if they have to share some of the risks, and helping to keep the British film industry alive?'

George was adamant. The ultimate aim of the union was to nationalize the industry. The struggles of budding film companies were not their worry.

My father and brother generously and loyally dipped into their capital and we selected Port Talbot as our centre. It had a derelict cinema that I rented for £1 a day. Two borrowed standards of timber levelled the floor and sound-proofed the shooting area, and I fixed up lodgings for the crew. Then I spent hours with Jill casting local people, since our story was built round a local family. When we gave Philip Burton, the head of BBC Wales and a most helpful and gifted adviser, the part of a colliery official, he implored us to find a place in the cast for his foster son, Richard. But Emrys Jones was already signed up for the only suitable role and there was no way we could have known how great a future star had slipped through our fingers.

On the first day of filming, the unions called a joint meeting in our basic studio. A chairman was elected and lost no time in addressing the gathering: 'Comrades and brothers,' he commenced, 'we must stand united against the management,' and went on to enumerate demands.

For a start, the accommodation was unsuitable. They should be put up in a first-class hotel in Cardiff, thirty-five miles away. Pay was to start from the moment they left their hotel and continue until they returned to it. Tea breaks and hot meals must be provided during the day wherever they were on location. Protective clothing must be supplied for the special conditions under which they would be obliged to work.

Eventually his litany drew to a close. I stood up and said, 'Brothers and sisters, I've good news for you. I can see that you don't like the idea of working on this film and you'll be pleased to learn I'm of the same opinion. The unit will return to London in the morning. The deal is off.'

They were all people whom I knew and liked. We had worked together on many films. After a few minutes' huddled conversation they gathered around me.

'Come on, guv,' they said. 'Let's get on with it.'

The story-line concerned a small mining village before and after the nationalization of coal: the daughter of a mining family wants to be a singer and forsakes her girlhood sweetheart for a man who can offer opportunities and a life in London. My chief interest in filming was always to see how things were done: it was a part of my insatiable curiosity. Love stories, including my own, are of the mind, powerful but difficult to convey visually. Yet, we were advised, a love story was essential if we were to gain the feature distribution we were hoping for.

Working with the miners went smoothly. They were intelligent, artistic and full of good ideas to enable us to achieve realistic results. I invited them to watch the filming, and they sat intrigued in the unaltered circle of the converted cinema. Their initial view that filming was a simple business soon changed and they began to say it was harder than working at the coal face. The preparation for each shot and the number of takes to get the scene right so involved them that they became emotionally exhausted and many fell asleep.

Jo Jago, our cameraman, shot beautiful material and enjoyed his liberation from the confines of the commercial studios, for to make a feature film outside a proper studio was at that time unheard of. It said much for Jo's work that, having finished with us, he was immediately invited to be cameraman for *Whisky Galore* on location in the Hebrides. One shot that I plotted myself was made with my faithful Newman Sinclair strapped, pointing upwards, on top of the lift cage. As the cage went down in the shaft, the camera recorded the circle of light at the top growing smaller and smaller until it finally disappeared, so creating for the audience the feeling of making the descent.

We became friends with the miners, who invited us to their working men's clubs, where we joined in the drinking and singing and experienced all the warmth of Welsh hospitality. Dances and parties heralded the end of shooting, and on this occasion at least the people were sorry to see the last of a film crew. The new floor, so carefully put in, was just as carefully lifted and returned to the timber control, where it was no doubt used to build new homes.

Back in London our editor, Kenneth Hume, editing his first feature in *Blue Scar*, already had a rough cut and it was clear that the film had not suffered from being made on location. Eventually we had our show copy to display proudly to the Wardour Street distributors. They could hardly have been less interested. The situation began to look desperate. I had borrowed thousands of pounds from my father and brother on the strength of my previous films; I had foolishly gone ahead without a distribution guarantee. I had, moreover, audaciously produced a new film from scratch with finance from outside the trade at a time when the industry was at a low ebb. Yet all I asked was for the public to be able to make up its own mind. Jill was even more upset and drummed up excellent articles in the press while I arranged two sneak previews, one at the Granada, Slough, and the other at Tooting. Of the 400 opinion cards handed out to an audience of 2,000, 80 per cent were favourable. I then spent hours talking to influential people, including Rank General Film Distributors and Sir Arthur Jarrett, head of the ABC chain. 'You don't even speak our language,' was Sir Arthur's comment.

Eventually we arranged a meeting with Alexander Korda and Harold Wilson, then Minister for the Board of Trade. Wilson had just set up the National Film Finance Corporation with £5 million to encourage British film production. Korda, who had Sir Winston Churchill under a script-writing contract of £5,000 a year, was to receive a proportion. We sat in Korda's plush private viewing theatre in Park Lane, and at the end of the film Wilson turned to his driver. 'I always rely on my driver's opinion about films,' he explained.

The driver said he liked it. Fascinated, I watched Korda, almost half of whose large cigar was grey ash. He flicked his finger and the ash fell on the expensive carpet. A bad omen, I thought. 'How much did it cost?' Korda asked.

'Forty-five thousand,' I said.

'How did you make it for so little?' he asked, his eyes observing me shrewdly.

'I paid cash for everything,' I said.

'Great mistake,' said Korda. 'Never pay cash. I'll speak to Arthur Jarrett.'

A few days later I had a distribution deal with British Lion, who finally got ABC to show it in seven towns on condition that, if takings warranted, the film would have a general release. The film did well, but went out as a co-feature, and all I received was £18,000. Happily I paid back my father and brother, but Outlook Films was left heavily in debt. It was the last film Jill and I made together. She married Michael Foot and I continued the battle alone.

A month later Ripley said his business had expanded and he needed more space. Could I manage to find somewhere else? Fortunately I had been offered a lovely house in Hampstead that belonged to the owner of the Cooling Gallery, where some of *Out of Chaos* had been shot. Originally the Watch House, the old Hampstead police station, it had ten rooms, two to a floor on five floors, rather like a lighthouse. The splendid views from the roof had originally enabled the watch to see that all was well. Luckily I was also able to get a little plot opposite with a garden room and garage.

Soon after this a letter from an advertising agency arrived, asking me to produce a short film for Kensitas to promote 'Lucky Strike' cigarettes. Kensitas were to supply the manufacturing film, I would provide the entertainment. It was just what I needed: a piece of guaranteed work into which I could throw myself. I asked Ray Elton to be cameraman-director, and our main scenes were shot at Merton Park, where Geraldo and his orchestra played 'Deep Purple Night' and 'Keep Your Sunny Side Up' with a choir of seventy. It was a big scene that stretched across the largest stage, which meant that the gantries appeared in the shot and needed to be skilfully removed by Pappa Day, the famous special-effects man. He blacked out the offending area, which was then reshot on a painted screen. The final effect was of the band playing in a huge theatre.

The picture was designed to be run in small suitcase viewers that the company's salesmen set up in bars, offices or wherever, hopefully to sway the customers. It was a simple picture to make, and when John Boor, the Kensitas executive, arrived from the United States the film was ready. 'My,' he said, 'you're a fast mover, but you've not had our specifications yet and all our films must conform to head-office rules.'

Dear God, I thought, all that money down the drain. I arranged to show him the film in the morning, and took Kensitas's bulky instruction book with trembling hands, though I never had the courage to open it. Next day Mr Boor sat silently through the screening and remained silent a long while afterwards. I fell into despair: my first commissioned film ruined, my reputation in tatters. As Jarrett had said so cuttingly, 'You don't even speak our language.' I stole a glance at Boor. He was crying. 'It's wonderful,' he said, 'as good as our best,' and in his relief he added, 'Boy, I want you to have something to remember this by.'

'I'd like that too,' I said. 'Can I have your pants?' for he was wearing a pair of superbly cut US colonel's fawn trousers.

We ended the day uproariously that evening in the Coconut Grove Night Club in Regent's Street, and I wore his trousers for many years afterwards.

Back in Belfast, death had claimed Sarah Collins, who had left my father to attend her ailing mother, only to suffer a stroke that paralysed her left side and die seven weeks later in hospital. My father himself had several falls – once when getting out of the Bangor train on the wrong side and tumbling on to the track, though miraculously without injury. He was still managing director and attended business three days a week – and always had a lift home in the paper-delivery van, for he was a simple frugal man and never saw the need to do the 'big pot', as he called it. When a letter came from him saying that he was passing a little blood in his urine, I went home at once. He looked frail but was in good spirits. In the morning he took me into the bathroom. 'I'll show you what it's like,' he said.

The crimson stream shocked me, though I pretended it was no great worry and he seemed highly relieved. My brother and I consulted the doctor, and we reached the unanimous conclusion that it was not worth frightening a nervous old man of eighty-two with an exploratory operation that would cause him great distress and would not necessarily help his condition. Shortly afterwards I was in Dublin when a call came from James saying that Father was seriously ill in Newtownards Hospital. I hired a car and drove through the night. When I arrived he was unconscious, but I talked to him as reassuringly as I could.

He had, James told me, been found on the floor of his bedroom, his back against the brass screen that protected the gas fire. He had gone to turn up the gas and fallen, receiving second-degree burns. On the way to hospital he joked with the ambulance men that they were taking him to the workhouse, for the hospital was indeed a converted workhouse and he had always joked that it was in the workhouse he would die. It was 6 April, and he did not survive the day. On the 24th he would have been eighty-three. His departure left James and me with a deep sense of loss as the last of the MacQuittys. Though we had often disagreed with his rigid opinions and found him difficult, he was a warm-hearted, loving father who had devoted his life to his sons' welfare.

I remembered, too, his sense of play and humour in his earlier years. At our first home there was a large tree of cooking apples, and at the end of each season Mother would carefully pick the fruit and wrap each apple in paper for storing in the pantry. 'Henny, you haven't picked all the apples,' said Father one year.

'Indeed I did, I brought in every one,' said Mother indignantly.

We all went out to take a look. To Mother's astonishment, there were three apples remaining at the very top of the tree. Thoroughly put out, she went at once to fetch the ladder and climbed back up with difficulty. Father had tied them on! He could make pennies appear and disappear, handkerchiefs change colour and objects arrive out of thin air, performing these tricks to the accompaniment of his characteristic little dance, his legs revolving like corkscrews.

As we carried his coffin to join Mother's in the cemetery, John the gardener walked beside me. 'Man,' said John, 'I beat him,' referring to the joke that he and Father had often shared as to which would outlive the other. 'I'll be round in the morning with the barrow. There'll be a few old boots and a couple of shirt he won't be needing.'

The Watch House seemed very empty when I returned to London. I found my thoughts returning to India. Why not ask some chaps in, run it as a chummery? The more I thought about the idea, the better I liked it. After a month's search I was lucky to find three likely companions to share my life: Louis Le Brocquy, a talented Irish painter who used the garden room as his studio; John Chandos, writer, actor, wine connoisseur and excellent cook; and Walter Goetz, a lively cartoonist. We got on well together, considering the volume of creative work in progress, and our Mrs Harding, a large cockney lady, 'did for us' and continually grumbled. John, when he felt inclined, produced memorable meals, and our distinguished guests included Father Cameron and Father Brown from the Farm Street Jesuits, who hovered in the hope of recapturing the soul of John, a 'spoilt' Catholic. A steady stream of girlfriends in the meantime earned us the title of the Monastery of the Monks of the Loose Habits.

Blue Scar continued to receive publicity. An illustration in a review by Richard Winnington, the film critic of the *News Chronicle*, showed J. Arthur Rank of Denham Studios saying to Joseph A. Rank of the Odeon cinema chain, 'We're not monopolists, are we?' This prompted an invitation from the Students' Union of London University to show *Blue Scar* and talk on the problems of the producer in the film industry. The lecture was held in the New Theatre at the London School of Economics, and after I had talked and answered questions, members of the Students' Union took me to a pub where we continued talking till closing time. I little knew that the evening would have a consequence to change my life.

20

A Union Man

I was asked to a bottle party at which a loving cup was provided. The elixir, mixed in the nose cone of an unexploded bomb that had fallen on the Royal Marsden Hospital, was rumoured to contain alcohol left over from the hospital lab. It was, to be sure, a lethal thirst-making mixture, and as I was helping myself to a beaker of water in the kitchen, a slim dark-haired girl came in through the door.

'Like a drink of water?' I asked.

'Yes, please,' she smiled. 'Aren't you the chap who gave the talk on films at the LSE?'

'Yes,' I said, thinking what a pretty and well-poised impression she created.

We drank wordlessly. When will she say something more, I wondered as the silence hung over us. All at once I heard myself asking, 'What did you think of it?'

She paused a moment before she said, smiling more prettily than ever, 'I thought it stank.'

Shocked and hurt I said, 'I didn't see you at the lecture.'

'I had a train to catch, otherwise I'd have talked to you afterwards.'

'Do you belong to the Students' Union?' I asked.

'I'm vice-president,' she said.

'What are you reading?' I asked.

'Economics,' she said, 'but I'm lucky to have Professor Laski as my tutor.'

I was overawed and fascinated. We talked on. Her name, I discovered, was Betty Bastin, and she had a brother in the RAF. Her parents' home was in Reading, where she spent her weekends, and she lived in Robert Adam Street. I found her irresistible.

'I'd like to see you again,' I said. 'May I give you a ring?'

'Not for a while,' she said. 'I'm preparing for my finals.'

Rank had meanwhile closed the Shepherds Bush studios, leaving Sydney to produce at Pinewood, where he was carrying an excessive work-load. I returned to a subject I had often broached with Sydney. Why didn't he and I set up a film company with his wife Muriel Box, who had started as a continuity girl and knew the industry well? Since he had given opportunities to so many unknown directors, why not to Muriel, who had worked on all his productions and won an Oscar into the bargain? I could produce and he could promote new subjects. All we needed was to make a good film every year or even one every two years and win time to make better pictures and enjoy life and freedom of choice. Sydney, ready by now for such a proposal, resigned from Rank and we set up a new production company called London Independent Producers.

Our first venture was *The Happy Family*. John Woolf, who was putting in £50,000, was nervous at having a woman director but happy if Sydney co-directed. Our cast, consisting of Stanley Holloway, Kathleen Harrison, Naunton Wayne, George Cole, Dandy Nichols and Miles Malleson, was engaged. Space was booked; the production team was readied. All went smoothly until, a week before our shooting date, John Woolf withdrew. It was the same old story: cheaper *in extremis* to put in money than close the show. We all subscribed and bought two weeks' grace, during which we got a deal with a new independent company and an agreement from Lloyds Bank to put up £50,000. The film opened in the United States under the title *Mr Lord Says No*, was well received and made a profit.

While the production was in progress I began to see a lot of Betty, who had, like me, left home at eighteen. In her case she had played Elvira in *Blithe Spirit* in repertory, joined ENSA in the Middle East and played the lead in *Lovers Leap*, a Lonsdale play, acting under canvas and in various venues, including the Cairo Opera House. I met her family. Her father had been a farmer and a great countryman, her mother a teacher. After much consideration and trepidation we decided we would marry at Hampstead Register Office on 15 September 1951; and since I was dubbing *The Happy Family* at the time, I left all the arrangements to Betty. As we turned to leave the registrar said, 'You owe me 6s. 6d.'

'Why?' I asked, fumbling for the money.

'Mrs MacQuitty paid only a shilling deposit.'

I thought this a sign of commendable prudence, but Betty said it was only what the registrar had requested. After that we had a short ceremony at Hampstead Parish Church, just below the Watch House, and when the Revd Herbert Carnegie asked Betty what he was to do, she said, 'Give us your blessing, but please make it brief.'

'It's good of you to bring God into it,' he said.

As we walked back down the aisle, I slipped a fiver into his hand, and he looked at me with a broad smile. 'Ah now,' said he, 'what you need for this job is a good sense of humour.'

I took it he was referring to marriage.

Nine months later, on 15 June 1952, Jonathan was born in Queen Charlotte's Hospital. Neither of us wore rings and the severe bemedalled matron said privately to Betty, 'Why don't you marry him? He seems a nice chap.' Manny Lederman and my brother and his wife Irene were godparents.

Betty had chaired political meetings at the university, was well versed in government affairs and could have had a safe seat as an MP. Now, however, she chose to put Jonathan and the family first. Before our marriage, when we had a special dinner together to celebrate her degree in economics, I had said, 'What we really want is a *cordon bleu*,' and she promptly went out and did that as well.

After a time we came to realize that a house on five floors of two rooms each was no suitable place for raising a child. We moved to Mill Hill – to Mote Mount, an old country house on two floors of five rooms each. It belonged to Sydney, who lived next door, and thus was convenient for work. Other attractions including a three-acre garden and fresh air. The three acres were at first a daunting prospect, but we were fortunate to persuade Paddy Dunn, an Irish gardener who had helped us in Hampstead, to come to our new home. 'I'll make ye a garden,' he promised.

We converted the stables into a little studio and here made a short film called *Les Mains Joly*, in which the white-gloved hands of four French puppeteers formed and re-formed in beautiful movements against a black-velvet backing. The artists wore black so only the hands were visible. Their movements, in time to Debussy's *La Mer*, depicted marine life. Following from this small venture, LIP was to produce fifteen successful feature pictures. Our office was in the coach house, our staff two personal assistants with two telephones. Nearly all our organization was done by phone. Letters were too slow and only important issues were confirmed in writing.

We kept a constant eye open for likely subjects, and a phenomenon that caught my attention was the number of press advertisements

for recruiting policewomen. This was mainly, I discovered, because they were skilled but attractive and soon married. Sydney and
Muriel used this as a basis to write *Street Corner*, a dramatic feature
about policewomen. The police were sensitive to the idea because of
innacuracies in the way they had been depicted in other films, but
after many script alterations they agreed to it and Muriel and I went to
make a reconnaissance of Paddington Police Station. A young
policeman, detailed to show us round, opened the door of the first cell
to reveal an old man sitting on the far end of a bunk. 'Wake up,
grandad,' he said. 'Here's your tea.'

The old fellow paid no attention. The policeman gave him a nudge.
The old man keeled over and slid to the floor: a meths drinker who
had consumed his last drink. Later an elderly prostitute was brought
in and Muriel requested that she be formally charged so she could
note the correct procedure.

'What's your name?' the duty sergeant asked.

'Sure, ye know me name, sergeant,' the old woman retorted.

The sergeant repeated his request.

'Sure ye know me name, sergeant. I've been coming here thirty
years.'

She was nearing seventy. Tears flowed down her cheeks as she
heard the charge: 'You have been apprehended as a common
prostitute . . .' The public have little notion what the police do for the
submerged tenth of our society. They are, for many, their only
friends.

Street Corner, shot in the autumn of 1952, included a scene where a
policewoman plunged into the Thames to rescue a small boy who had
fallen in and was being carried off by the current. It was a night scene
and the police required stringent safety measures. I had completed a
diving course myself, and had already bought the rights to *Above Us
the Waves*, an account of the disabling of the German battleship
Tirpitz by British midget submarines. This enabled me to ask James
Benson, one of the authors and a distinguished submariner who had
been on the raid, to stand by in diving gear with me. The take
prepared, we slipped into the icy river. The boy ran about on the
barges on Chelsea Reach and duly fell in. Eleanor Summerfield's
double dived to the rescue. On 'cut', Jimmy and I swam to the couple,
who were better swimmers than we were and needed no assistance.
The Thames was heavily polluted and anyone swallowing water had
to be stomach-pumped. Luckily we got the shot on the first take.

Peggy Cummins and Anne Crawford were our stars, and the film
did excellent business besides receiving good reviews. In fact *Street
Corner* came to be Muriel's favourite among all her pictures. After this

success, there was no problem with her being accepted as a director in England, though for some reason, despite successful distribution in the United States, no American producer offered her work.

Our next picture, *The Beachcomber*, was another screenplay by Sydney and Muriel. This one was based on Somerset Maugham's *Vessel of Wrath*. We decided to work on location in Ceylon and Muriel and I flew out on one of the first Comets. We refuelled *en route* at Bahrain, and after a brief wait strapped ourselves in for take-off in our seats up front behind the cockpit. The plane was roaring down the runway when, a hundred yards to lift-off, its inside port engine exploded. The sea at the end of the runway lay before us and a crash seemed inevitable. 'Brace your feet against the bulkhead!' I shouted.

Muriel did nothing. I thought the flames and the noise of the explosion must have dazed her. I yelled again, and this time she spoke. 'Why?' she asked, looking at me calmly. 'I always thought it was safer to be in a relaxed position.'

No one was hurt, but fire engines tore out and it was found that the explosion had been caused by a burst in one of the high-pressure fuel pipes to the engine. A spare engine was produced, but the cowling had buckled and no efforts could close it. Four days went by before a red-headed Scots engineer flew in from Calcutta and requested a sledge hammer. As six men held the cowling down, he struck it a massive blow and, with a crisp *clunk*, the cowling fitted back into place.

At last we approached Ceylon and, as we stepped down from the plane, I was assailed by mental images from twenty years before: of Lione, of the bo tree, of Storm Lodge. I went straight to the Chartered Bank to open an account. 'You already have one,' said the clerk, the very one who once threatened suicide and was now in charge.

The account had been kept open by long-forgotten pre-war dividends from rubber companies.

When we arrived with Jonathan at Mote Mount in 1952, the house was dark and grimy and the grass on the lawn grew three feet tall. There were great mature cedar and beech trees in the grounds. Wildlife was abundant. Foxes, badgers, rabbits, squirrels, stoats, jays, rooks, magpies, woodpeckers and owls found sanctuary with us, besides the more usual robins, blue tits, sparrows, blackbirds and thrushes and the less welcome rats and mice. Some doors from the main house, which caught fire in 1933, had been salvaged and used to panel three ground-floor rooms. For some reason there were five lavatories, two of which we gutted to add their space to the adjoining rooms. Central heating came from a huge Britannia coke-burning boiler, hot water from a smaller boiler. Each year we shovelled seven to eight tons of coke into their hungry maws and removed vast quantities of ash and cinders that were used to surface the overgrown garden paths.

Paddy Dunn, who brought his long-handled heart-shaped spade with him when he left County Cavan, was a slight, wiry Irishman, full of a love for the soil and an ability to make things grow. In his efforts he was indefatigable. We grew to love him and he us. Inside the house Betty found help in Mrs Jordan, who lived with her husband in a cottage near by. Mr Jordan managed a timber yard and was away all day. They were to become second parents to our family. In a field next to us, Sydney kept a pedigree herd of Guernseys. We bought their thick creamy milk from the Miss Wheedons, who ran the farm and also supplied us with fresh eggs and butter. Before long we were growing our own vegetables and fruit. I took a course in bee-keeping and installed two hives, and from then on we had our own honey.

Our second child, Jane, born at Queen Charlotte's Hospital in October 1953, already had long dark hair when she arrived just two hours before the 15th of the month. In this she remained the odd one out in a family where the rest of us were born on a 15th. Her godparents were Stanley Spencer, Peggy Cummins, my brother and Irene. Ten days later I had to leave for Ceylon for eight weeks, leaving Betty with much to contend with, including the winter heating. Our total direct costs on *The Beachcomber* were already calculated at £146,000, which meant we could afford to take only a small production team on location. The union insisted that I include a carpenter. I offered to pay him his salary and leave him at home, but this was not acceptable. Once in Ceylon we had to find doubles for our stars, Robert Newton and Glynis Johns. Marjory Murdoch, sister-in-law to the well-known British radio comedian 'Stinker' Murdoch, made a convincing stand-in for Glynis, though Robert Newton was less easily simulated. We searched everywhere until, eventually, Muriel and Bob Attwool, our production manager, told me, 'It's got to be you, Bill.'

It was to prove a strange experience in role shifting. As the dresser spent hours getting me kitted out to look like Newton, the crew dropped all their arguments about the uncomfortable situations I was forcing them into and overflowed with consideration. For the moment I was no longer at everyone's beck and call but a cosseted star.

One scene required a jetty in a beautiful bay. George Provis, our art director, found the ideal situation where a sand spit divided a lagoon from the sea, and here he built a small jetty for the mission boat to land. The night before we shot the scene, I went down to check that all was well. There was a full moon, and the jetty certainly looked romantic in its lovely setting as the palms leant gracefully beside the waters of the lagoon. A couple of old men walked slowly across the sand and stopped near by. As one of them began to dig with a spade, I watched with interest, assuming he was after bait. He continued digging in more or less a straight line, but seemed to find nothing and finally grew tired and handed the spade to his companion. The other carried on until he reached the lagoon, when a trickle of water filled the trench and the men stepped back. The trickle grew to a stream and in seconds became a torrent. I hurried to safety and turned to watch the sandbank swept away and our jetty with it. We had not known it was the custom each year, when the lagoon waters rose too high, for the villagers to release them to the sea. The immediate consequence for us was that we needed a new location fast. My solution was less idyllic yet practical. Next day I took the unit to Negombo, the fishing bay I had known so well before the war.

On our last night I sat above Negombo harbour with a monk of the La Salle Mission, whose mission house we had used for the governor's residency. The good father suffered from angina and, unable to lie down, passed each night in a cane chair. He accepted his agonizing condition as the will of God and his faith in life after death was total. When he asked me about my own beliefs, I said I kept an open mind about an after-life but wondered whether I could be useful if there were such a thing. I liked to be able to use the brains nature had given me, and they did not suggest to me that a loving God would allow his children to suffer so dreadfully. Was there not enough to do here on earth in trying to help others, and might not the purifying of one's own soul for eternal life be a selfish, even an arrogant pursuit? I could see the sadness in his expressive eyes as he looked at me in the moonlight and said, 'You have my profound sympathy.'

Back in London we started work on studio takes to match up with our location rushes. There were problems. In one of the long shots I had picked up 'Glynis' and carried her off. In the studio, Newton found that picking up Glynis was beyond his strength. Worse than that, he had started to drink heavily and it was almost impossible to use him after lunch. I kept a close watch and discovered his source of alcohol: a bottle concealed in a lavatory cistern. In the meantime, the Rank Organization had run out of pictures and laid off most of its carpenters, and as a result a mass meeting was called for all unions on 'E' stage. The chairman made a rousing speech and speaker after speaker called on their unions to strike. It seemed certain that the studios would close, yet we only needed a week to finish. It was every producer's worst nightmare.

Before he took the vote, the chairman asked if anyone else wished to speak. I held up a hand and took the rostrum, for was I not also a union man? 'Brothers and sisters,' I said, 'I am the lodger in the house who brings in the rent. I need a week to finish the picture. Your dispute is with Rank, not with me. Your livelihood depends on making pictures. If I don't complete this one, my backers won't put up money for the next. I hope you'll try to settle your differences without closing the studio.'

The dead silence that followed was broken by the chairman saying, 'Those in favour of striking, stay where you are. Those against striking, walk to the other side of the stage.'

'E' stage, the largest in Pinewood, seemed bigger than ever as I left the crowd and walked slowly across to its empty side. My mind was filled with bitterness and black despair. I had striven in the film industry for ten years, had risked my own money in backing films. Sydney, Muriel and myself had expended precious time and effort in setting up a movie that now required one more simple week if we were to reap the rewards. Without that week we had no film, though everyone working on it except ourselves would be paid in full for their labours. I thought of the carpenter I had been forced to take to Ceylon – a decent chap, but faced with work beyond his capabilities and only able to watch as the locals built the ill-fated jetty and a village of thatched huts. I walked on, not daring to look back.

The majority followed me; we finished on schedule.

21

Seas and Sands

Our first priority at Mote Mount had been to reduce the appalling draughts, for its exposed position invited high winds to blow freely through the house. First we sealed all the open fireplaces, except for one magnificent grate in the hall where we put in a spit to take advantage of log fires in winter. One complete window was removed from each room and replaced by a single double-glazed pane. The oak panels in the door leading to the hall were replaced with glass, through which we could see the garden. An arch was cut through the wall separating the dining room from the kitchen. A thick layer of glass wool was laid under the rafters to retain the heat. In due course, the ancient boilers were replaced by a new Trianco gravity-fed anthracite boiler which took two hundredweight in its large hopper and ran for days without refilling. The walls, deprived of their dark panelling, were painted white. Suddenly our home was filled with light and warmth.

The time had come to turn attention to the rights I had bought in *Above Us the Waves*, the story of the disabling of the pride of the German navy, the battleship *Tirpitz*, co-authored by C.E.T. Warren, a submariner, and Jimmy Benson. Our script treatment had been through several stages and now we needed to work out the visual images the story needed. Our director was Ralph Thomas, who had just completed *Doctor in the House*, the first of the very successful 'Doctor' series produced by Betty Box. Ralph and I duly set out for

Portsmouth in his Jaguar to search for locations suitable for a film intended to be a thrilling adventure. We soon had one ourselves when, without warning, a farm tractor pulled out of a concealed opening. We were doing 80 m.p.h. at the time, and there was barely room to squeeze past, but the tractor was towing an unseen harrow and, just as we thought we had made it, the nearside front tyre caught the harrow and burst. The car lurched from side to side of the narrow lane and seemed certain to overturn, but Ralph's superb driving kept control and eventually we screeched to a halt. We changed the wheel and continued our journey, shaken but unharmed. Ralph, a former tank major in the North African campaign, assured me it was the nearest he ever came to being killed.

Our reconnaissance with the Royal Navy went smoothly and Commander Donald Cameron VC, who was in command of X Craft 6 which disabled the *Tirpitz*, was appointed our naval adviser. HMS *Maidstone*, depot ship for the submarines, became our HQ, and when two extras arrived dressed as vice-admirals, and it had not occurred to me to inform the watch, they were accepted as real and alarmed to find themselves being piped aboard as signals whizzed about the ship warning everyone of the momentous event. On another occasion, as I walked along the quay with Betty, a sailor emerged from the front hatch of a moored submarine, singing at the top of his voice, 'Got no money, got no luck, got to go to Gosport to get a . . .' till he saw Betty, stopped in mid sentence and saluted smartly.

The cameraman on the craft sequence was Peter Hennessy, who had worked with me on *Out of Chaos*. He was a robust, hearty character who overflowed with excellent photographic ideas and was as experienced in shooting such scenes in confined spaces as Stanley Spencer was in painting the long shipyard scenes in his small bedroom. (I am sorry to say poor Peter met an untimely end years later when he swallowed a wasp in his home-brew and died from shock when the insect stung him.) The X-craft, the midget submarines, were fifty feet long with an interior some thirty feet long by five in diameter. Every inch of space was crammed with machinery and equipment. In the still waters of the original Norwegian fjord where the real-life drama was enacted, Peter shot the X-craft diving and surfacing, the crew coming on deck and going below.

The submarines had a wet and a dry compartment to enable one man at a time to enter or leave to cut a way through anti-torpedo nets, clear obstacles or place explosive charges. Our cast, John Mills, John Gregson, Donald Sinden and Michael Medwin, had already undergone the full diving routine from the bottom lock of a diving tower. When the lock was flooded, they stepped into the tower and shot to the surface, but on the way up needed to remember to breathe out all the time to bring the pressure in their lungs down to surface pressure. They were all courageous and dedicated, but John Mills stood alone in convincing the sailors that he was a navy man.

The shooting finished on time and I felt very happy with the result, but Earl St John, executive producer for Pinewood, told me the sales forces were worried and asked me to talk to them. I met them at the Odeon Theatre, Hammersmith, where their spokesman said, 'We are very concerned, Mr MacQuitty, that you have no female stars or any females at all in this picture. Never before have we had to sell a picture with no interest for women, who make up more than half our audience.'

'Gentlemen,' I said, 'let me allay your fears. The film has the one ingredient to appeal to all women.'

'And what is that?' they asked.

'Courageous men,' I replied.

After the exhausting work of filming, I took Betty for a holiday in Sicily, where I was tracked down by a cable from Earl St John saying that the film was to have its world première at the Embassy Theatre in Malta. Proceeds were going to the Playing Fields Association, and their patron, the Duke of Edinburgh, would be present. Could I see, please, that all went smoothly? When we arrived in Valetta, I hired tails in a second-hand clothes shop and Betty bought long white gloves. Happily I reached the cinema in time to dissuade the manager from a proudly announced plan to get things off to a good start by showing a new American wide-screen comedy (obtained with enormous difficulty) first. The contrast would have been disastrous for our small-screen black-and-white movie, and heaven knew what the naval top brass would have had to say.

I put up a fiver to anyone who could spot a naval mistake in the film, but neither of the C-in-C's of the combined Home and Mediterranean Fleets, Sir Charles Grantham and Sir Reginald Denny, nor their officers came up with a challenge after the showing. Were there any, they asked. There were. John Mills's cap badge was 'ER' when it should have been 'GR' and the *Maidstone* had flown her ensign while at anchor in harbour.

was held at the Odeon, Leicester Square, on 31 March 1955, before a celebrated audience headed by Queen Elizabeth and Lord Mountbatten. The Band of the Royal Marines played. There was a fanfare of trumpets. The evening was a heady one for Betty and me, but as I listened to the rapturous applause and Elgar's *Pomp and Circumstance*, my mind went back to *Blue Scar*. The film was also a success in the United States, though there the title had to be changed to *Secret*

318 CHAIRMAN OF TALENTS

Submarines. WAVES formed the initials of the Women's Auxiliary Volunteer Service, and the sexual implications of *Above Us the Waves* were more than the American cinema's moral code could cope with.

Brian Desmond Hurst, when he departed from *On Approval*, had predicted we would work together again. The chance came with *The Black Tent*, based on a short story, 'The Promissory Note', by Robin Maugham, nephew of Somerset. Robin's uncle had once offered him £500 a year to give up writing, perhaps for fear that the great name might be downgraded. The screenplay was written by Robin with Bryan Forbes; the story embroidered out of the fact that, as Robin knew from his war service, officers in the desert were authorized to sign promissory notes of up to £100 to pay for help from the bedouin if separated from their regiment. In the story, many years after the war one such note turns up, and the brother of the officer concerned goes to the desert to discover the truth, which emerges in flashback. His wounded brother strayed into the tents of a bedouin tribe, to be nursed back to health by the sheikh's daughter. He married her, but then was killed in a guerrilla raid on the Germans, and later his wife gave birth to a son. The boy, heir to a grand title and estate in England, must decide whether to claim his inheritance. He renounces the title and remains with his tribe.

This mainly visual drama demanded a talented director of photography, and I was fortunate to obtain Desmond Dickinson. We used wide-screen Technicolor VistaVision, which gave a larger picture by running the film sideways in the camera. To reach our locations in Libya, the unions required first-class travel for their members, so I chartered a plane and we *all* went first class, setting out in August 1955, the hottest month of the year. Our film travelled in special Thermos containers that needed to be kept cold, and I arranged for these to go straight into a local brewery's cold room, and also to be free of customs duty, since we would be taking the film out of the country afterwards. At San Benito Airport, the customs refused to let us move the containers out of the scorching heat until we paid duty at 50 per cent. Strenuous efforts to have the duty refunded failed, and the Libyan customs owe me £3,000 to this day.

The unions had also placed me under heavy pressure to take a plasterer to Libya, but I refused, unable to see what use we would have for a plasterer in a picture set among tents and sand. In this I had reckoned without Brian Hurst, who was capable of turning up any morning with a pair of alternative scripts under his arm. To try to curb his urge to rewrite everything, I made him initial each page in

London, but the freedom of the desert had a fertile effect on his agile brain. One of the new dramatic situations he dreamed up required the machine-gunning of the ancient ruins of Sabratha. I had to hire a local plasterer to provide a plaster stone with pockets for the explosive charges to simulate machine-gun fire.

A pool was needed for the wedding sequence, and George Provis, my art director, found a lovely oasis with a suitable large well but no pool. 'Build one,' I said grandly, 'and make it permanent. It will be a useful local water supply.'

The pool was beautifully situated beside the well in the shade of date palms. Tankers filled it with water and the well kept it topped up. We duly shot the scene. The bridal procession proceeded with music and dancers to the pool, where the bride was ceremoniously bathed, so prompting the Arab press to run a leader next day about naked orgies in the desert. When I came to pay the headman for the use of his oasis, I told him graciously that it gave us great pleasure to leave the concrete-lined pool as a small gift that we hoped his people would enjoy for many years. To my astonishment he became very angry and demanded that the pool, which desecrated the oasis, should be removed and the sand restored to its original purity.

One of my most pressing problems was keeping the unit free from 'Libya's revenge', for the desert was full of flies. Black and fearless, they attacked our food and fought for it even into the eater's mouth. Washing before meals was essential, and water, soap and towels were kept in constant readiness, as were two first-aid units. This did not prevent a consistent tenth of the crew being off sick. The flies, besides contaminating our food, made multiple retakes necessary as they landed on artists' faces or even lips in the love scenes, or simply buzzed around the microphone. Anthony Steel, our hero, faced a hard time injecting passion into the love scenes. He had to contend not only with the flies but also with the constant presence of Valeria Materza Nini, the mother and chaperone of our nineteen-year-old Italian starlet, Anna Maria Sandri. The fact that Anna Maria's English vocabulary did not extend beyond the one word 'Yes' added to everyone's tribulations, until Nanette Newman, newly married to Bryan Forbes and supposedly in North Africa on her honeymoon, came spiritedly to the rescue and expertly dubbed Anna Maria's lines on to our working soundtrack as we went along. In the end we decided to disregard all difficulties and re-dub the lot when we got back to England.

Betty was meanwhile booked on a BOAC Argonaut to come out to visit me on 21 September. She became convinced that the plane would crash and wore for the flight easy shoes to kick off in an emergency and a warm vest in case of a landing in the sea. Sydney Box drove her to Heathrow, but they arrived three minutes late through traffic delays and found BOAC had allocated her seat to another passenger. Despite Sydney's pleading that her husband had been in the desert for months, the staff were immovable and Betty declared in a fury that she would claim the first available seat on an alternative flight even if the passenger were only one minute late.

I drove out to meet her at Idris Airport in a gathering sand storm and watched her plane land. In fact her flight came in first. The Argonaut arrived shortly afterwards. We watched the Argonaut approach, then turn away, then do the same for its second and third approaches. On the fourth approach it came in low, ploughed through the tops of some tall eucalyptus trees and crashed short of the runway. A fire had broken out before the aircraft stopped moving, and a fire engine standing by dashed out with rescue squads. 'I knew it was going to crash,' said Betty.

We returned to the hotel in a state of shock.

Next morning we visited the scene. The plane was badly burnt; liquid metal filled footprints in the sand. The ground was strangely scattered with visiting cards as well as with passengers' baggage and pieces of aircraft. The flight crew had escaped through the cockpit exit, but the port emergency exits had been locked by the plane's angle of settlement. Passengers managed to scramble out of the two starboard exits, however, until one became blocked by an African chieftain in bulky ceremonial robes. Sitting next to the other was a lady on her first flight who forgot to release her safety belt. Frantic passengers, led by the cabin steward, scrambled across her, and only after the last one left could she undo her belt and succeed in struggling out. She showed Betty her bruised and trodden thighs. Fifteen were dead, their bodies, awaiting identification, laid out in an airport building.

The high point of *The Black Tent* was a battle between a Panzer division and a Royal Horse Artillery gun site on the Gafara plain near Azizia. The wasteland selected for our battle site was liberally seeded with explosives, and as the filming began a most realistic battle erupted as guns and tanks blazed, flames leapt and explosions shook the ground and flung tons of debris high into the air. I watched the scene with exhilaration and satisfaction, but slowly became aware that a tall bedouin in flowing white robes stood at my side, respectfully waiting to speak. When the action stopped, I turned to him. 'Why, sire, do you destroy my cornfields?' he asked.

Flabbergasted, I protested that we had been preparing the ground for this battle for weeks and had dealt with all possible objections. I had never seen such a bleak and arid landscape in my life.

The man continued to look at me with patient reproach as he said, 'This is where my corn is planted, and when the rains come, by the grace of Allah, it will spring up and I shall reap my harvest, but now you have blown it all away.'

I took the matter to our legal adviser, Arni Dejarny. Arni said, 'The man is right. You will have to meet him with the magistrates and agree compensation.'

After many cups of coffee, £200 changed hands and the matter was settled with honour.

Betty's birthday, 15 March 1956, was the date fixed for *The Black Tent*'s première in Leicester Square. It had a strong score by William Alwyn, conducted by Muir Matheson, who was a magical conductor of film music. Muir possessed the knack of timing the music perfectly for the soundtrack as he watched the film on a large screen behind his orchestra. He was also full of fun, and mischievously asked Brian Hurst if he expected the music to save this one as Richard Addinsell's 'Warsaw Concerto' had his earlier film, *Dangerous Moonlight*.

Brian, too, was wonderful company, and I was glad circumstances should have once again brought us together to work on a film. He was meticulous in getting his way as a director and possessed an astounding ability to lay bare the psyche of anyone who opposed him. Generously he gave me a piece of his share in the picture – surely a unique gesture by a director to a producer. The unions, for their part, had me on the mat for not taking a plasterer and for feeding them with macaroons rather than slab cake. I explained that macaroons were packed in sterile tins and slab cake covered in flies was unhealthy. They forgave me, as a union man and brother.

22

A Night to Remember

Besides running the home, looking after the children and garden and periodically entertaining a dozen or so guests at our large round dining table, Betty had grown to be closely involved in reading our scripts, discussing and solving problems and typing letters and manuscripts. She had become a good judge of ideas, and when in June 1956 she returned from Queen Charlotte's Hospital after the birth of our third-born, Miranda Irene Nancy Yeats (called after Nancy Astor, Jack Yeats and my sister-in-law, Irene), she brought with her not only the new addition to the family but also a preview of a book that she thought could make a good movie. *A Night to Remember* was the first full and true account of the sinking of the *Titanic*, cross-checked and verified by its author, Walter Lord, over a period of twenty years. The subject appealed to me at once. The *Titanic* legend had been part of me from childhood, from the ship's triumphal launch to its trials in Belfast Lough and the profound national impact of the disaster. What was more, Sir Frederick Rebbeck, chairman of Harland & Wolff, had often suggested I ought to make a film in Belfast. I had no doubt that he would place the shipyards at our disposal.

First I optioned the rights and gave the author a share in the film, an act that at once prompted questions from the Rank Organization. Was not the story in the public domain, and why did we need the book at all? It was a good title, but there was no copyright to a title. In reply I argued that Walter Lord had researched his subject for twenty years and would work with me on the film, and that, unless we told the authentic story, we were bound to fail at the box office. Since good library material existed, I then decided to keep the film in small-screen black and white, a fact displeasing to the distributors, who would have preferred the wide-screen Technicolor VistaVision approach used for *The Black Tent*.

With these initial difficulties out of the way, I paid Sir Frederick a visit, and to my astonishment found him deeply upset after reading about the project in the newspapers. 'Bill,' he said immediately, 'you surely don't intend to make money out of this tragedy? I wouldn't mind it being done in fifty years' time, but not now.'

In my pleading I pointed out that the disaster had been caused through no fault in the ship, and the *Titanic*'s sister ship, the *Olympic*, completed thirty years' service without mishap. Besides, weren't great subjects often tragic and wouldn't the building of this splendid ship be good publicity for the firm?

'We don't need advertising,' he said immovably.

'May I use the film of the launch?' I finally asked.

'Certainly not, and I won't have any film people near the yard.'

Several of the shipyard workers who built the *Titanic* were still alive and I managed by talking to them to get all the information I needed. I called in on Richard Hayward and members of the Group Theatre – Harold Goldblatt, Joseph Tomelty, Bee Duffell – there would be parts for them all. I asked Eric Ambler to write the shooting script and Roy Baker to direct. Geoffrey Unsworth would direct the photography and our art director would be no less a person than Alex Vetchinsky, famous for creating immortal sets, not least among them the Irish station halt of Buggleskelly in the best of the Will Hay comedies, *Oh, Mr Porter!* 'Vetch' was a stout, vigorous man, an impatient perfectionist. His brief was to build a full-size section of the ship that would need a vast concrete foundation to carry its weight. On this the crowd scenes would be shot: hundreds of people on deck, lifeboats being lowered, and passengers jumping overboard. The deck angle had to be such that the camera could shoot it level to start with, then gradually increase the tilt as the ship began to sink; each page of the script showing the angle required. The grand reception and dining rooms had to be constructed on reinforced floors controlled by powerful hydraulic jacks so they could also tilt as the bows sank.

The cast of forty-nine was led by Kenneth More, and many of the several hundred extras had speaking parts, but I was clear from the start that the real star was going to be the ship and that the authenticity we were aiming for would be all-important, whatever the production complexities. I was in for a shock, however, when, on 26 August 1957, Steve Fallon, head of accounts, brought me the budget. Steve was a small, cheerful man who had costed Pinewood pictures for many years, but this was the largest budget he had ever produced and we were only talking about a small-screen black-and-white movie with no international star names. He estimated running time at 113 minutes and costs at £499,670. It was an enormous sum. Even *The Black Tent*, with its overseas location and glorious large-frame colour, had cost only £223,000. I began to wonder if I would ever get this past John Davis, the managing director of the Rank empire who was virtually blood brother to Arthur Rank. When I went to see Earl St John, the executive producer on all Pinewood pictures, and he told me that 'JD' was coming next day and wanted to speak to me about the *Titanic* project, I asked him what he thought of my chances.

'Not great, I think,' said Earl. 'It's been done before and it's the hell of a budget.'

JD had started as an office boy and come up the hard way. He was direct to the point of ruthlessness, and had fired so many staff, including members of his board, that they formed a club called the Rank Outsiders. One evening they invited him to a dinner and asked him to speak afterwards. 'I know why you've invited me,' he said. 'You're afraid you'll run out of new members. Have no worries, there'll be plenty more!'

Nevertheless I found John's direct approach refreshing and I knew that he never went back on his word. When I entered the room he was sitting behind his desk with his advisers grouped around him. 'Why do you want to make this film?' he asked. 'It's been made before.'

'It's a well-known subject,' I said, 'but, like the Lord's Prayer, no one has lived up to the truth of it.'

'Say what you mean without the Irish blarney. It's just another shipwreck.'

'It's more, much more than that,' I said. 'It's the end of an era, an era of privilege. There were no lifeboats for the steerage passengers, and the names of the dead on the *Titanic* memorial in Belfast appear in order of importance, unlike those on the war memorial right beside it, which are in alphabetical order.'

'Check that out with our Belfast manager,' JD ordered one of his cohorts, and continued, 'It's the most expensive film we've ever considered and you're asking Roy Baker to direct. You realize he's eight weeks behind schedule on *The One That Got Away*?'

'He'll be on time with this one, provided no one interferes,' I said, and thought I caught the glimmer of a smile on JD's face, for he was known to have interfered quite a lot on certain pictures.

Before long Belfast confirmed my information about the memorials and JD gave me the go-ahead. I thanked him, but then, as I reached the door, he called out to ask whether there was anything else I'd like to tell him before I left. It seemed he had not quite managed to exorcize all his doubts. 'I'm sure you know this already,' I said, 'but the bank rate went up 2 per cent this morning.'

'You're joking,' he gasped.

'No,' I said, 'I heard it on the car radio.'

'If I'd known I wouldn't have given you a penny.'

We both laughed.

Our first location shots were to show the lowering of the lifeboats. The Shaw Savill Line's colours matched the White Star colours of the *Titanic* and we were promised the use of one of their liners while it was in the Royal Albert Dock between voyages to South Africa. I purchased lifeboats identical to the *Titanic*'s from the *Franconia*, Churchill's secret HQ during the Yalta Conference, then being broken up in Scotland. They were brought down by road to be hung on the Shaw Savill liner's davits. Alongside we moored barges with arc lights and generators. Our extras were hired and dressed and three night's filming was scheduled to begin on Friday. On the Thursday morning I was telephoned by an embarrassed Shaw Savill port captain to say that the company chairman had suddenly decided against the film. Finding myself in an alarmingly expensive situation, I cancelled everything while I sought another location.

Doing the rounds of many other shipping companies, including my old friends, the P&O, produced only refusals. Sinking a ship was bad for business. I phoned Lloyds. 'Try Thomas Ward, the Clyde shipbreakers,' they advised. The same day I flew up to Helensburgh, where Ward's were breaking up the *Asturias*. Her starboard side was still intact, and, though she was painted white, she had the same davits as the *Titanic*. We only needed the starboard side at night, I told the manager, and he would remain free to work on the port side, next to the dock, during the day. 'How much do you want for ten nights?' I asked.

'You can have it for £100,' he said, thoroughly excited by the idea.

The jungle telegraphs of the shipping world would, I had a shrewd idea, be humming by this stage, so I asked him for a signed agreement as I could not afford another 'gentlemen's agreement' fated to fall through. He laughed as he scribbled it on the receipt. Next morning he showed me a telegram advising him not to give me assistance. 'They're too late,' he said with obvious pleasure.

The stunt men who did the eighty-foot jump into the Clyde's chilly waters were paid £1 a foot. The first arrived dressed in an original heavy cork life-jacket reaching from groin to chin. I was just in time to stop him jumping. If he had, the jacket would have struck him under the chin and broken his neck. The jumpers were now all fitted with similar-looking jackets, but made of kapok rather than cork. A team of Glasgow art students helped to paint the White Star colours. The port side of the ship was created by manipulating a mirror on the camera and using mirror writing.

The lifeboat sequence itself was shot on the more domestic waters of Ruislip Reservoir, not far from the studios. By good luck the weather was bitterly cold. The breath of the artists showed up nicely. To save us time, I had rooms made up on the bank that were super-heated with hot-air blowers designed for drying out buildings. These quickly brought the freezing cast back up to temperatures where they were glad to plunge in again. Kenneth More, who wore a thick seaman's sweater, had to spend longer in the water than anyone. I asked if he wasn't cold. He pulled back a sleeve to reveal a wet-suit underneath. We made sure that the lifeboats were filled with the correct numbers of people, all dressed in authentic costumes.

Everything possible was done to recreate the scene accurately. Joseph Boxhall, fourth officer of the *Titanic*, was my technical adviser throughout, and many survivors came to watch the filming and helped with first-hand knowledge. The two I saw most of were Edith Russell and Lawrence Beesley. Edith became a great friend of the family and spent her Christmases with us until she died aged ninety-six in 1976. Her real name was Rosenbaum, and as a fashion buyer for a New York store, she had reserved two cabins, one for herself and one for Paquin gowns bought in Paris. It was rumoured that she had been something more than good chums with Bruce Ismay, chairman of the White Star Line, and that her mother was a mistress of Disraeli's. During her frequent visits to the set, she expressed her delight with the accuracy of the work, especially with a scene where she sent her stewardess back for her lucky pig but abandoned her abundant jewellery.

The weather was even colder by the time we moved on to the lot to shoot the vast centre section of the ship. The set incorporated two funnels and four lifeboats. Batteries of arc-lights stood fifty feet above the ground on towers of tubular scaffolding, and the electricians had to climb vertical ladders to reach their lamps. Round the ship's side thousands of cardboard boxes were piled to a depth of twelve feet to break the falls of passengers leaping overboard. They did the job most effectively, taking the impetus out of the impact by a gradual collapse. Hot soup and drinks were in constant supply and there was an atmosphere of electric excitement, almost as if the scenes were real. Every night I visited the first-aid department, run by Dr Black with a matron and two nurses, but despite the dangerous work we had no serious accidents.

The main filming proceeded, but the model work was meanwhile keeping pace in a large indoor tank. Our smallest model was twenty feet long and accurate in every detail, its interior beautifully lit with electricity. The lifeboats were built to scale and propelled by electrically operated rowers. The sinking, when it was finally filmed, was remarkably moving as the lifeboats pulled away. The little models seemed to come to life.

Work on the filming had started on Pinewood's twenty-first birthday and shooting ended five months later. William Alwyn composed a score that was played by the Sinfonia of London under the baton of Muir Matheson. The première was held on 3 July 1958 at the Leicester Square Odeon. The reviews were the best ever received for a product of the Rank Organization, and among the accolades was a letter I received from John Davis:

4th July 1958

My dear Bill,

Some people in this industry can write fulsome letters, but I am afraid that I am not one of those people. However I do not want you to think that although this letter is brief it is any the less sincere.

May I thank you most sincerely for the great contribution you have made to the making of a great film, *A Night to Remember*. I have watched with pleasure the untiring effort which you put into this gigantic production and the great organizing work you put in to help the director in his work.

Many thanks.
Yours sincerely,
John.

Still glowing from the tributes, Roy Baker said to me, 'The door is wide open. We don't even have to push.'

The film was hailed as one that 'lends new lustre to the British film industry' and went on to win many awards. Two days after the letter from John Davis, Connery Chappel, a new Pinewood administrator I had never seen before, sent for me. He looked up as I entered and offered me a chair. 'The company's not renewing your contract,' he announced in a matter-of-fact tone. 'It expires at the end of this month.' Then he concluded, because I must have looked puzzled,

'It's company policy and has been ordered by the managing director, John Davis.'

I said nothing. I went back to my office, collected my things and thanked my devoted secretary, Genia Kaye, who was in any case moving into production. I had joined the ranks of the Rank Outsiders. 'When one door closes another opens,' said Betty.

She has an amazing gift of extra-sensory perception and I am convinced she knows the manner, hour and place of my death, though that is a matter she always refuses to confirm.

23

The Little Gem

Sydney, who joined Tyne Tees Television in 1957, felt I ought to have a go for the Northern Ireland franchise that the Independent Television Authority planned to set up at the end of 1958. I had no desire to return to Ireland, but my brother James liked the idea and I suggested he form a group and Sydney and I would give whatever help and advice we could. As far back as 1955, several people had thought about applying for the contract – among them my father's old paper, the *Belfast Telegraph*, and the *News Letter* – but soon began to harbour doubts about financial viability, leaving the *Northern Whig*, and its managing director, Lieutenant-Colonel Cunningham, the sole local applicant.

My brother met with scant enthusiasm for his proposals, and grounds for doubt certainly existed. At that stage, the BBC was producing only a few minutes of broadcasting time a day for the region. In theory a million people would be able to receive the new channel, but the set count so far stood at only 80,000. This would yield an annual income from advertising of about £400,000, out of which the winning contractor would have to pay a licence fee of £100,000, produce seven hours a week of local programmes and buy in enough product to fill the rest of the air time with material as good as that of the big stations whose incomes ran to many millions. It was also going to be necessary to build and equip expensive hi-tech studios, recruit highly skilled, highly paid and heavily unionized staff and maintain harmonious relations with a dangerously divided community. Small wonder if the response to my brother's appeal evoked a thunderous silence.

In August 1958 I needed to go to Belfast to see George Lodge, who had first shown *Simple Silage*, to arrange the Ulster première of *A Night to Remember*. During our conversation he invited me to go in with the *Northern Whig* group of contenders, of whom he was one. 'We need someone who knows about film,' he said, 'and you'd be ideal, being also an Ulsterman.'

The idea did not, however, appeal to the Cunninghams. They had by that stage already approached an American TV company to put the station on the air. It began to look as if our project was truly doomed, but I still had one card left to play. I had brought with me Sydney's application for the Tyne Tees contract, and with this to serve as a blueprint went to look up Paddy Falloon, my old friend of the castle-hunting expedition. 'Paddy,' I said, 'here is the last chance of a real bonanza. We need daring, tough Ulstermen with a gambling spirit. It's risky, but it could be a winner.'

The next day he took me to meet the Catherwoods, father and son, and Major George McKean, who had interests in transport and building work. They grilled me up and down, especially about any English shareholders who might gain control of the company. Eventually I suggested a shareholding of 51 per cent for Ulster, 25 per cent held in reserve for a local newspaper and, for the English investors, including myself, 24 per cent. On this basis McKean said he would put in money, and the others followed suit. A steering committee was formed with my brother in the chair, and Paddy suggested Lord Antrim for our group's chairman. The *News Letter* and *Belfast Telegraph* were invited to join and turned the proposal down, but Commander Oscar Henderson and his two sons, Captain Bill and Brumwell 'Brum' Henderson, part-owners of the *News Letter* came in, as did two of my Baird cousins who were part-owners of the *Belfast Telegraph*.

It became obvious that it would help our application if we could back up our representative spread of influential Northern Ireland people with some entertainment talent from London. I therefore invited Sir Laurence Olivier, Betty Box, Bea Lillie (herself of Ulster stock) and Sir John Rothenstein, Director of the Tate Gallery, to join us, which they did. Sydney came over and he and Brum spent two days at Paddy's Inn at Crawfordsburn creating our application. The name we chose for our company was 'Ulster Television'. Our apt and unique logo, the track of a flying spot zigzagging across the screen, was the result of a competition.

Our interview with the Independent Television Authority came about on the afternoon of 4 November 1958, and we fielded a team that consisted, besides myself, of Lord Antrim, Bill Henderson and our accountant, George Cameron. The Cunninghams, the Duke of Abercorn at their head, had already been in to put their case that morning. Sir Ivone Kirkpatrick, chairman of the ITA, said that his committee liked the look of our application but wanted to know who, when it came to it, was actually going to take off their coat and get the station working. We had, I assured him, lined up a top programme producer from one of the big companies who would more than satisfy them, but Sir Ivone pressed smartly ahead with his next question: 'Mr MacQuitty, will you be prepared to take time off from film production and put the company on the air?'

My worst fears had come to pass. Above all else except my family, I valued my freedom, and I hated any form of contract and future commitment. The last thing I wanted was to become involved in the day-to-day business of setting up a new TV station – a colossal task compared with producing a film. But then, if I said no, we looked likely to lose the contract. The team all gazed at me expectantly. From somewhere up by the ceiling I heard a strange voice saying, 'I will.'

To ensure a representative board, we had appointed eighteen directors who were top people in their own fields. This still left me as the only one with any inside knowledge of films or television. I could see myself, as managing director, beginning to drown before long in drafting lengthy reports on the merits of this or that system and endeavouring to explain the rights of the numerous trade unions without whom no TV company can exist; not to say yearning for the simplicity of my partnership with Sydney Box and our ability to make headway without ever holding a board meeting.

My contract ran for a year from 1 January 1959. The first six months were to be full-time, the second six months half-time on half-pay. After that I would be free again. Besides setting up the station, there was the prospect that I would have to take on and nurse along someone to succeed me as managing director. This was perhaps the most daunting prospect of all. Anyone handling Ulster affairs was walking a tight-rope, and a skill in local politics combined with a liberal instinct was an essential attribute. As I told the board, we were all now like goldfish in a bowl, and everything we did would be seen and speculated upon, our judges the people of Ulster. I added that while I hoped we might leave some footprints in the sands of time, our first thoughts must be for the people of Ulster as a whole.

In England I approached a range of electronic companies and executive managers about equipment and running requirements.

None of those I spoke to were sanguine. Finance was going to be very tight. I began to think I must have been mad ever to touch this venture. Here was I in charge. Here were eighty solid Ulster folk putting up £100,000, with a call for twice that amount, who would be bitterly upset to lose their money. Yet, as with producing a film, the main task was to choose the best people. I settled on George Kelsey of Marconi for equipment; on Howard Steele of ABC to work with our architect, Brian Hewitt, to equip Havelock House, an old clothing factory found for us by Paddy Falloon. Gradually a magic forest of TV artefacts grew up through concealed floor ducts into an air-conditioned control room ingeniously fitted between the old building's iron-pillar supports. Two modest studios came into being, as did a small fixed-camera newsroom.

I was perplexed to know how we could set up our own sales office in London without using our call on the shares, which was something I wanted to avoid at all costs. Happily I persuaded the head of ABC, Howard Thomas, my chief mentor, to let me have Mike Hutcheson, his sales manager. Frank Brady, a first-class engineer, we obtained from ABC Manchester, and from the same source we recruited S.E. Reynolds, our programme controller. He had been in television since it started at Alexandra Palace in London and proved a wonderful teacher and adviser for our new staff. Apart from these key people, our policy was for all staff to be local.

My successor was yet to be found, and the board felt he should be someone highly qualified from across the water. Several likely candidates were interested, including Huw Weldon, who at that time had an urge to leave the BBC and run his own show. The more I thought about it, however, the more I was convinced that only an Ulsterman was going to be able to cope with Ulster politics. From that point of view, the choice narrowed down to Brum Henderson, MA of Trinity College, Dublin, who had worked on the *News Letter*, Ireland's oldest newspaper, and had a wide grasp of Ulster affairs. Against him was the fact that he was still only twenty-nine and had no previous experience of television, and that two of his family were already on the board. Moreover, he shared my instinctive reluctance to tie himself into an all-devouring and uncertain enterprise. In the end he accepted the situation, and his father, in a graceful gesture, resigned from the board in his favour.

Our temporary office was small, but furnished with a king-size chair and table. I placed Brum firmly in the hot seat and sat at his side as we interviewed local applicants. The first to be appointed was our company secretary, Barry Johnston, and the next our press man, Paddy Scott. Later we took on a programme director, Derek Bailey, who, like many of our young hopefuls, moved on from our modest station to become internationally famous. (Indeed, he eventually headed an application to oust us.)

Dummy programmes began to run and we started to wonder what we could do to mark our opening night, 31 October 1959, in a way sufficiently memorable. We had no money, but we did have Larry Olivier and Bea Lillie. I talked to S.E. Reynolds and we worked out a little Hallowe'en sketch for which we planned to invite in a group of children off the street to participate. It was not going to be too expensive so long as Larry and Bea refrained from asking their usual fees. The sketch was warm and modest and more appealing, I thought, than some of the spectacular openings I had witnessed. I went to see Larry and Bea, who agreed at once to do the opening. It would be an honour. They wanted no payment and wished the company every success. Betty, who had been my alternate director from the beginning, and who had worked with me through all the decisions, thought they had done very well in being offered shares in the company. In her view, this was likely to be the only performance we got out of them. It was.

Then, just as we were in the midst of our pre-opening activities, the ITA and the Independent TV Companies Association mounted a conference for the European Broadcasting Union. Every independent company was requested to come up with its best programme to impress the Europeans with the superior quality of British commercial TV. In vain did I protest that we had as yet no working studio, much less a programme. Bill Ward, who was putting the show together, was adamant that the smallest, newest and only British overseas station had to be seen and heard. 'What props can you give me?' I asked.

'All I can give you is a map of the British Isles,' he said.

It was clear that we could not compete directly with the other companies' blockbusting productions of Shakespeare, ballet, orchestral performances, operas and general cultural uplift. Our only chance lay in contrast. It came down to me and the map. I commenced by showing exactly where Ulster lay on it and talked about the general lack of television sets. I told how it had therefore been a great delight to me to find an antennae rising from the roof of a thatched cottage in the lonely Mountains of Mourne. I knocked on the door and was invited in, happy to spot a small TV receiver in the corner, but since one has to be devious in Ireland, I asked the old couple who lived there, 'Are you not lonely here, so far from everyone?'

'Not a wee bit,' said the husband in his broad Ulster accent. 'We have the electric television.'

'Do you like it?' I asked.

'Man,' he said, 'if ye shut yer eyes it's every bit as good as the wireless.'

I asked the wife what she thought. 'Ah,' she said, 'it's well enough, it keeps the ould fella quiet, but it's a terrible bad light for reading by.'

After the respectful silences and refined clapping for the big shows, the European audiences roared their applause with unrestrained laughter. Ulster's shoestring item was a success.

We were now on course for our own celebration, but I remained apprehensive that some minor technical hitch could cause signal failure on the big day. Kelsey reassured me that, if we were not fully operational and secure, he would have a mobile unit on standby to keep the station going. Betty was given the responsibility of shepherding Larry and Bea into a press reception in the VIP lounge at Heathrow Airport, by which we hoped to obtain maximum publicity. Despite her frantic efforts, neither of our stars showed up, and it was not until the last call for passengers that Larry and his agent Cecil Tennant, both wearing trilbys pulled well down on their heads, were spotted sidling past on their way to the plane. Bea was even later. She arrived leaning on the arm of her faithful companion, John Huck – 'Huck with an H' as she always introduced him. 'Where have you been?' asked an indignant Betty.

'You're lucky she's here at all,' said Huck. 'She's stoned.'

Somewhere above the Irish Sea, Bea recovered sufficiently to sway up and down the aisle, singing 'Does your mother come from Ireland?' to Sir Ivone Kirkpatrick and his retinue. In due course the embarrassing flight ended and, at the airport, Rolls-Royce after Rolls-Royce drew up on the tarmac to whisk Sir Ivone and his ITA colleagues off to Government House, where they were to stay. As each Rolls arrived, Larry asked Cecil with mounting wrath, 'Is this ours?'

I had told Brum to be sure to have a Rolls for the stars, but the government had bagged the lot and the best he could come up with were ancient Pontiacs stained with years of marriages and funerals and smelling of drink and vomit. In these our stars drove to the Grand Central Hotel, where Larry demanded his key. The pretty receptionist looked at him closely and said, 'Who are you?' in the broadest of Belfast tones.

Betty cut in hastily, 'This is the famous Sir Laurence Olivier, who has very kindly come from London to open our new television station.'

'You're not a bit like your picture,' said the girl unabashed.

The following day ITA laid on a grand celebration lunch in the hotel. The distinguished guests included Lord Wakehurst, the Governor of Northern Ireland, Lord Brookeborough, the Prime Minister, and the Lord Mayor of Belfast. Bea was sitting at the far end of one of the side-tables and Betty, thinking this must be an oversight, asked a union representative on the local ITA committee, who was sitting beside her, if she should offer to change places. 'I think the Authority would be most upset if you tried to alter their arrangements,' he said.

After lunch we adjourned to the studio, and here the opening programme commenced at 4.45 p.m. The little sketch went off smoothly and we all congratulated ourselves. A few minutes later I was told there was someone on the phone for me. At least there's one person who likes the programme, I told myself. Up till now, my name had not been mentioned in any of the laudatory speeches, and I lifted the handset in pleasant anticipation of at last receiving recognition. A strong male Belfast voice rattled the diaphragm of the receiver. 'Are you Mr MacQuitty?'

I said I was.

'You don't know me,' the voice continued, 'but ye'll rue this day's work.'

'Who are you?' I asked.

'Never ye mind who I am, but ye'll rue this day.'

'What is your complaint?' I asked.

The voice continued, 'Ye know the chidler ye had round the barrel?'

'No, I don't,' I said. 'They were just ordinary children we brought in who were playing in the street outside the studio.'

'Them's not ordinary childer. Them's Catholics, all of them, ye right Papist bastard.'

The line went dead. On the side of the red railway bridge across the street from the studio was written in white letters two feet high:

GOD IS LOVE – LOVE EVERYBODY

The evening progressed; the drinks flowed. Bea ended up sitting on the Governor's knee. Larry, persuaded to read the epilogue, asked for a Bible. We had to send out for one. Finally, after giving the matter much thought in the solitude of the secretary's office, he read the first two verses of Genesis, on which reverberant note the great day ended. Bea was invited to stay with the Governor and Betty and I walked back through the empty streets. I thought how much my father would have appreciated the evening, how my mother would have relished it all. A year of constant effort had culminated in a good launch. The ITA were pleased. The smallest station, the 'little gem', as I dubbed it, was on the air. My task was almost done.

Towards the end of my year as managing director, a deputation of influential shareholders came to lobby me in London. They wanted me to continue; I could name my fee. I explained that I had specifically contracted for only one year as there were films lined up and waiting for me. 'I'm sure UTV will continue to be a success,' I told them, 'and if you have any suggestions, you can bring them up at the annual general meeting.'

They duly did so, but the meeting was satisfied that the company was on the right course. I moved that Brum be made managing director and Mike sales director. The motion was passed, and the board invited me to be deputy chairman with Sir Francis Evans, a cultured diplomat who lent dignity and elegance to our meetings. It was an honour I gladly accepted, and it represented the start of a tradition of strong family links with UTV. Betty was made a director on my eventual retirement, and later became vice-chairman; when Lord Antrim died, my brother James became chairman. Brum Henderson, having been a prodigious and talented managing director, took over the chairmanship when James retired. Brum himself retired after thirty-two years' service in the company and his deputy John McGuckian became chairman. John is pro-chancellor of the Queen's University and chairman of the International Fund for Ireland. His father was a founding director of the company, and, like three other sons who followed their fathers on to the board, has given the company great stability.

From the outset, public opinion has been firmly on our side. The UTV announcers spoke in broad Ulster accents, for I cautioned them not to adopt the standard English of the BBC, but to emphasize that we were an Ulster station for Ulster people. There was yet another phone call before I was through with my year's commitment. It sounded very like the man who first complained about the children.

'Is that Mr MacQuitty?' asked the voice.

'It is,' I said.

'I want to tell ye something, mister.' There was a pause. 'Are ye still there?'

'I am,' I said.

'Yer television's useless till nobody!'

The double negative was the highest praise Ulster could bestow.

24

Khartoum to Abu Simbel

One evening in December 1959, I was instructed by Betty to pick her up from the Gas Council showroom in Kilburn. Without knowing the reason, I did as asked, and took the children with me. We found ourselves sharing in a wonderful occasion. She had been awarded the title of Britain's champion cook, and her triumph kept us supplied with all our kitchen equipment for the next thirty years. The terms of the competition were to provide a meal for four people costing not more than £1. This was her winning menu: cream-of-leek soup; fillet of beef in pastry, served with red cabbage and creamed potatoes; pudding surprise made of sponge, ice-cream, meringue and cherries, served *flambé*.

My work with Ulster Television continued, but before long I was back to looking at film ideas. Two were based on books on which I had collaborated with Gerald Sparrow, whom I first got to know during my time in Siam. The third was *Death of a Snout*, written by Douglas Warner in association with John Gosling, the head of Scotland Yard's so-called 'Ghost Squad', a section of the police who worked with informers and had a special relation with the under-world. The Sparrow books were, respectively, *Gordon, Mandarin and Pasha*, a life of General Gordon, and *Opium Venture*, about the 'Golden Triangle' or opium cultivation in Burma, Laos and Siam. The one about Gordon of Khartoum looked particularly promising.

I flew to Khartoum, but the Sudan was at the time governed by a junta of generals who feared the Mahdi's followers and would give no help with a film. The Mahdi's people, by contrast – descendants of the one who defeated Gordon – were eager to co-operate. I imagined they thought that as soon as we reached the battle scenes they could seize the chance to push the generals into the Red Sea. Khartoum itself was full of mementoes of Gordon. His desert motor-car, fitted with railway wheels so it could run on railway tracks, was in the local museum together with other relics. The relief ship was the head-quarters of the Khartoum Yacht Club. The palace steps, on which Gordon died, shone in the clear sunlight. It was magnificent material, but politically it was obviously impossible to set up the film in the Sudan. I decided I would have to try Egypt.

Bill Reed, a marine biologist stationed at Port Sudan, then invited me to go diving with him in the Red Sea, and in the evening he took me to the Red Sea Club, a small wooden house with a tin roof and cannon on either side of the door. Inside the club the expatriates, as they called themselves, preserved, like the sahibs of India, their way of life: long-chairs, magazines and a busy bar. The talk was all of home, while about them were the Nubians and their customs, which had so fascinated the ancient pharaohs – the Land of Ghosts, filled with rare animals, spices and treasures of ivory and gold.

Later we went to a village in the desert, a 'village of ladies'. It looked drab and dusty. There was not a tree or bush in sight and mud paths ran between mud-built huts. Bill led the way through the narrow lanes and knocked at a rough wooden door. A Nubian girl servant opened up, and a moment later the lady of the house, black as ebony and magnificently proportioned, welcomed us into a lounge fitted with fans, expensive carpets, luxurious chairs, a large record player and a well-stocked fridge. Here we sat and drank iced beer as Bill was rebuked for neglecting his girlfriend. 'I'll fetch her now,' said our hostess in perfect English.

In came a stunningly beautiful Nubian girl, who embraced Bill after scolding him for his long absence. There seemed to be a beguiling innocence in the situation. We sat and talked and sex was never mentioned. On the way back, the biologist in Bill returned to the fore and he said, 'Funny thing, but the girls seem immune to VD, though most of their clients are sailors.'

'Anything to do with female circumcision?' I asked.

'I don't think so, but they do have a host of native medicines. Anyway, they've a great reputation for being OK with the sailors.'

The next day we visited the deserted city of Suakin, the old port of Sudan, which is still used for the embarkation of pilgrims to Mecca. Tall white empty buildings lined the three-mile channel that led from its deep inland harbour to the sea. I walked through the cemetery, whose tombstones recorded the short lives of British soldiers and sailors who had died for the Empire. The caretaker showed me the tattered record book:

Private Ashby   18.3.85   Killed in action, Hasheen.
Private John Quinn   17.3.85   53rd Shropshire Regiment, enteric fever.
Ed. William Collier   8.8.85   Nav. Lieut., HMS *Grappler*, heat apoplexy.
Patrick Moglan   2.8.85   Lance-Cpl., sunstroke.

Five centuries before Christ, the Persian forces of Cambyses II had suffered greater losses hereabouts when overtaken by a sandstorm while trying to reach the oasis of Siva, then the site of the temple of Amon. Tens of thousands vanished completely in the sea of sand. (Not until 1977 were their remains discovered: thousands of skeletons with their swords and spears.) I found everything moving and exciting in these ancient lands of the pharaohs. 'You should see Abu Simbel before it's inundated,' said Bill as we parted.

I took a plane to Wadi Halfa, where I hired an old Packard and set out at 3 a.m. to reach Abu Simbel before sun-up. At first our journey lay through cultivated fields, but these soon gave way to desert and our speed increased to avoid becoming stuck in patches of sand. Skirting the early Merotic cemetery of Gebel Adda, then being excavated by the Smithsonian Institute to save the burials from inundation, we entered Abu Simbel village. In the pre-dawn darkness, I hired a *felucca* and set sail across the Nile towards the western bank where the temples lay.

At first all I could see was the dark outline of the tall cliffs of buff sandstone lining the river. As we approached the sun rose out of the eastern desert and its rays struck the temples head-on. There were two days each year when it shone directly into the inner sanctuary, 23 February and 23 October, and I was there on 23 February 1962. The boatman ran his *felucca* – the design of which was almost unchanged since the time of the builder of the temples, Ramesses the Great – on to a narrow strip of sand. I gazed up at the colossal figures of the pharoah. The giant heads were extraordinarily impressive.

Inside the temple, eight huge Osiride figures of Ramesses lined the first chamber and caught the sun's rays, which then struck on through two more chambers before entering the sanctuary, cut 180 feet within the living rock. Here four gods, Ptah, Amen-ra, Ramesses himself and Re-Horachty, sat in equal dignity on one massive throne. Round the walls, like a Bayeux tapestry engraved and painted on stone, flowed scenes from the pharoah's many exploits: Ramesses killing his enemies; Ramesses charging superior forces alone in his chariot, his pet lion running beside him; Ramesses being presented with the hands of the slain; Ramesses returning triumphant to Thebes.

A few yards away was a smaller temple dedicated to his favourite wife, Nefertari, whose name meant 'Beautiful Companion'. She was one of his sixty-seven daughters, three of whom he married – a practical way of ensuring the purity of the line and a system still in force during the reigns of the Ptolemies. He also had 111 sons, two by Nefertari, and despite his prodigious output lived to the ripe age of ninety-seven, keeping most of his hair and teeth. I stayed in the temples until the sun set, aware of being surrounded by history made over 3,000 years before and yet as vivid and fresh as the day it happened. Before long all of this was to be submerged by the rising waters of the Aswan High Dam. As I drove back through the night to Wadi Halfa, I wondered what could be done.

In Cairo I talked with the heads of the Egyptian film industry about my Gordon project. They had good studios available and could supply all the extras I needed as well as soldiers and cavalry. They were friendly and helpful. The Nile was the Nile, the desert the desert. Why bother with Khartoum? I returned to London full of an enthusiasm which the Rank Organization shared. Unfortunately, when the budget came to nearly half as much again as *A Night to Remember*, they turned it down regretfully. At this point Julian Blaustein, an American producer who had by curious chance become interested in the same subject, asked me to go and see him. I was slightly taken aback to enter his apartment and find him holding a copy of *Gordon, Mandarin and Pasha*. He read out Gerald Sparrow's acknowledgement aloud:

'Artists, including authors, are no longer fortunate in having a patron to encourage and protect them. The best modern substitute is a friend with a lively critical faculty. I have had this in William MacQuitty, who first suggested writing this book to me.'

'Mr MacQuitty,' he said, 'I congratulate you. This is the best book I've read on Gordon, and I've read the lot.'

Mr Blaustein commanded resources beyond the wildest dreams of the British film industry. His lead in the resulting film, *Khartoum*, would be no less a star than Charlton Heston. I warned him of the problems of shooting in the Sudan and offered him my contacts in Egypt. I spoke to him about Abu Simbel, of which in due course he had a magnificent scale model constructed. The loss of the film was a major personal disappointment, but on the rebound I wrote to *The Times*, suggesting that the temples might be saved by leaving them underwater. They could be protected by a skin dam containing clean water so as to be visible to tourists from submarine passages. Artificial sunrises with suitably placed lights would then reveal the inner sanctuary – a cool modern miracle at a relatively low cost.

At that time there were three other contending plans for saving the temples: the French, to build a large dam to hold back the waters; the Italian, to cut away the surrounding cliff, enclose the temples in reinforced concrete boxes and, using 650 hydraulic jacks, to raise them a sixteenth of an inch at a time until they were lifted above the danger line; and the Egyptian, to cut the temples into blocks and reassemble them on top of the cliff, safe from the rising waters. The consideration and sponsorship of the plans was in the hands of UNESCO.

All three schemes were extremely expensive, their costs ranging between £16 million and £60 milion. Mine would have cost less than a million and it had the added attraction of preserving the temples from erosion. The idea swept the world press, and to my astonishment I found myself in demand. I spoke first to old friends, the architects Jane Drew and Maxwell Fry, and together we approached Ove Arup, then completing the engineering work for the new Sydney Opera House. Sketch plans were prepared, and we took these to the famous archaeologist, Sir Mortimer Wheeler, who thought the idea original and exciting. Experts went to Abu Simbel and brought back specimens of Nile water and the sandstone cliffs for analysis. We asked the Pilkington Glass Company if they could supply glass windows able to withstand a water pressure at 200 feet or more, and received confirmation.

In March 1962, we saw Dr Salah el-Din Tewfik, permanent representative of the United Arab Republic at UNESCO. He pronounced himself delighted with the scheme, which he thought would be of even greater interest than the statues. Other representatives were impressed by the plan, but obviously reluctant to see their own pet schemes abandoned. Meanwhile newspapers around the world, including *Newsweek* and *Time* magazine, showed pictures of our designs and gave us high praise. On 24 April the Italian plan fell through for lack of funds. The French plan failed likewise. As the Egyptian plan hung in the balance, we continued our struggle. I wrote to Edward Heath, who was then Lord Privy Seal, and spoke to the conservative MP George Hutcheson, making the point that the residual bad will left by the Suez débâcle in 1956 might be dissipated a little by helping to save the Egyptians' temples.

Evenutally, on 6 June 1963, I received a letter from Nicholas Ridley saying that the Ministry of Education had agreed to meet a deputation from both sides of the House to discuss my plan. Sir Hamilton Kerr and he would represent the Conservative side, Dr Barnett Stross and Dr Horace King the Labour side. I was to present my case before them. This I did and it went down well. 'Spike' Marlin, senior director of the United Nations Office of the High Commissioner for Refugees, sent the plans to René Maheu, secretary-general of UNESCO, but pointed out that when officials make proposals they become wedded to them and their *amour propre* makes it extremely difficult for them to accept any alternative. On the 19th 'Spike' commented in a letter to me:

> UNESCO cannot be overjoyed by your idea to save money on the Abu Simbel project. When I saw Mahew the other day he looked glumly at me without mentioning your idea. However, as you say, they may be driven to accepting it for lack of money.

On the 21st a letter came from D.G. Allen, private secretary to the Lord Privy Seal. It said:

> The scheme that you devised was brought to the notice of the United Nations Educational, Scientific and Cultural Organization, but it was not formally considered by the Executive Committee of the Campaign to Save the Monuments.

And there the matter ended. More than a year's hard work by many experts, and the plan had not even been considered by the elected representatives of the fifty-seven nations who were putting up the money to save the temples and who, according to international press coverage, gave our scheme enthusiastic support. It seemed incredible that our future heritage could lie in the hands of such people. D.J. Pinto, the engineer, wrote to me:

> Compared with the pedestrian scheme for cutting up the statuary or the other impractical solutions that have been proposed, your idea resembles the Columbian egg standing on its end.

However, it was not altogether the end so far as I was concerned. Norman Fisher, chairman of the BBC *Brains Trust*, asked me if I would write a book about my plan for saving the temples of Abu Simbel. I said I had never written a book but would like to try. He introduced me to Walter Parrish, editorial director of the publishers Macdonald, and my book *Abu Simbel* was published on 25 August

1965. It sold 40,000 copies and received wonderful press reviews as well as letters of praise from the White House, the Smithsonian Institute and the Boston Museum of Fine Arts among other illustrious sources. Sir Mortimer Wheeler wrote:

> The Ancient Nubia has been destroyed to feed the living, but itself lives again in this splendid picture book. Not without help from Ramesses II, Mr MacQuitty has produced a masterpiece.

Walter invited me to dinner and said, at the end of the meal, 'We're in a rather embarrassing position with regard to your contract.'

'Why?' I asked.

'Our legal department tell me that you failed to ratify it as you did not cash the cheque for £100 which was your advance on the book. Why not?' he asked somewhat apprehensively.

'I didn't know whether or not I could write a book,' I replied, 'and I didn't want to take the money until I knew you were satisfied.'

He smiled. 'We're going to improve on the terms, and now, what about your next book?'

I said I had no plans for another, but, having taken photographs since childhood, would rather be a photographer than a writer.

'That would suit us very well. We want to produce a book on Irish gardens by Edward Hyams. Would you like to be the photographer on the project?'

'Very much,' I said, 'but at the moment I do have a film to make.'

'When will you be free?'

'In eight months,' I said.

'It's a deal,' said Walter, and we shook hands on it.

Julian Blaustein, when he finished work on the production of *Khartoum*, asked me if I would like the scale model of Abu Simbel – a sort of consolation prize, I supposed. 'It's beautiful,' he urged me.

I thanked him graciously. A week later a heavy transport lorry ground its way slowly up our drive, bearing a ten-foot cube of wood encased in steel bands. 'Where are the crew to unload?' asked the driver.

I said I was very sorry, but there had been a misunderstanding, and would he please return the load to the studio? I rang Julian and apologized, but promised I would find the model a good home. This I did, and anyone visiting the Egyptian Room of the Leicester Museum today will see it set against a large backing of one of my photographs and at the front a small card that reads: 'On permanent loan from William MacQuitty'.

25

Gardens and a Lost Lion

The Rank Organization gave me the go-ahead to make a film of *Death of a Snout*, but did not like the book's title and insisted on it being changed to *The Informers*. To my mind, this was altogether too close to *The Informer*, John Ford's classic of the 1930s, and the use of 'snout' seemed appropriate enough to me, being underworld slang for an informer. (For the American distribution it was, in any case, retitled yet again to *Underworld Informers*.) John Gosling, the retired head of the Ghost Squad and the book's co-author, became my consultant and, with his powerful but genial personality, he guided me around his former manor. The use of informants meant a system of rewards and an unwritten code of conduct between police and criminals, and many crimes were uncovered that would otherwise have stayed unsolved. As it laid down in my old Punjab Light Horse manual, 'Never lose touch with the enemy,' but doubtless there were abuses and the idea of policemen mingling so closely with criminals caused disquiet in certain quarters. John Gosling forecast that the discontinuation of the information fund would lead to a rising crime rate.

My director, Ken Annakin, and I had first worked together at Merton Park when we made a documentary called *Breast Feeding*, progress on which was much interrupted by flying bombs. Now I was fortunate to get him. He was in international demand and would soon be directing that most blockbusting of comedy epics, *Those Magnificent Men in Their Flying Machines*. Ken was a dedicated and unwearying film-maker, whose quick temper cut through the web of union delays that by then was plaguing the industry. It took ten unions or so to make one film, and the rule books had grown so complicated that workers sometimes came to me to ask whether they ought or ought not to be doing such and such a job. The already enormous risks taken by producers were meanwhile multiplied by the possibility of strikes against which there was no insurance.

Nigel Patrick played the lead in *The Informers*, and the excellent supporting cast included Catherine Woodville, Maggie Whiting, Colin Blakely, Derren Nesbitt, Frank Finlay and Harry Andrews. The film emerged as an unsentimental, hard-edged account of the framing of a police inspector, and, released in 1963, attracted a huge audience.

With the film out of the way, my commitment to take the photographs for *Irish Gardens* became a source of delight. The author of the text, Edward Hyams, was one of our most prolific writers on horticulture as well as a novelist and a commentator on the social and political scene. Dapper and neatly bearded, short, slim and agile, Edward displayed an astounding, sometimes wicked wit combined with learning on an awesome scale. We got on well from the start. With his writer's reserve, he did not like to approach people without, first, an exchange of letters, formal introductions and an edifice of courtesy. As an unabashed organizer, I cleared a path for us round the great Irish gardens with little difficulty. Half-way through our itinerary we reached Birr Castle, the home of Lord and Lady Rosse. During lunch the sun came out and I asked to be excused so I could take advantage of the light. 'You're just like my son, Tony. He's a keen photographer,' said Lady Rosse.

Tony, as Lord Snowdon, is now one of the world's best photographers.

On our way to our next garden, Ilnacullin, I suddenly said to Edward, 'We're wasting our time.'

'What do you mean?' he asked.

'The Irish don't buy books. We should be doing a book on the great gardens of the world.'

Edward looked at me closely. 'Bill,' he said, 'you're absolutely right. One day we'll do it. You realize it'll mean going round the world at least twice for you to catch the seasons? What an excellent idea.'

Macdonald's gave *Irish Gardens* a splendid launch in London, but hung fire on the idea of the big book. They said they would need to find a publishing partner.

'Don't worry,' said Edward, 'it will come to pass, though it may take time. I have our title already: *Great Botanical Gardens of the World*.'

Ulster Television had been running strongly and making a handsome profit. I continued to attend board meetings on the first Friday of each month, and although the many problems that beset us increased enormously as bitter political divisions and tensions engulfed the area, these were always exuberant occasions. One of Ulster Television's greatest successes had been an idea I originated in which teaching members of the Queen's University covered such subjects as medicine, law, literature, music, physics, history or economics. The series, called *Midnight Oil*, went out between 10.40 and 11.15 in the evening and ran to forty-two broadcasts. *Midnight Oil*'s successor was *The Enquiring Mind*, which offered popular introductions to, for instance, microbiology, architecture, aviation, the visual arts and Ulster's contribution to the history of the United States. In its history of independent television in Britain, the ITA commented:

> Although the description of 'First University of the Air' is an excusable exaggeration, such enterprise from a diminutive regional company certainly merited Sir Ivone Kirkpatrick's comment 'a very remarkable effort'. The Authority was sufficiently impressed seriously to contemplate making Northern Ireland the area in which to experiment with the future possibilities of an educational channel.

By now I had succeeded in enthusing Rank with the idea of a film based on *Opium Venture* to the extent where they agreed to finance a trip to the Far East to search out a beautiful Oriental girl to play the lead. They also accepted Jack Cardiff as director. Jack, a first-class cameraman as well as an excellent director who had made the highly regarded screen version of *Sons and Lovers*, had no idea of time or order. When we landed in Bangkok I discovered he had forgotten to have his injections and rushed him into a clinic to get immunization for cholera, typhoid and polio. We then continued with our trip through Siam, Laos, Singapore, Hong Kong, Manila and Japan. The girls we saw were all heavily escorted, and they and their agents were so concerned about being turned down that every meeting needed to be devised in secret. These elaborate farces made it difficult to compare talents, but we collected photographs and essential details to boil down later to the two or three hopefuls who would be offered a film test. I was, at the same time, able to add to my extensive collection of photographs, but began to have doubts about our exotic Oriental story. When I got back from Japan I found the Rank Organization were also having second thoughts, and for once I agreed with them.

A few months later, two important opportunities presented

themselves. The government decided to sell its costly venture into films, British Lion, and ITA was inviting applications for programme contractors for the new period, 1964–7. Sydney and I discussed our chances and decided that London Independent Producers should bid for British Lion while we formed a new company, London Independent Television Producers, to bid for the London TV area, presently held by Associated Rediffusion.

Besides myself and Sydney, our group behind the television bid consisted of Norman Fisher, chairman of the *Brains Trust*, Ted Willis, James Carr of World Wide Pictures and a hundred very well-known associates, including film and television directors and producers, artists and writers. We even had our own symphony orchestra, conducted by Muir Matheson. The *Observer* saw this 'star-studded group as showing the dissatisfaction of creative people at the way things were run'. In certain quarters we were regarded as over-reaching ourselves in making our television bid at the same time as we were trying to acquire British Lion, yet British Lion was exactly what we needed for production facilities. It promised, integrated with the TV network, to make a powerful force to counteract the film-distribution monopoly of Rank and ABC.

Sydney's bid for London television, the best application he had ever put together, had the potential to change the face of British television for the better. Lord Hill said that it showed 'a vigour and freshness of approach and a liveliness of imagination'. Unfortunately the selling of British Lion turned into a débâcle involving a tremendous row about selling off a public asset to private interests. The controversy thereafter undermined our chances of the television contract.

Not long after this, David D'Ambrumenil, who handled insurance for Greek shipping companies, invited me to lunch and said he and some friends wished to back films. I responded at once. 'Don't touch them. Ships rarely sink but films seldom float.'

He was not to be persuaded. 'We intend to have a go. Who would you recommend?'

'Sydney Box,' I said without hesitation.

A week later Sydney and I were invited to St Moritz by the shipping magnate Stavro Niarchos, who had had a wide cinema screen installed at the far end of his magnificent indoor swimming pool. There, after dinner, we watched a feature film beautifully projected, but also reflected upside down in the pool – a distraction that had me wondering about ill-omens.

At the behest of D'Ambrumenil's associates, a new company, London Producers Association, was duly formed, with offices in the

West End, and in due course twelve films were announced. The offices were filled with scriptwriters, directors and the complexities of a large production company. It all seemed a far cry from my original notion, long ago, that Sydney and I would produce a picture every year or so, but Sydney was in his element, a magnificent catalyst in the midst of the humming machinery of creation.

Alas, it was not to last. The pressures on Sydney were enormous. He needed to make a hasty trip to New York and returned exhausted. He had already suffered one massive cerebral haemorrhage back in 1959, and had then been harried, even in hospital, by worried producers and directors who felt unable to proceed without his advice. Now, his doctors told him, his one chance was to make a complete break. At the end of 1967 he retired, moved to Australia and settled in Perth. I was heartbroken. We had worked together since 1941 and during the whole of that time had spoken together almost daily. He was a man who had filled many seats, and now they were all empty. Muriel was even more distressed. For some time she and Sydney had been drifting apart on account of his interest in another lady.

I said to Betty that I would like to get away for a while. 'Why don't we go to Abu Simbel,' she suggested, 'and see how the work there's progressing?'

It was exactly the right thing to do. We flew to Cairo, took the plane to Aswan and went by hydrofoil to Abu Simbel. We swept past Nubian villages submerged in the very waters that had for thousands of years supported them. The temples were already being resited on top of the cliff, and behind them an artificial cliff was in process of construction. But the temples looked forlorn in their new setting, and it was a feeling I shared.

Months had gone by, yet still Macdonald had failed to come up with the partner they needed for an ambitious project like the botanical gardens book. Edward Hyams and I grew restive and fearful that someone else would step in ahead of us with the same notion. In the end our patience ran out. We went to see Jocelyn Baines, managing director of Thomas Nelson, and within twenty-four hours had a deal. For me it was going to mean two trips round the world to cover the seasons in the northern and southern hemispheres, avoiding, like the swallows, the winters. To my regret, Edward was only going to be able to travel with me in Australia and the Argentine.

My first assignment was at Kew Gardens, where I kept vigil while the great Victoria lily, with its giant soup-plate leaves, produced her midnight flowers, at first a delicate white, but gradually turning pink and finally vanishing in a droop of tattered brown as the sun rose; a *memento mori* if ever there was one. The director of Kew, Sir George Taylor, could hardly have been more helpful. He had lived in the East, knew the Himalayas well and agreed to write the foreword. He gave me introductions to his colleagues, and armed with these I was able to go, like a frog leaping from lily pad to lily pad, to the fifty cities in the world that had botanical gardens. As I soon discovered, the directors and staffs of these places formed a universal brotherhood which was, like their plants, close to nature. Everywhere that I went I received a warm welcome as a link with the mother garden at Kew.

The seasonal flowering of plants ordered my movements – a difficult timetable, further complicated by the need for fine weather. I was unprepared for the extravagant abundance of nature. What strange force had produced this enormous variety of species, each striving for supremacy, each adapting to its environment? As my quest continued, I found myself having the time of my life in a kingdom without frontiers that bound the whole world together in harmony.

A note of human discord, however, was sounded when the Tashkent Tourist Office refused to let me travel the ten kilometres to the botanical gardens unless they received clearance from the director. The young official was clearly enjoying my frustration, so I asked him to telephone the director, Professor F.N. Rusanov. He did so most reluctantly and said there was no reply. At this point a group of American tourists arrived in the office and, taking advantage of an audience, I demanded, 'Please connect me with the director of the Ministry of Agriculture in Moscow, under whose authority I am taking photographs of the Russian botanical gardens, so that he may approve your decision. I wish you to be properly rewarded for your concern.'

For a moment he was taken aback, and then asked ominously, 'Are you travelling alone?'

'Certainly not,' I said. 'I am here with the full approval of the British Foreign Office and Sir Fitzroy Maclean, President of the Great Britain–USSR Association, and your own government.'

Shortly afterwards a large black limousine arrived with a sinister driver in a black uniform. When we reached the gardens the professor apologized for his telephone being out of order. It had not, in fact, worked for several weeks. I passed on greetings from Sir George as well as some tablets that he needed for one of his children.

One of the numerous uncertainties for the traveller in Russia is that he does not know which hotel has been assigned him until he reaches his destination. I returned to Moscow at eleven at night to discover that mine was the huge Hotel Russia. My lucky number was much in evidence, I noted with relief. I planned an early start the next day to see the botanical gardens before catching an afternoon plane at 3.30, and fully expected to be back at the hotel by noon. In the event, the director kept me talking, and it was one o'clock before I returned. I dashed up to the fifth floor and asked the formidable floor lady for key No. 515. She looked at me with stern disapproval and replied, to all my frantic inquiries, '*Nyet.*'

In my room were my cameras, films, copious notes, tickets, passport, travellers' cheques. I hurried down to reception and was told in chilling tones that in the whole of that vast hotel there was no room of that number. Suddenly I felt invisible. It was as if I were living out a nightmare in a story by Kafka. This is what comes of having an altercation with an official at Tashkent, I thought, and said to the girl, 'I signed in late last night and slept in room 515. I have to catch a plane at 3.30. May I please have my key?'

The girl looked at me stolidly. 'There is no room numbered 515.'

'Look up my name in the register,' I pleaded.

Reluctantly she turned the pages of the heavy tome.

'Is a Mr Maguitray,' she said, 'but he 'as room 5115.'

The lady in charge of my floor handed me key No. 5115 with a look of withering scorn and I dashed to the room. On the door the number was clear: '515'. I looked at the neighbouring door. It was numbered '5116'. In my case when the second 1 fell off 5115 became 515! Inside, everything was as I had left it. I was still shaking like a leaf when I reached the airport.

26

Nothing to Fear

While travelling and taking the photographs for *Great Botanical Gardens of the World*, I seized the chance to gather material for my book *Buddha* which Nelson were also to publish. It was at Nelson, in fact, that I first met Peter Ford when he was one of the team who worked on seeing *Great Botanical Gardens of the World* through the press and edited the text for *Buddha* in the days before he moved on to becoming an author in his own right with *The True History of the Elephant Man* among other publications. (It is most rewarding for me that he should now be applying his brilliant and wide-ranging talents to the editing of the present book.)

All of this time, the arthritis in my hip-joints was growing steadily worse: a price exacted for the energetic activities of my youth. Kneeling was practically impossible, and when I met the Zenkei Shibayama Kancho, the head of the Zen sect, in Kyoto, he courteously invited me to sit beside him with my legs stretched out while he and my interpreter knelt. The interpreter, a young student overcome with awe, kept banging his head on the floor in an excess of humility. Our talk led up to the question to which, I had been told, I would be very lucky to get an answer: 'Is there a life after death or is there simply nothing?'

The old man, who was then over eighty, put an arm round my shoulder and said with a broad smile that showed all his gold teeth, 'My dear friend, there is no such thing as nothing!'

My search for Buddha took me back to many scenes of my past, to the sacred sites of Buddhism and finally to Dharmsala. I had last been here forty years before, when I drove up into the cool hills with Kim in the Grand Prix Salmson to escape the dusty clangour of Amritsar. Since then the population had doubled. Much was unchanged, but there were too many people and the road was packed with over-crowded, evil-smelling buses. I stayed at the rest-house and in the morning went to call on the Dalai Lama, for this was his place of exile.

He was younger than I had expected, and he exuded a twinkling boyish air from behind his large round glasses. He seemed little affected by his dramatic, almost miraculous escape from the Chinese forces. We talked about Buddhism and I promised to send him a copy of my manuscript, for which I hoped he might write a foreword. He said he would like to. As we sat together in his small room, he asked me about world affairs, about the chances of Tibet becoming free so that he and his followers could return to their old way of life. In my view, I said, there was so much common ground between the Four Noble Truths of Buddhism and Christianity that I would try to arrange meetings for him with the Pope, the Archbishop of Canter-bury and the Dean of Westminster Abbey. (In time, all of these meetings came to pass.) As I left he gave me his blessing and we exchanged white silk scarves. Outside, Indian troops guarded the encampment, while inside Tibetan children went to school and artists dressed in their national costumes acted in their Tibetan theatre. Life went on briskly, though some of the elderly were preoccupied with elaborate preparations for the next world.

To protect our children from over concern with an afterlife, I pasted a huge map of the world on the ceiling of their bedroom. The sooner they realized it was all one world, the better. The time came when we asked ourselves what more we should do for them. The answer seemed obvious: let them see for themselves the wonders of the world; and so, at the end of 1969, we made a family trip to Egypt and stayed in Shepheards Hotel, Cairo. Egyptians love children and were delighted we had brought ours with us, especially since the war of 1967 had frightened so many tourists away. From our balcony we were able to watch the sun setting across the Nile and showering the distant pyramids in a blaze of colour.

We spent Christmas Day in the old Cataract Hotel, Aswan, where a little church, beautifully made of icing sugar and lit inside by a red lamp, welcomed us into the dining room. The children were impressed by the majestic waiters in their long *galabiyas* as they served a traditional dinner, unchanged since the days of the Victorian visitors who wintered in Egypt. The turkey was flanked by sausages, the plum pudding flamed in local brandy. On Boxing Day we travelled by hydrofoil to Abu Simbel. The temples had been skilfully rebuilt, but there was no avoiding an artificiality in their ancient majesty and mystery. 'Your plan would have been better,' said Betty. 'They're already becoming eroded.'

We caught a plane to visit and explore the great temples of Karnak and Luxor, and the following day took a little steamer north to Dendera. The voyage took four hours to reach Dendera with the current, and an extra two hours coming back against it. Since the temple lay two miles from the river, I asked our captain Said (who was also chief engineer and, except for an old man and a tea boy, ran the boat himself) to find me a quiet donkey. My hip joints were now so stiff that I could not separate my legs and had to ride side-saddle. Said helped me to mount and then, holding me securely on the animal, walked beside me all the way to the temple and back. No Egyptian to whom I related this thought such customer-care was anything out of the ordinary. The Egyptians have a great streak of hospitality, and back in Cairo, when we visited the mosques of Sultan Hassan, the Citadel and the Blue Mosque, I was everywhere helped up the steps by strangers.

The family suggested that I stay on and try the Helwan sulphur baths for my hips. By that stage I was ready to try anything. In Helwan I found a room at the Evergreen Pension, run by two Italian sisters, Eva and Berta Laurella. They had lived in Egypt most of their lives and looked like Gibson girls in the early photographs of themselves they showed to me.

'Why did you never marry?' I asked them.

'We were too independent,' they said. 'We prefer to live our own lives.'

Next morning Fikri Shaaban, a powerfully built masseur, gave me short-wave, infra-red physiotherapy treatment and finally, laying me on a table, took a foot in each of his large hands, moved them slowly apart and held them. The pain was intense, but gradually he managed to get one of my feet on either side of his broad waist. He looked triumphant as he said, 'Before you leave, we'll do better than a metre.'

I was thoroughly alarmed at the idea. The lining between the head of the femur and the socket had ceased to exist and bone ground on bone. Nature set up inflamation, possibly to prevent movement and hoping no doubt that the bones would fuse together and leave me still but free from pain. I was given a series of exercises. Next day my joints were less stiff, and I was taken to the bath, a fifteen-foot-square concrete tank full of a steaming yellow, sulphurous liquid at 100°F. It was a comforting stew, and I did my exercises in its weightless embrace. Half an hour later I was called out, wrapped in a large towel and, still soaking, put to bed in a small cubicle. For a week the treatment continued. I rested each afternoon in a long-chair in the sun at the *pension* until, greatly refreshed, I said goodbye to the sisters and returned to Cairo and thence home to Mill Hill.

Betty and the children welcomed me back to Mote Mount. After that I went to see my bees. They were tightly clustered against the cold. Here and there there were small movements. Perhaps, I thought, they took turns relieving each other on the cold exterior of the group.

Shortly after this we were invited to a dinner at which I met Ramesh Sanghvi, an Indian barrister and adviser to the Shah of Iran. He was in the midst of arranging a magnificent celebration for the 2,500th anniversary of the Persian Empire in 1971. 'There will,' he explained, 'be a vast caravanserai of elaborately furnished tents at Persepolis to accommodate the crowned heads of Europe and a host of international celebrities. There will be banquets and speeches followed by displays of events in Persian history with a magnificent march-past of Persian armies through the ages.'

'What will remain,' I queried, 'when the show is over, after the caviar and peacock have been flushed down the gold-plated loos, the electric-light bulbs and bunting dismantled and the 10,000 firs specially imported from France left to battle with the desert's dusty drought?'

'It is all being filmed for posterity.'

'But films get old and damaged, and the Shah, however important his guests, would inevitably grow bored with the repetition. Why not produce a splendid book on the history of the country with beautiful pictures, print it in many languages, give it a beautiful Persian binding? The Shah can then present it to important guests.'

Six weeks later they asked me to prepare a dummy. This I did with the help of Peter Kindersley, a first-class designer who had worked with me on *Great Botanical Gardens of the World* and today owns his own publishing company, Dorling Kindersley. Accompanied by Betty and Peter Kindersley, I arrived in Teheran, where my first require-ment was a letter from the Iranian authorities to open all doors and grant me facilities. The government of Iran worked downwards from the Shah through his parliamentary Prime Minister on the one hand and his Minister of Court on the other. We waited a long time in the elegant reception room of the latter before, eventually, an exquisitely dressed young man emerged from the inner room. 'You are the Irish photographer?' he inquired.

I said that I was.

'I also take photographs,' he said. 'I don't know why they sent for you.'

'I'm delighted to hear it,' I said. 'Please inform the minister that I'm leaving the matter entirely in your hands and will return to London. You have my full agreement to take the photographs for the book for His Imperial Majesty.'

The young man retreated in baleful silence. After a suitable pause – essential for the proper conduct of Eastern business – I was ushered into the presence of His Excellency Amir Motaghi, a charming, slender and diplomatic man. The letter was duly typed, signed and embossed with the official seal.

The government were prepared to supply a car and driver, but Ramesh agreed with me that it would be better not to ask for anything we could supply ourselves. I therefore hired a driver with a Buick for a six-week tour, but, when we went down next morning, we found another driver awaiting us. His name was Terani, he said, and since his friend's wife was expecting a baby, he would take his place. Terani, a thick-set, beaming Iranian, had boxed for Iran against Singapore, was a game warden and occasionally worked for the Shah when he went shooting. I took to him at once, but Betty swore he was a secret agent. So much the better, I thought. As we put our suitcases in the boot, I noticed a shotgun and an automatic rifle neatly slung inside.

When we reached the Caspian, I particularly wanted a sunrise shot of fishermen bringing in the sturgeon. At Bandar Palavi we therefore went straight to the fishery headquarters and asked for the director. He would be there at six the next morning, we were told, and we duly arrived at his office on time. The director, a big bull of a man, then stated that photography was out of the question. I listened in despair as the sun slowly rose. 'Please put me through to His Imperial Majesty,' I said. 'It seems it is easier for me to photograph the King of Iran than the king of fish.'

Terani then said something in Farsi, and the director reluctantly gave permission, but insisted I be accompanied by one of his assistants. The assistant, as burly as his director, immediately told me I was not to photograph the fish coming in. I hung my camera round his neck. 'You take the pictures,' I said. 'I'm sure the Shahanshah will be very pleased.'

He was nonplussed. After this I was given a free rein. 'These very sad peoples,' said Terani.

While Betty and Peter returned to London, I continued alone to Mashhad. Here I met the Governor-General, HE Bagher Pirnia, who controlled the Province of Khorasan and was also imam of the shrine of Imam Reza, second in importance only to Mecca, being the shrine of the Shiah sect of Islam. No unbeliever, let alone an Irish Buddhist photographer, had ever before been allowed inside this sacred place, and my guides refused to stay with me. Ignoring their protests, I struggled up the steep stairs of an adjoining building to the roof. Here I traversed a narrow ledge thick with pigeon droppings and obtained a fine view of the mosque. But the ledge was too narrow for me to turn round, so I had to shuffle backwards on my return journey, the camera bag becoming heavier and heavier all the way.

Descending by another stair, I found myself in the great courtyard in front of the shrine. No one paid me any attention and I walked in with the worshippers. As I slowly circumambulated the shrine, I realized I was being followed. Glancing behind me apprehensively, I saw four men carrying a coffin. I continued to move quietly round with the throng, and did this three times, but without managing to shake off the pall-bearers. Eventually I stopped. At this they stopped as well and placed the coffin carefully at my feet. I watched with pounding heart as they slowly removed the lid to reveal the body of an old man, all but his face covered with a white shroud. Reverently they lifted a corner of the carpet and gently shook some of the sacred dust on the face. Greatly relieved, I placed myself on the edge of the worshippers and took flash pictures of the scene. No one acknowledged my presence and I followed the pall-bearers out into the sunshine.

That afternoon I drove to Nishapur through a blinding sandstorm to pay my respects to the grave of Omar Khayyám. Above the tomb soared a tall narrow tower of open geometrical design, and beneath its diamond points a polished black marble slab marked the resting place of my favourite poet. The walled garden was filled with roses and perfume. I picked a rose and laid it on the slab. A cat stretched out on the warm marble and purred as I stroked it.

Finally I was to photograph the imperial family at the square and modern Saadabad Palace. I was cleared by security guards who released the shutter of my Nikon camera and examined the flash with concern. In the vestibule I was surprised to find half a dozen photographers already waiting, equipped with strobe lights, white reflecting umbrellas, tripods, boxes of equipment and assistants. I was asked to go in first. The drawing room, a magnificent double cube, was richly furnished and carpeted with priceless Persian carpets. The tall French windows led on to a series of shallow white marble steps that descended into the garden. The room was empty. I took some shots. When the Shah came in with Queen Farah Diba, Ramesh introduced me. The Shah looked disappointed as he asked, 'Is that your camera?'

'Yes, Your Imperial Majesty,' I replied.

'It's very small,' he said.

'It is the finest camera in the world, Your Imperial Majesty. Small things are often the best.'

He looked at me searchingly. 'What is your background?'

'I was a trooper in Indian Cavalry, Your Imperial Majesty.'

'Ah,' he said, 'my father was a cavalry man, and so am I. Where do you wish us to be?'

I led them to the steps in the clear sunshine. I stood Queen Farah on a lower step, since she was the taller of the two, and the Shah above her, angling them into the light so that it melted part of his large nose into his cheek. 'Look towards each other,' I whispered, and quickly ran off five frames.

He seemed apprehensive, but she was quiet and reassuring as if enjoying some private joke. The children joined them and the family tried to present a uniform front, but, despite parental prompting, it was some time before the children ceased bending and turning. Just as all seemed well, Prince Ali Reza began to pick his nose. We were all relieved when it was over and the Shah called for his dogs. A large black Labrador bounded up, followed by a red Irish setter and a long-haired white husky. They joyfully frisked and frolicked with the family, giving me the chance of some homely shots. 'Please don't include these in the book,' said the Shah. 'Dogs are regarded by Muslims as being unclean.'

Persia, the Immortal Kingdom was published in ten languages. It contained three sections: 'The Classical Age' by Professor Roman Ghirshman; 'The Medieval Age' by Vladimir Minorsky; and 'Iran Today and Tomorrow' by Ramesh Sanghvi. For the modern section of the book, I photographed the Atomic Research Centre, where I was allowed a free run of the establishment and spent some time focusing on a strange blue light at the bottom of a large tank of water. Later, in the laboratory, the staff pointed out that I had been within the danger area, but they had not liked to interfere with such an eminent scientist. My pictures of the Shah and his queen were hung in Iranian embassies and the Shah used them for Christmas cards. My one regret was that, despite my best endeavours, Omar Khayyám was not included. The Shah did not regard him as an important poet. When we parted I had asked if I might quote a quatrain. The Shah nodded. I said quietly:

'The Worldly Hope men set their Hearts upon

> Turns to ashes – or it prospers; and anon,
>   Like Snow upon the Desert's dusty Face
> Lighting a little Hour or two – is gone.'

He listened attentively and after a time shook his head and said, 'We have better poets.' I never saw him again, but I took away the sense of a man trapped by events beyond his control. Six months later I received a handsome volume from 'His Imperial Majesty Muhammad Reza Pahlavi Aryamehr, Shahanshah of Iran', entitled: *Iran: Philosophy Behind the Revolution*. The sole picture in the book was one of those I took of him on the palace steps. Within ten years his own revolution would be, 'Like Snow upon the Desert's dusty Face', swept aside by another even more formidable.

In 1972, Roy Thomson (Lord Thomson of Fleet), then the owner of *The Times* and Scottish TV as well as of my old publishers, Nelson, brought the 'Treasures of Tutankhamun' exhibition to London for display in the British Museum. My photograph showing the funerary mask was selected for the official poster, and I also wrote the book, *Tutankhamun: The Last Journey*. It was published by Sphere and Nelson, and when, some years later, the exhibition moved to the United States, I suggested to Sphere that they might reprint it. By that stage Anthony Cheetham, my former editor at Sphere, had moved on to found Futura Publications, and the new editor turned the idea down. He did, however, graciously sell me the plant for £100. Then I had a tremendous stroke of luck. At a party I met Naim Attallah, who told me that his company, Quartet, were looking for a book to lead them into the American market. I showed him *Tutankhamun*, and he accepted it instantly. To our mutual delight it sold half a million copies.

The year after the Tutankhamun exhibition in London, Betty and I made two trips to the Far East. The first was prompted by the Royal Academy's announcement of its forthcoming 'Treasures of China' exhibition, which Betty foresaw was going to be another 'Tutankhamun' and suggested I cover it. On 14 April 1973 we set off for Peking by air. There had been many changes in China since I was last there. The old landlord class had vanished, along with the thieves and prostitutes. Dutifully we made our rounds of youth palaces and schools, where children of all ages gave glowingly uninhibited displays of music, singing, dancing, dramatics and gymnastics. We saw crèches filled with chubby, red-cheeked babies watched over by cheerful grandmas. Young boys went through commando courses as elderly citizens sat peaceably in community rooms, reading, playing chess or cards, smoking and drinking innumerable mugs of the green tea without which no one in China seemed at ease. It was rumoured that the tea had an anti-aphrodisiac effect, and we wondered if that could account for the universal calm pervading the country. There was no sign whatever of the yelling, jostling crowds that had filled Shanghai in my youth. The calm seemed to have spread even to the animal kingdom. Gradually it dawned on us there were no birds, cats or dogs, and very few flies. Everything inessential to the community had been swept away.

Something else we saw nothing of were open signs of love or affection. No lovers strolled hand in hand through the beautiful people's parks or cuddled on the numerous benches. When I asked an eighteen-year-old girl interpreter when she would marry, she replied confidently, 'When I am twenty-six.'

'Who will you marry?' I pursued.

'One of my classmates,' she replied.

'Which one?' I asked.

'Oh, I have not made up my mind. Things can change in eight years.'

'But what would you do if you were walking along the bund, looking at the moonlight on the river, and you suddenly saw a handsome young man coming towards you and fell madly in love with him?'

She regarded me in blank astonishment. 'That could not happen,' she said, and she and her companions all laughed heartily at such a crazy notion.

In Hanchow we attended the May Day celebrations, held in the Flower Pond Park in pouring rain. Several thousand people turned up despite the weather, and settled happily under huge varnished-paper umbrellas. There were good acrobatic performances and colourful dances. After it was over, I plodded back through the glutinous clay to my car, only to find when I got there that the rubber ferrule had come off my stick. To my surprise, the hall porter handed it to me when we reached the hotel. I said I should like to give the finder something for his trouble, but the suggestion was laughingly brushed aside. 'He was a small boy,' the porter said, 'and we have no idea where we might find him. It was his duty to return it.'

The same level of concern was evident throughout the trip. In Shanghai, after we had gone out for the day, I realized I had left my notebook and fountain pen on the breakfast table. Since the notebook contained critical material, I was worried about whose hands it might fall into, but when we returned that evening, it was exactly where I had left it. Other travellers found their discarded shampoo bottles carefully returned to them at their next hotel.

The film I was using was Kodakrome II, which could only be processed by Kodak, who had no facilities in China. I explained this to the Chinese authorities on arrival, but they were adamant that any film must be developed in China so it could be examined before leaving the country. In vain I sought reassurance, and received no response to various ideas that I put forward, such as getting the Chinese to send the film to their London embassy who could then have it developed and returned for a censorship check. As a result I was in a perpetual state of anxiety that reached a high pitch as we approached the customs at Shanghai before boarding the plane for London. I was convinced by then that all my work – several thousand photographs – was about to be lost. But the customs officials handed back my film. 'Have the regulations changed?' I asked.

'No, but you are our friend,' they said with immense warmth.

The result of the trip was *Princess of Jade*, in which my pictures were accompanied by a text by Edmund Capon, Assistant Keeper of the Far Eastern Section of the Victoria and Albert Museum. It told the story of Lieu Sheng, a prince of the Han Dynasty, and his consort, Princess Tou Wan (AD 205–20). Their bodies had disintegrated into dust, but the beautiful jade pieces that formed their 'suits for eternity' had survived to become the centrepiece of the 'Treasures of China' exhibition at the Royal Academy, where ten huge enlargements of my photographs lined the entrance-way.

I had been steadfastly refusing to let the drastic deterioration in my hip bones cramp my style. A normal hip-joint is made up of a ball, about the size of a small tangarine, on the end of the femur, or thigh bone, which fits into a similar-sized cartilage-lined socket in the hip bone, called the *acetabulum*. The joint, lubricated with synovial fluid, carries a tremendous workload, and the only surprising thing about my hips was that they should have lasted so long after my strenuous athletic pursuits. Man was not created to stand upright and the hip-joint was not designed to carry the additional weight. I was told not to rest, but to take as much exercise as I could bear, and this advice I followed for some fifteen years. But by this time movement was excrutiatingly painful to me and my mobility was limited to a hundred yards a day. With careful planning I nevertheless managed to get by. In the morning I moved to my office, which was on the same floor as my bedroom. I came downstairs for lunch, then drove to London in a Bedford Camper, fitted with a table, seats and a small stove on which I could brew up coffee for clients. On special occasions I would park on the meter outside Fortnum & Mason's, where I arranged for lunch to be brought out for my guests and myself, complete with a bottle of chilled champagne. When we went travelling, the family, 'my horses', supported me.

All at once our children became adults. Jonathan, at twenty-one, was reading chemistry at Magdalen, Oxford; Miranda, at seventeen, was planning to read marine biology at London University; and Jane, at twenty, was working with *House and Garden* and complaining about having to pay tax to keep her layabout brother and sister at university. I still had an ambition to show them my 'university of the world' before they finally took up their own lives. 'With your hips,' said Betty, 'the sooner we go the better,' and so our second trip in 1973 came about.

On 16 December we set off for Colombo and went to stay at Mount Lavinia. The smells were the same and the crows still flew into the rooms to snatch food off the breakfast trays. The roar of the surf on the reef lulled us to sleep. We wandered through my old home, Storm Lodge, transformed into a swimming club where Sinhalese and Europeans mixed freely, the colour bar entirely vanished. We drove to Anuradhapura along the old narrow road, though the lush green vegetation was blackened by the exhaust fumes of heavy lorries and buses. Anuradhapura itself was unchanged, and we mingled with the worshippers at the foot of the oldest tree in history, but in general I had the feeling that the old magic had disappeared under a wave of modernization. High-rise buildings flanked the Galle Face Green; a huge power station thrust its chimneys into the heavens.

In Colombo we dined with our old friend Arthur C. Clarke, who had visited Ceylon at my suggestion in 1954 and remained there entranced. On his roof terrace stood a huge TV receiving dish, a gift from the government of India in recognition of his contribution to the knowledge of space. This served to keep him in touch with the rest of the world. The one thing he missed, he said, was conversation with his space-related colleagues, but a constant flow of visitors from all parts of the globe, his writing and an underwater safari company he had founded left him little time to spare.

Finally we called on a delighted Kartar Singh, my old clerk at Amritsar, who introduced us to his family and who was, as a living link with my past, questioned closely by my children about their father's youth. 'I never met a sahib so interested in the mysteries of India,' said Kartar Singh, 'always asking questions.'

After this I made a small pilgrimage on my own to Ashoka's Pillar.

The park was deserted, but as I approached the pillar I saw a figure seated at its base and, as I drew closer, I saw it was a *sadhu*. My heart raced. I stood before the *sadhu* as he sat, his legs folded under a blue loin-cloth and his hands, with long finger-nails, resting on his knees. His hair and beard were iron grey, and the latter fell over necklaces of coral and sacred wooden beads. His body was strong yet slight. His eyes held mine as he said at last in a low voice, 'It has been a long time.'

I was dumbfounded, wondering if it really could be the same man. After another long pause he said, 'Your mind was torn when we parted in Gulmarg.'

The years rolled back and all I could do was wait for him to break the silence again, which he did after a while. 'You followed the Way,' he said. 'You have nothing to fear,' and added after another long silence, 'We will not meet again, but I will be with you as I have been since the beginning.'

'This is true of all the people I have met,' I said. 'All are a part of me, but you formed my thinking. I owe you a great debt.'

'You owe me nothing,' he said. 'We are all part of Brahma. There is abundance for everyone, but few perceive it.' At last he said again, 'You have nothing to fear.'

I thanked him and gave him money, as I had done in the past. 'I will give this to my *chela*,' he said. 'He is now in Benares, but will return to me.'

There was a finality in his voice and, feeling I was being dismissed, I walked slowly away, leaning heavily on my stick, though finally stood still with a longing to see more of him. I hurried back along the path as fast as my hips would allow. The little figure had gone. I searched around the pillar, but there was no sign of him. The whole of my past already had a dream-like quality. Forty years hence, where would today's realities be; where would I be? Life was in the mind. Past, present and future were all one to Brahma. Whichever way I turned, all my life was with me. 'When me ye fly, I am the wings.'

Next day we flew home. Mote Mount was damp but welcoming, and a letter was there to say that my hip operation was scheduled for Monday, 24 June.

The operation was something Betty and I had awaited for over a year, but now we greeted the prospect with mixed feelings. It was this or a wheelchair, though as Sir Henry Osmond-Clark, the doyen of hip surgery, had often said during my annual consultations, 'What's wrong with a wheelchair?' We had explored the various options for hip-replacement, including that of a Burmese surgeon who used an ivory prosthesis, but the easy winner was Professor John Charnley, head of the Centre for Hip Surgery, Wrightington Hospital, Wigan. He was a surgeon who had the additional merit of being a professor of engineering. As well as creating a superb joint (the Charnley prosthesis allowed for great flexibility of movement and in this respect was an improvement on the natural joint), he had designed a sterile operating theatre that had reduced the rate of post-operative infection to less than one in two hundred (the London average being far higher). Above all, I liked his sense of humour. When he first examined me, I asked him if he were the right age for this operation. 'Yes,' he replied, 'you are just the right age.'

'Professor Charnley,' I said, 'my question was, are *you* the right age?'

Charnley, who was then sixty-four, laughed and said, 'It's like going three rounds with Muhammad Ali, but I still do six hips a day when I operate.'

In my case he was going to replace both hips at once. This would give me a balanced start and the bonus of not having to undergo a second operation.

We were silent on the 200-mile drive to Wigan that Sunday, 23 June 1974. There was not much to be said. The Wrightington Hospital itself was an old single-storey TB hospital with long passages creating a sense of isolation. My room looked on to a grass square, beyond which lay the sterilizing plant. I got into bed and after tea Betty was ushered out and a beautiful sister with one eye and a jolly fat nurse with two produced Gillette razors. Without soap, they proceeded to shave off every hair from navel to knees. The scrotum was difficult to dry shave, but eventually, with my help and a lot of giggling, we completed the task. Next I was sent for a bath, followed by another session of shaving to make sure not a single hair remained. 'Tomorrow, when you're painted with iodine, anything we've missed will show up, and if there's one hair left the professor will have our heads!' they exclaimed.

Betty was allowed back and watched me have my last meal and an allergy test for iodine, followed by a glass of Ovaltine and two sleeping pills, which I did not take. Finally we said goodnight and she went off to the local hotel to join the other anxious relatives. Lying in bed in the darkness I could see, across the grass, steam rising from the sterilizer into the night sky. I'm in good hands, I reassured myself, and the *sadhu*'s words came back to me: 'You have nothing to fear.'

Next morning my chest and hips were X-rayed and Betty came back. At 1.30 p.m. I was given my 'pre-med' sedation shot. At 2 p.m.

a hypodermic needle was taped into a vein in the back of my left hand. The porters arrived, lifted me on to a trolly and wheeled me to the operating theatre. By that stage Betty was feeling far worse than I was. She had given Charnley a copy of her book, *The Battle for Oblivion*, about the discovery of anaesthesia, and presuming she had medical experience, he had invited her to watch him operate. Despite being frightened, she courageously watched from a corner, closing her eyes at the worst bits.

I woke up lying on my back, and tried to turn into my usual sleeping posture on my side only to find my legs separated by a V-shaped bolster and my ankles tied to the end of the bed. 'Waggle your feet.' A blonde nurse was looking down at me. 'Waggle your feet up and down,' she commanded.

'I'd like to turn over,' I said. 'I'm not used to sleeping on my back.'

'You've had your operation,' she said, looking hard at me to see if I understood. 'You've had your operation,' she repeated, 'and now you must waggle your feet.'

'I know I've had my operation,' I said, 'I just want to go to sleep.'

It took some time to dawn on me that I had not been briefed on an important post-operative requirement: that I would have to sleep on my back for some months. I looked around the intensive-care ward and saw a dozen or so patients all waggling their feet up and down, and joined in. Every four hours there was an injection of morphia and a period of blissful, pain-free tranquillity.

At 9 a.m. the next day I was wheeled back to my room. Betty, as she came in, said how well I looked, but was concealing the shock she felt at the sight of three half-litre bottles dangled from either side of my bed. These were filled with body fluids that would otherwise have swollen my legs to twice their normal size. On Wednesday morning, two buxom ladies in bright-yellow uniforms came in and announced, 'We're your physiotherapists. Sit on the side of the bed,' and lifted the bedclothes.

I slithered round cautiously and lowered my feet to the floor. Well-supported by one on either side, I managed a few steps. 'Very good,' they said, full of encouragement, and produced a walking frame.

Walking was an effort. My top and bottom halves were separated by plastic and stainless steel, and messages from my brain had difficulty in getting through. After several false starts, I made a slow circuit of the room. Then I was ordered back to bed and a smooth board was placed at my feet. My heels were lowered into circular pads made from rolled-up tights discarded by the nurses. 'Move your feet away from one another as far as possible, and then slide them together again,' they said. 'It's a very good exercise. Keep on doing it.'

I felt better after this, and pulled myself into a sitting position with the toggle bar above my head. I had brought with me the draft of my next book, *Island of Isis*, which I had started in May. Writing helped me to forget the aches and pains as I concentrated on the life of Cleopatra VII, her identity with the goddess Isis and her love affairs with Julius Caesar and Mark Antony. Each day I became stronger and was doing a variety of exercises to strengthen disused muscles. On 1 July, Charnley removed the deep stitches, which had been kept under pressure by five resilient pads on either side of the incision. On the 8th the external stitches were removed. Betty was there whenever she could manage it.

On 12 July, the 'Glorious Twelfth' celebrated in Ulster to commemorate the victory of William of Orange at the Battle of the Boyne, I was allowed home. Betty arrived at midday to collect me. We thanked everyone and gave presents. My manuscript was almost finished, for Charnley's secretary had kindly typed up each day's work for me. We made our farewells, and as we drove to the gate Betty asked if I had forgotten anything. 'I don't think so,' I said.

Then I remembered that I had asked Mike Wroblewski, Charnley's colleague, to save my femur heads. We went back and I retrieved them, neatly labelled in a little white box.

27

'What to Do?'

I have started to write this chapter on 24 June 1990, sixteen years to the day after receiving my new hip-joints from John Charnley. John has since joined the majority, though each year Mike Wroblewski, his brilliant successor, checks his master's long-lasting replacements. The hips were like new tyres to a tyreless car. I found myself restored to complete mobility, the wide world once again open to me. The operation enabled me to write more books, to photograph new countries and, above all, to meet more people. *Island of Isis*, partly written in hospital, was dedicated to 'Professor John Charnley and his colleagues'. A number of the photographs in it, including that on the jacket, had been taken by Betty, who, with her excellent eye, saw to those shots that my hips made difficult for me.

Betty, besides being beautiful, is one of life's practical realists. She carried my heavy camera bags round the world and, when my pre-Charnley hips gave out, climbed minarets, descended into Ancient Egyptian tombs and braved the flooded temple of Philae to take the photographs herself. From the inception of Ulster Television, she was my alternate; and is still vice-chairman. Together we discussed ideas for programmes, including the famous *Midnight Oil*, and in fact shared our lives completely, the one exception being her book, *The Battle for Oblivion*, about the discovery of anaesthesia by William Morton. This, which she found time to write and research without reducing her other activities, was a best-seller in Britain and the United States, where it was called *The Conquest of Pain*.

The entrance of Betty into my life had been its watershed. We were both very much afraid that marriage might not work out, but our fears were quite unfounded and she remains, as she always has been, the pivot round which our family life revolves. Our family is close-knit, though often widely separated. Jonathan is president of GenPharm International, a company engaged in animal genetics, and married to Laurie Hunter, a business consultant. They were classmates at Stanford and their son Alexander, thanks to his parents, has, for a three-year-old, a remarkable vocabulary of more than 5,000 words. On him the future of the family name depends. Jane is wine correspondent on *The Times* and *Good Housekeeping*, writes books covering the wines of the world, and is married to Philip Hedges, who has his own corporate finance company specializing in helping young enterprises to succeed. They have a beautiful daughter, Alicia. Miranda is a doctor of marine biology who writes books on animals and articles to encourage the protection of the environment. She has also worked with Oxford Scientific Films and the St Louis Zoo.

Whenever time allowed, Betty and I continued to travel the world extensively, as often as not in the company of our closest friends, Dr Emanuel 'Manny' Lederman and his wife, Dr Vera Dalley. I first came to know Manny during the war when he was a specialist in cancer of the throat at what is today the Royal Marsden Hospital. The silence and fear surrounding cancer was something I felt strongly about after my experience with my mother's illness and death, and I had sought his advice on an unrealized project for a film that might help to overcome these aspects. One of the happiest journeys we made together was one of our later trips to China, where the medical profession laid out red carpets and laid on banquets for Manny, who was world-renowned for his treatment of cancer of the head and neck.

During this journey, Betty and I spent many hours in hospitals and clinics, photographing operations where anaesthesia was produced by acupuncture. Chinese surgeons were not given to mirth, but in the Shanghai Second Medical School, when I was photographing the removal of a thyroid tumour, I asked the surgeons, one male, one female, if I was tiring the patient by my frequent questioning through the interpreter. 'Oh, no,' the woman surgeon giggled. 'While he talks we know that we have not divided his vocal chords!'

In March 1975, when Betty and I went to Papua New Guinea, we made a small pilgrimage to Kim's grave. Kim, after remarrying – an army captain this time – had settled in New Guinea amid all the tropical sunshine, flowers and fruit she could desire. We were never to meet again, though we wrote regularly until, in 1972, her usual birthday letter to me failed to arrive. Betty said at once, 'Something dreadful has happened,' and a week later I received a letter to say she had died on my birthday. 'I'll write to Bill as soon as I get out of hospital,' she had told her friend. There was no stone on her grave, just a number and a beautiful tropical shrub to mark the place. Her husband, who had died a year before her, was buried in the military cemetery near by. We also visited her pretty bungalow, whose garden, surrounded by a fringe of coconut palms, was still full of flowers. Her servants wept as they spoke of the old days.

The first of the books to come about after my wonderful new-found freedom was *The World in Focus*, the text for which I was asked to write by Barry and Mark Austin. It was a book that their father, George Austin, the founder of Colour Library International, had always wanted to produce from its huge collection of photographs, though he tragically died from a brain tumour before that life-long ambition could be realized. I decided to avoid politics and had maps prepared without boundaries. I then wrote short descriptions of the birth of planet earth, her countries and the arrival of man and civilization. In other words, it was planned as a handsome sort of handbook for visitors from another planet, and my old friend, Arthur C. Clarke, was kind enough to write the Foreword – something he had previously never done for anyone. We then took the book to Bartholomew, who said they would publish it if it could contain a higher proportion of human-interest photographs. They selected 440 of mine, and Colour Library International asked permission to handle the rights in those particular pictures. This I was happy to give, but unfortunately it came about that Colour Library International changed hands to become the Telegraph Colour Library and in the process 149 of my best pictures went missing and have never so far been rediscovered.

From my first visit to Egypt in 1926 I was in love with the Ancient Egyptians and their approach to life. Over the course of many years I accumulated ancient sayings that appealed to me, and these were in due course published under the title: *The Wisdom of the Ancient Egyptians*. Then, since I seldom got commissions, I was delighted when Mitchell Beazley invited me to write the sections on Iran and China for their stupendous *The Joy of Knowledge*, published in the United States as *The Random House Encyclopedia*.

I had known James Mitchell and John Beazley when they were respectively editorial director and production manager of Thomas Nelson, and had watched with interest their dynamic progress as one of the most lively London publishing teams of the 1970s. They also commissioned me to write a book about my favourite Pharoah, Ramesses II, who had been the subject of my first book, *Abu Simbel*. Tragically, *Ramesses, the Great Master of the World*, was to be the last book on which I worked with them. Both those independent-minded, energetic and forward-looking publishers – first John, then James – were to die at the early age of forty-five.

When I retired from Ulster Television, Betty said, 'I'm not going to have you getting under my feet all day. I think you should join a club. You can let on that you're going into town on some work project.'

'I'm not a club man,' I protested. 'I had all that in the Orient.'

Nevertheless I joined the Garrick. Over lunch one day, the author Eric Newby said to me, 'Bill, I want to write about China. You know the country, so why not do a book with me on modern China?'

I could hardly believe my good fortune. Eric was a most sought-after writer and a sparkling companion. It looked like a splendid enterprise, and our contracts and advance cheques promptly arrived from Charles Pick, chairman of Heinemann. I obtained permits for our journey and, as usual, got on well with the Chinese authorities, but even as I was arranging matters with my travel agent, a letter arrived from Eric saying that he felt unable to proceed and had returned his part of the advance. I was stunned. Charles Pick said, 'It's not the eleventh hour, it's a second off midnight.'

'All right,' I said, 'I'll find another writer.'

Charles said, extremely dubiously, 'He'll have to be good.'

I went home, talked with Betty and rang Malcolm MacDonald, with whom I had been friends since we met at his house at Frognal during the war. 'I'm in the middle of a book,' he said, 'but I'd love to do this one.'

Next day Charles welcomed him with open arms. He said to me later, 'You seemed to produce him like a rabbit out of a hat.'

Inside China was a huge success, in Britain and the United States. Malcolm and I joked about whether we would live to see it published. We did. Sadly, however, he died from a heart attack shortly afterwards. He was a great and trusted friend of the peoples of South-East Asia and Africa, and no one was too small to receive his help. They came in droves to his celebration service in Westminster Abbey, which was filled with orchids from his friends in Singapore.

Since the Festival of India was due to open in England in 1982, I suggested to Charles Pick that this would make a good subject for a book to be called *The Glory of India*. The large-format sixty-four-page collection of colour pictures I had in mind did not, however, fit the Heinemann style, so I took it to Christopher MacLehose at Collins, who suggested I ask John Masters for a foreword, since he was the fifth generation of his family to have served in India. To my delight, he sent me a magnificent 7,000 words from his retirement in New Mexico, and his text fitted my pictures as if he had seen them. Chandra Kumar, the Commonwealth Institute's charming and meticulous consultant for the festival, then supplied the commentary for the photographs, and during the festival itself I had the honour of presenting a copy to Mrs Gandhi.

While I was still in my eighty-fifth year, Ulster Television threw a little party in London to launch a selection of sixty of my early black-and-white photographs, chosen by Zelda Cheatle for an exhibition at her prestigious Zelda Cheatle Gallery, near Leicester Square. She had delved through several boxes of my old Rollieflex negatives, many of which had never been printed up, and on her advice I sent them to Grove Hardy Ltd, run by the famous photographer Bert Hardy, where Charlie Keeble and Paul Knights produced stunning prints from them. 'But why,' I asked Zelda in bewilderment, 'should anyone want to buy black-and-white prints, which can so easily be duplicated?'

'It's a very important market today,' she explained patiently. 'There are collectors all over the world, and some photographs sell for $50,000 or much more.'

'What will you charge for mine?' I asked nervously.

'Framed, £160 each.'

I was incredulous, but by the end of the month fifty-seven had been sold, fifteen to the Imperial War Museum, ten to the National Portrait Gallery, six to Ulster Television, bless their hearts, and the remainder to various collectors. Shortly after this, Nouvelles Images, the leading French art firm, bought one from which to print postcards and posters. It was all a heart-warming experience, and it opened yet another new horizon. I do, after all, have 26,000 black-and-white negatives!

My parents certainly started something when, on my eighth birthday and I went away to school, they gave me the Kodak Box Brownie camera. Its tiny view-finder became a protective shield, and the fact that everything was reduced in size gave me confidence. My films were developed at my father's printing works, but I printed the positives on daylight paper and watched the pictures form with delight. Even at that early age I realized that it was possible for me to capture precious moments, and I have never stopped taking pictures. Today the MacQuitty International Collection handles rights in a quarter of a million of my photographs.

My earliest recollection of myself is of a timid, frightened, very emotional child, clinging to the love and affection of his family. I grew up in a world of religious fear: fear of Satan, hell and damnation; fear that the neighbours might point the 'finger of scorn' at me for my shortcomings. I pictured God as an enormous eye, which sat on my head like a halo and followed me wherever I went, even, embarrassingly, into the lavatory. The blinds of my father's home, in his youth, had been drawn on Sundays, and reading was, in the semi-gloom, confined to the Bible and religious books. His only escape from the house was going to church and Sunday school, so not unnaturally he held strong views on questions of right and wrong. There were no doubtful areas in his philosophy, though he did, on the other hand, counsel, 'Moderation in all things.' He was anxious to see me follow him into printing and publishing, or to become a doctor like my namesake Uncle William, the renowned physician whose medical watchword was, 'Leave well alone.' Both these precepts I found to be of great value.

Yet, as I grew older, I realized that there was an exciting world beyond Belfast of which I knew nothing. I yearned to be part of it and by the age of fourteen was determined to explore it. I was fearful, but I also had a highly developed fear of being afraid. Everything I was afraid of became a challenge to me. I vividly remember bathing from the pier at Brighton, then compulsively climbing up to the high dive, twenty feet above the water, simply to take a look. When I got there I walked to the end of the board, and though I had never before dived off anything higher than a few feet, dive I must. I was afraid to turn back. It was this overwhelming curiosity that constantly drove me forward. I wanted, like Kipling, to know the 'What, why, when, how, where and who' of everything.

What have I learnt? Chiefly that we human animals, for all our warring creeds and colours, are the same. With notable exceptions we are stupid, superstitious and given to wild bouts of rage and hatred, but also capable of tenderness and love. As Wilhelm Stekel said, emotions are bi-polar. Nature I loved, but I loved mankind more, and during my wanderings I was fortunate to meet a great variety of talented and lovable people who were generous with their knowledge. I should also acknowledge my multitude of ancestors, some million of them, who provided the continuous chain of life to get me here. I stand on the peak of their pyramid of hopes and fears as, through me, their genes and cells continue their lives.

What did I want from life? Love, affection and knowledge. I have been fortunate in the first two and have also had the good luck to live at a time when nature's secrets were being revealed. Who would have dreamed of a child born in 1905 that he might live to see the conquest of space and of so many fatal diseases. On television I have seen the far side of the moon, and the earth from outer space. The search for knowledge has revealed the secret of life in the spirals of DNA. The evolution of man and of the earth is being read in the story of the ancient rocks, though certain religious sects would seek to deny it.

I have found myself in positions of authority, but power never appealed to me. I have seen the problems that wealth brings. Chang Ch'ao, the Chinese philosopher, said: 'Only those who take leisurely what the people of the world are busy about, can be busy about what the people of the world take leisurely.' You belong to your possessions, they do not belong to you.

Like Ulster Television, the *Titanic* lives on. Two American societies, the Oceanic Navigation Research Society and the *Titanic* Historical Society, issue magazines covering every aspect of the disaster and hold annual gatherings where they serve the menu of the final dinner and arrange for a wreath to be dropped on the spot where she sank. Occasionally I am asked to speak at these functions. The rediscovery of the wreck in 1985 led to a world-wide renewal of interest, and Betty and I, attending the Maritime Museum in Paris, found it thronged with people looking at salvaged artefacts. Many felt that the ship ought not to be disturbed, but should remain a tomb for the dead. I do not feel this. It is good that the past should live again, a lesson for the future.

My affairs are in order, my bags are packed. I am not too concerned about my departure, except the manner of it and the leaving of my family, whom I love deeply. Nature provides only one entrance to this world, but unfortunately has a thousand exits, some pleasant, others not. Most of my friends have already departed, but all are with me still, though I think personal survival after death unlikely. Yet it is a mystery, so who knows? I sleep soundly and find oblivion comforting. As the great scientist, J.B.S. Haldane, wrote in his article 'On Being Finite':

> I should find the prospect of death annoying if I had not had a very full experience, mainly stemming from my work . . . For example I was one of the first two people to pass forty-eight hours in a miniature submarine, and one of the first few to get out of one under water. I doubt whether, given my psychological make-up, I should have found many greater thrills in a hundred lives. So when the angel with the darker drink at last shall find me by the river's brink and, offering his cup, invite my soul forth to my lips to quaff, I shall not shrink.

Why are we here? Answers to that question have promoted innumerable beliefs and faiths, whose unfortunate effect has been to enable handfuls of people to control vast numbers of the human race. The saddest chapters of history have been written by those who believe they have absolute knowledge. In needing help to face the terrible injustices of the laws of nature, people have accepted their edicts. The truth may be that nature had to produce humans to discover her own secrets. However, I remain optimistic. We have barely arrived on our planet, yet have achieved so much. In the years to come, if our gains are not lost through foolishness, we may yet achieve eternal life and paradise on earth.

Betty and I travelled to Sri Lanka to visit our old friend Arthur C. Clarke. He had not been well, but an initial diagnosis of motor neuron disease had been changed to one of an earlier polio infection. I found my erstwhile tranquil paradise filled with warring sects, maiming and murdering with unrestrained brutality in the name of freedom. Yet, despite the dreadful situation, we found Arthur in good form, on the mend and working on three books. I reminded him of his 'Replicator' in *Profiles of the Future*. This was a device that, when fed the correct information, could produce anything man required. Material objects thereupon became relatively worthless, leaving our descendants free to 'remember what most of us have forgotten – that the only things on earth that really matter are such imponderables as beauty, wisdom, laughter and love'. When I asked him about immortality, he said, 'We go out like candles.'

'And religion?' I asked.

'I'd like to repeat a quotation. I once heard Pandit Nehru say, "Politics and religion are obsolete. The time has come for science and spirituality." '

He escorted us round the Arthur C. Clarke Space Centre, and we gazed in wonder at the huge dishes and advanced technical areas that brought the thoughts of the world into this quiet room. 'Is there anyone out there?' we asked.

'There is no hard evidence that earth has ever been visited from space,' he said. 'If the terrestrial experiment started all over again from Time Zero, there might be intelligence on this planet – but it would not look like us. In the dance of the DNA spirals, the same partners would never meet again. Loren Eisley wrote this thirty years ago: ". . . nowhere in all space or on a thousand worlds will there be men to share our loneliness. There may be wisdom; there may be power; somewhere across space great instruments may stare vainly at our floating cloud wrack, their owners yearning as we yearn. Nevertheless, in the nature of life and in the principles of evolution we have had our answer. Of man elsewhere, and beyond, there will be none for ever." '

For myself, I feel happier with the Irish poet James Stephens' philosophy:

> No thought have I save that the moon is fair,
> And fair the sky and God is everywhere.

So, 'What to do?' as Allah Dad would have said. Perhaps the only possible answer is written in great white letters on the old Belfast railway bridge next to Ulster Television:

GOD IS LOVE — LOVE EVERYBODY

'Have you finished your manuscript?' Betty asked.

'Almost,' I said.

'Well, you'd better start looking for a publisher.'

'No problem,' I said. 'I've had fifteen books published successfully as well as fifty illustrated articles distributed to thirty-five countries by Camera Press. My library of a quarter of a million of my photographs is used worldwide.'

'Don't be lulled,' said Betty shrewdly. 'Publishing today is not the same as it used to be. There have been so many amalgamations of publishers that they only accept books with massive appeal, and even then they still spend thousands hyping them.'

'Watch me,' I said.

Some time later the penny dropped. My acquaintances in the publishing world said that the only autobiographies being published were of internationally famous people – movie stars, dictators, statesmen and so forth. 'You're a nice chap, Bill, but you're not a household name.'

'What to do?' I asked Betty.

'Take it to Naim Attallah,' she said.

I climbed the steep stairs to Naim's office. Half-way up I paused and found myself looking into a large room filled with pretty secretaries and pictures of film stars. At the far end sat Theo Cowan, who had been head of Rank publicity in my day, though he too joined the Rank Outsiders. He was now head of his own prestigious PR firm within Naim's Namara Group. For thirty years I had received his famous 'Cowgram' greetings for my birthday and on our wedding anniversary. It seemed a good omen and I hurried up the final flight. Naim rose from behind a large black desk, arms outstretched, and embraced me warmly. It was nearly twenty years since we first met, but he was quite unchanged by his huge success.

'I'll publish your book,' he said. 'You are my friend.'

Epilogue

I asked the family what they thought of my manuscript.

'You've forgotten something,' they said.

'Like what?' I asked, rather indignantly.

'Like your funeral,' they said. 'Anyway, why did you write it?'

'I wrote it to answer some of the questions you are likely to ask when it's too late, as happened to me with my own parents and many friends. Also I would like to rescue some of my life from oblivion, and to say sorry and give thanks. As for my funeral, I'd like a quiet cremation, just the family. Make sure my steel hips are removed before they put the bones in the grinder. They might wreck it.'

'What would you like done with your ashes?' they asked.

'When we were first married, I wrote in my will that Betty was to scatter my ashes over the Himalayas above the snow-line. She was to travel by ship and my calculation was that she might meet a suitable successor on the outward or the return voyage. When we left Mill Hill and came to live by the river in Putney, I suggested she should simply drop them into the Thames on a dark night, but she said she would like both our ashes ultimately to be mingled, and then to let the children decide how to dispose of them.'

'What about the service?' they asked.

'I'd like it to be short and jolly and to include "John Brown's body".'

'And a celebration?' they asked.

'First I must assure you that none of you could have done more for me than you have done, so no remorse. Regarding a celebration, Betty and I have been to our quota of celebration services for many friends – Nancy Astor, Norman Fisher, Malcolm MacDonald, Huw Weldon, Larry Olivier and Gerald Gardiner among others – and found them somewhat overpowering. I would like you to arrange an evening at the Hurlingham Club, invite all our friends to eat, drink and be merry, and especially to talk a lot, for, as the Ancient Egyptians said, "To speak of the dead is to make them live again"; and I do so very much enjoy talking.'

Index